Caminos 1

Teacher's Book

segunda edición

Alan Wesson

Published in 2002 by:
Nelson Thornes Ltd
Delta Place
27 Bath Road
CHELTENHAM
GL53 7TH
United Kingdom

02 03 04 05 06 / 10 9 8 7 6 5 4 3 2 1

A catalogue record for this book is available from the British Library

ISBN 0 7487 6781 9

Page make-up by Tech-Set Ltd

Printed and bound in Great Britain by Antony Rowe

Contents

INTRODUCING CAMINOS SECOND EDITION 4

Using *Caminos 1, second edition* 5

- Presentation 5
- Practice 6
- Differentiation 7
- Grammar 8
- Other opportunities 8
- Assessment policy 9
- Teaching units overview 10
- QCA Key Stage 3 Scheme of Work coverage 24

1	Nuevos amigos	25
2	En clase	33
3	La familia	41
4	¿Cómo eres?	51
5	Vamos al insti	58
1–5	¡Repaso!	65
6	Mi ciudad	68
7	¿Cómo es donde vives?	76
8	Hogar, dulce hogar	87
9	Los ratos libres	95
10	La rutina	103
6–10	¡Repaso!	112
11	Comer fuera	115
12	¡A comprar!	123
13	La salud	133
14	¿Qué hiciste?	142
15	¡Bienvenidos!	149
11–15	¡Repaso!	156

- Assessment answers 158
- Assessment tapescripts 163

INTRODUCING CAMINOS

Caminos is a three-stage course written by practising teachers, designed to meet the requirements of the National Curriculum 2000 for Modern Languages at KS3 / 4.

- It supports a wide range of students through its unique differentiation scheme, providing material and tasks for students of differing educational needs.
- It ensures a steady and spiral progression across both key stages, incorporating revision and recycling of language.
- It covers all aspects of the revised curriculum and lays good foundations for the new GCSE examination requirements.

CAMINOS 1, second edition: OVERVIEW

Caminos 1, second edition, is a beginner's Spanish course which equips students with all the basic skills necessary for successful understanding and communication. Listening, speaking, reading, writing and dictionary skills are carefully developed to enable students to cope in the target language, both in the classroom and in a Spanish-speaking environment. It is a flexible resource which can be used successfully as a one-year course and, if fully exploited, also offers ample material for those who wish to extend it into a second year.

- Student's Book
- Teacher's Book
- Resource and Assessment File
- Audio CD pack
- Flashcards

Student's Book

Structure of each unit:

Objectives
Each spread opens with a list of objectives in English. Topics and grammar throughout both *Caminos 1 second edition* and *Caminos 2 second edition*, cover the QCA scheme of work.

Teaching spreads
Each spread presents and develops related linguistic objectives offering activities for practice and consolidation.

Acción: lengua
Focus on specific grammar points covered in the preceding unit, providing clear explanations and differentiated exercises.

After every five units:

¡Repaso!
Double-page revision spread, reinforcing language covered in preceding units, transferring it to new contexts in the form of differentiated exercises.

Lectura
Independent reading activities, using language from the previous five units.

Táctica: lengua
Strategies to improve the four skills and language learning techniques.

Práctica: lengua
Single page with differentiated grammar drills.

At the back of the book:

Gramática
Grammar explanations, in English, with examples.

Vocabulario
Spanish–English and English–Spanish vocabulary, using simple dictionary conventions.

Resource and Assessment File

Presentation materials
Clear black and white visuals which can be made into OHP transparencies or photocopied onto card, cut up and used in games.

Hojas de actividades / Worksheets
Worksheets which support each objective in the Student's Book and give further differentiated practice in all skill areas. There are worksheets designed to support lower attainers throughout.

Hojas de vocabulario / Vocabulary sheets
Each contains the core language, with an English translation, of the objectives in each unit. These can be photocopied and given to students to stick in their exercise books at the start of each unit. Encourage students to tick the words they have learnt thoroughly; partners can test each other before ticking the box to confirm that words are known.

Assessment materials

Evaluación A Revision and testing for Units 1–2
Evaluación B Revision and testing for Units 3–5
Evaluación C Revision and testing for Units 6–8
Evaluación D Revision and testing for Units 9–10
Evaluación E Revision and testing for Units 11–13
Evaluación F Revision and testing for Units 14–15
Evaluación G End of book test (Units 1–15)

Further details of the assessment materials are given later in the Teacher's Book.

Caminos 1, second edition, supports assessment in different ways. The *Hoja de vocabulario* for each unit gives an opportunity for peer-assessment. The Teacher's Book highlights those opportunities in the Student's Book and worksheets which are useful for ongoing assessment, and the seven more formal assessment tests offer a 'snapshot' of pupil performance at different points throughout the year.

Audio CD pack

CD 1:	Student's Book, Units 1–5 and ¡Repaso! 1–5
CD 2:	Student's Book, Units 6–10 and ¡Repaso! 6–10
CD 3:	Student's Book, Units 11–15 and ¡Repaso! 11–15
CD 4:	Worksheets, Units 1–7
CD 5:	Worksheets, Units 8–15
CD 6:	Assessment Worksheets A–G

Flashcards

Numbers 1–29 and 42–80 are bold black-and-white line images, with numbers 30–41 as full colour photographs.

1 un supermercado
2 una tienda
3 una panadería
4 un videoclub
5 un cine
6 una piscina
7 una discoteca
8 un polideportivo
9 un colegio
10 un instituto
11 una iglesia
12 un parque
13 un bar
14 una cafetería
15 un hotel
16 un restaurante
17 un café con leche
18 un café solo

19 un té con leche
20 un té solo
21 un té con limón
22 un chocolate
23 una limonada
24 una naranjada
25 una Coca-cola
26 un zumo de naranja
27 una agua mineral con gas
28 una agua mineral sin gas
29 un batido de chocolate, un batido de fresa
30 una hamburguesa
31 un perrito caliente
32 un bocadillo de jamón York
33 un cruasán de queso
34 un cruasán vegetal
35 un bocadillo de chorizo
36 una tortilla española
37 calamares
38 patatas fritas
39 pescado frito
40 churros
41 aceitunas
42 ir a la bolera
43 ir a las salas de juegos
44 ir de compras
45 ir de paseo en bici
46 ir a la playa
47 ir a los partidos de fútbol
48 ir de excursión
49 ir de pesca
50 un regalo
51 una camiseta
52 un jersey
53 un reloj
54 un póster
55 un compact-disc
56 un videojuego
57 un cinturón
58 un vale-regalo
59 un Walkman
60 el gazpacho
61 la tortilla
62 el pastel
63 sangría
64 los pimientos
65 los huevos
66 las patatas
67 una botella de vino
68 un litro de limonada
69 medio litro de leche
70 una lata de sardinas
71 medio kilo de tomates
72 una caja de pañuelos
73 un bote de mermelada
74 un kilo de naranjas
75 100 gramos de queso
76 200 gramos de jamón
77 un tubo de pasta de dientes
78 una bolsa de bombones
79 una barra de pan
80 un paquete de café

USING *CAMINOS 1, SECOND EDITION*

The sections below contain activities and suggestions for using and exploiting the *Caminos* material: they are not intended to be prescriptive in any way, but simply offer ideas which have proved useful in the classroom.

1 PRESENTATION

Caminos caters for a wide variety of teaching and learning styles by providing different ways in which students can meet and understand new language. The picture story in the Student's Book, with the Audio CD, can be used to introduce new language as an alternative to the OHT visuals or flashcards for each unit, or can act as an authentic example of language already presented. The visuals can be used in a subsequent lesson for reinforcement or revision.

Picture story

The picture story presents the new language in the Student's Book. Listening and reading together helps students to focus on pronunciation and intonation, presents language in context with a range of voices and emotions, is a good 'settling' activity, and helps to cater for the wide variety of student-learning styles. Students can be encouraged to listen and read twice through: some suggestions for aiding comprehension and exploiting the story follow.

Checking comprehension
- Help students to work out who is involved in the episode: list the names of all the main characters and let students choose the relevant ones.
- Say a line of the dialogue, with appropriate intonation – students tell you which character you are. Useful for highlighting key language.
- Mime a facial expression, body pose, or action – students work out who you are. This is good for helping students to see how gesture can help to convey meaning and mood.
- Ask students how they think the different characters are feeling. Although language for moods is not introduced until Unit 9, much can be conveyed using the language from Unit 1A: e.g. *¿Qué tal está Tomás? ¡Fatal!*

Exploring the new language
- Highlight the key words by writing them on the board, and ask students to work out the meaning.
  The context in the story will have helped, but other useful techniques include spotting cognates, using stick drawings for clarification (e.g., to highlight the difference between brother and sister), and checking by asking *¿Cómo se dice ... en inglés?*
- Occasionally, use the picture story as an opportunity for dictionary work or, having clarified most of the meaning together, leave three or four words which students can look up for themselves: this encourages independence and gives them confidence so that they are not totally reliant on the teacher.
- Students can listen and repeat after the recording, or read along in groups with the recording if you designate certain groups or rows to take the parts of the different characters. This helps students' intonation and gives the less able confidence because, in reading aloud with others, they feel less exposed.
- Students may enjoy doing their own 'dramatised reading' in small groups. The picture story text offers support, but allows students to express emotion, moods and feelings.

Flashcards and the OHP
Presentation
When presenting new language using the OHP or flashcards, revealing only one item at a time will help students to focus more clearly. If possible, include the written language with it, either on the OHP or on cards stuck to the wall or board, since some students really need this as a memory aid. As soon as possible, pass the activity over to the students: having seen you model it with the whole class, they can then do it in pairs. Two or three minutes is often enough, since short bursts of pairwork interspersed with presentation keeps students alert and occupied.

Responding

Allow students to hear new words plenty of times before they have to say them, but get them involved quickly – physical responses give students something active to do. Avoid games which involve only a few students or allow others to coast. Encouraging students to respond as a class sometimes rather than individuals, even if the response is slightly 'ragged', gives the less able the confidence to speak along with everyone else. You may find some of the following activities useful.

- Accompany new language with a mime which students imitate and do every time you say it.
- Stick flashcards in different places around the room: students point to the one you mention.
- Stand up / sit down: if what you say matches the visual, students sit. If not, they stay standing.
- Thumbs up / down: if what you say matches the visual, students give the thumbs up – and if not, they give the thumbs down.
- Sí / no card: students hold up a card with either sí or no, depending on whether what you say matches the language or not.
- Hands up: allocate a new word to different tables in the room. Every time students hear 'their' word, they put their hands up.
- Teacher calls out the new language and pupils write down the number or the letter of the OHT item or flashcard mentioned: a good 'settling activity' which provides a brief respite in the oral work.
- Students give the number or letter of the visual. Accept responses from the less able in English. Make it more challenging for more able students, by pointing at two visuals at once – students can choose to give one or the other or both.
- Students repeat the new language if it matches the visual and stay silent if it doesn't. If playing as a game where if you make a mistake you are 'out', allow everyone two chances – the more able are unlikely to make a mistake and the less able can stay 'in' for longer.

2 PRACTICE
Target language

Spanish is used in core units with objectives in English. English is used whenever grammar or a specific language point is explained or reinforced, i.e., on Acción: lengua, Táctica: lengua and Práctica: lengua pages. Classroom language displayed on the walls of the room, or hanging from the ceiling on cardboard speech bubbles, acts as an aide-mémoire and encourages students of all abilities to use the target language effectively.

Student's Book activities

These incorporate all four skills, and give students an opportunity to work at their own level. The diamond activities can be attempted by all students, and focus on the core language of the objective. The club activities focus on extra details or information, encourage 'reading between the lines' for feelings, may have more intellectual challenge and often recycle language from earlier units in the new context. They are useful for the fast finishers and more able students; but all students should be encouraged to tackle at least some of them. There are always speaking activities, often with a game or challenge element, in the Student's Book and the visuals on the OHT sheet which accompanies many objectives, give further opportunities for speaking practice.

Communication games

Students need plenty of opportunities to practise and recycle language, if they are to learn it thoroughly. Activities and games give a sense of purpose, achievement and fun. Repetition often follows the presentation phase and is useful for pronunciation practice – students repeat after you in funny voices or in a variety of ways (slowly, fast, loudly, softly, in robotic voice, happily, sadly), clapping or clicking fingers to a rhythm, breaking long words into syllables and chanting in turn, in groups, or in rows. Repetition, however, does not always help vocabulary to stick in the memory – a number of students can happily repeat 'on automatic pilot'. The desire to communicate can be a more powerful mechanism in learning new language than repetition.

Supporting communication

Games are an enjoyable vehicle for practising new language, whether on the OHP or with flashcards, as long as there is a genuine information-gap or a reason for communicating. However, students need support in this: we often expect them to go straight from repetition to production without helping them to bridge the gap.

- Leave the new language visible in written form, either on the OHP or on the board.
- Have the words written large on sheets of A4 down the side of the board at the front if there is no room on the board or OHP itself or you want to use the space.
- Give students the Spanish and English written in large letters on an A4 sheet, one between two, at the start of the lesson as a prop. This relieves the anxiety some students undoubtedly feel.
- Give students the Hoja de vocabulario at the start of the unit and allow them to refer to it whenever they need to.

Games and challenges

Many of the following games can be played in teams and involve an element of guessing.

- Flash the flashcards, or slip a piece of A4 in and out between the OHP mirror and the acetate.
- Hold the acetate underneath the OHP mirror so that the image is blurred, and gradually lower it to bring it into focus.
- Use a piece of A3 with a hole in it and move it from side to side above the surface of the acetate. The hole could be made to look like a keyhole, or as if looking through binoculars. This can be done with pictures or new language.
- Position smaller OHT pictures round the edge of the OHP, with only part of them visible. Move them further towards the middle to help students to guess.
- Hide flashcards in a drawer and students guess which one is next; on the OHP place a cut-out shape appropriate to the topic (e.g., a pencil case for classroom objects or a basket for shopping) and the smaller acetate pictures on top: students guess what is 'inside'.
- Stand a tall book in front of the OHP and place small real objects on the screen: students guess what the silhouettes are.
- Beat the teacher: slide small OHT drawings from one side of the OHP to the other. If students say the appropriate Spanish before it reaches the other side, they win. If they don't, you do! Vary the speed to keep them on their toes. Cheat by doing one or two impossibly fast so that you win – for some reason they always enjoy this!
- **Kim's Game**: show a set of pictures for 1–2 minutes, then remove one or more items. Students have to guess what has been removed.
- A variant of Kim's Game for teams: remove all the items and time how long it takes the team to name all the missing items, or see how many they can name within a

minute. Change a few each time so that the last group does not have the advantage of having seen them all several times. Can also be done as a whole-class activity: can we do it faster than last time?

- In reverse, cover each picture with a small piece of paper, and remove them as the items are guessed.
- Like **Battleships**: put items in a grid which is lettered vertically ABC and horizontally 123. Cover the items: students give co-ordinates and then guess what the item is. How many direct hits in two minutes? Then allow a student to set it up, and challenge you to guess the co-ordinates and items – although you have the advantage of knowing the vocabulary well, you may not be as good at guessing where they are!
- The **Generation Game**: a volunteer stands at the front and watches while you slide a selection (6–10) of pictures of the new language across the screen and name each in turn. They then have one minute in which to name them all from memory. It adds to the fun and the amount of language generated, if you allow the class to call out to the volunteer – they can help either by calling out items s/he has forgotten, or by calling out items not included to put them off the track. Good in teams, with volunteers from each team. Score one point for every correct item and add them up at the end to give a grand total – the team with the most correct items wins.
- **Noughts and Crosses**: good on a grid of nine, more mileage on a grid of 16. Mark the Xs and Os on a clear acetate placed on top of your picture, or shine the visual sheet onto a white board and draw the Xs and Os on top of the image. Scoring: 1 point for 3-in-a-row, and 2 points for 4-in-a-row.

Once they are familiar with the activity, students are perfectly capable of running it themselves – leaving you free to watch who is responding, or to sit in the seat vacated by the student and encourage the students around you. A small group could use the OHP or flashcards to play any of these games during a session of carousel-type activities, leaving you free to monitor other activities.

Games with small cards

The design of a number of the *Caminos 1, second edition*, OHT sheets, with pictures and language, allows them to be photocopied onto A4 card, cut into smaller cards and used for matching games. You will need to add the language to OHT sheets with pictures only: divide an A4 sheet into six or nine as appropriate and write the matching language in large, clear letters. Photocopy it onto card and use with the picture cards. If stored in small resealable plastic envelopes, they will last longer and can be reused by students for revision or by the fast finishers. Give all small cards on an A4 sheet the same number on the back, so that if you find one on the floor (as you inevitably will) you know which pack it comes from. All the activities below can be done in pairs after modelling by the teacher.

- Reading recognition: students use only the word cards. The teacher calls out the language, and the students put the cards in the order in which they hear them.
- Listening practice: as above, using pictures only. In pairs, one student can read from the word cards, while the other orders the pictures.
- Reading practice: students match word and picture cards. Good as a whole-class game, with students racing against each other in pairs, or trying to beat their previous time score. Students can also time each other.
- Pelmanism: all cards are placed face down, and students take it in turns to turn over two. If they don't match, the other partner has a turn. If they do match, the successful player keeps the pair of cards and has another turn. The student with most pairs wins.

- Speaking practice: one student puts down the picture cards for a partner, who has to say the appropriate language.
- A pairwork variant on 'guess the flashcard': one partner holds all the picture cards in a pile, and the other guesses what the one on top is. They then change over: the one who guesses the language for all cards in the fastest time is the winner. The game can also be scored according to the number of guesses, which can be recorded as ticks on a piece of paper. The person with the fewest number of guesses wins.
- A trick-your-partner game. Partner **A** puts down a picture card and says a word or phrase: partner **B** has five seconds to decide, by saying *Verdad* or *Mentira*, whether the language matches the picture correctly. If partner **B** makes a mistake, partner **A** keeps the card: the game ends when one player loses by having no cards left.

Songs

Songs help to reinforce vocabulary, structures and pronunciation in an enjoyable and relaxing way. There are many songs and raps in *Caminos 1, second edition*, with activities which help to sensitise the student's ear, foster good listening skills and provide a pleasant change of pace in a lesson. Some teachers are happy to play them while students are working quietly on reading and writing tasks. You might like to copy all the songs together on the same tape to facilitate this. Here are some ideas for presenting them, before tackling the activities suggested in the Student's Book or worksheets.

- Invent actions to accompany the song which students do along with you.
- Allow students to hum the tune or clap the rhythm as they listen.
- Give a group or row of students a key word to listen for: they wave both hands in the air when they hear their word.
- Pick out two or three key words which are repeated; ask students to copy them down and put a tick beside them every time they are sung.

Using displays

Displays are not only decorative: they can provide material which helps to teach and practise language. Enlarge pictures from the OHT masters by shining the OHP onto a sheet of A2, tracing round the outlines and adding the new language as an aide-mémoire for the current teaching unit.

Make sure students' work is read by devising a 'quick quiz' on it, displayed alongside 'Lost Property' notices (Unit 2 might generate questions such as *¿Cuántos bolis perdidos?*). A few small prizes or merits could be awarded for correct answers in Spanish: have a cardboard box or *buzón* pinned on the wall in which students can post their answers, with a daily or weekly collection.

Encourage students to devise their own puzzles: number games, crosswords, word-searches, sentences to decode, etc. Mounted on card and slipped into a cardboard wallet pinned to the wall, they act as a resource for fast finishers.

3 DIFFERENTIATION
Whole-class work

During the presentation and practice with the whole class, there are opportunites for meeting the different needs within the classroom:

- **By activity**: choose an activity every lesson which requires minimal use of Spanish so that less able students are able to operate and be successful on the same terms as everyone else. Use a variety of short activities to keep the interest of those with brief attention spans, and alternate between lively and 'settling' type tasks.

- **By skill**: a number of the activities can also be done as listening and reading tasks: you decide how many times to 'flash' the cards, or at what point you won't lower the blurred acetate any further, and allow students to write their replies. This helps those whose reactions are slower, or need more time to think. Allow them to use word cards which they simply have to place in the correct order.
- **Within an activity**: give the more able the chance to extend by adding in an extra layer of difficulty. For instance, you might point to two visuals and allow students to give the number or language for either or both. More able students can be encouraged to focus on additional features in their responses, e.g., gender ('un' or 'una' boli?).
- **By grouping**: use a variety of ways of grouping students so that they are used to working with others, even for five or 10 minutes. Pair up able and less able students for some activities so that the latter have a greater chance of experiencing success. Most of the activities above can be done as pairs co-operating together. Have a five-second pause before you ask for answers, to give pairs time to confer.
- **By outcome**: allow minimal responses from less able students, or allow them to use their *sí / no* card. Use smiles and praise to help them feel that you value their contribution as much as that from more able students who can say more. Accept partial guesses or incorrect pronunciation.
- **By level of support**: allow the support of the written language. More able students will simply do without it when they are ready because it is quicker not to look, but it acts a security blanket for those who need it.

Worksheets: core and extension

Each objective in the Student's Book is further supported by a visual sheet which can be used for OHP presentation, further reinforcement or card games, and worksheets. These practise all four skills through differentiated activities and are clearly referenced within the spreads of the Student's Book. Práctica: lengua pages provide grammar worksheets with English instructions. Where appropriate, there are worksheets to support lower attainers when tackling activities in the Student's Book (e.g., worksheet 4.2).

Reading pages

The *Lectura* pages, placed after every fifth unit, provide a range of extra reading material for pleasure and interest.

4 GRAMMAR

Caminos 1, second edition has an enhanced grammar focus, in line with the National Curriculum 2000. Grammar objectives are listed in the Student's Book and within each spread, grammar points are highlighted using a fast-forward button which refers students to a fuller explanation in the Grammar summary at the back of the book.

Acción: lengua pages

The main grammar point is picked up and explored with activities in the Acción: lengua page at the end of each unit. Each page offers a short presentation of the grammar point, followed by differentiated exercises. All pages introduce full paradigms of verbs for less able students, while higher attainers are required to recognise and manipulate the part of the verb that has been met in the core material.

Práctica: lengua pages and worksheets

These offer differentiated exercises on grammar points met in preceding units after every fifth unit. Grammar is recycled, often in a different setting or situation, so helping students to develop transferable skills, and instructions are in English.

Táctica: lengua pages

These also come after every fifth unit and focus on language learning strategies. English is used in *Caminos 1, second edition*, in order to help students to access the ideas and suggestions easily for themselves. A brief explanation is followed by an activity – listening, speaking, reading, writing or learning vocabulary – which enables students to put into practice what they have learnt.

¡Repaso! pages

Consist of a double-page spread with exercises at two levels of difficulty after every five units, revising language met previously in new contexts.

5 OTHER OPPORTUNITIES
Using Information Technology

There are many good reasons for encouraging ICT use in the Spanish classroom: it provides a welcome change of activity and pace for you and the students; students find it motivating; it enables them to work at their own pace on differentiated activities in what they perceive as a non-threatening environment and many can display their considerable skill.

Suggestions for incorporating or using ICT are given in the introductory notes to each objective, under ICT opportunites. These may involve word-processing, redrafting, building up a data-bank, or preparing work for display. They are not intended to be prescriptive, but merely to highlight and give examples of possibilities: many more will occur to you as you use the course and much will depend on the resources available in your department or school, along with the frequency or ease of access to them. Some general ideas follow.

Word-processing, desk-top publishing, and graphics packages

- **Homework**: students can be encouraged to word-process written activities either at home or at lunchtimes, if they have access to the computer room: an initial attempt can be corrected by you and students can then redraft and use the final version in their homework books.
- **Visual support**: classroom language (Unit 2) or rules can be typed up and printed large to act as memory-joggers.
- **Project work and creative writing**: many of the activities suggested in the Student's Book provide opportunities for using ICT. A number of students are sophisticated users of graphics and design packages, and their talents can be harnessed to provide collections of poems, booklets and leaflets.

Text manipulation

A number of commercial text manipulation and authoring packages add variety to the activities offered to students in the Spanish classroom: Fun with Texts, Word Sequencing, Gapkit (all from Camsoft), Modern Languages Developing Tray (ILECC) and Storyboard (Wida) are very popular. These packages allow teachers to type in texts which students can then manipulate for consolidation and practise in a variety of ways. However, a number of the activities suggested below can also be done on a conventional word-processor, requiring students to use the cut-and-paste facility and move blocks of text around. Many of the texts from *Caminos 1, second edition*, can be typed in as separate files and used in a variety of ways for consolidation: this will save you time inventing and writing material yourself. Some suggestions follow.

- *Learning vocabulary*: new vocabulary for the objective or unit can be accessed quickly from the *Hojas de vocabulario* and typed up for use in a variety of ways:
  - Instruct the package to hide the genders, so that students have to type in the correct *un* or *una*.
  - Type in the English as well and remove the Spanish or English word at random: students have to reconstruct the bilingual list.
  - Type up a list of key vocabulary, and give students a photocopy of the pictures from the relevant OHT: they have to reorder the vocabulary list to match the sequence or numbering of the pictures.
  - Use a scrambling activity so that the words appear as anagrams, or in code: students reconstruct the Spanish version.
- *Consolidating grammar*: many of the activities from the Acción: lengua pages can be used, as can tasks from the Práctica: lengua pages and worksheets. Once typed in, instruct the package to hide whatever it is you want them to practise (verb endings, adjectival endings, genders, etc.), and students have to put them in again correctly. Verb tables can be used in the same way.
- *Mixed skill tasks for reinforcing / revising language in context*
  - Reuse the picture stories from the Student's Book. Type in the text with the characters' names in front, and underline any words which could be altered later by students to make a new dialogue (e.g., names of drinks, colours, adjectives, types of houses, etc.). Instruct the package to jumble the order of the lines. Firstly, students reorder them correctly: this encourages reading for meaning. Next, students invent their own version, substituting other known vocabulary for the underlined words. Finally they can role-play it. (Reading > writing > speaking)
  - Type in a dialogue from the Student's Book, or one of the question-and-answer matching tasks, but giving the questions only and in the wrong order. Give students a separate list of the answers on the OHP or on a page: they have to reorder the questions on screen to match the answers. If you alter the text as you type it in, so that some of the information in the answers is different from the original recorded version, students can subsequently listen to the recording, underline the differences, and then substitute other known vocabulary to create and record a new dialogue themselves. (Reading > listening > writing > speaking)
  - Type in one of the tapescripts for a listening exercise from the worksheets. Instruct the package to give only the initial letter of each word. First, play the recording to students several times and allow them to take notes: they then work in pairs, from their notes, to reconstruct the full tapescript on screen. Fast finishers can be given a printout of the original dialogue with only the first letter of each word, or a gapped version, to do orally from memory. (Listening > reading > writing> speaking).

Fast tracking

For second-language learners wishing to complete the course in less than a year, the following activities from the Student's Book will provide a core of material which will enable students to fulfil all the objectives.

(SB – Student's Book; AL – Acción: lengua; TL – Táctica: lengua; WK – Worksheet; PL – Práctica: lengua worksheet)

PB Unit	Obj. A	Obj. B	Obj. C	Obj. D	Obj. E	Other
1	1, 2, 3	1, 3, 4	1, 3, 4	1		
2	1, 3, 4	1, 3, 4	1, 3, 4, 5	2, 3		
3	1, 2, 3	1, 2, 3	1, 3, 5	1, 2	1, 2	
4	1, 3	1, 2, 3b	1, 2, 5	1, 2		
5	1, 3	1, 2, 3, 4	1, 2a, 2b	1, 2		TL
6	1, 2	1, 2, 3	1, 3	1, 2		
7	1, 3, 5	1, 2, 6	1, 2, 3	1, 2		
8	1, 2, 3, 4	1, 3, 4	1, 3	1		
9	1, 2, 3	1, 2, 3	2, 3, 5	1, 2		
10	1, 2, 4, 5	1, 2	1, 2	1, 2, 3	1, 2	TL
11	1, 2, 4	1, 2, 5	1, 2, 3	2, 3		
12	1, 2	1, 2, 3	1, 5, 6	1, 4, 5, 6	1, 2	
13	1, 2, 3	1, 2, 3	1, 2, 3, 4c	1, 2, 3		
14	1, 2, 3	1, 2, 3, 5	1, 2	1, 2		
15	1, 2, 4	1, 3, 4	1, 3			TL

6 ASSESSMENT POLICY

Assessment is in the target language in harmony with the rationale of this course. In order to give the most detailed picture of student performance, we have adopted a three-pronged approach, so that you can build up a portfolio of evidence during the year for each individual from these different sources.

First, assessment opportunities are suggested at the beginning of each unit in the Teacher's Book. These activities can be used unobtrusively during classroom teaching to monitor progress, or selectively at the discretion of the classroom teacher, and the results can be recorded to give additional evidence of attainment.

Second, there are vocabulary sheets which have a section designed for students to test each other on new language. They provide an opportunity for revision and a means of checking progress while at the same time encouraging students to take more responsibility for their own learning. The vocabulary sheets are contained in the Resource and Assessment File and can be photocopied. The degree of formality with which these checklists are used will of course depend on the individual teacher or department.

Finally, there is more formal assessment at regular intervals throughout the book. Using the mark scheme provided, the level at which each student is working in each of the four skills – listening, speaking, reading and writing – can be assessed. These mark schemes are designed for ease of operation and to give sensible totals. Levels 1-6 in the four attainment targets are catered for. The answers to the assessments given on pages 158–162 of this book suggest the levels which can be attained.

To monitor standards, it is also recommended that each department compile a dossier of samples of students' work covering all the attainment targets.

UNIDAD 1: NUEVOS AMIGOS

	OBJECTIVE	KEY LANGUAGE	GRAMMAR / SKILLS	PoS	ATs	Scottish 5–14 National Guidelines Levels
1A	¡Hola! ¿Cómo te llamas? introducing yourself	¡hola!, ¿cómo te llamas?, me llamo … ¿y tú?, ¿qué tal?, estupendo, muy bien, bien, regular, fatal, sentaos, callaos, levantaos, hay que …, sacar los libros, recoger todo, aprender, escribir, repetir, dibujar, escuchar (la cinta), mirar (la pizarra, el retroproyector), trabajar (en parejas)	listening attentively; identifying and pronouncing vowel sounds	1 a, b, c 2 a, b, c, d, e 3 b, c, e 4 a 5 a, b, c, d	1, 1–2 2, 1–2 3, 1–2 4, 1–2	Listening A–B Speaking A–B Reading A–B Writing A–B
1B	¿Cómo se escribe? spelling your name	yo, sí, no está alphabet a–z ¿cómo se escribe? mi / tu nombre mi / tu apellido	distinguishing consonants clearly and pronouncing them correctly; spelling words	1 a, b, c 2 a, b, c, e 3 b, c, e 4 a 5 a, b, c, d, f		
1C	¿Cómo se dice …? coping with language problems; numbers 1to19	numbers 1 to19 ¿cómo se dice en español / en inglés? no lo sé, ni idea se me ha olvidado otra vez, por favor	beginning to cope with redundant language; coping with simple linguistic problems in the target language	1 a, b, c 2 a, b, c, d, e 3 b, c, e 4 a 5 a, b, c, d, f		
1D	Los días de la semana the days of the week; spelling words with accents	lunes martes miércoles jueves viernes sábado domingo	asking for help with vocabulary and pronunciation; expressing simple opinions; spelling words with accents	1 a, b, c 2 a, b, c, d, e 3 b, c, e 4 a 5 a, b, c, d		

UNIDAD 2: EN CLASE

	OBJECTIVE	KEY LANGUAGE	GRAMMAR / SKILLS	PoS	ATs	Scottish 5–14 National Guidelines Levels
2A	¿Tienes …? schoolbag items; questions; the indefinite article	¿tienes?, ¿me dejas …? sí, toma, tengo, lo siento, no tengo, un boli / un bolígrafo, un cuaderno, un estuche, un lápiz, un libro, una hoja, un sacapuntas, una agenda, una goma, una mochila, una pluma, una regla	asking for things, and replying appropriately; using the indefinite article; un / una	1 a, b, c 2 a, b, c, d 3 a, b, c, d, e 4 a 5 a, b, d, f	1, 1–2 2, 1–2 3, 1–2 4, 1–2	Listening A–B Speaking A–B Reading A–B Writing A–B
2B	¿Se hace …? classroom instructions; the definite article 'the'; classroom furniture and equipment	se hace por delante se hace por detrás se hace en limpio se hace en sucio se hace en la hoja se hace en el cuaderno ¿qué se hace ahora? ¿qué página es? la pizarra, la puerta, la ventana, abre / cierra, enciende / apaga, pon … bien / limpia la silla, la mesa, la luz, el cassette, el retroproyector, el ordenador, el vídeo el magnetofón, el tablón el borrador el estante el suelo el armario	coping with everyday classroom situations in the target language; using the definite article el / la	1 a, b, c 2 a, b, d, e 3 a, b, c, d 4 a 5 a, b, c, d		
2C	Números y fechas numbers 20 to 31; months of the year; the date	the numbers 20 to 31 ¿a quién le toca? me toca a mí te toca a ti enero, febrero, marzo, abril, mayo, junio, julio, agosto, septiembre, octubre, noviembre, diciembre	suggesting whose turn it is; asking / giving the date	1 a, b, c 2 a, c, d, e 3 a, b, c, d 4 c, d 5 a, b, c, d		
2D	Los plurales forming the plurals of nouns; forming the plurals of articles	plurals of nouns and articles already introduced	understanding instructions; forming plurals	1 a, b, c 2 a, b, d, e 3 a, b, c, d 4 a 5 a, b, c		

	OBJECTIVE	KEY LANGUAGE	GRAMMAR / SKILLS	PoS	ATs	Scottish 5–14 National Guidelines Levels
	UNIDAD 3: LA FAMILIA					
3A	**¿Tienes hermanos?** talking about brothers and sisters	hermano / hermana mayor / menor hermanastro / hermanastra hermano gemelo / hermana gemela hijo único / hija única tengo / no tengo / tienes soy / eres se llama / se llaman que ...	the relative pronoun **que** ...	1 a, b, c 2 a, b, c, d 3 a, b, c, d, e 4 a 5 a, b, c, d	1, 1–3 2, 1–3 3, 1–3 4, 1–3	Listening A–C Speaking A–C Reading A–C Writing A–C
3B	**¿Cuántas personas hay en tu familia?** talking about members of the family	¿cuántas personas hay en tu familia? somos ... personas mi ... padre / padrastro madre / madrastra mamá / papá tío / tía primo / prima amigo / amiga hijo / hija / hijos abuelo / abuela mis padres ... ... están divorciados ... están separados	carrying out a small survey and drawing up results	1 a, b, c 2 a, b, c, d, e 3 a, b, c, d, e 4 a 5 a, b, c, d, f		
3C	**¿Cuántos años tienes?** numbers from 31 to 100; people's ages	numbers 31 to 100 ¿cuántos años tienes? tengo ... años ¿cuántos años tiene? tiene ... años	listening for key numbers; saying people's ages	1 a, b, c 2 a, b, c, d, e 3 a, b, c, d, e 4 a, d 5 a, b, c, d, f		
3D	**¿Tienes algún animal?** talking about pets; saying what kind of pet you would like	¿tienes algún animal? ¿qué tipo de animal es? ¿cuántos años tiene tu animal? ¿cómo se llama tu animal? ¿te gustaría tener un animal? me gustaría tener ... no me gustaría tener ningún animal un perro un gato un hámster un ratón un conejo un pájaro un gerbo un pez un insecto palo una serpiente una cobaya una lagartija una tortuga	writing a simple letter using a model **me gustaría**	1 a, b, c 2 a, b, c, d, e 3 a, b, c, d, e 4 a, d 5 a, b, c, d, f		
3E	**¿Cuándo es tu cumpleaños?** talking about birthdays; singing 'happy birthday'	¡feliz cumpleaños! ¿cuándo es tu cumpleaños? es el ... lo siento, no sé	revision of months and numbers 1 to 31; apologising and saying you don't know	1 a, b, c 2 a, b, c, d, e 3 a, b, c 4 a, d 5 a, b, c, d		

UNIDAD 4: ¿CÓMO ERES?

	OBJECTIVE	KEY LANGUAGE	GRAMMAR / SKILLS	PoS	ATs	Scottish 5–14 National Guidelines Levels
4A	**¿Qué colores te gustan?** names of colours likes / dislikes	lila, naranja, rosa, azul gris, marrón, verde amarillo/a, blanco/a negro/a, morado/a rojo/a ¿te gusta …? me gusta me gusta mucho no está mal no me gusta no me gusta nada	extending your ability to agree and disagree	1 a, b, c 2 a, b, c, e 3 a, b, c, d, e 4 a, c 5 a, b, c, f	1, 1–3 2, 1–3 3, 1–3 4, 1–3	Listening A–C Speaking A–C Reading A–C Writing A–C
4B	**¿Cómo soy?** personality; adjectives; verb 'to be'	soy / eres / es un poco, muy, a veces, bastante, normalmente hablador(a), gracioso/a, extrovertido/a, simpático/a, alegre, optimista, tímido/a, pesimista, callado/a, serio/a, antipático/a, perezoso/a, trabajador(a)	verb **ser** (to be); singular adjectives; expressing enthusiastic agreement or vehement disagreement	1 a, b, c 2 a, b, d, e 3 a, b, c, d, e 4 a 5 a, b, c, d, e		
4C	**Mi físico** descriptions of build; hair and eye colour	¿cómo es tu físico? ¿cómo tienes el pelo? ¿cómo tienes los ojos? ¿de carácter, cómo eres? Soy / eres / es … alto/a, bajo/a, delgado/a, gordito/a, pelirrojo/a de talla media tengo / tienes / tiene … llevo / llevas / lleva … el pelo negro, rubio, moreno, castaño los ojos grises, azules, marrones, verdes pecas, barba, gafas	adjective agreement	1 a, b, c 2 a, b, c, d 3 a, b, c, d, e 4 a, d 5 a, b, c, d, f		
4D	**Somos …** to be (plural); adjectives	plural of ser (nosotros) somos (vosotros) sois (ellos, ellas, ustedes) son plurals of adjectives already encountered serios / serias alegres optimistas trabajadores / trabajadoras tonto/a(s) divertido/a(s) molesto/a(s) imposible(s) majo/a(s) pesado/a(s) el cuervo	using the verb **ser** (to be); forming plural adjectives	1 a, b, c 2 a, b, c, d, g 3 a, b, c, d, e 4 c, d 5 a, b, c, d, f		

	OBJECTIVE	KEY LANGUAGE	GRAMMAR / SKILLS	PoS	ATs	Scottish 5–14 National Guidelines Levels
UNIDAD 5: VAMOS AL INSTI						
5A	**¿Qué asignaturas estudias?** school subjects; what's on what day	¿qué tienes hoy / el (lunes)? tengo … ¿tienes …? Es … / son … (el) deporte, (el) dibujo, (el) francés, (el) español / (la) lengua, (el) inglés (la) biología, (la) música, (la) historia (la) geografía, (la) física, (la) química (la) tecnología, (las) ciencias, (las) matemáticas, (la) ética el campo de deportes, el gimnasio, el patio, el salón de actos, la biblioteca, el comedor / la cantina, la enfermería, la piscina, la sala de ordenadores, despachos, laboratorios, pasillos, aulas, servicios, cocinas (revision of likes and dislikes, and descriptions, e.g. aburrido)	asking and responding to questions, and contradicting a wrong answer	1 a, b, c 2 a, b, c, g, h 3 a, b, c, d, e 4 a, d 5 a, b, c, d, f	1, 1–3 2, 1–3 3, 1–3 4, 1–3	Listening A–C Speaking A–C Reading A–C Writing A–C
5B	**¿Qué opinas?** subjects; reasons for likes / dislikes	(no) me gusta (el inglés, el francés, etc.) (no) me gustan (nada) … el / la … es (divertido / aburrido, etc.) las / los (matemáticas, etc.) son … el / la profe es … simpático/a divertido, aburrido, difícil fácil, interesante porque …, pero, aunque	**gustar** (to like) revision of plural adjectives; expressing more sophisticated opinions and backing them up with reasons	1 a, b, c 2 a, b, c, d, f, g 3 a, b, c, d, e 4 a 5 a, b, c, d, f		
5C	**¿Cuándo tienes …?** time; subjects – where and when	a las (diez) … es la una …, son las (diez) … en punto, y cinco, y diez, y cuarto, y veinte, y veinticinco, y media, menos veinticinco, menos veinte, menos cuarto, menos diez, menos cinco la mañana, la tarde el aula, el campo de deportes el laboratorio, la sala de ordenadores tengo … horas la mañana / tarde luego … ¿qué tienes el … por la mañana / tarde? ¿cuántas horas de … tienes? tengo … horas de … la mañana / tarde / el lunes / a la semana (etc.) ¿cuándo tienes …?	asking and telling the time and using time phrases confidently	1 a, b, c 2 a, b, c, d, f 3 a, b, c, d 4 a 5 a, b, c, d, f		
5D	**¿Te interesa …?** likes and dislikes revision of **gustar**	revision of language encountered in the first three spreads of the unit	recognising and using the present tenses of **gustar** and **encantar**	1 a, b, c 2 a, b, c, d 3 a, b, c, d, e 4 a 5 a, b, c, d, f		

REPASO 1–5	Revision section looking back over language studied in Units 1–5	**PoS**	1 a, c 2 a, b, c, d 3 b, c, e 4 c, d 5 a, c, d, f
1–5 LECTURA	Reading for pleasure and information	**PoS**	2 h, i 3 d 4 a 5 g
1–5 TÁCTICA: LENGUA	Recognising masculine and feminine nouns, developing listening skills, learning vocabulary	**PoS**	2 h 3 d 5 g
1–5 PRÁCTICA: LENGUA	Summative grammar tasks based on grammar items encountered in Units 1–5	**PoS**	1 b 3 d, e

	OBJECTIVE	KEY LANGUAGE	GRAMMAR / SKILLS	PoS	ATs	Scottish 5–14 National Guidelines Levels
UNIDAD 6: MI CIUDAD						
6A	¿Dónde vives? where you live	¿dónde vives / vive? vivo / vive en … una ciudad, una ciudad grande, un pueblo, el centro un barrio, las afueras, el campo, cerca de …	attracting someone's attention	1 a, c 2 a, b, c, d 3 b, c, e 4 c, d 5 a, b, c, d, e, f	1, 1–4 2, 1–4 3, 1–4 4, 1–4	Listening A–D Speaking A–D Reading A–D Writing A–D
6B	¿Dónde está exactamente? where you live (in detail); points of the compass	¿dónde está? está en … el norte / el sur/ el este / el oeste el noreste / el sureste / el noroeste / el suroeste las Islas Británicas, Escocia, Gales Irlanda del Norte, Irlanda del Sur, España en la sierra, en la costa, en el centro de … junto al río	giving more detailed information about a particular area; the points of the compass	1 a, c 2 a, e–g, h, i 3 a, d, e 4 c, d 5 a, b, c, d, e		
6C	¿Qué hay en tu barrio o ciudad? what there is in your area	¿qué hay en tu barrio? hay / no hay … … donde comer… donde comprar lugares públicos un supermercado un mercado una tienda una panadería un videoclub un cine un instituto un parque un colegio una discoteca una iglesia un bar un hotel un restaurante una cafetería una piscina, un polideportivo	writing a letter using a model	1 a, c 2 a, d–g, h, j 3 a, c, d, e 4 c, d 5 a, b, c, d, e, f		
6D	¿Qué tiempo hace? weather and seasons	¿qué tiempo hace (en …) ¿hace buen tiempo? (sí,) hace buen tiempo (no,) hace mal tiempo el clima es … casi tropical hace (mucho) calor hace frío hace sol hace viento hay niebla hay nieve hay tormentas llueve (mucho)	phone-call structures and language	1 a, b, c 2 a, b, d–g, i 3 a,c, d, e 4 c, d 5 a, b, c, d, e, f		

UNIDAD 7: ¿CÓMO ES DONDE VIVES?						
	OBJECTIVE	KEY LANGUAGE	GRAMMAR / SKILLS	PoS	ATs	Scottish 5–14 National Guidelines Levels
7A	**¿Cómo es?** describing where you live; saying where you would like to live; opinions	¿qué te parece? me parece … moderno turístico bonito tranquilo divertido limpio antiguo industrial feo ruidoso aburrido sucio ¡de acuerdo! ¡qué va! no sé ¿dónde te gustaría vivir? me gustaría vivir en … a (X) le gustaría vivir en …	expressing opinions, agreeing and disagreeing; giving preferences; coping with redundant language in listening comprehension	1 a, b, c 2 a, d–g, h, i 3 a, b, c, d, e 4 c, d 5 a, b, c, d, e, f	1, 1–4 2, 1–4 3, 1–4 4, 1–4	Listening A–D Speaking A–D Reading A–D Writing A–D
7B	**Lo bueno y lo malo** the good and bad points of where you live	¿te gusta? me gusta me gusta mucho no me gusta no me gusta nada no está mal lo bueno es que … lo malo es que … ¿por qué? porque … hay mucha movida hay mucha diversión hay mucha cultura hay mucho tráfico hay mucho turismo tiene mucha historia tengo muchos amigos	giving balanced reasons, both positive and negative	1 a, b, c 2 a, c–f, h 3 a, c, d, e 4 c, d 5 a, b, c, d, e, f		
7C	**¿Qué se puede hacer?** what there is to do in your town or area; what you like doing	¿qué se puede hacer? se puede … ir al cine ir al polideportivo ir a la bolera ir a la playa ir a las salas de juegos ir a los partidos de fútbol ir de compras ir de excursión ir de paseo en bici ir de pesca salir con amigos nadar visitar los pueblos típicos	al ('to the')	1 a, b, c 2 a, d–g, i 3 a, c, d 4 c, d 5 a, b, c, d, e, f		
7D	**¿Qué deportes te gusta hacer?** which sports you like to play or do; which sports you would like to play or do	hacer los deportes acuáticos hacer atletismo jugar al hockey hacer alpinismo jugar al voleibol hacer ciclismo hacer piragüismo hacer deportes jugar al fútbol jugar al squash hacer esquí hacer alpinismo hacer footing hacer vela hacer atletismo y ciclismo	more dictionary skills	1 a, b, c 2 a, e–f, j 3 a, d, e 4 c, d 5 a, b, c, d, e, f		

		UNIDAD 8: HOGAR, DULCE HOGAR				
	OBJECTIVE	KEY LANGUAGE	GRAMMAR / SKILLS	PoS	ATs	Scottish 5–14 National Guidelines Levels
8A	¿Vives en una casa o un piso? what kind of house or flat you live in; how near or far away it is; where it is in relation to other places	una casa una casa doble una casa adosada un chalé un piso un bloque nuevo un bloque antiguo una torre una finca la calle la plaza está … cerca (de) lejos (de) a unos cinco minutos andando a tres kilómetros prepositions: delante (de); detrás (de); al lado (de); encima (de); debajo (de); enfrente (de); entre; en …	saying something is near or far away; **del** (of, from the)	1 a, b, c 2 a, d–f, h, 3 a, b, c, e 4 c, d 5 a, b, c, d, e, f	1, 1–4 2, 1–4 3, 1–4 4, 1–4	Listening A–D Speaking A–D Reading A–D Writing A–D
8B	¿Qué hay en el piso? naming the rooms in your house and saying what facilities it has	hay / tiene … una entrada una cocina un salón con balcón un comedor un cuarto de baño un aseo escaleras un dormitorio una terraza un lavadero un porche un sótano un jardín un garaje un desván	asking what words mean in another language	1 a, b, c 2 a, d–g, h 3 a, b, c, d, e 4 c, d 5 a, b, c, d, e, f		
8C	¿Cómo es por dentro? saying where rooms are in your home	¿cuántas plantas tiene …? ¿cuántas habitaciones tiene? ¿cuántos dormitorios tiene? en la planta baja en la primera planta en la segunda planta arriba abajo a la derecha a la izquierda al final	recognising Spanish handwriting	1 a, b, c 2 a, d–g, h 3 a, b, c, d, e 4 c, d 5 a, b, c, d, e		
8D	¿Qué hay en tu dormitorio? what there is in your bedroom; explaining where things are	el dormitorio grande pequeño no está mal … la cama la mesilla de noche la lámpara el armario el guardarropa el pupitre la butaca la cómoda la alfombra la estantería	making descriptions and explanations	1 a, b, c 2 a, d, e, f 3 a, b, c, d 4 c, d 5 a, b, c, d, f		

UNIDAD 9: LOS RATOS LIBRES						
	OBJECTIVE	KEY LANGUAGE	GRAMMAR / SKILLS	PoS	ATs	Scottish 5–14 National Guidelines Levels
9A	¿Qué tal estás? saying how you are feeling; saying what you want to do; the verb **querer**	estoy / estás / está … cansado/a contento/a decepcionado/a deprimido/a egoísta enfadado/a estresado/a extrovertido/a harto/a (de) ilusionado/a optimista preocupado/a triste querer (quiero / quieres etc.)	attracting people's attention and making suggestions	1 a, b, c 2 a, d–g, h, i 3 a, c, d, f 4 c, d 5 a, b, c, d, e, f	1, 1–4 2, 1–4 3, 1–4 4, 1–4	Listening A–D Speaking A–D Reading A–D Writing A–D
9B	¿Estás libre? say where you're going; asking if someone is free and replying; saying you can't, and giving excuses	¿quieres ir / venir …? voy / vas / va al cine al polideportivo al parque de atracciones al club de jóvenes al estadio de fútbol al centro comercial no tengo mucho tiempo / dinero no puedo … porque … a la bolera a la pista de hielo a la piscina por la mañana / la tarde / la noche vale, gracias (lo siento), (el problema) es que … no tengo ganas tengo un montón de deberes no quiero … porque …	saying where you go / are going, and asking others; accepting and declining invitations	1 a, b, c 2 a, d–g, h, j 3 a, b, c, d, f 4 c, d 5 a, b, c, d, e		
9C	¿Dónde y cuándo nos vemos? arranging where and when to meet	¿estás libre? (no) estoy libre ¿dónde nos vemos? ¿cuándo nos vemos? ¿a qué hora nos vemos? a la una / a las (dos) ¡estupendo! ¡hasta luego! adiós	arranging where and when to meet; revision of prepositions (place)	1 a, b, c 2 a, d–g, h, j 3 a, b, c, d, e 4 c, d 5 a, b, c, d, f		
9D	¿Qué vas a hacer? saying what you're going to do; saying where you're going and with whom	voy / vas (etc.) a … ¿con quién …? ¿adónde vas a …? ¿cuándo vas a …? ¿Qué vas a hacer? voy a … quedarse	asking and answering questions and using the simple future	1 a, b, c 2 a, d–g, h, j 3 a, b, c, d, e 4 c, d 5 a, b, c, d, e, f		

	OBJECTIVE	KEY LANGUAGE	GRAMMAR / SKILLS	PoS	ATs	Scottish 5–14 National Guidelines Levels
UNIDAD 10: LA RUTINA						
10A	**¿Qué tienes que hacer?** saying what you have to do at home and asking others	¿qué tienes que hacer? (no) tengo / tienes / tiene que … ayudar, hacer la / mi cama, lavar los platos, compartir, quitar la mesa, quitar el polvo, pasar la aspiradora, planchar, lavar la ropa, limpiar el cuarto de baño, preparar la comida, poner la mesa, recoger mi dormitorio, sacar la basura, todos los días, el fin de semana, de vez en cuando, nunca, la pocilga	**tener que** (to have to); expressions of frequency; negatives	1 a, b, c 2 a, d–g, h, j 3 a, b, c, d 4 c, d 5 a, b, c, d, f	1, 1–4 2, 1–4 3, 1–4 4, 1–4	Listening A–D Speaking A–D Reading A–D Writing A–D
10B	**¿Cómo es tu rutina diaria?** saying what you have to do as part of your daily routine	hay que … cenar, ir a la cama, trabajar mucho, coger el autobús, desayunar, estudiar, hacer los deberes, ir al instituto, tener exámenes, ver la tele (un poco) llegar a tiempo, volver a casa, escuchar, leer, escribir, comer, ir al instituto (andando), ir al polideportivo, salir un rato pronto, temprano	Saying what you have to do	1 a, c 2 a, d–g, h, j 3 a, b, c, e 4 c, d 5 a, b, c, d, e, f		
10C	**Normalmente** describing what you do	verbs in the present tense, including: me levanto (temprano), desayuno (zumo de naranja), cojo (el autobús), voy (al instituto), llego (a tiempo), escucho (a los profesores), trabajo (mucho), vuelvo (a casa), escribo (en mi carpeta), como (con la familia), salgo (con mis amigos), juego (al tenis), veo (la televisión), leo (una revista), hago (mis deberes), ceno (en la cocina), voy (a la cama)	present tense verbs;	1 a, b, c 2 a, c–g, h, i 3 a, d, e 4 c, d 5 a, b, c, d, e		
10D	**Preguntas** asking questions about daily routine	question forms, including the following: ¿qué desayunas?, ¿cómo vas al instituto?, ¿a qué hora llegas?, ¿dónde comes al mediodía?, ¿sales mucho con tus amigos?, ¿cuántas horas de deberes haces?, ¿qué desayunas en Gran Bretaña?, ¿vuelves a casa?, ¿a qué hora te levantas?, ¿tienes tiempo para desayunar?, ¿vas al instituto andando?, ¿qué haces en el recreo?, ¿llevas un bocadillo para comer?, ¿y después de las clases?, ¿haces algún deporte?, ¿ves mucho la tele?	asking questions about daily routine; present tense (**tú**)	1 a, b, c 2 a, d–g, h 3 a, b, c, d, e 4 c, d 5 a, b, c, d, f		
10E	**Hablando de otra persona** talking about what other people do	verbs in the third person singular, including: ¡es un desastre!, se levanta tarde, no desayuna, no llega a tiempo, no estudia en clase, no escribe los deberes, sale al parque, vuelve a casa a las diez, va a la cama a las once de la noche, come una tostada y es todo, llega tarde también, estudia nueve asignaturas, no escribe nada en sus cuadernos, ve cuatro horas de tele cada noche	transferring sentences into the third person form	1 a, b, c 2 a, d–g, h, j 3 a, b, c, d, e, f 4 c, d 5 a, b, c, d, e		

			PoS	
6–10 REPASO	Revision section looking back over language studied in Units 6–10		PoS	1 a, c 2 a, b, c, d 3 b, c, e 4 c, d 5 a, c, d, f
6–10 LECTURA	Reading for pleasure and information		PoS	2 h, i 3 d 4 a 5 g
6–10 TÁCTICA: LENGUA	Finding your way around the dictionary, note-taking, sentence-building		PoS	2 h 3 d 5 g
6–10 PRÁCTICA: LENGUA	Summative grammar tasks based on grammar items encountered in Units 6–10		PoS	1 b 3 d, e

	OBJECTIVE	KEY LANGUAGE	GRAMMAR / SKILLS	PoS	ATs	Scottish 5–14 National Guidelines Levels
11A	**¿Qué quieres beber?** ordering a hot or cold drink; asking others what they want to drink	¿qué quieres?, quiero … una bebida caliente / fría algo frío / caliente un agua mineral, un café con leche, un café solo un té solo, un té con leche / con limón un chocolate, un granizado, un batido de chocolate / de fresa, una limonada, una naranjada una coca-cola, un zumo de naranja con gas / sin gas, con hielo camarero / camarera, cliente, ¡oiga camarero! dígame, ¿algo más? sí, por favor, no, nada más gracias, es todo, en seguida, ¿cuánto cuesta …?	exchanging information orally	1 a, b, c 2 a, d–g, k, l 3 a, c, d 4 c, d 5 a, b, c, f	1, 1–4 2, 1–4 3, 1–4 4, 1–4	Listening A–D Speaking A–D Reading A–D Writing A–D
11B	**¿Qué quieres comer?** how to order something to eat; other ways of saying what you'd like; asking what there is for vegetarians	¿para quién es? para mí / él / ella, para mi amigo/a ¿quieres probar …? ¿hay algo para vegetarianos? soy vegetariano/a una hamburguesa, un perrito caliente un bocadillo de jamón York un cruasán de queso, un cruasán vegetal un cruasán / bocadillo de chorizo, una tortilla española, calamares, patatas fritas, pescado frito, churros, aceitunas ¿tienes hambre / sed?, (no) tengo hambre / sed	**para mí, ti, él, ella,**etc.; memorising words	1 a, b, c 2 a, d–g, j 3 a, c, d 4 a, c 5 a, b, c, d		
11C	**¿Cuánto es?** asking how much something is; paying the bill; numbers from 100 to 1000	numbers from 100 to 1000 la cuenta, por favor ¿cuánto es en total? un billete, una moneda, un duro sólo tengo no tengo cambio	how to say what you want (**querer**); numbers from 100 to 1000	1 a, c 2 a, d–g, j 3 a, c, d, e 4 a, c 5 a, b, c, d, f		
11D	**En el restaurante** how to order a three–course meal	¿nos trae más pan, por favor? ¿qué van a tomar (de postre)? ¿y de segundo? ¿y para beber? de primero para mí, quisiera … voy a tomar prefiero … filete de ternera / cerdo, gambas al ajillo, pisto manchego, sopa de verduras tortilla de champiñones trucha con almendras flan, fruta (del tiempo), helado de fresa helado de vainilla zumo de naranja / piña una botella de agua mineral con / sin gas una botella de vino blanco / tinto / rosado	how to order a three-course meal; the verb **preferir** (to prefer)	1 a, c 2 a, d–f, g 3 a, c, d, e 4 c, d 5 a, b, c, d, f		

	UNIDAD 12: ¡A COMPRAR!					
	OBJECTIVE	**KEY LANGUAGE**	**GRAMMAR / SKILLS**	**PoS**	**ATs**	**Scottish 5–14 National Guidelines Levels**
12A	**¡Vamos de tiendas!** different types of shops; names for different types of items to buy	el tomate, el azúcar, el ajo, el pan, el café, el filete, el limón de cerdo, el vino, el gazpacho, el zumo de fruta los pasteles, los pimientos, los pañuelos, los huevos, los antibióticos la mantequilla, la aspirina, la harina, la leche la revista, la naranja, la cebolla, la limonada la carne picada, la tortilla, la comida, la ropa, la pasta de dientes las patatas, las patatas fritas, las sardinas frescas el periódico, el supermercado, el almacén, el detergente, el hipermercado, el champú, el barrio, el mercado, el quiosco la farmacia, la panadería, la pescadería, la droguería, la pastelería, la carnicería, la tienda (de alimentación), la frutería	singular and plural forms of **comprar**	1 a, b, c 2 a, c–g, h, j 3 a, d, e 4 c, d 5 a, b, c, d, f	1, 1–4 2, 1–4 3, 1–4 4, 1–4	Listening A–D Speaking A–D Reading A–D Writing A–D
12B	**¿Por dónde se va?** asking for and giving directions	perdone, ¿por dónde se va a ...? tome la primera / segunda (calle) a la izquierda / derecha cruce la plaza, baje la calle, suba la calle coja la segunda a la derecha siga todo recto, está al final, está allí, hasta los semáforos tuerza a la izquierda en el cruce	asking for and giving directions; positive commands: **tú, usted**	1 a, b, c 2 a, c–g, h, j 3 a, d, e 4 c, d 5 a, b, c, d, f		
12C	**¿Qué desea?** buying groceries; talking about quantity and containers	¿qué desea?, quisiera ... un kilo de, un litro de, medio kilo de, medio litro de, cien gramos de, un bote de, una caja de, una botella de, una lata de, un tubo de, una bolsa de, un paquete de, una barra de tomates, mermelada, pañuelos, vino, sardinas pasta de dientes, bombones (revision of food items, ¿algo más?; nada más; ¿cuánto es?; en total, son ...; aquí tiene; ¿tiene ...?)	developing your transactional skills in shops; quantities and containers	1 a, b, c 2 a, c–g, h, j 3 a, c, d, e 4 c, d 5 a, b, c, d, e		
12D	**Quisiera comprar un regalo** buying a present; saying whether it's a little, very or too expensive, large, etc.	¿cuánto es?, qué desea?, ¿qué te parece este plato?, ¿tiene algo más barato?, aburrido, algo de cerámica muy, un poco, barato, bonito, caro, demasiado caro, enorme, grande, pequeña lo dejo, gracias ¡Oiga por favor! un cinturón, un compact disc, un estéreo personal, un jersey, un pegatín / pegatina, un póster, un reloj, un tarro, un vale–regalo, un videojuego, una caja de turrón, una camiseta	say whether something is a little, very or too expensive, large, etc.; revision of agreement of adjectives; expressing your opinion	1 a, b, c 2 a, d–g, h, j 3 a, d, e 4 c, d 5 a, b, c, d, f		
12E	**¡No lo como nunca!** saying what you don't eat, and why	¿hay algo que no comes / tomas? ¿no te / me gusta(n)? (soy) alérgico(a) a / al ... el queso el trigo la leche la miel las nueces los mariscos los productos (con) ... los productos lácteos los yogures porque es ... no como / tomo vegetariana (estricta)	expressing negative opinions and imparting negative information; direct object pronouns	1 a, b, c 2 a, c–g, h, j 3 a, d, e 4 c, d 5 a, b, c, d, f		

UNIDAD 13: LA SALUD						
	OBJECTIVE	KEY LANGUAGE	GRAMMAR / SKILLS	PoS	ATs	Scottish 5–14 National Guidelines Levels
13A	**Me duele …** saying you don't feel well and where it hurts; naming the parts of the body	¿qué te pasa? no me siento bien me duele el / la … me duelen los / las … el brazo, el estómago, el oído, el ojo, el pecho, el pie la boca, la cabeza, la espalda, la garganta la mano, la muela, la nariz, la pierna	**me duele(n)**; excuses	1 a, b, c 2 a, d–g, h, j 3 a, b, c, d 4 c, d 5 a, b, c, d, f	1, 1–4 2, 1–4 3, 1–4 4, 1–4	Listening A–D Speaking A–D Reading A–D Writing A–D
13B	**Tengo fiebre …** giving further reasons for feeling unwell; saying what's wrong with others	tengo / tienes / tiene le duele(n) fiebre, tos, un catarro, náuseas la fiebre del heno, una picadura una ampolla	recognising / using **le** to talk about other people	1 a, b 2 a, d–g, h, j 3 a, b, c, d 4 c, d 5 a, b, c, d, f		
13C	**Debes …** what you have to do	Debo / debes / debe … tomar … una aspirina, una pastilla, un antibiótico un poco de agua, un jarabe poner(me/te) … una crema, una tirita llamar / ir … al médico, al dentista, al hospital, a la cama descansar	the modal verb **deber**	1 a, b, c 2 a, d–g, h, j 3 a, b, c 4 c, d 5 a, b, c, d, f		
13D	**La vida sana** what you or others ought to do to be / stay healthy	andar, correr debes beber / comer / hacer (etc.) decir 'no' el azúcar, el ejercicio físico, el pescado hacer … veces por semana / día hacer deporte, hacer footing hay que beber (etc.) la agua, la carne, la fruta y verduras la grasa, las cereales las colas … muchos contienen azúcar, las naranjadas, los colorantes artificiales los dulces, los edulcorantes, los gaseosos los pasteles, los productos lácteos los refrescos más, menos practicar deporte repite … veces ver (demasiado) la tele	revision of **hay que** and **tener que**	1 a, b, c 2 a, d–g, h, j 3 a, b, c 4 c, d 5 a, b, c, d, f		

UNIDAD 14: ¿QUÉ HICISTE?						
	OBJECTIVE	KEY LANGUAGE	GRAMMAR / SKILLS	PoS	ATs	Scottish 5–14 National Guidelines Levels
14A	¿Adónde fuiste? where you went, how, and with whom; when, and how long for	¿(por) cuánto tiempo fuiste? ¿adónde fuiste? ¿cómo fuiste? ¿con quién fuiste? ¿cuándo fuiste? en autobús / en autocar / en coche / en avión / en tren / en barco / en barco de vela / en taxi / en aerodeslizador / en metro / en bicicleta / en taxi / en globo / en ciclomotor / en motocicleta fui a / en / con … me quedé en casa	recognising and forming the preterite tense of **ir**	1 a, b, c 2 a, b, c, d, e, f 3 a, c, d, e 4 c, d 5 a, b, c, d, f	1, 2–5 2, 2–5 3, 2–5 4, 2–5	Listening B–E Speaking B–E Reading B–E Writing B–E
14B	¿Qué hiciste? describing things you did on holiday or at the weekend	¿qué hiciste? bebí (un refresco) cogí (el autobús) comí (algo en una cafetería) conocí (a una chica inglesa) di (una vuelta) escribí (una postal) leí (una revista) salí (a las diez) vi (una película) volví (a casa) me aburrí (un poco) me divertí (mucho)	recognising and forming the preterite tense of **-er** and **-ir** verbs	1 a, b, c 2 a, d–g, h, i 3 a, c, d, e 4 c, d 5 a, b, c, d, f		
14C	¿Qué tal lo pasaste? talking about further holiday activities; using time phrases	¿qué compraste? compré un regalo para X alquilé una bici … tomé el sol visité … bailé en la discoteca cené en un restaurante compré recuerdos conocí a un chico el agua estaba muy fría lo pasé fatal / bomba / muy bien me aburrí mucho monté a caballo nadé (en la piscina) no comí nada no hubo nada yo lo pasé fatal / muy bien yo me quedé en el hotel fuimos a … charlamos	recognising and forming preterite tense of **-ar** verbs; time phrases	1 a, b, c 2 a, e–g, h, j 3 a, c, e 4 c, d 5 a, b, c, d, f		
14D	¿Qué hizo? saying what someone else did, or didn't do	¿adónde fue X? ¡X ha ido a Londres! hizo /compró / comió leyó / visitó / fue robó / dio / cogió vio / salió / insistió que … vi a … volvió	preterite tense of **-ar, -er, -ir** verbs (**él, ella, usted**)	1 a, b, c 2 a, d–g, h, i–j 3 a, c, d, e 4 c, d 5 a, b, c, d		

UNIDAD 15: ¡BIENVENIDOS!						
	OBJECTIVE	KEY LANGUAGE	GRAMMAR / SKILLS	PoS	ATs	Scottish 5–14 National Guidelines Levels
15A	**¿De qué nacionalidad eres?** saying what country you're from; saying what nationality you are	¿de qué nacionalidad eres? yo soy … nací en … nació allí Alemania, Escocia, Canadá, Francia, Gales, Gran Bretaña, Irlanda del Norte, Italia, India, Inglaterra, Estados Unidos, Marruecos, América del Sur, Paquistán, Portugal alemán / alemana, americano/a, británico/a canadiense, escocés /escocesa, español/a francés / francesa, galés / galesa, indio/a italiano/a, marroquí, portugués / portuguesa, paquistaní, inglés / inglesa	more about adjectival agreement	1 a, b, c 2 a, d–g, h, j 3 a, d, e 4 c, d 5 a, b, c, d, f, h	1, 2–5 2, 2–5 3, 2–5 4, 2–5	Listening B–E Speaking B–E Reading B–E Writing B–E
15B	**¡Encantado!** making formal and informal introductions; inviting someone to eat and drink	¿conoce usted a mi mujer …? ¿qué quiere(s) tomar? ¿quiere(s) comer algo? ¿un café?, ¿un pastelito?, ¿una galleta? para mí, nada, gracias buenas tardes encantado/a, igualmente, siéntese / siéntate aquí te / le presento a mi mujer …, lo / la conozco con mucho gusto	indirect object pronouns; the personal **a** formal / informal forms of address	1 a, b, c 2 a, c–g, h, j 3 a, c, d, 4 c, d 5 a, c, d, f		
15C	**Agradecimientos y disculpas** using exclamations; apologising to, thanking and congratulating others	¡ay, perdón!, ¡ay, qué bien!, ¡ay, qué ilusión!, ¡felicitaciones!, ¡qué amable!, ¡qué suerte!, ¡qué ilusión!, ¡y qué …!, ¡qué bien!, ¡qué sorpresa!, ¡qué asco!, ¡qué disgusto!, ¡qué horario más desagradable!, ¡qué horror!, ¡qué pena!, ¡qué rollo!, ¡y, qué susto! ¿qué tal está …? lo siento (mucho), te pido perdón por … (muchísimas) gracias por todo no hay de qué, no importa (ahora)	exclamations; apologising to, thanking and congratulating others	1 a, b, c 2 a, d–g, h, i 3 a, c, d, e 4 c, d 5 a, b, c, d, e, f		
15D	**Adiós …** using further exclamations	¡qué bonita! ¡qué guapa es! la boda el bautizo	further exclamations	1 a, b, c 2 a, d–g, h, j 3 a, d, e 4 c, d 5 a, b, c, d, e, f		

11–15 REPASO	Revision section looking back over language studied in Units 11–15	PoS	1 a, c 2 a, b, c, d, e 3 b, c, e 4 c, d 5 a, b, c, d, e
11–15 LECTURA	Reading for pleasure and information	PoS	2 h, i 3 d 4 a 5 g
11–15 TÁCTICA: LENGUA	Reading skills (looking for clues); looking up present / preterite tense verbs in the dictionary	PoS	2 h 3 d 5 g
11–15 PRÁCTICA: LENGUA	Summative grammar tasks based on grammar items encountered in Units 11–15	PoS	1 b 3 d, e

QCA KS3 Scheme of Work coverage

QCA Unit	New language	Caminos unit(s)	New contexts	Caminos unit(s)
1	Simple questions 1st / 2nd person singular verbs Numbers 1-31 Pronunciation / spelling rules Indefinite articles Plurals of nouns *(No) hay*	1, 2, 5, 9, 10, 12 1, 5, 6, 7 1, 2 1 2 2 6, 7	Formal / informal meetings / greetings Personal information (name, age, birthday) The alphabet Months, dates, days of the week Classroom objects Classroom instructions	1, 1, 3 1 1, 2 2 1, 2
2	3rd person singular & all plurals of regular –ar and –ir verbs Possessive adjectives Questions with *¿cómo?, ¿cuánto?, ¿quién?* *tener, ser* (all persons) Definite article Adjective agreement Intensifiers (*muy, bastante*) Numbers 1-100	3 1, 3 1, 4 3, 4, 5 2 4, 5, 15 4 3	Other people Family, friends, pets descriptions Nationalities Fiestas	3 3 15 3
3	Likes, dislikes, preferences Stem-changing verbs e -> ie + noun and *pensar* Adverbs of frequency *¿a qué hora?* questions Regular –er verbs Irregular verb *hacer*	4, 5 10 11 5, 10 5 10 6, 7	School subjects and timetables Telling the time Mealtimes; simple food / drink items	5 5 10, 11, 12
4	Reflexive verbs Stem-changing verbs (o -> ue) Introduction to *ser* and *estar* Numbers above 100 Ordinal numbers Prepositions	10 5 11 8 8	Daily routine Simple descriptions of homes	10 8
5	The irregular verb *ir* Positive imperative form of regular verbs (2nd / 3rd person singular)	9 12	Places in town Points of the compass and maps Directions Seasons Weather	6, 7 6 12 6 6
6	*gustar, preferir* + infinitive Present continuous tense Modal verbs *poder, querer* Interjections Subject pronouns *él, ella, usted* *ir a* + infinitive (immediate future)	11, 12 7, 9 15 12 9	Leisure, hobbies, sport, music Family activities	7, 9 7, 9
7	Quantifier *poco* Regular comparative and superlative adjectives Formation of adverbs with -mente Direct object pronoun with persons (*le, la, les, las*)	12 15	Character descriptions Meeting people formally and informally Being, and welcoming, a guest Thanking (speech / letter)	 15 15 15
8	Direct object pronoun with things (*le, la, les, las*) Expressions of quantity *tener hambre / sed* Disjunctive pronoun with preposition (e.g. *para mí*)	12 12 11 11, 15	Food and drink Likes, dislikes and preferences Following and preparing recipes Buying food Restaurant / *tapas*	11, 12 12 12 11
9	Parts of the body Structure with *doler* Further expressions with *tener* Structures using (*no*) *deber* (*no*) *hay que*, (*no*) *tener que* + infinitive	13 13 13 13 13	Ailments, illnesses and remedies Visiting the doctor, chemist or dentist Healthy lifestyle	13 13 13
10	Expressions of size Demonstrative adjectives and pronouns (*este, ese, aquel*) Use of interrogative (*¿cuál?*)		Shopping for clothes and presents Discussions of fashions Consideration of appropriateness of clothes	14
11	Preterite tense of *ir* Preterite tense of regular –ar verbs	14 14	Holidays and tourism Outings and trips Modes of transport	14 14 14
12	All forms of the preterite tense of regular –er and –ir verbs, e.g. *comer, salir* and irregular verbs *hacer, ver, estar* Imperfect tense (receptive use) using *había / hacía / era(n)*	14 14	Entertainment Concerts, cinema, theatre, sport Ordering and buying tickets Recounting a past event or an outing	14 14 14 14

Objectives

Students learn – to greet people
– to say how they are and ask how others are
– to recognise classroom commands (extension)

Key language

¡hola!
¿cómo te llamas?
me llamo … ¿y tú?
¿qué tal?
estupendo
muy bien
bien
regular
fatal

Extension language

sentaos / levantaos
callaos
hay que …
sacar los libros
recoger todo
aprender
escribir
repetir
dibujar
escuchar (la cinta)
mirar (la pizarra, el retroproyector)
trabajar (en parejas)

Skills / Strategies

Students learn – to listen attentively
– to identify and pronounce vowels (*a, e, i, o, u*)

ICT opportunities

Students can – create and save a simple poem on computer, format it and print it for classroom display (Student's Book, Activity 5)

Ways in

Greetings and feelings – Picture story in Student's Book, page 4
Classroom instructions – OHT 1A

Assessment opportunities

AT1,1   Student's Book, Activity 3: students listen and match the photos with the speakers.
AT2,1   Student's Book, Activity 4: target a small group of students during whole-class walkabout.
AT3,1   Worksheet 1.2: Activity 1: students match the pictures to the language.
AT4,1   Student's Book, Activity 5: students write a poem – essentially copy-writing.

STUDENT'S BOOK, pages 4–5

1 Me presento

Some of the key characters in the story introduce themselves. Students can then introduce themselves to the class. If you want to give them Spanish names, they could use these to introduce themselves here, playing a memory game with them, perhaps with forfeits for those who forget names they have been told!

PILAR:	¡Hola! Me llamo Pilar.
ISABEL:	¡Hola! Me llamo Isabel.
JOSÉ LUIS:	¡Hola! Me llamo José Luis.
CARLOS:	¡Hola! Me llamo Carlos.

You can extend the activity by playing a version of the Generation Game. Choose a number of students to stand in a row and, with a real or imagined microphone, 'interview' each student quickly, e.g., *¿Cómo te llamas?* and let them reply. Each 'contestant' (or other student) has to move along the row and name everyone correctly by saying *Te llamas (Claire)*, etc. Give the students an example by being the first contestant. Turn it into a competition by timing how long each contestant takes. Remember to change the students in the row from time to time.

2 En el patio

Picture story

The friends all meet up, and it's obvious that Tomás is unhappy.

○ Students write down the characters' names (or the first letter) and draw the appropriate picture symbol beside them.

○ Students can work out Isabel's nationality.

Answers: ○ *Tomás – fatal; José Luis – fenomenal; Isabel – muy bien; Carlos – regular; Pilar – bien.*
○ *Isabel es inglesa.*

PILAR:	Carlos, ¡hola!
CARLOS:	Pilar, ¿Qué tal?
PILAR:	Bien.
	Isabel es inglesa, de Liverpool.
CARLOS:	Hola, Isabel, ¿qué tal?
ISABEL:	Muy bien, ¿y tú?
CARLOS:	Regular.
PILAR:	José Luis, ¿qué tal?
JOSÉ LUIS:	¡Fenomenal!

JOSÉ LUIS:	¡Hola! ¿Cómo te llamas?
ISABEL:	Me llamo Isabel.
JOSÉ LUIS:	Y usted ¿qué tal?
TEACHER:	Muy bien, gracias.
PILAR:	¿Tomás? ¿Qué tal está Tomás?
ISABEL:	Fatal, Pilar, fatal.

Preparatory or follow-up activities could include OHT presentation and games with gesture. Recycle new language in a different context: ask students their opinions of current TV programmes, or football teams, e.g., *¿Qué tal los programas en la televisión? Para mí (Neighbours) – ¡fatal! ¿Para ti (Karen)?* This can then be practised in pairs. Additional phrases such as *¡estupendo!* or *¡no muy bien!* could be included.

3 ¿Qué tal los jóvenes?

Students write down numbers 1–5, look at the photos, listen to the five friends saying how they are, and work out who's speaking.

Answers: *1 – Belén; 2 – Alicia; 3 – Carlos; 4 – David; 5 – Elena.*

1	CHICO:	¡Oye!
	BELÉN:	¡Hola!
	CHICO:	¿Qué tal?
	BELÉN:	¡Muy bien! ¿Y tú?
2	ALICIA:	¡Hola!
	CHICO:	¡Hola! ¿Qué tal?
	ALICIA:	¡Pues fenomenal! ¿Y tú?
3	CARLOS:	¿Mamá?
	MAMÁ:	¡Hola! ¿Qué tal?
	CARLOS:	Bueno, regular.
4	CHICO:	¡Hola! ¿Qué tal?
	DAVID:	Bien, gracias.
5	ABUELO:	¡Hola!
	ELENA:	Hola, abuelito.
	ABUELO:	¿Qué tal?
	ELENA:	¡Fatal!

4 ¿Y tú?

Working in groups, students take turns asking and explaining to each other how they feel. Try to encourage gesture and a little play-acting. If circumstances allow, students could go on a brief class walkabout to do this activity. More able students can use the photos from Activity 3 as a basis for an extension activity where they adopt the roles of various people and ask further questions.

5 **Poema**

🌑 An opportunity for students to write in simple Spanish. The poems could be word-processed, attractively designed and put on display. Practise the words and phrases aloud first.

♣ Using photos from newspapers and magazines, or their own drawings, students can create a speech-bubble dialogue with a famous person or people they identify with (or loathe!). Alternatively, they can invent an improbable conversation between two famous people or characters (e.g. Mussolini and Scooby-doo). The language could be handwritten or computer-generated, and presented as a collage in their exercise books or on paper.

Gramática

A brief explanation could be given here of the usage of the formal and familiar forms *tú* and *usted*. Students are referred to the grammar summary, section 9 on p.149.

SUPPORT MATERIALS

OHT 1A ¿Qué hay que hacer?

This presents the language for the extension objective – understanding classroom instructions. You may prefer to introduce classroom instructions gradually, a few at a time, over a series of lessons. The *'hay que ...'* structure is suggested because it can be used by students themselves to clarify with you what they have to do, e.g., *¿Hay que recoger todo?* They can be photocopied on to card, cut up, and used in games. Worksheet 1.2 supports this language.

Worksheet 1.1 ¡Bienvenidos!

1 **En el instituto**

🌑 An activity practising the greetings structures. Students listen and draw happy or sad faces to represent how the speakers feel.

♣ This activity entails listening to see if the formal or familiar forms are used. Students write *tú* or *usted*.

Answers: 🌑 *1 –* ☺ *; 2 –* ☹ *; 3 –* ☺ *; 4 –* ☹ *.*

♣ *1 – usted; 2 – tú; 3 – tú; 4 – usted.*

EJEMPLO	
CHICO:	¡Hola, Felipe! ¿Qué tal?
CHICO:	Bien gracias ¿Y tú?
1 SEÑOR:	¡Buenos días! ¿Qué tal está?
SEÑORA:	Bien, gracias. ¿Y usted?
2 CHICA:	¡Ana! ¿Qué tal?
ANA:	¡Fatal! ¿Y tú?
3 CHICO:	¿Qué tal, Juanita?
CHICA:	Regular, gracias. Y tú, ¿Qué tal estás?
4 SEÑORA:	¡Buenas tardes!
SEÑOR:	Buenas tardes. Y usted, ¿qué tal?
SEÑORA:	No muy bien.

2 🗨 **¡Hola!**

🌑 A simple oral activity in which students substitute words from a grid to modify a model dialogue, and practise the new dialogues obtained with a partner.

♣ Students make up their own dialogues, using a substitution grid containing a mix of young people and adults, and information about how the people feel. They then practise the dialogues with a partner, taking care to use *tú* or *usted* as appropriate.

3 **Javi y Sarah**

A gap-fill activity in which students complete a dialogue with words from a given menu.

Answers: *1 – tal; 2 – bien; 3 – fenomenal; 4 – llamas;*
5 – llamo; 6 – Qué; 7 – gracias.

Worksheet 1.2 ¡El español es estupendo!

This extension sheet can be used after, or in conjunction with, OHT 1A. The numbered pictures could be used for presentation, in the absence of an OHP. If you prefer to use the *vosotros* command form, the visual sheet can still be used: you will need to adapt the extension worksheet, rewriting the instructions for Activity 1. The song will still work as a rap in the *vosotros* command form, if you adapt the lyrics.

1 **Las instrucciones**

Students match the pictures and instructions. They could stick a copy in the inside cover of their exercise books for reference, or design a large version of it for classroom display. An extra pairwork activity can be added by having Student **A** hold his/her sheet up, with an exercise book behind it to make the sheet opaque, and pointing to one of the pictures on the sheet. Student **B** has to guess what has been selected.

Answers: *1 – c; 2 – j; 3 – d; 4 – a; 5 – l; 6 – h; 7 – k; 8 – e;*
9 – f; 10 – i; 11 – g; 12 – b.

2 **¿Qué hay que hacer?**

The rap can be exploited in a number of ways. Students can be encouraged to use gesture along with the lyrics to help them to memorise the language.

> Levantaos y sentaos,
> Callaos ¡atención!
> Todos los días
> Es la misma canción.
>
> ¡Sacad y recoged!
> ¡Y trabajad y aprended!
> Mirad y escuchad.
> Dibujad y copiad.
>
> Todos los días
> aprendiendo
> ¡que el español
> es estupendo!

Objectives

Students learn – the alphabet in Spanish
            – to answer the register
            – to spell words and ask others

Key language

yo, sí, no está
Alphabet a–z
¿cómo se escribe?
mi / tu nombre
mi / tu apellido

Skills / Strategies

Students learn – to distinguish consonants clearly and to
            pronounce them correctly
            – to spell words

ICT opportunities

Students can – create a database featuring the names of the
          students in their class

Ways in

Alphabet   – Student's Book, Activity 1 (with recording);
            children's magnetic letters on OHP to give
            shadow shapes

Assessment opportunities

AT1,1   Worksheet 1.5, Activity 1: students listen and pick out
        names.

AT2,1   Student's Book, Activity 4: target a small group of students
        doing the activity.

AT3,1   Worksheet 1.3, Activity 1: students read the names.

AT4   Worksheet 1.3, Activity 1: students read and list names.

STUDENT'S BOOK, pages 6–7

1 **El alfabeto**

The listening activities are recorded, but you may prefer to read them aloud yourself.

a Students listen to the whole alphabet, following the text in the Student's Book, and repeating each letter.

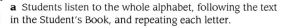

a b c d e f g h i j k l m n ñ o p q r s t u v w x y z

b Students listen and decide which of the two names is being spelt each time.

Answers: *1 – Paco; 2 Toñi; 3 – Juan; 4 – Gabi.*

P-a-c-o   T-o-ñ-i   J-u-a-n   G-a-b-i

c The alphabet is sung as set out in the Student's Book. There is no redundant language and the music is repeated afterwards so that students can sing along by themselves.

2 **Pasando lista**

Picture story

Tomás arrives as the register is being taken, and introduces himself to the teacher. He meets Pepa for the first time.

Students read the picture story and note who is present and who is absent.

Answers: *25 ✓; 26 ✓; 27 ✓; 28 ✗; 29 ✓; 30 ✓.*

PROFESORA:	¡Chhhh! ¡Callaos! ¿Fernando Pretus?
FERNANDO:	Yo.
PROFESORA:	¿Juanita Talavera?
JUANITA:	Sí.
PROFESORA:	¿Ana? ¿Ana Velázquez?
ALUMNO:	No está.
PROFESORA:	¿Tomás Willou … Willou …
TOMÁS:	Tomás Willoughby.
PROFESORA:	Ahhh – de Liverpool, en Inglaterra, ¿no?
TOMÁS:	Sí.
PROFESORA:	¿Cómo se escribe Willoughby? W-i-l-l-o-u …
TOMÁS:	… g-h-b-y.
PROFESORA:	… g-h-b-y. Vale, gracias. Siéntate, Tomás.
PEPA:	¡Hola! Me llamo Pepa.
TOMÁS:	Hola, ¿qué tal?
PEPA:	¡Fatal! ¿Y tú?
TOMÁS:	¡Fatal!

3 **¿Cómo se escribe?**

Picture story

Isabel explains who she is to her new teacher.

ISABEL:	¿Cómo se llama usted?
PROFESOR:	Sr. Romero. ¿Y tú?
ISABEL:	Mi nombre es Isabel. Mi apellido es Willoughby.
PROFESOR:	¿Cómo se escribe tu apellido?
ISABEL:	W-i-l-l-o-u-g-h-b-y.

a Students listen to the brief dialogue between Isabel and Sr. Romero, following the text at the same time.

b ⚫ This simple activity involves listening to six further conversations where students (both younger and adult) are enrolling for a course or excursion. In each case the teacher is checking the names individually as people arrive, and writing them down on the register. Students who have problems writing fast enough should be given some support if possible.

Answers: *1 – Conde; 2 – Saez; 3 – Victor; 4 – Benjumea;*
                5 – Zurita; 6 – Marisa.

1	PROFESORA:	¿Celia?
	CELIA:	¿Sí?
	PROFESORA:	Celia, ¿cuáles son tus apellidos?
	CELIA:	Adriano Conde.
	PROFESORA:	¿C-O-N-D-E?
	CELIA:	Sí.
	PROFESORA:	Vale, gracias.
2	PROFESOR:	¿Gabi?
	GABI:	¿Sí?
	PROFESOR:	¿Cuál es tu apellido?
	GABI:	Saez Melo. Se escribe: S-A-E-Z …
	PROFESOR:	Y Melo. Ya lo tengo. Vale, gracias.
3	PROFESORA:	¿El señor Damas Lozano?
	SEÑOR:	Sí.
	PROFESORA:	Señor Damas, no tengo aquí en la lista su nombre.
	SEÑOR:	Victor. V-I-C-T-O-R.
	PROFESORA:	Gracias.
4	PROFESOR:	¿Rosario García está?
	ROSARIO:	Sí, soy yo.
	PROFESOR:	Rosario, ¿cuál es tu segundo apellido?
	ROSARIO:	Benjumea.
	PROFESOR:	¿Cómo se escribe?
	ROSARIO:	B-E-N-J-U-M-E-A.
5	PROFESOR:	Jaime, sólo tengo aquí en la lista tu segundo apellido. El primero, ¿cuál es?
	JAIME:	Zurita. Z-U-R-I-T-A.
	PROFESOR:	Gracias.

6 PROFESOR:	¿Usted es la Señora Cruz Arjona?
SEÑORA:	Sí.
PROFESOR:	¿Y su nombre?
SEÑORA:	Marisa.
PROFESOR:	M-A-R-I-S-A.
SEÑORA:	Eso es.

c Students now listen again and decide whether each dialogue is in the formal or the familiar form.

Answers: *1 – tú; 2 – tú; 3 – usted; 4 – tú; 5 – tú; 6 – usted.*

4 **Tú pasas lista**

A pairwork activity which entails exchanging and spelling names with members of an imaginary school exchange, using names from the menu given on p.7.

○ Less able students concentrate on dialogues in the familiar form.

♣ More able students do dialogues using the formal variants.

Gramática

There is a brief résumé in the Student's Book here of the use of the reflexive verb *llamarse* (to be called) in the second person familiar and formal forms. Students who require further explanation of reflexive verbs are referred to the grammar summary section 13 on p.150 and to *Acción: lengua 1* on p.11.

SUPPORT MATERIALS

OHT 1.3 Vamos a pasar lista

1 **La excursión**

A pre-dictionary skill, ordering the names alphabetically, in preparation for the listening activity. Students who find this amount of copying difficult can be given the 10 names on separate slips of paper which they move around on their desks until they have the correct order.

Answers: *Itziar; Javi; Juanjo; Laura; Maite; Margarita; Pepe; Toni; Toñi; Yoli.*

2 **En el autobús**

○ Using their list from Activity 1, students listen to the teacher on the coach trip checking the register and write a tick for those who are present, and a cross for the absentees.

♣ More able students listen and work out whether *sí* or *yo* occurs more frequently.

Answers: ○ *Itziar ✓; Javi ✓; Juanjo ✗; Laura ✓; Maite ✓; Margarita ✓; Pepe ✗; Toni ✓; Toñi ✓; Yoli ✗.*

♣ *4 students use Yo and 3 use Sí.*

PROFESORA:	¿Este es el autobús número dos?
CONDUCTOR:	Sí, Señora.
PROFESORA:	Bueno ... Chhh. Callaos todos. Vamos a pasar lista. ¿Vale?
ALUMNOS:	Sí ... vale ...
PROFESORA:	Itziar ... ¿Está? Itziar?
ITZIAR:	Yo.
PROFESORA:	¿Javi?
JAVI:	Sí.
PROFESORA:	¿Y Juanjo? ¿Juanjo?
CHICA:	No está.
PROFESORA:	¿Juanjo no está? Bueno ... ¡Laura!
LAURA:	Yo.
PROFESORA:	¿Maite?
MAITE:	Sí.
PROFESORA:	¡Margarita!

MARGARITA:	Yo.
PROFESORA:	Un momento ... ¡Pepe! ¿Pepe?
VOCES:	¡No está!
PROFESORA:	Pepe no está ... Vale. Toni – ¿Toni está?
VOCES:	¡Toni!
TONI:	¡Yo!
PROFESORA:	¡Vale, gracias! Y Antonia – ¿Toñi?
TONI:	Sí.
PROFESORA:	Vale ... ¡Yoli! ¿Yoli?
CHICO:	No está.
PROFESORA:	Yoli no está. Bueno.
CHICA:	¡Yoli está con Juanjo!
PROFESORA:	Oye, por favor ...

Worksheet 1.4 Práctica: lengua Mi / Tu / Su

This grammar worksheet sets out and explains the singular possessive forms *mi*, *tu* and *su*. There is a brief practice activity to help students work out the new point and use it.

Answers: *1 – mi; 2 – tu; 3 – mi; 4 – su; 5 – tu; 6 – mi.*

Worksheet 1.5 ¿Cómo se llama?

1 **Otra vez**

○ This activity comprises people giving their names. Students pick which of two names from a menu is the correct one each time.

♣ Students listen to the same tapescript, but this time they have to fill in the gaps with the speakers' surnames.

Answers: ○ *1 – Daniel; 2 – Raquel; 3 – Emilia; 4 – Antonio.*

♣ *1 – Arjona; 2 – Cruz; 3 – Gallego; 4 – Arroyo Gil.*

EJEMPLO	
CHICA:	¿Mi nombre? Se escribe C-O-N-C-H-I-T-A.
SEÑORA:	¿Y tus apellidos?
CHICA:	Valverde Melo.
SEÑORA:	Valverde Mero.
CHICA:	No, Melo. M-E-L-O.
SEÑORA:	Vale, gracias.
1 CHICO:	¿Mi nombre? Se escribe D-A-N-I-E-L. Y mis apellidos son Elizalde Arjona.
SEÑORA:	¿Cómo se escribe Arjona?
CHICO:	A-R-J-O-N-A.
SEÑORA:	A-R-J-O-N-A. Gracias.
2 CHICA:	¿Cómo se escribe? R-A-Q-U-E-L.
SEÑORA:	¿Y tu apellido es Parejo ...
CHICA:	Cruz. Se escribe C-R-U-Z.
3 CHICA:	Mi nombre se escribe E-M-I-L-I-A.
SEÑORA:	Y tus apellidos son Garrego Guerra.
CHICA:	No. Gallego Guerra. Se escribe G-A-L-L-E-G-O.
4 CHICO:	Mi nombre es A-N-T-O-N-I-O.
SEÑORA:	¿Y tus apellidos?
CHICO:	Arroyo Gil. A-R-R-O-Y-O.
SEÑORA:	Arroyo. Vale. ¿Y tu segundo apellido se escribe G-I-L?
CHICO:	Sí. G-I-L es correcto.

2 **En clase**

○ Students match sentences to a series of visuals.

♣ A slightly longer reading activity. Students read sentences and decide if they are true or false.

Answers: ○ *a – 3; b – 6; c – 2; d – 4; e – 1; f – 5.*

♣ *a ✗; b ✓; c ✗; d ✓; e ✗; f ✓.*

Objectives

Students learn – numbers 1–19
- to ask how to say something in Spanish or English
- to say that they don't know or have forgotten something
- to ask someone to repeat something

Key language

Numbers 1–19
¿cómo se dice en español / en inglés?
no lo sé
ni idea
se me ha olvidado
otra vez, por favor

Skills / Strategies

Students learn – to begin to cope with redundant language
- to cope with simple linguistic problems in the target language

Ways in

Numbers – number shapes / magnetic letters on OHT; Student's Book, Activity 1a

Assessment opportunities

AT1,1 Worksheet 1.6, Activity 1: students listen for numbers.
AT2,1 Student's Book, Activity 6b and Worksheet 1.6, Activity 2: target a small group each time.
AT3,1 Worksheet 1.7, Activities 1, 2, 4.
AT4,1 Worksheet 1.7, Activities 1, 2 and any puzzle which the student invents in Activity 5.

STUDENT'S BOOK, pages 8–9

1 Los números

a Presentation of numbers 1-10: they are said twice, with a pause for students to repeat.

```
uno, uno
dos, dos
tres, tres
cuatro, cuatro
cinco, cinco
seis, seis
siete, siete
ocho, ocho
nueve, nueve
diez, diez
```

b ◐ This listening activity helps students to cope with redundant language. Students listen for the correct gate number for each flight only. During the first hearing you could ask them simply to raise their hands when they hear the key words *puerta número ...*, to help them focus on the vital information. For greater clarity, they may find it helpful if you write the whole of the first announcement up on the board.

♻ Students listen and work out which is the correct flight number for Valencia.

Answers: ◐ *Bruselas – puerta 3; Dublín – puerta 6; Edimburgo – puerta 9; Londres – puerta 5; Río de Janeiro – puerta 10; Valencia – puerta 4.*
♻ *The flight to Valencia is AV 715.*

BRUSELAS:	Vuelo Iberia, con destino Bruselas: embarquen por la puerta número tres por favor – puerta tres.
DUBLÍN:	Vuelo Aer Lingus, con destino Dublín – embarquen por la puerta número seis. Puerta seis, por favor.
EDIMBURGO:	Vuelo British Caledonian, con destino Edimburgo – embarquen por la puerta número nueve. Puerta nueve.
LONDRES:	Última llamada para el vuelo British Airways, con destino Londres – puerta número cinco. Puerta cinco.
RÍO DE JANEIRO:	Iberia anuncia la salida de su vuelo a Río de Janeiro – embarquen inmediatamente por la puerta número diez. Puerta diez.
VALENCIA:	Es el último aviso para los señores pasajeros del vuelo AV 715 para Valencia. Puerta de embarque número cuatro. Puerta cuatro, por favor.

2 El juego de los dedos

A brief pairwork activity: students can hold up fingers or, if you prefer, trace numbers on the desk with a finger. Their partner says the number.

3 Los deberes de inglés

Picture story

Pilar, Carlos and José Luis are doing the first English homework of the term, and having trouble with the spelling. Isabel is watching and helping.

◐ This activity encourages students to focus on the active language of the objective, drawing a parallel between the already known *¿cómo se escribe?* and the new *¿cómo se dice?*

♻ Students work out the meaning of four of the key phrases.

Answers: ◐ *1 – José Luis; 2 – Pilar; 3 – Carlos; 4 – Carlos.*
♻ *1 – I've forgotten; 2 – homework; 3 – English; 4 – good! / how nice!*

PILAR:	Inglés, ¡qué bien!
JOSÉ LUIS:	Isabel, ¿cómo se dice 'se me ha olvidado' en inglés?
ISABEL:	Se dice: 'I've forgotten'.
JOSÉ LUIS:	I've forgotten everything.
CARLOS:	Isabel, ¿cómo se dice 'rápido' en inglés?
ISABEL:	Se dice 'quickly'.
CARLOS:	'Quickly'... ¿y cómo se escribe?
ISABEL:	Q-u-i-c-k-l-y.
PILAR:	Q-u-i ... ¿otra vez por favor?
ISABEL:	Q-u-i-c-k-l-y.
PILAR:	'Beautifully' – se escribe con una 'l' o con dos 'll'?
CARLOS:	No lo sé, ni idea. ¿Isabel?
ISABEL:	Con dos.
JOSÉ LUIS:	Con una 'l'... con dos 'll'... ¿Cómo se dice 'deberes' en inglés?
ISABEL:	¿Deberes? – 'homework'.
JOSÉ LUIS:	Isabel – my homework – quickly and beautifully – please?

4 Con tu pareja

A quick pairwork activity which recycles the numbers 1-10 within the new structure. Students can time themselves against the clock to see how many correct responses they can achieve within a minute, or you can announce when a minute is up and students change over.

5 **Juegos**

a Presentation of the numbers 11-19: they are said twice, with a pause for students to repeat. You could extend this activity with a variety of number games: counting up in even numbers, counting back in odd numbers, writing the numbers on the board and getting students to come forward and wipe off or circle the correct one. They could also be organised as team games.

once, once	
doce, doce	
trece, trece	
catorce, catorce	
quince, quince	
dieciséis, dieciséis	
diecisiete, diecisiete	
dieciocho, dieciocho	
diecinueve, diecinueve	

b Students jot down any six numbers between 1 and 19. They listen to the lottery computer – has anyone got all six numbers? You might like to have a few small prizes ready!

Answers: *4; 5; 11; 13; 15; 18.*

PRESENTADOR:	¡Bienvenidos a nuestra lotería! Ordenador – los números, por favor!
COMPUTADORA:	Cinco.
PRESENTADOR:	Cinco.
COMPUTADORA:	Trece.
PRESENTADOR:	Trece.
COMPUTADORA:	Dieciocho.
PRESENTADOR:	Dieciocho.
COMPUTADORA:	Quince.
PRESENTADOR:	Quince.
COMPUTADORA:	Cuatro.
PRESENTADOR:	Cuatro.
COMPUTADORA:	Once.
PRESENTADOR:	¡Once! Vamos a poner los números en el orden correcto: cuatro, cinco, once, trece, quince, dieciocho ...! Si tienes todos los números, llámanos ...

c A radio game *¡Otra vez!*, in which contestants choose six numbers which are then scrambled into a different order by the computer and the contestant has to guess the correct order in the fewest possible guesses. The audience participates by shouting out *¡Otra vez!* when the contestant gets it wrong. Students listen and note the order of the numbers.

Answers: *11; 5; 18; 2; 16; 14.*

PRESENTADOR:	Bienvenidos al juego '¡Otra vez!'. ¡Hola, Juan!
JUAN:	Hola.
PRESENTADOR:	¡Bien! Ordenador, pon los números de Juan en un orden diferente. Vale – Juan: ¡a jugar!
JUAN:	Amm ... dos.
PÚBLICO:	¡Otra vez!
JUAN:	Ehh ... once.
PRESENTADOR:	¡Sí – once es correcto!
JUAN:	Mmm ... dieciocho.
PÚBLICO:	¡Otra vez!
JUAN:	Cinco.
PRESENTADOR:	¡Sí – cinco es correcto!
JUAN:	Ahh ... dieciocho.
PRESENTADOR:	¡Bien! Dieciocho es correcto!

JUAN:	Ahh ... catorce.
PÚBLICO:	¡Otra vez!
JUAN:	Dieciséis.
PÚBLICO:	¡Otra vez!
JUAN:	Dos.
PRESENTADOR:	¡Sí – dos es correcto!
JUAN:	Ehh ... catorce.
PÚBLICO:	¡Otra vez!
JUAN:	Dieciséis.
PRESENTADOR:	Sí – dieciséis es correcto.
JUAN:	Catorce.
PRESENTADOR:	Claro – catorce es correcto. Juan – en total: once aciertos. Gracias Juan.

6 **Más y menos**

a In this reading and writing or speaking activity, students do some simple sums in Spanish.

➕ An open-ended activity in which students invent some more sums of their own.

Answers: ◐ *1 – cinco; 2 – dieciséis; 3 – diez; 4 – catorce; 5 – trece; 6 – diecisiete.*

b Finally, students work in pairs to make up mathematical problems.

SUPPORT MATERIALS

Worksheet 1.6 ¡Acorazados!

1 **El juego de Raúl**

Students listen to Raúl and Amaya playing a game of Battleships (*Acorazados*): they write the other three numbers in the appropriate squares. A cross in a square could indicate a miss.

Answers: *Square A2 – 8; Square A1 – 19; Square B3 – 6; Square C2 – 15.*

RAÚL:	¿Amaya? Te toca a ti.
AMAYA:	Mmm ... A2.
RAÚL:	¡Sí! A2 es correcto.
AMAYA:	¿Y el número?
RAÚL:	Número ocho.
AMAYA:	Número ocho. Vale.
RAÚL:	¡Otra vez!
AMAYA:	¿B1?
RAÚL:	¡No!
AMAYA:	¿A1?
RAÚL:	¿A1? – ¡correcto!
AMAYA:	¡Qué bien! ¿Y el número?
RAÚL:	Número diecinueve.
AMAYA:	¿Diecinueve?
RAÚL:	Sí.
AMAYA:	Mmm ... C3.
RAÚL:	¡No!
AMAYA:	¿B3?
RAÚL:	Sí – ¡B3 es correcto!
AMAYA:	¿Y el número es?
RAÚL:	Seis.
AMAYA:	Seis – ¡fenomenal! Mm ... B2.
RAÚL:	¿B2? ¡No! Otra vez.
AMAYA:	Vamos a ver ... C2.
RAÚL:	¡Sí! C2 es correcto.
AMAYA:	¿Qué número es?
RAÚL:	Número quince.
AMAYA:	Quince. Muy bien. ¡Gano yo!

2 **¡Otra vez, por favor!**

Battleships with numbers: students write down four numbers from 1–19 in any squares they choose on their own grid entitled *yo*, then take turns to guess each other's squares and numbers. They use the grid entitled *mi pareja* to note where their partner's numbers are. Once Partner **A** scores a direct hit, Partner **B** has to give the appropriate number and Partner **A** jots it down in the correct place. The first person to find his/her partner's four locations and numbers wins. Compare grids afterwards – if there are any errors, the other person wins. Practise the game on the OHP or board first, and encourage the use of *¿otra vez, por favor?* if they want to hear the number again.

Worksheet 1.7 Puzzles

A worksheet of number and word puzzles: you might like to give students a free choice.

1 **¡Qué desorden!**

Ten anagrams of numbers which need to be rewritten correctly.

Answers: *1 – once; 2 – dos; 3 – tres; 4 – doce; 5 – catorce;
6 – diez; 7 – quince; 8 – nueve; 9 – trece;
10 – cinco.*

2 **Matemáticas**

Students do the addition and subtraction in order to supply the missing number in the gap which will make each sum correct.

Answers: *1 – seis; 2 – siete; 3 – cuatro; 4 – catorce; 5 – uno;
6 – diecinueve.*

3 **Las letras**

In each of the five combinations of numbers there is a common letter. Students may need to refer back to the numbers on Student's Book p.8, or write out the numbers, in order to find out what the letter is.

Answers: *a – s; b – t; c – u; d – c; e – e.*

4 **Las cuentas**

Students find the equivalents and pair them.

Answers: *a – vii; b – iii; c – v; d – i; e – iv; f – ii; g – vi.*

5 **¡A inventar!**

Students can invent a puzzle for their partner to do, such as those in Activities 1, 2 or 4. These might be word-processed or written out neatly, and put into a bank of filler activities for other students to do.

Objectives
Students learn – to say the days of the week
– to spell words with accents

Key language
lunes
martes
miércoles
jueves
viernes
sábado
domingo

Skills / Strategies
Students learn – to ask for help with vocabulary and
pronunciation
– to express simple opinions
– to spell words with accents

ICT opportunities
Students can – create a week planner or calendar

Ways in
Days of the week – A Spanish calendar
Alphabet – Student's Book, Activity 2 (with recording);
children's magnetic letters on OHP to give
shadow shapes

Assessment opportunities
AT1,1 Student's Book, Activity 2b: students listen and fill in the gaps.
AT2,1 Student's Book, Activity 3: target a small group of students doing the activity.

STUDENT'S BOOK, page 10

1 **El rap de la semana**

The rap of the week! Students first listen, then sing along and finally do the gestures and possibly modify the rap for their own purposes, according to how brave they feel!

> ¿Lunes? ¡Fatal!
> ¿Martes? ¡Peor!
> ¿Miércoles? No es mucho mejor ...
> ¿Jueves? Bien.
> ¿Viernes? ¡Tremendo!
> ¿Sábado? ¡Fenomenal!
> ¿Domingo? ¡Estupendo!

2 **Con acento**

a Students read and listen to the vowels with accents being read out clearly and slowly.

> á – é – í – ó – ú.

b Students now listen and fill in the gaps in a series of names. Some of the missing letters have accents.

Answers: 1 – Ramón; 2 – Andrés; 3 – Aránzazu; 4 – Joaquín;
5 – Raúl; 6 – Marifé; 7 – Ana María; 8 – Concepción.

1	voz 1:	¿Cómo se escribe tu nombre?
	voz 2:	R-A-M-O con acento-N.
2	voz 1:	Eres Andrés, ¿no?
	voz 2:	Sí, A-N-D-R-E con acento- S.
3	voz 1:	¡Qué bonito es tu nombre – ¡Aránzazu! ¿Cómo se escribe?
	voz 2:	A-R-A con acento-N-Z-A-Z-U.
4	voz 1:	¿Cómo te llamas?
	voz 2:	Joaquín.
	voz 1:	¿Cómo se escribe?
	voz 2:	J-O-A-Q-U-I con acento-N.
5	voz 1:	Oye, ¿'Raúl' se escribe con acento o no?
	voz 2:	Sí. R-A-U con acento- L.
6	voz 1:	¿Cómo se escribe tu nombre?
	voz 2:	M-A-R-I-F-E con acento.
7	voz 1:	Tu nombre se escribe: A N A ...
	voz 2:	M-A-R-I con acento-A.
8	voz 1:	¿Te llamas Concha, no?
	voz 2:	Bueno, sí, pero mi nombre es Concepción. C-O-N-C-E-P-C-I-O con acento-N.

3 **Con tu pareja**

A pairwork activity in which students ask each other the Spanish for, and sometimes the spelling of, various words.

Acción: lengua 1, page 11

Students learn

– to use and understand the familiar and formal forms of the second person

– to recognise and understand the reflexive verb *llamarse* (to be called)

1 ○ Students work out which singular form to use in a variety of situations.

○ A similar activity, but including the plural forms *ustedes* and *vosotros*.

Answers: ○ 1 – tú; 2 – tú; 3 – usted; 4 – tú; 5 – tú.

○ 1 – vosotros; 2 – usted; 3 – tú; 4 – ustedes;
5 – vosotros.

2 This activity covers the usage of the remaining subject pronouns.

Answers: 1 – yo; 2 – él; 3 – usted; 4 – ella; 5 – tú; 6 – ellos;
7 – nosotros; 8 – ustedes; 9 – ellas.

3 ○ An activity practising *llamarse*. The verb is given in full above as a reference.

○ Students supply the correct form of *llamarse* to complete a gap-fill activity.

Answers: ○ 1 – te llamas; 2 – me llamo; 3 – se llama;
4 – se llama; 5 – me llamo.

○ 1 – os llamáis; 2 – nos llamamos; 3 – te llamas;
4 – me llamo; 5 – se llama; 6 – se llaman;
7 – se llama.

Objectives
Students learn – the names for schoolbag items
– to ask if someone has an item and reply
– to use the indefinite article

Key language
¿tienes?   *un libro*
¿me dejas ...?   *una hoja*
sí, toma   *un sacapuntas*
tengo   *una agenda*
lo siento, no tengo *una goma*
un boli / un bolígrafo *una mochila*
un cuaderno   *una pluma*
un estuche   *una regla*
un lápiz

Skills / Strategies
Students learn – to ask for things, and reply appropriately
– to use *un / una*

ICT opportunities
Students can   – create a lost property notice with an attractive
border (Worksheet 2.1, Activity 2b)

Ways in
Schoolbag items – OHT, real objects; Student's Book, Activity 1
and picture story
un / una   – unobtrusively via item presentation, or through
exploitation using Student's Book Activity 3,
and Worksheet 2.1 Activity 1

Assessment opportunities
AT2,1   Student's Book, Activity 2: target students working in
pairs.
AT3,1   Worksheet 2.1: Activity 1: students match the pictures with
the items.
AT4,2   Worksheet 2.1, Activity 2b: students write an
advertisement for lost property.

STUDENT'S BOOK, pages 12–13

1   La mochila de Pepa

a Presentation of schoolbag items: students listen and
follow. Each item is said twice.

> 1 un boli / un bolígrafo
> 2 un cuaderno
> 3 un estuche
> 4 un lápiz
> 5 un libro
> 6 un sacapuntas
> 7 una agenda
> 8 una goma
> 9 una hoja
> 10 una mochila
> 11 una pluma
> 12 una regla

b ◐ Students write the numbers of the items 1–8 and
listen as Pepa's exasperated Dad is helping her to check
her bag for school. They put a tick if she has got the item,
and a cross if she hasn't.

Answers: *1 – ✗; 2 – ✓; 3 – ✗; 4 – ✓; 5 – ✓; 6 – ✗; 7 – ✗; 8 – ✗.*

PAPÁ:	Vamos a ver ... ¡Pepa! ¿tienes un boli?
PEPA:	¿Un boli? ¡No!
PAPÁ:	¿Un cuaderno?
PEPA:	Un cuaderno. Mm, sí.
PAPÁ:	¿Tienes un estuche?
PEPA:	No.
PAPÁ:	¿Un lápiz?
PEPA:	Sí, tengo un lápiz.
PAPÁ:	¡Qué bien! ¿Tienes un libro?
PEPA:	Ah–h ... libro, sí.
PAPÁ:	¡Fenomenal! ¿Un sacapuntas?
PEPA:	Un sacapuntas ... no.
PAPÁ:	¿Una agenda?
PEPA:	Mm, no. Agenda, no.
PAPÁ:	¡Fatal! ¿Una goma?
PEPA:	No. No tengo goma.
PAPÁ:	Pepa, ¡eres un desastre!

2   Juego de memoria

♣ A pairwork or group speaking activity in which Partner
A looks at the visuals shown beside the activity and says
numbers, and Partner **B** has to say the Spanish word for
that item without looking at the book.

3   El diccionario

A basic dictionary skills activity in which students check to
find out whether each of the 10 nouns given is masculine
or feminine, and write the English translation of each.

Answers: *1 – una bebida: a drink; 2 – una calculadora: a
calculator; 3 – una carpeta: a folder; 4 – un clip: a
paper clip; 5 – un compás: a pair of compasses;
6 – una grabadora: a tape recorder; 7 – una llave: a
key; 8 – un monedero: a purse; 9 – una taladradora:
a pneumatic drill; 10 – un rotulador: a felt-tip pen.*

Gramática

Students are referred to the grammar worksheet on the
indefinite article. Talk students through how the indefinite
article works, referring them to the brief Student's Book
item as necessary. Then move on to the activities on the
worksheet, which provide practice at both basic and higher
level. If students need further assistance they could refer to
the grammar summary, section 2 on p.148.

4   ¿Tienes ...?
Picture story

Tomás suffers at the hands of Roberto and his mates.
Students should initially listen to the recording and read
the text before going on to the exploitation activities.

◐ A straightforward true or false activity checking
comprehension of the text.

♣ A slightly more challenging exploitation activity
involving a gap-fill which practises the verb *tengo*.

Answers: ◐ *1 – mentira; 2 – verdad; 3 – mentira; 4 – verdad;
5 – mentira; 6 – verdad.*

♣ *1 – tengo; 2 – tiene; 3 – tienes; 4 – tengo;
5 – tiene.*

PEPA:	¡Psst! ¿Tienes un boli?
TOMÁS:	Sí, toma.
PEPA:	¡Oye! ¿Tienes una regla?
TOMÁS:	Sí, toma ...
PEPA:	¿Tienes un sacapuntas?
TOMÁS:	Lo siento, no tengo. Pepa, pero ¿no tienes un estuche?
PEPA:	¿Yo? ¡No! ... Oh-oh – Roberto.
ROBERTO:	¡Ah! ¿Un estuche inglés? ¡Qué bien!
AMIGO 1:	¿Tienes una pluma, Tomás?
ROBERTO:	¿Tienes una hoja, Tomás?

AMIGO 2:	¿Tienes una goma, Tomás?
AMIGO 1:	¿Tienes un lápiz, Tomás?
PROFESOR:	¡Silencio! ¡Sentaos!
ROBERTO:	¿Usted tiene un lápiz?
PROFESOR:	No, no tengo. ¡Y no tengo mucha paciencia!

Gramática

Students are referred here to the entry for *tengo* in the grammar summary, section 11 on p.149, and to Acción: lengua 3, p.29.

SUPPORT MATERIALS

OHT 2A ¿Me dejas?

Schoolbag items. The 12 items correspond to those used in listening Activity 1a in the Student's Book. This sheet can be used for presentation or subsequent practice, and photocopied on to card for games.

Worksheet 2.1 La mochila

1 **¿Qué hay en la mochila?**

O Students write the correct word for each of the items pictured.

Answers:
a – un sacapuntas; *b* – un rotulador; *c* – un compás; *d* – una agenda; *e* – un lápiz; *f* – un estuche; *g* – una pluma; *h* – una carpeta.

2 **He perdido ...**

a **♣** Students read the texts to work out who each of the two bags pictured belongs to.

Answers:
Bag 1 – Ana Belén Sánchez;
Bag 2 – Arantxa Menéndez.

b An open-ended writing activity in which students describe a bag they have 'lost', using the notices in the preceding receptive activity as a model.

Worksheet 2.2 Práctica: lengua un / una

This grammar worksheet presents and provides practice in the use of the indefinite article *un / una* (see also Student's Book, p.12).

En clase

O Students fill in the correct form of the indefinite article for each item listed.

♣ Students fill in the gaps in a longer text.

Answers:

O *1 – un; 2 – una; 3 – un; 4 – una; 5 – un; 6 – una; 7 – una; 8 – un; 9 – una.*

♣ *1 – una, una, un, nothing, nothing; 2 – nothing, nothing, una, un, nothing.*

Homework opportunity

Apart from learning the vocabulary of the objective, students could be encouraged to carry out a research homework using the English–Spanish section of the dictionary. After reminding students which part of the dictionary to use for this activity, ask them to look up the Spanish for between five and 10 other things they carry around with them in their bags or pockets. If students don't have their own dictionary, they could use dictionaries in the school library.

Extra

Make small cards from OHT 2A, and use them for a game of Happy Families. Put a list on the board of all 12 items divided into four 'families'. In groups of four, each student tries to collect a 'family' by asking *¿Tienes un boli?*, to which the reply will be either *Lo siento, no tengo* or *Sí, toma*. More fun with another four or eight items to give 'families' of four or five cards: you or your students could decide on the most useful ones for your class from the selection on the Student's Book pages.

Objectives

Students learn – to ask how to do their work
– to understand and give classroom instructions
– to use the definite article 'the'
– to identify classroom furniture and equipment

Key language

se hace por delante	*la silla*
se hace por detrás	*la mesa*
se hace en limpio	*la luz*
se hace en sucio	*el cassette*
se hace en la hoja	*el retroproyector*
se hace en el cuaderno	*el ordenador*
¿qué se hace ahora?	*el vídeo*
¿qué página es?	*el magnetofón*
la pizarra	*el tablón*
la puerta	*el borrador*
la ventana	*el estante*
abre / cierra	*el suelo*
enciende / apaga	*el armario*
pon ... bien	
limpia	

Skills / Strategies

Students learn – to cope with everyday classroom situations in the target language
– to use *el / la*

ICT opportunities

Students can – enter instructions and classroom objects on to computer and practise 'copy' and 'paste' functions to create different classroom instructions (Student's Book, Activity 4)

Ways in

Classroom activities – OHT 2B, Picture story (Student's Book page 14)
Classroom objects – the actual items in the room

Assessment opportunities

AT1,1 Worksheet 2.3 Activity 1: students listen and match the visuals.
AT2,1 Worksheet 2.4, Activity 4: students invent a conversation.
AT3,1 Worksheet 2.4, Activity 1: phrase assembly / recognition activity.
AT4,1 Worksheet 2.4, Activity 2: simple copying.
AT4,2 Student's Book, Activity 4: students write simple instructions used regularly in class.

STUDENT'S BOOK, pages 14–15

1 ¿Qué se hace ahora?

Picture story

José Luis, Carlos, Isabel and Pilar are in class. The friendship between José Luis and Isabel is developing, but under the watchful eye of Pilar.

○ Students match up the phrases with the correct pictures.

✿ Some straightforward questions relating to the tapescript and picture story.

Answers: ○ *1 – f; 2 – d; 3 – c; 4 – a; 5 – e; 6 – b.*

✿ *1 – página 15; 2 – número 3; 3 – Look at the board / I've finished / What do we do now?*

PILAR:	¡Sentaos aquí!
PROFESOR:	Página quince, número tres, por favor.
ISABEL:	¿Se hace en sucio?
PILAR:	No – en limpio.
JOSÉ LUIS:	¿Se hace en la hoja?
CARLOS:	No – en el cuaderno.
JOSÉ LUIS:	¿Se hace por detrás?
CARLOS:	No – por delante.
JOSÉ LUIS:	Isabel, ¿qué página es?
ISABEL:	La página quince.
JOSÉ LUIS:	¿Qué número es?
CARLOS:	¡Mira la pizarra!
JOSÉ LUIS:	Ya he terminado. ¿Qué se hace ahora?
PROFESOR:	No es la actividad dos, es la actividad tres.
JOSÉ LUIS:	¡Qué desastre!
PROFESOR:	Deberes para el viernes – número cuatro. ¿José Luis ...? ¡Números tres y cuatro, por favor!

2 La queja de los profes

A song to practise the new language – you might point out that you like students to ask questions, but want them to do it in Spanish! The song is heard twice.

¿Se hace en limpio?
¿Se hace en sucio?
¿Se hace por delante?
¿Se hace por detrás?
¿Se hace en la hoja?
¿Se hace en el cuaderno?
¿Se hace aquí en clase?
¡No puedo más!
Estoy hasta la coronilla
con las explicaciones
¡Hay que escuchar
las instrucciones!

3 En clase

Further practice in using the vocabulary section at the back of the Student's Book, or an actual Spanish–English dictionary. Since the correct *el / la* is given, students only need to be aware that there are two words for 'the' and don't need to understand the concept of masculine and feminine yet. If you want to exploit it at this point, there is an explanation in the grammar summary, section 3 p.148, and it is dealt with in Acción: lengua 2, p.19 at the end of this unit. A little pronunciation practice of the new words would be helpful.

Answers: *a – board; b – door; c – window; d – chair; e – table; f – light; g – cassette player; h – video recorder; i – overhead projector; j – computer; k – tape recorder; l – board; m – rubber; n – shelves; o – floor, ground; p – cupboard.*

4 Los robots

○ Presentation of common classroom instructions.

The robot voice gives instructions to all the little robots. With the aid of the sound effects and pictures, students should complete the phrases using one of the words from the list in Activity 3.

✿ An open-ended activity in which students use stimulus language from Student's Book p.14–15 to make up their own commands.

Answers: ○ *1 – la ventana; 2 – la puerta; 3 – la silla; 4 – la luz; 5 – el ordenador; 6 – la mesa.*

> **1** – Abre la ventana.
> **2** – Cierra la puerta.
> **3** – Pon la silla bien. ¡Ay!
> **4** – Enciende la luz.
> **5** – Apaga el ordenador.
> **6** – Limpia la mesa.

Gramática

This brief item draws students' attention to the definite article, which is taught via a worksheet in this unit – see Práctica: lengua Worksheet 2.5. Students may also want to refer to the coverage of the point in the grammar summary section 3 on p.148 and Acción: lengua 2, p.19.

SUPPORT MATERIALS

OHT 2B ¿Se hace ...?

This sheet presents the key phrases for introducing and practising classroom instructions. The images can be photocopied onto card and used for pairwork practice.

Worksheet 2.3 ¿Qué se hace ahora?

 ◐ Students listen to the conversations and match each one to the appropriate visual.

✚ Students listen again and select the appropriate sentence from a menu of three each time.

Answers:	**◐** *A – 1; B – 3; C – 6; D – 2; E – 5; F – 4.*
	✚ *1 – a; 2 – b; 3 – c; 4 – a; 5 – c; 6 – a.*

1 CHICA: Oye, ¿qué actividad es? ¿Seis?
   CHICA: No, es la actividad siete.
   CHICA: Vale, gracias.

2 CHICO: Oiga, ¿se hace por delante?
   PROFESOR: Sí, por delante. ¿Cómo te llamas?
   CHICO: Juan.
   PROFESOR: Después de hacer esto, Juan, puedes escuchar el cassette ...

3 CHICO: Por favor, ¿qué hago ahora?
   PROFESOR: ¿Has terminado?
   CHICO: Sí.
   PROFESOR: A ver ... ¿No tienes bolígrafo?
   CHICO: No, no tengo.
   PROFESOR: Toma éste, y hazlo otra vez ...

4 CHICA: ¿Se hace en limpio?
   PROFESOR: Sí, en limpio. Eres Rosa, ¿no?
   CHICA: Sí.
   PROFESOR: ¿Y tu apellido es García?
   CHICA: No, Garfía. G-A-R-F-Í-A.

5 CHICO: Oye, Ana, ¿qué página es?
   CHICA: Es la página quince.
   CHICO: Quince. Vale.

6 CHICA: ¿Se hace en sucio, esta actividad?
   PROFESOR: ¿En sucio? ¿Por qué?
   CHICA: Es que no tengo mi cuaderno.
   PROFESOR: Bueno, hay que hacerlo en sucio entonces.

Worksheet 2.4 Instrucciones

1 **¿Tiene sentido o no?**

◐ Students read a series of sentences and select the most plausible combination of words for each.

Answers:	*1 – b; 2 – a; 3 – c; 4 – b; 5 – b; 6 – a.*

2 **¿Qué dicen?**

◐ A text-completion activity practising the classroom instruction language.

Answers:	*1 – ¿Qué página es? 2 – ¡Cierra la ventana! 3 – Apaga el ordenador. 4 – Abre la puerta. 5 – Enciende la luz. 6 – ¡Limpia la mesa!*

3 **Hasta la coronilla**

✚ In this gap-fill activity students fill in the gaps in a conversation between a student and a teacher.

Answers:	*1 – página; 2 – cuatro; 3 – la; 4 – por; 5 – delante; 6 – tengo; 7 – bolígrafo; 8 – un.*

4 **Te toca a ti**

✚ An open-ended writing activity involving writing similar scenes to the one in the preceding activity. Students then practise their dialogues with a partner.

Worksheet 2.5 Práctica: lengua – El / la

This sheet presents and practises the definite article in the masculine and feminine singular. If necessary, students should refer to the grammar summary section 3 on p.148 for further help.

¿De quién es?

◐ A basic gap-fill activity using *el* and *la*.

✚ A gap-fill activity practising *el* and *la*, but also revising *un* and *una*, and checking students' knowledge of when to use each form of article.

Answers:	**◐** *1 – El; 2 – La; 3 – la; 4 – el; 5 – La; 6 – El; 7 – La; 8 – El.*
	✚ *1 – el; 2 – un; 3 – la; 4 – una; 5 – la; 6 – una; 7 – el; 8 – la; 9 – la; 10 – un.*

Extra

To reinforce the classroom language and instructions, students could prepare labels and signs for display around the walls. Doors, windows and lights could be labelled in Spanish and the student questions could be displayed on card or posters somewhere near the board. It is helpful to number such items, so that they can be referred to more easily. When a student asks one of the key questions in English, simply point to the relevant sign and say *¡Número (4) por favor!* You could also include some of the student language from the previous objective.

Objectives
Students learn – the numbers 20–31
– to ask and say whose turn it is
– the months of the year
– how to ask/give the date

Key language
The numbers 20–31
¿a quién le toca?
me toca a mí
te toca a ti

The months of the year
*enero, febrero, marzo,
abril, mayo, junio,
julio, agosto, septiembre,
octubre, noviembre, diciembre*

Skills / Strategies
Students learn – how to suggest whose turn it is
– how to ask / give the date

ICT opportunities
Students can – create / complete a crossword using the
appropriate crossword-production package

Ways in
Numbers   – Student's Book, Activity 1
Taking turns – Student's Book, Activity 3

Assessment opportunities
AT1,1 Worksheet 2.7, Activity 1: students listen for numbers and
spell the names.
AT2,1 Student's Book, Activity 2: assess a small group of
students playing the multiplication game.
AT3,1 Student's Book, Activity 4b: students listen and read the
months in Spanish.
AT4,1 Student's Book, Activity 5: students write out the dates in
Spanish.

STUDENT'S BOOK, pages 16–17

1 **Más números**

Presentation of the numbers 20–31. Students listen to the
recording and repeat the numbers. For further
reinforcement you could use a selection of number games
and recycle numbers below 20 too, so that the pattern
becomes clear. Each number is repeated.

```
veinte
veintiuno
veintidós
veintitrés
veinticuatro
veinticinco
veintiséis
veintisiete
veintiocho
veintinueve
treinta
treinta y uno
```

2 **Multiplicación**

A basic open-ended oral production activity in which
students set multiplication tasks for their partner.

3 **La audición**

◗ Students listen to the auditions being called and work
out which person has each number.

➕ A picture-matching activity practising the instruction
language featured in the dialogues.

Answers:
◗ *Ahmed 23; Catalina 30; Felipe 19; Juanjo 25;
Margarita 31; Sohora 27.*

➕ *Ahmed c; Catalina e; Felipe b; Juanjo a;
Margarita f; Sohora d.*

AHMED
ENTREVISTADOR:	¡Número veintitrés! ¿Veintitrés?
CHICO:	Sí – ¡me toca a mí!
ENTREVISTADOR:	Eres Ahmed, ¿no?
CHICO:	Sí.
ENTREVISTADOR:	Oye, Ana, no veo nada. Enciende la luz, por favor.

CATALINA
ENTREVISTADOR:	¡Treinta! ¡Te toca a ti! Treinta, por favor.
CHICA:	¡Ya voy!
ENTREVISTADOR:	¡Hola, Catalina! Ven, siéntate aquí en la mesa.

FELIPE
ENTREVISTADOR:	¿A quién le toca?
ANA:	Número diecinueve.
ENTREVISTADOR:	¡Hola! ¡Pasa, pasa!
CHICO:	¡Hola! Tengo el número diecinueve.
ENTREVISTADOR:	No leo bien tu apellido, Felipe. ¿Cómo se escribe?
CHICO:	Es inglés. Se escribe M – O – R – R – I – S – O – N.

JUANJO
ENTREVISTADOR:	¡Veinticinco!
CHICA:	¡Juanjo! ¡Te toca a ti! Veinticinco.
JUANJO:	¿Me toca a mí? Ya voy.
ENTREVISTADOR:	¡Hola! ¿Qué tal?
JUANJO:	Mm ... Regular. Un poco nervioso, si te digo la verdad.
ENTREVISTADOR:	Bueno, vamos a ver ...

MARGARITA
CHICO:	Aquí viene.
CHICA:	¡A que me toca a mí!
ENTREVISTADOR:	¿Treinta y uno?
CHICA:	¿Treinta y uno? ¡Soy yo!
ENTREVISTADOR:	Ven, pasa. No tengo papel. ¡Ana! ¿tienes una hoja de papel, por favor?
ANA:	Sí, toma.

SOHORA
ENTREVISTADOR:	¿A quién le toca?
ANA:	Le toca a ... veintisiete. ¡Veintisiete!
ENTREVISTADOR:	¡Hola! Pasa, pasa por favor. Ana, cierra la puerta. Gracias.

4 **Los meses del año**

a First of all, students listen to the names of the months
on the recording, to give them a good grasp of the
pronunciation.

```
enero, enero
febrero, febrero
marzo, marzo
abril, abril
mayo, mayo
junio, junio
julio, julio
agosto, agosto
septiembre, septiembre
octubre, octubre
noviembre, noviembre
diciembre, diciembre
```

b Students listen and write down the names of the months mentioned in each of the six dialogues.

Answers: *1 – noviembre; 2 – septiembre; 3 – junio; 4 – enero; 5 – marzo; 6 – diciembre.*

---

1 CHICO: ¿Qué fecha es?
  CHICA: El doce de noviembre.
  CHICO: El doce de noviembre. Gracias. Y hoy es martes.
  CHICA: Sí, es martes. No me gustan nada los martes porque ...

2 CHICA: Martín, ¿qué fecha es? ¿El quince, no?
  CHICO: Sí. El quince de septiembre.
  CHICA: El quince de septiembre. Y es lunes.
  CHICO: Sí, es lunes. ¡Qué horror!

3 CHICO: Íñigo, hoy es el veintisiete de junio, ¿no?
  CHICO: Sí, el veintisiete de junio.
  CHICO: Jueves, el veintisiete.
  CHICO: Hoy es viernes.
  CHICO: ¿Seguro?
  CHICO: ¡Sí, seguro!
  CHICO: Bueno. Viernes, el veintisiete de junio.

4 CHICA: Alicia, ¿qué fecha es?
  CHICA: El once.
  CHICA: De enero.
  CHICA: Claro, ¡de enero!
  CHICA: Gracias. Jueves, el once de enero. Alicia, ¿tienes un boli? El mío no funciona bien ...

5 CHICO: ¿Sabes qué día es?
  CHICA: Sí, es sábado.
  CHICO: Pero, ¿qué fecha es?
  CHICA: El veintinueve de marzo.
  CHICO: Y ...
  CHICA: ¿Y qué? ¿Es una fecha importante, el veintinueve de marzo?
  CHICO: Es el cumpleaños de la abuela. ¿Le has comprado algo?

6 CHICA: ¿Es el catorce de diciembre?
  CHICO: Sí. Es domingo, catorce de diciembre. ¿Por qué?
  CHICA: Porque tengo el dentista mañana.

---

c ◐ Students listen again and write down the date.

◑ Students listen again and write down the day of the week instead of, or in addition to, the date.

Answers: ◐ *1 – 12 noviembre; 2 – 15 septiembre; 3 – 27 junio; 4 – 11 enero; 5 – 29 marzo; 6 – 14 diciembre.*

  ◑ *1 – martes; 2 – lunes; 3 – viernes; 4 – jueves; 5 – sábado; 6 – domingo.*

5 🖊 **El calendario**

A writing activity in which students write out a selection of dates in full.

Answers: *1 – el doce de enero; 2 – el veintitrés de febrero; 3 – el treinta y uno de marzo; 4 – el ocho de abril; 5 – el primero de mayo; 6 – el veintiséis de junio; 7 – el ocho de julio; 8 – el dos de agosto; 9 – el veintiuno de septiembre; 10 – el siete de octubre; 11 – el diecinueve de noviembre; 12 – el veinticinco de diciembre.*

SUPPORT MATERIALS
Worksheet 2.6 Preguntas

This is an information-gap activity in two halves. The sheet should be cut along the dotted line and one half given to each of a pair of students. The students then question each other to find out the information on their partner's half-sheet. There are two questions on the sheet, and roles are swapped so that each student plays the questioning and the answering role.

Worksheet 2.7 Repaso

1 💿 **El cursillo de inglés**

Students are being registered for English classes by the native English speaker, Karen Jones. Students listen and write down each student's enrolment number ◐ and first name as it is spelt out ◑. There is redundant language here, and this is the first occasion that students hear the formal address with *usted*. You may wish to point this out to your students, but since it does not affect the activity, you may prefer to deal with it later.

Answers: ◐ *1 – 15; 2 – 27; 3 – 25; 4 – 30.*

  ◑ *1 – Belén; 2 – Jorge; 3 – Zeneida; 4 – Gari.*

EJEMPLO SR AV: Por favor – ¿el cursillo de inglés?
  KAREN: Sí – aquí. Me llamo Karen Jones. Soy la profesora de inglés. ¿Su número de matrícula?
  SR AV: Treinta y uno.
  KAREN: Treinto y uno. Muy bien. Y ¿usted es ...?
  SR AV: Ignacio Alvarez Villarejo.
  KAREN: Ignacio. I-g-n-a-c-i-o. Vale. La clase dura dos horas ...

1 STA D: ¡Hola! Buenos días.
  KAREN: Buenos días. Soy Karen Jones. ¿Su número de matrícula?
  STA D: Mm, quince.
  KAREN: Quince. Vale, gracias. ¿Y su nombre?
  STA D: Me llamo Belén Díaz Menéndez.
  KAREN: ¿Cómo se escribe?
  STA D: B-e-l-é-n. Oye, ¿no soy un poco vieja para aprender el inglés ...?

2 KAREN: ¡Hola! El Sr García López, ¿no?
  SR GL: Sí, soy yo.
  KAREN: ¿Su número de matrícula, por favor?
  SR GL: Veintisiete ... ah ... sí, veintisiete.
  KAREN: ¿Y su nombre?
  SR GL: Me llamo Jorge.
  KAREN: J-o-r-g-e. Muy bien. Hay clases cada miércoles ...

3 SRA G: Buenas tardes. ¿Es usted la señorita Karen Jones?
  KAREN: Sí, soy yo. ¿Tiene su número de matrícula?
  SRA G: Sí, veinticinco.
  KAREN: Veinticinco. Vale, gracias. ¿Cómo se llama usted?
  SRA G: Zeneida Guerra Velázquez.
  KAREN: ¿Zeneida? ¡Qué bonito! ¿Cómo se escribe?
  SRA G: Z-e-n-e-i-d-a. Mire, ¿a qué hora empieza la clase el miércoles?

4 KAREN: ¡Hola! Soy Karen, la profesora de inglés.
  SR R: ¡Hola! Soy Gari Roldán.
  KAREN: Gari – ¿se escribe como en inglés – G-a-r-y?
  SR R: No. G-a-r-i. Mi nombre es vasco.
  KAREN: Vale, gracias. Y ¿el número de matrícula?
  SR R: No lo sé.
  KAREN: ¿Me deja la tarjeta? Es treinta.
  SR R: ¿Treinta? Ah, sí ... perdone ...

2 Crucigrama

The crossword recycles some of the key vocabulary covered so far. Students use a mixture of visual and written clues to fill in the squares.

Answers:

Objectives
Students learn – how to form the plurals of nouns
– the plurals of articles

Key language
Plurals of nouns and articles already introduced

Skills / Strategies
Students learn – to understand instructions
– to deduce plural forms from known singulars

ICT opportunities
Students can – modify singular texts via word-processing to
produce plural versions (Student's Book, Activity 3)

Ways in
Plurals of nouns – Student's Book, Activity 1
Plural articles – Student's Book, Activity 3

Assessment opportunities
AT1,1 Student's Book, Activity 1: students listen and write the
number of items.
AT3,2 Student's Book, Activity 3: mixed-skill reading/writing
activity.
AT4,1 Student's Book, Activity 2: simple copywriting activity.

STUDENT'S BOOK, page 18

1 **Objetos perdidos**

◯ A listening activity which entails listening and writing down the number of things mentioned in a conversation at the lost property office.

✚ Students listen again to work out what additional item to those listed has been lost, and whose it is.

Answers: ◯ *agendas – 23; bolígrafos – 31; estuches – 15; gomas – 23; lápices – 30; magnetofones – 2; rotuladores – 11; sacapuntas – 26.*

✚ *A rucksack. It belongs to Pepa Yessef*

MUJER:	Objetos perdidos ... Inventario.
HOMBRE:	¿Agendas?
MUJER:	Sí.
HOMBRE:	Mm ... veintitrés agendas.
MUJER:	Veintitrés ... bien. ¿Bolígrafos?
HOMBRE:	¡Uff! Treinta y uno.
MUJER:	Treinta y uno. Y ... ¿estuches?
HOMBRE:	Mm ... quince.
MUJER:	Quince estuches.
HOMBRE:	Y gomas ... veintitrés.
MUJER:	Veintitrés gomas.
HOMBRE:	Lápices ... treinta.
MUJER:	Treinta lápices. ¿Y magnetofones?
HOMBRE:	Dos.
MUJER:	Dos magnetofones.
HOMBRE:	¿Rotuladores?
MUJER:	Once.
HOMBRE:	Once. Luego, sacapuntas.
MUJER:	¿Cuántos hay?
HOMBRE:	Vamos a ver ... Veintiséis.
MUJER:	Veintiséis. ¿Es todo?.
HOMBRE:	Sí. ¡Ay, no! Hay una mochila.
MUJER:	¿Una mochila? ¿De quién es?
HOMBRE:	No lo sé. Hay un nombre ... P – e – p – a. Pepa ... Y – e – s
MUJER:	Pepa Yessef. ¡Claro! ¡Es un desastre, esa chica!

2 **El inventario**

An activity which provides initial copywriting practice of the plural forms. Students fill in a form saying what needs to be cleaned, painted, repaired, etc.

Answers: *5 ventanas; 3 puertas; 2 ordenadores; 30 sillas; 2 vídeos; 4 estantes; 6 tablones; 8 luces.*

3 **En el almacén**

A gap-fill activity practising the plural forms of the definite article.

Answers: *a – los; b – los; c – los; d – las; e – los; f – las; g – las; h – los; i – los; j – los.*

Gramática

The table on p.18 summarises the point being learnt and refers students to the appropriate section of the grammar summary, section 4 on p.148 if they need further explanation. Finally, a brief résumé of the plurals of the definite and indefinite article is given at the bottom of p.18.

Acción: lengua, page 19

Students learn
– the singular and plural of indefinite articles
– the usage of indefinite and definite articles in the plural

1 ◯ This activity practises the indefinite article forms in the singular.

✚ Students classify plural words according to whether they are feminine or masculine.

Answers: ◯ *un; un; una; un; un; una; un; una.*

✚ *unos: rotuladores, bolis, vídeos, cassettes, borradores, lápices.*
unas: carpetas, luces, reglas.

2 ◯ Students fill in the gaps in the stage manager's instructions with the appropriate form of *el* or *la*.

✚ Students insert the correct form of the definite article in the singular or plural as necessary.

Answers: ◯ *1 – el, el; 2 – la, la; 3 – la; 4 – el; 5 – la; 6 – la.*

✚ *la puerta; el ordenador; los tablones; las ventanas; las sillas; los estantes; la pizarra; las mesas.*

3 ◯ An activity which involves choosing the correct form of the definite or indefinite article in response to a given prompt.

✚ A longer piece of writing in which students insert the correct indefinite or definite articles.

Answers: ◯ *1 – un; 2 – un; 3 – un; 4 – la; 5 – un; 6 – un; 7 – la; 8 – una; 9 – la.*

✚ *una (silla), unos (estantes), el (ordenador), el (suelo), una (mesa), un (armario), el (dormitorio), una (ventana), unos (profesores), la (clase).*

3A ¿Tienes hermanos?

Objectives
Students learn – to talk about their brothers and sisters and ask others

Key language
hermano / hermana
hermanastro / hermanastra
hermano gemelo / hermana gemela
hijo único / hija única
tengo / no tengo / tienes
soy / eres
se llama / se llaman
que …

Skills / Strategies
Students learn – to use the relative pronoun *que …*

ICT opportunities
Students can – import images, clip-art, or photos into documents to create an illustrated and annotated description of their brothers and sisters

Ways in
Brothers and sisters   – OHT 3A; Student's Book, Activity 1
Have / has, relative pronoun *que* – Student's Book, Activity 1

Assessment opportunities
AT1,1   Student's Book, Activity 3: students note the number of brothers and sisters.
AT2,1   Student's Book, Activity 4: assess students while working in groups of three.
AT3,2   Worksheet 3.1, Activity 1: students match up the sentence halves.
AT4,1: Worksheet 3.1, Activity 2: students complete the speech bubbles.

STUDENT'S BOOK, pages 20–21

Picture story
Pepa is introduced to Isabel and Pilar, and Tomás meets José Luis and Carlos. As they all walk home, they find out about each other's brothers and sisters.

1 ¿Tienes hermanos?
○ Students read and listen to the picture story and write down who said each of the five phrases.

✚ The emphasis here is on the phrases *se llama* and *se llaman*, which will enable students to talk about their own brothers and sisters. Students pick the correct words to fill in the gaps. You may like to point out the function of *que* at this point.

Answers: ○ *1 – Pilar; 2 – Tomás; 3 – José Luis; 4 – Carlos; 5 – Pepa.*
✚ *1 – se llama; 2 – se llama; 3 – se llaman; 4 – se llama.*

TOMÁS:	Isabel, mi hermana, y Pilar.
PILAR:	Hola, Pepa.
ISABEL:	Mi hermano, que se llama Tomás.
ISABEL:	José Luis, ¿tienes hermanos?
JOSÉ LUIS:	Sí, tengo un hermano y una hermana que se llaman Rafael y Ana.
ISABEL:	¿Y tú, Pepa? ¿Tienes hermanos?
PEPA:	No, soy hija única.
TOMÁS:	¿No tienes hermanos? ¡Qué bien!
ISABEL:	¡Qué pesado eres, Tomás! Y tú, Carlos, ¿eres hijo único?
CARLOS:	No, tengo tres hermanos y tres hermanas.
ISABEL:	Pilar – tu hermano, Juan … ¿no está?
PILAR:	No …

2 ¿Cómo se dice en inglés …?
A dictionary skills activity. Encourage students to use the Spanish–English section of the vocabulary to find the meanings of these four phrases.

Answers: *1 – stepbrother; 2 – stepsister; 3 – twin brother; 4 – twin sister.*

3 ¿Cuántos hermanos tienen?
○ Students listen to the four dialogues and jot down how many brothers and sisters each person has.

✚ Students study the eight pictures and try to identify who the four people speaking are.

Answers: ○ *1 – 1 brother and 0 sisters; 2 – 0 brothers and 0 sisters; 3 – 0 brothers and 2 sisters; 4 – 1 brother and 2 sisters.*

✚ *1 – Arancha; 2 – Paco; 3 – Sofía; 4 – Gari.*

1	CHICO:	¿Tienes hermanos?
	CHICA:	Sí.
	CHICO:	¿Tienes un hermano?
	CHICA:	Sí.
	CHICO:	¿Tienes hermanas?
	CHICA:	No.
	CHICO:	¡Ah! ¡Eres …!
2	CHICO:	¿Tienes hermanos?
	CHICO:	No.
	CHICO:	¿Y no tienes hermanas?
	CHICO:	No.
	CHICO:	¡Ah! Eres hijo único – eres …
3	CHICO:	¿Tienes hermanos?
	CHICA:	Bueno, hermanos no, pero …
	CHICO:	¿Tienes hermanas?
	CHICA:	Sí.
	CHICO:	¿Tienes una hermana?
	CHICA:	Mm …
	CHICO:	¿Tienes dos hermanas?
	CHICA:	Sí, tengo dos hermanas.
	CHICO:	¡Ah! ¡Eres …!
4	CHICO:	¿Tienes hermanos?
	CHICO:	Sí.
	CHICO:	¿Tienes un hermano?
	CHICO:	Sí.
	CHICO:	¿Tienes hermanas?
	CHICO:	Sí.
	CHICO:	¿Tienes una hermana?
	CHICO:	Mm, no.
	CHICO:	¿Tienes dos hermanas?
	CHICO:	Sí.
	CHICO:	Ah – ¿eres …?

4 **En un grupo de tres**

A groupwork activity. Student **A** pretends to be one of the eight people pictured in Activity 3, and Students **B** and **C** take it in turns to ask how many brothers and sisters Student **A** has until they can identify the correct picture. Student **A** can only reply by saying *sí* or *no*.

5 **¿Quién soy?**

Written follow-up of the previous activity. Students identify the six people from the same eight pictures, and write their names.

Students write speech bubbles for the remaining two people.

Answers: *1 – Paco; 2 – Arancha; 3 – Sofía; 4 – Felipe; 5 – Gari; 6 – Reyes.*

a – Me llamo Zohora. Soy hija única.
b – Me llamo Charo. Tengo una hermana.

SUPPORT MATERIALS

OHT 3A ¿Tienes hermanos?

Presentation of brothers and sisters. Reveal the pictures one by one to introduce various combinations of these, as well as two people without brothers and sisters.

Worksheet 3.1 Los hermanos

1 **¿Cuántos hermanos tienen?**

Students join together a series of sentence halves which give information about how many brothers and sisters people have, using the picture cues.

Answers: *1 – e; 2 – c; 3 – f; 4 – a; 5 – d; 6 – b.*

2 **¡Imagina!**

An open-ended activity where students use artwork and cues to generate their own sentences describing how many brothers and sisters the people pictured have, and what they are called.

Worksheet 3.2 Carlos

1 **¡Pobre Carlos!**

A picture story about Carlos, his family and two girls who pass by his house. Students fill in the gaps in the speech bubbles using appropriate words from the box.

Answers: *1 – ¡Fatal!; 2 – Tienes; 3 – hermanastros; 4 – toca; 5 – hermanas; 6 – lápiz; 7 – puerta; 8 – gemela; 9 – hermano; 10 – somos.*

2 **Puzzles**

By completing the sentences and writing the answers in the grid, students will reveal the answer to number 7. Poor Carlos!

Students use the words given in the box to complete the letter correctly.

Answers:

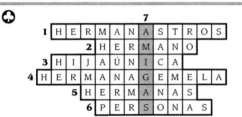

1 – Tengo; 2 – hermanos; 3 – tres; 4 – un; 5 – llaman; 6 – gemela; 7 – tienes; 8 – único.

Objectives

Students learn – to talk about members of their family and ask others about theirs

Key language

¿cuántas personas hay en tu familia?	*primo / prima*
somos … personas	*amigo / amiga*
mi …	*hijo / hija / hijos*
padre / padrastro	*abuelo / abuela*
madre / madrastra	*mis padres …*
mamá / papá	*… están divorciados*
tío / tía	*… están separados*

Skills / Strategies

Students learn – to carry out a small survey and draw up results

ICT opportunities

Students can – design a personal family tree using imported photos / images / clip-art (Student's Book, Activity 3)
– present the results of the survey using the appropriate software package (Worksheet 3.3, Activity 2)

Ways in

Family members – OHT 3A; actual photos or slides of Spanish or British families; Student's Book, Activity 1

Assessment opportunities

AT1,2   Worksheet 3.3, Activity 1: students note down the numbers of people in the family.

AT2,2   Worksheet 3.3, Activity 2: target certain pairs as the whole class does the activity.

AT4,1   Worksheet 3.4, Activity 1: students copy single familiar words correctly.

STUDENT'S BOOK, pages 22–23

Picture story

Pepa is visiting Tomás at home. They talk about their respective families and we learn why Tomás's father is not in Seville.

1 **La familia Willoughby**

a Students read and listen to the picture story and then fill in gapped sentences which contain information about the characters' relationship to each other.

Answers: *1 – hermana; 2 – hermano; 3 – madre; 4 – padre; 5 – cuatro; 6 – separados.*

b Students now adapt the information from Activity 1a (sentences 1–5 only) so that it applies to the Álvaro Vallejas family, who appear on the family tree on p.23.

Answers: *1 – Pilar es la hermana de Juan; 2 – Juan es el hermano de Pilar; 3 – Carmina es la madre; 4 – Omar es el padre; 5 – Hay cuatro personas en la familia.*

TOMÁS:	Somos cuatro personas en mi familia.
PEPA:	¿Quiénes son?
TOMÁS:	Yo, mi madre Teresa y mi hermana Isabel …
PEPA	¿Y tu padre?
TOMÁS:	En Londres. Se llama Michael. Mis padres están separados.
PEPA:	Mis padres están divorciados …
CARMINA:	¿Teresa? Teléfono – Michael, de Londres.
TOMÁS:	¡Mi padre!
PEPA:	Bueno, gracias. Adiós.
TOMÁS:	Vale, adiós …

2 **¿Quiénes son?**

A speaking activity in which small groups of students ask about each others' families. You could change the groups round after a few minutes to give students the chance to practise their questions and answers with increased confidence. A menu of sentences is given on the page for students who need support.

3 **El árbol genealógico**

a ◐ This is an opportunity for students to use the English–Spanish vocabulary section at the back of the book. They look at the given forms and deduce the missing ones, which are similar in form except for the endings, and

can easily be deduced. Ensure that they appreciate the significance of the masculine and feminine forms of the words.

♣ Students look at the family tree and complete the gapped sentences relating to it.

Answers: ◐ *el hijo; la tía; el primo; la abuela.*

♣ *1 – tío; 2 – prima; 3 – abuelo; 4 – tía; 5 – sobrina; 6 – primo.*

b ◑ Students fill in the gaps with the correct family member. They should refer to the family tree to check who's who. As an additional activity, students could write about the important people in their own lives, with a photo or drawing of themselves surrounded by thought bubbles.

♣ Students invent some more similar phrases for their partner.

Answers: *mi madre Teresa; mi padre Michael; mi prima Pilar; mi hermana Isabel; mi tío Omar; mi tía Carmina.*

c ♣ Pupils draw up their own full family tree.

SUPPORT MATERIALS

OHT 3B Las familias Álvaro Vallejas y Willoughby

This sheet shows the Álvaro Vallejas and Willoughby family tree which also appears on p.23 of the Student's Book.

Worksheet 3.3 Familias

1 **En la clase de Isabel y Pilar**

This listening activity provides preparation for a survey that students can carry out themselves. By listening to the eight people talking about their families, students should be able to fill in the correct number of people in each category. Some of the squares will remain blank. The first two are done as examples. It is worth reminding the students to listen very carefully for the difference between *hermano* and *hermana*. As a final activity they can list the number of families with more than six people in them, the number of only children and the number of additional people mentioned.

Answers: *(NB: the total number includes the speaker)*

	Número de personas	Padre padrastro	Madre madrastra	Hermanos hermanastros	Hermanas hermanastras	Otras personas
Unai	4	1	1	–	1	–
Carlos	9	1	–	3	3	abuela
Alicia	5	1	1	2	–	–
Mohamed	5	1	1	–	1	tía
Curro	6	1	1	2	1	–
Emi	2	1	–	–	–	–
Concha	7	1	1	1	3	–
Matilde	4	–	1	–	–	abuelo / abuela

There are three families with six or more people; there are two with only children; there are four additional people mentioned.

1
PILAR: Oye, Unai, ¿cuántas personas hay en tu familia?
UNAI: Somos cuatro: mi padre, mi madre y … mi hermana.
PILAR: Cuatro – padre, madre, una hermana – vale, gracias.

2
ISABEL: ¡Carlos!
CARLOS: ¿Sí? Ah, Isabel.
ISABEL: ¿Cuántas personas hay en tu familia?
CARLOS: Somos nueve.
ISABEL: ¿Nueve? ¡No me digas!
CARLOS: Sí – mi padre, mis tres hermanos y mis tres hermanas y también mi abuela – y yo.

3
PILAR: Alicia, ¿cuántas personas hay en tu familia?
ALICIA: Somos cinco: yo, mi padre, mi madrastra, y mis dos hermanos.
PILAR: Un momento – padre, madrastra y dos hermanos … Gracias.

4
ISABEL: Mohamed, díme – ¿cuántas personas hay en tu familia?
MOHAMED: Somos cinco.
ISABEL: ¿Cinco?
MOHAMED: Sí – mi padre, mi madre, y mi hermana.
ISABEL: Tu padre, tu madre, tu hermana …
MOHAMED: Y mi tía, también.
ISABEL: Tía … vale, gracias.

5
ISABEL: Curro – ¿cuántas personas hay en tu familia?
CURRO: Somos seis.
ISABEL: ¿Seis?
CURRO: Sí – mi padre, mi madre, dos hermanos y una hermana … y yo.
ISABEL: Vamos a ver – tu padre, madre, una hermana y dos hermanos. Bien.

6
PILAR: Emi – ¿cuántas personas hay en tu familia?
EMI: Somos dos. Mi padre y yo.
PILAR: ¿No tienes hermanos?
EMI: Mm, no …

7
ISABEL: Concha – ¿cuántas personas hay en tu familia?
CONCHA: ¡Muchas! Somos siete.
ISABEL: ¿Siete?
CONCHA: Sí – mi padre, madrastra, mi hermano …
ISABEL: Un momento. Padre, madrastra, un hermano …
CONCHA: Y mis tres hermanas.
ISABEL: ¡Tres hermanas! ¡Uf!

8
ISABEL: ¡Matilde! Oye – ¿cuántas personas hay en tu familia?
MATILDE: Somos cuatro.
ISABEL: ¿Cuatro? Y ¿quiénes son?
MATILDE: Bueno, mi madre …
ISABEL: Madre …
MATILDE: … y mis abuelos.
ISABEL: ¿Tus abuelos?
MATILDE: Sí – mi abuelo y mi abuela.

2 **En tu clase**

Focus on the key questions and phrases which Isabel and Pilar used to interview their classmates in Activity 1. Write them on the board for reinforcement or highlight them in the Student's Book. (*¿Cuántas personas hay en tu familia? Somos … ¿Tienes …? Tengo …*) Students then interview each other in pairs until they have completed a total of eight interviews. As a follow-up, the students should complete the statistics at the foot of the sheet, comparing their results with those of Pilar and Isabel.

Worksheet 3.4 Árboles genealógicos

1 **La familia de los gatos**

○ Using the phrases supplied, students complete the cat's family tree.

Answers: *1 – mi abuelo; 2 – mi abuela; 3 – mi padre; 4 – mi madre; 5 – mi hermano; 6 – mi hermana.*

2 **El rap**

○ ◑ The song helps to reinforce the vocabulary of the family. It could be used either as a reading activity (based on the family tree in the Student's Book) or a straight listening activity before going on to sing it. If students need extra help, write the missing words up on the board first.

Answers: *1 – personas; 2 – padre; 3 – hermana; 4 – madre; 5 – tío; 6 – prima; 7 – Tomás.*

¿Cuántas **personas** hay en mi familia?
¡Muchas, muchas, muchas!
En primer lugar, mi **padre** Omar
También mi **hermana**, que se llama Pilar.
Mi tía Teresa, la hermana de mi **madre**,
Mi **tío** Michael, el amigo de mi padre.
Mi **prima** Isabel y mi primo **Tomás** –
¡Gracias a Dios que no hay más!

3 **El crucigrama**

○ With the help of the clues and some of the letters already supplied in the grid, students complete the crossword which is based on the family tree on p.23 of the Student's Book.

◑ Students fill in the gaps in the sentences.

Answers: ○

◑ *2 – padre; 3 – hermana; 4 – abuela; 5 – tía; 7 – abuelo; 9 – hijo.*

Homework opportunity

Using pictures and photographs cut out of newspapers and magazines, students can make up an imaginary family tree which can be as ridiculous as they like (featuring film stars, rock stars, soap stars, politicians, entertainers, etc.). They can stick them on to card or paper and label them with *mi hermana / mi padre / mi abuela*, etc., or write a short description underneath: *En mi familia somos cinco …* The final posters could then be displayed on the classroom walls under a title such as *La familia ideal*.

Extra

By using the images on OHT 3B, cut into sets of small cards with one face on each, you could organise a game based on Happy families. Divide the class into groups of three or four and give them 20 cards (two sets of the pictures). Shuffle and deal four cards to each player. The object is to make a complete foursome (e.g., one each of Omar, Carmina, Pilar and Juan; or Teresa, Michael, Isabel and Tomás, and so on).

Students take it in turns to ask another player *¿tienes (el padre de Juan)?* The other player says either *sí, toma* and hands it over in exchange for a card the first player wants to discard, or *lo siento no tengo*, whereupon the turn passes to the next player *(¡te toca a ti!)*. Alternatively, the player takes a card from the top of the pile and then discards one. The winner is the first person who can say *¡Tengo una familia!*

3C **¿Cuántos años tienes?**   **Unidad 3** *La familia*

Objectives
Students learn – the numbers from 31–100
– to ask / say how old someone is

Key language
Numbers 31–100
¿cuántos años tienes?
tengo … años
¿cuántos años tiene?
tiene … años

Skills / Strategies
Students learn – to listen for key numbers (Worksheet 3.5, Activity 1)

ICT opportunities
Students can – add to their database if it was created in Unit 1B, sort students in the class by age, etc., and produce a graph of age distribution

Ways in
Numbers – Number cards; Student's Book, photos and Activity 1
Ages – Student's Book, Activity 3

Assessment opportunities
AT1,3 Worksheet 3.5, Activity 1: students listen and complete the information given.
AT2,3 Worksheet 3.6: information-gap activity.
AT3,3 Worksheet 3.5, Activity 3: reading a brief letter.

STUDENT'S BOOK, pages 24–25

1 **Más números**

a Students listen to the numbers 40, 50, 60, 70, 80, 90, 100 and look at the photos.

b The numbers are read out a second time, this time twice and in a different order. Students point to the number they hear.

> **a** cuarenta
> cincuenta
> sesenta
> setenta
> ochenta
> noventa
> cien
> **b** setenta, setenta
> cuarenta, cuarenta
> noventa, noventa
> cien, cien
> sesenta, sesenta
> cincuenta, cincuenta
> ochenta, ochenta

Answers: *b 1 – 70; 2 – 40; 3 – 90; 4 – 100; 5 – 60; 6 – 50; 7 – 80.*

2 **Con tu pareja**

Student **A** traces one of the new numbers, either in the air or with a finger on the desk, and Student **B** guesses what it is and has to pronounce it correctly. This can also be done as a silent mouthing activity.

3 **Los deberes**

This activity enables students to talk about their age. Since most of the students in the class will be more or less the same age, you may wish to include the number of months as well as years (*Tengo 13 años y 2 meses*).

Picture story

Pilar is doing her English homework and needs to know everybody's age.

◑ Students listen and read in order to find out the age of each person.

♣ Students write short answers to the four questions.

Answers: **◑** *Juan – 12; Carmina – 41; Isabel – 14; Omar – 45; Pilar – 13; Teresa – 39; Tomás – 13.*

♣ *1 – No, está en Londres; 2 – ¡Fatal!; 3 – Tengo trece años; 4 – Bien.*

PILAR:	Edades de la familia … ¿cómo se dice en inglés?
ISABEL:	Ages of the family. Tía Carmina, ¿cuántos años tienes?
CARMINA:	Tengo cuarenta y un años.
ISABEL:	¿Y tú, Mamá? ¿Cuántos años tienes?
TERESA:	Tengo treinta y ocho …,¡ay no! treinta y nueve años.
ISABEL:	Mamá, ¿qué tal está el bebé?
TERESA:	Bien.
PILAR:	Yo tengo trece años e Isabel tiene catorce …
CARMINA:	¡Omar y Juan!
PILAR:	¡Papá! ¿Cuántos años tienes?
OMAR:	¡Cien!
PILAR:	¡Papá!
OMAR:	Tengo cuarenta y cinco años.
ISABEL:	Juan, ¿tienes once o doce años?
JUAN:	Doce.
PILAR:	Y tú, Tomás – tienes trece años, ¿no?
TOMÁS:	¡Sí!
OMAR:	¿Qué le pasa?
TERESA:	Tomás no tiene a su padre aquí – Michael está en Londres. Es muy difícil …

4 **Un puzzle**

◑ This activity helps to reinforce higher numbers. Students write out the numbers, in numerical order, either in figures or in words.

♣ An activity requiring basic deduction skills to work out some mathematical problems.

Answers: **◑** *23, 31, 46, 48, 52, 61, 74, 83, 97.*

♣ *1 – Mi hermana tiene veinticuatro años; 2 – Mi madrastra (or Ella) tiene cuarenta y dos años; 3 – Tengo trece años; 4 – Mi madre tiene treinta y seis años.*

5 **¿Y tú?**

◑ Students match up the questions and answers.

Answers: *1 – c; 2 – f; 3 – a; 4 – d; 5 – e; 6 – b.*

6 **La entrevista**

Students invent and write down the name, age and family details for one of the photographs and then prepare to interview their partner. They can use the questions in Activity 5 for support and add others. The interviews could be taped or acted out. Students could use prepared scripts, notes or try without either.

Gramática

This is a brief résumé of use of the verb *tener* (to have) in the first, second and third person forms. Students who require further explanation are referred to the grammar summary, section 11 on p.149.

SUPPORT MATERIALS

Worksheet 3.5 La lotería

1 **Lotería**

Radio Sol has organised a prize draw in different age groups for a holiday in Disneyland. Once the disc-jockey has pulled the winner out of the hat, his assistant rings the telephone number on the card and checks the person's details.

♦ Students write down the person's age and telephone number.

♣ Students write down the number of people in the family and who they are.

Answers: ♦ *Grupo 1 – tel: 4.47.21.50, aged 14;*
Grupo 2 – tel: 4.25.13.18, aged 36.

♣ *Grupo 1 – four people: Alicia, Mum, Dad, brother;*
Grupo 2 – three people: Jesús, two sons.

PRESENTADORA:	Buenos días, y bienvenidos a la lotería Radio Sol.
PRESENTADOR:	Grupo 1: el primer número de teléfono es ... el cuatro, cuarenta y siete, veintiuno, cincuenta.
PRESENTADORA:	El cuatro, cuarenta y siete, veintiuno, cincuenta.
ALICIA:	¿Diga?
PRESENTADOR:	¿Alicia?
ALICIA:	Sí. Soy yo ...
PRESENTADOR:	Radio Sol aquí. Oye Alicia – ¿cuántos años tienes?
ALICIA:	Tengo catorce años.
PRESENTADOR:	Catorce años ... ¿Y cuántas personas hay en tu familia?
ALICIA:	Somos cuatro – mi madre, mi padre y mi hermano.
PRESENTADOR:	Bueno – tu madre, tu padre, tu hermano ¡van todos a Disneylandia en Florida contigo!
ALICIA:	Ay, ¡estupendo!
PRESENTADORA:	Ahora, grupo 2: el número de teléfono es ... cuatro, veinticinco, trece, dieciocho.

PRESENTADOR:	Cuatro, veinticinco, trece, dieciocho ... ¡Hola, aquí Radio Sol!
JESÚS:	¡Radio Sol – qué bien!
PRESENTADOR:	¿Cuántos años tienes, Jesús?
JESÚS:	Tengo treinta y seis años.
PRESENTADOR:	¿Treinta y seis? Y ¿tienes familia?
JESÚS:	Sí – somos tres. Mis dos hijos y yo.
PRESENTADOR:	¿Dos hijos? Bueno – ¡vais todos a Disneylandia en Florida!
JESÚS:	¡Qué bien! Muchas gracias ...

2 **¿En qué grupo?**

Extracts from some of the competition entries.

♦ Students read the information on each card and put the person into the correct age group.

Answers: *Paco – Grupo 1 (14 años); Anita – Grupo 2 (25 años); Maribel – Grupo 4 (72 años); Andrés – Grupo 3 (48 años); Carmen – Grupo 3 (56 años); Tere – Grupo 1 (16 años).*

3 **En la revista**

This letter and photograph were sent in to the Sol Radio magazine by Lorena who won a trip to Disneyland.

Students read the letter and identify the members of the family and their ages.

Answers: *1 – Lorena (14 años); 2 – Marisa, madre (41 años); 3 – Pepe, hermanastro (3 años); 4 – Unai, padrastro (36 años); 5 – Gabriel, hermano (18 años); 6 – Rosario, abuela (72 años).*

Worksheet 3.6 Radio Sol

An information-gap activity. Cut the worksheet in half and give pairs of students a different part each. Partner **A** asks the questions and Partner **B** supplies the answers.

♦ Students check the people's ages.

♣ Students check the people's telephone numbers.

Answers: ♦ *Zeneida – 8; Trinidad – 35; Marta – 45; Jaime – 16; Ali – 62; Catalina – 22.*

♣ *Zeneida – 31.22.60.12; Trinidad – 93.43.56.21; Marta – 64.37.72.24; Jaime – 86.12.19.39; Ali – 72.19.46.87; Catalina – 85.31.63.24.*

Objectives

Students learn – to ask and talk about their pets
– to say what kind of pet they have or would like

Key language

¿tienes algún animal?
¿qué tipo de animal es?
¿cuántos años tiene tu animal?
¿cómo se llama tu animal?
¿te gustaría tener un animal?
me gustaría tener … / no me gustaría tener ningún animal

un perro	*una serpiente*
un gato	*una cobaya*
un hámster	*una lagartija*
un ratón	*una tortuga*
un conejo	
un pájaro	
un gerbo	
un pez	
un insecto palo	

Skills / Strategies

Students learn – to write a simple letter using a model (Student's Book, Activity 5)

ICT opportunities

Students can – draft and redraft their letter using a word-processing package (Student's Book, Activity 5)

Ways in

Numbers – Number cards; Student's Book, Activity 1 (visuals in book and recorded material); own pets (both teacher's and students'!); pictures from magazines or the Internet

Assessment opportunities

AT2,3 Student's Book, Activity 3: students interview each other about their pets.
AT3,3 Student's Book, Activity 4: students read a letter and fill in blanks.
AT4,3 Student's Book, Activity 5: students write about their animals and family.

STUDENT'S BOOK, pages 26–27

1 Los animales

a Students listen to Pepa and Tomás discussing pets and read the picture story on p.26.

PEPA:	¿Tienes algún animal en casa?
TOMÁS:	No, no tengo. ¿Y tú?
PEPA:	Sí, tengo un pájaro que se llama Nucho.
TOMÁS:	Me gustaría tener … un perro … un gato … un hámster … un ratón … un conejo … un pájaro … una serpiente … una cobaya … un gerbo … un pez … un insecto palo … una lagartija … y una tortuga.
PEPA:	¡Uf! ¡Te gustaría tener un zoo!

b ◑ There now follow six conversations between people discussing what kind of pet they have. Students write down the letters of the animals each person has.

♣ For this activity, students listen and answer a set of six questions in Spanish relating to the texts.

Answers: ◑ *1 – f, j; 2 – a, e; 3 – h, i; 4 – d, k; 5 – b, g; 6 – c, e.*

♣ *1 – Dino; 2 – 3 años, 1 año; 3 – una serpiente; 4 – ocho personas; 5 – dos hermanos; 6 – Quirri.*

1	VOZ:	Marta, ¿tienes algún animal en casa?
	MARTA:	Sí, tengo un pájaro y un pez.
	VOZ:	¿Cómo se llaman?
	MARTA:	Mi pez no lleva nombre, pero mi pájaro se llama Dino.
	VOZ:	¿Cómo se escribe? ¿D-I-N-O?
	MARTA:	Sí, eso es.

2	GABI:	¿Tú tienes algún animal, Antonio?
	ANTONIO:	Sí, tengo un perro, que tiene tres años …
	GABI:	¡Qué bien! ¡Un perro!
	ANTONIO:	También tengo un conejo.
	GABI:	¿Cuántos años tiene?
	ANTONIO:	¿El conejo? Un año.

3	ALBERTO:	Virginia, ¿tienes animales en casa?
	VIRGINIA:	Sí, tengo una cobaya y un gerbo.
	ALBERTO:	¿Una cobaya y un gerbo? ¡Uf!, no me gustan esos animales. ¡Son horribles!
	VIRGINIA:	¡Qué va! Pero no me gustaría tener una serpiente.
	ALBERTO:	¿Una serpiente? ¡Qué horror!

4	ÁLVARO:	Nando, tú no tienes animales, ¿verdad?
	NANDO:	Sí, tengo. Tengo un ratón y un insecto palo.
	ÁLVARO:	¿No tienes perro? Yo creía que sí.
	NANDO:	No, no tengo. Somos muchas personas en casa.
	ÁLVARO:	¿Cuántos sois?
	NANDO:	Somos ocho en total.
	ÁLVARO:	¿Ocho? ¿Quiénes son?

5	JOSÉ:	Me gustan los animales. Tengo un gato …
	ANA:	¿Un gato? ¡Ay, qué suerte!
	JOSÉ:	Un gato, y una serpiente.
	ANA:	¿Una serpiente?
	JOSÉ:	Sí, pero no les gustan a mis hermanos.
	ANA:	¿Cuántos hermanos tienes?
	JOSÉ:	Tengo dos.
	ANA:	No me sorprende que no les guste …

6	SUSANA:	Elena, ¿tienes algún animal en casa?
	ELENA:	Sí, tengo dos animales. Un hámster y un conejo.
	SUSANA:	¡Ah! ¿Cómo se llaman?
	ELENA:	El hámster es nuevo, y no tiene nombre, pero mi conejo se llama Quirri.
	SUSANA:	¿Quirri? ¡Qué raro! ¿Cómo se escribe? ¿Con K?
	ELENA:	No. Q-U-I-R-R-I.
	SUSANA:	Es bonito. Pero ¿qué nombre vas a dar a tu hámster?

3 ¿Tienes …?

In this pairwork activity students pick an animal from the visuals on the page and have a conversation with their partner about it, using the information given. There are six pets pictured, so each partner could play each role three times.

4 La carta electrónica de Pilar

◑ Students read the letter and fill in the blanks with the correct word from the selection given.

♣ Students read the letter again and answer the true / false / impossible to tell questions.

Answers: ◑ *1 – llamo; 2 – padre; 3 – personas; 4 – separados; 5 – tienes; 6 – trece; 7 – perro; 8 – animal.*

♣ *1 – verdadera; 2 – falsa; 3 – no se sabe; 4 – falsa; 5 – verdadera; 6 – no se sabe.*

5 **Mi familia**

Finally, students write a letter similar to the one written by Pilar, using Pilar's as a model if needed. They describe their own family and pets, giving as much detail as they are able.

SUPPORT MATERIALS

OHT 3C ¿Qué animal ...?

This OHT presents the animals taught in the unit, and can be used to discuss what pets students have, or would like to have.

Worksheet 3.7 Una encuesta: ¿tienes algún animal?

Students carry out a survey into who has what pets in their class, and record the results on the grid provided on the worksheet.

Objectives

Students learn – to say when their birthday is and ask others
– to sing 'Happy Birthday' in Spanish

Key language

feliz cumpleaños
¿cuándo es tu cumpleaños?
es el ...
lo siento, no sé

Revision of months and numbers 1–31

Skills / Strategies

Students learn – to apologise and say they don't know

ICT opportunities

Students can – generate a class birthday database and produce statistical information about whose birthdays are in which month, etc. (Activity 2)

Ways in

Numbers – Student's Book, Activity 1; students' own birthdays!

Assessment opportunities

AT2,3 Student's Book, Activity 2: students interview each other about their own and others' birthdays.

AT3,2 Worksheet 3.8, Activity 2: students match visuals to brief texts.

AT4,2 Worksheet 3.8, Activity 3: students write brief, cued pet descriptions.

STUDENT'S BOOK, page 28

1 **¿Cuándo?**

Picture story

It is Teresa's birthday. Students read and listen to the picture story and work out whose birthday is on which of the dates given.

Answers: *a* – 19/2 Isabel; *b* – 21/11 Tomás; *c* – 1/5 Carlos; *d* – 22/11 Pepa; *e* – 7/12 Pilar; *f* – 12/8 José Luis.

JOSÉ LUIS:	Feliz cumpleaños ...
ISABEL:	Es el cumpleaños de Mamá.
JOSÉ LUIS:	¿Cuándo es tu cumpleaños, Isabel?
ISABEL:	Es el diecinueve de febrero.
ISABEL:	¿Y tu cumpleaños, José Luis?
JOSÉ LUIS:	El doce de agosto.
PEPA:	¿Cuándo es tu cumpleaños, Tomás?
TOMÁS:	Es el veintiuno de noviembre.
CARLOS:	¿Y tu cumpleaños, Pepa?
PEPA:	¡El veintidós!
CARLOS:	Mi cumpleaños es el primero de mayo.
JOSÉ LUIS:	¿Y Pilar? ¿Cuándo es su cumpleaños?
ISABEL:	Es el siete de diciembre.
JOSÉ LUIS:	Una fiesta ...
CARLOS:	¡... para tu amiga especial – Pilar!
TOMÁS:	¡Estupendo!
CARLOS:	¿Isabel?

2 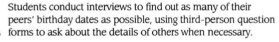 **¡Pregunta y apunta!**

Students conduct interviews to find out as many of their peers' birthday dates as possible, using third-person question forms to ask about the details of others when necessary.

Gramática

The brief grammar table on p.28 sets out the third person form *su* and refers students to the grammar summary section 7, p.148 and to Acción: lengua 3, p.29.

Acción: lengua 3, page 29

Students learn –
to understand and practise using all forms of the verb *tener* (to have) and possessive pronouns in the singular and plural forms.

Tener – to have

1 ◑ A gap-fill activity requiring the insertion of the correct form of *tener*.

◕ A substitution activity where students change the person of the verb form in response to a prompt.

Answers: ◑ *tengo, tiene, Tienes, Tengo, tiene, tiene.*

◕ *1 – Tú tienes dos perros – ¡qué bien! 2 – Sara tiene un insecto palo, ¿verdad? 3 – Y yo tengo una lagartija. 4 – ¿José? Tiene conejos. 5 – Vosotros no tenéis animales.*

Mi, tu, su

2 ◑ A gap-fill activity in which students fill in each gap with the appropriate form of *mi*, *tu* or *su*.

◕ Another gap-fill activity, this time in response to English language prompts.

Answers: ◑ *tu, mi, mi, tu, su, su.*

◕ *mi, tu, su, sus, mi, Tu, tus, Mis.*

SUPPORT MATERIALS

Worksheet 3.8 Cumpleaños feliz

1 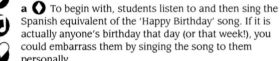 **Cumpleaños feliz**

a ◑ To begin with, students listen to and then sing the Spanish equivalent of the 'Happy Birthday' song. If it is actually anyone's birthday that day (or that week!), you could embarrass them by singing the song to them personally.

b Now students prepare a simple birthday card, using the phrases supplied if necessary.

> Cumpleaños feliz,
> Cumpleaños feliz,
> Te deseamos todos
> ¡Cumpleaños feliz!

2 **Mi animal favorito**

◑ A simple matching activity which provides practice of the animal vocabulary.

Answers: *1 – F; 2 – A; 3 – D; 4 – E; 5 – G.*

3 **Descríbeme**

◑ Students write five sentences giving details about pets, in response to the cued visuals on the worksheet.

Answers:
1 – Mi gato se llama Bubu, y tiene cinco años. Su cumpleaños es el diez de marzo.
2 – Mi hámster se llama Dani, y tiene dos años. Su cumpleaños es el once de octubre.
3 – Mi tortuga se llama Murillo, y tiene seis años. Su cumpleaños es el quince de junio.
4 – Mi serpiente se llama Pipa, y tiene cuatro años. Su cumpleaños es el nueve de abril.
5 – Mi conejo se llama Nieves, y tiene tres años. Su cumpleaños es el veintidós de septiembre.

Objectives

Students learn – the names of the colours
              – to say they like / don't like something, and ask others

Key language

lila	¿te gusta ...?
naranja	me gusta mucho
rosa	me gusta
azul	no está mal
gris	no me gusta
marrón	no me gusta nada
verde	
amarillo/a	
blanco/a	
negro/a	
morado/a	
rojo/a	

Extension language

los mejores / los peores

Skills / Strategies

Students learn – to extend their ability to agree and disagree

ICT opportunities

Students can – use different coloured fonts to write a poem about colours and design their own personal rainbow to illustrate it (Worksheet 4.1, Activity 2)

Ways in

The colours – Student's Book, Activity 1; a set of coloured pencils, colour spots drawn onto an OHT sheet with marker pens; coloured paper or card, etc.

Assessment opportunities

AT1,2   Worksheet 4.1, Activity 2: students listen and complete the gaps in the song.

AT2,3   Student's Book, Activity 3: a scripted conversation about colours.

AT3   Student's Book, Activity 3: reading the conversation and filling in the blanks prior to practising it.

AT4,2/3   Student's Book, Activity 2b: students write about the colours (and days of the week) they (don't) like.

STUDENT'S BOOK, pages 30–31

1 Los colores

Presentation of colours. You could accompany this with an OHT sheet which has colour spots drawn on it – try mixing the primary colours to create the range you need. Alternatively, use sheets of coloured paper or card as they are, or stick them onto a large sheet of paper (e.g., the back of a poster you no longer use) and create a kind of paint manufacturer's colour chart.

Picture story

a Pilar and Isabel are looking at tins of paint in a shop and trying to decide on a colour for Isabel's new room.

> PILAR: ¿Qué color prefieres tú, Isabel ...? Lila ...
>   ¿naranja? ... rosa ...
>   azul ... ¿gris? ... marrón ... verde ... amarillo ...
>   ¿blanco? ...
>   ¡negro! ... ¿morado? ... ¡rojo! ... ¡ay, madre!
> ISABEL: Pilar, ¡qué tonta eres!

b Students listen to Isabel giving her opinions on the colours, and complete each of the opinions with the appropriate colour.

> ISABEL: ¡Me gusta mucho el rojo! ¡Me gusta el verde!
>   No está mal el amarillo. No me gusta el
>   blanco. ¡No me gusta nada el color naranja!

Answers: 1 – el rojo;   2 – el verde;   3 – el amarillo;
                 4 – el blanco;   5 – el color naranja.

c A pairwork activity in which students give their opinions on various colours.

2 Yo y los colores

A basic open-ended writing activity in which students have a choice of activities.

a Students create their own personal colour balloon or umbrella, and say which colours would be nice and not so nice for it.

b This activity involves saying which colours are brought to mind by various days of the week. Students write a short poem on the subject.

3 Los novios

◐ An activity in which students fill in the gaps in a conversation between two people giving their opinions on colours.

♣ Students complete a grid with the appropriate information on colours given in the conversation.

Answers: **◐** In order: azul, verde, lila, amarillo, rosa, naranja.

♣

	Nuria	Raúl
Really likes	green	lilac
Doesn't mind	pink, blue	–
Really dislikes	lilac, orange	green, yellow

Gramática

Students are referred here to section 15 of the grammar summary on p.151, which deals with the verb gustar.

SUPPORT MATERIALS

Worksheet 4.1 Los colores

1 Los colores

◐ A colouring activity which focuses on combinations of colours. Students colour the segments of the circles by numbers.

♣ Students work out the four colour combinations.

Answers: **◐** 1 – red;   2 – yellow;   3 – blue;   4 – purple;
                 5 – orange;   6 – green;   7 – brown.

                 ♣ 1 – verde;   2 – naranja;   3 – morado;
                 4 – marrón.

2   Mi arco iris personal

Before listening to the song, students should solve the anagrams of the colours and insert them in the numbered gaps. The song revises familiar language of liking and disliking: *me gusta, no me gusta, me encanta*, as well as *fatal*, *no está mal* and *fenomenal*. The first verse also refers to the colours as the worst ones (*los peores*) and the third verse refers to the colours as the best ones (*los mejores*). You could point out these features when asking students to produce their own 'personal rainbow'. Students could produce coloured versions for display on the classroom walls, and those who wish to do theirs on computer could use drawing and painting software to design the rainbow and use attractive coloured fonts for the text.

Answers: *1 – verde; 2 – marrón; 3 – negro; 4 – gris; 5 – lila; 6 – azul; 7 – amarillo; 8 – rojo; 9 – blanco; 10 – rosa; 11 – naranja; 12 – morado.*

No me gusta el verde,
marrón y negro,
el gris me parece fatal.
Estos colores
son los peores
en mi acro iris personal.

Me gusta el lila,
azul y amarillo,
el rojo – no está mal.
Pero estos colores
no son los mejores
en mi arco iris personal.

Me encanta el blanco
rosa y naranja,
el morado – ¡fenomenal!
Estos colores
son los mejores
en mi arco iris personal.

Objectives
Students learn – to talk about their personality and ask others
　　　　　　 – Grammar: singular adjectives, *ser* – to be
　　　　　　 (singular)

Key language
normalmente
soy
eres
es
un poco
muy
a veces
bastante
normalmente
hablador(a)
callado/a
serio/a
gracioso/a
alegre
optimista
pesimista
tímido/a
extrovertido/a
simpático/a
antipático/a
trabajador(a)
perezoso/a

Skills / Strategies
Students learn – to express enthusiastic agreement or vehement disagreement

ICT opportunities
Students can　– design an Identikit™ person and word-process a description

Ways in
Student's Book Activity 1; photos of famous people collected from magazines or the Internet (give opinions on their personality and then invite students to join in; best to get controversial pictures!)

Assessment opportunities
AT1,1　Worksheet 4.4: students listen and work out who's who.
AT2,2　Student's Book, Activity 2: a pairwork activity, where students give opinions on people's characters.
AT3,2　Student's Book, Activity 3a: a text-sequencing activity.
AT4,2/3 Student's Book, Activity 3b: students write character descriptions of people, using a letter as a model.

STUDENT'S BOOK, pages 32–33

1 **¿Cómo soy?**

Picture story

Tomás is talking about his character in the company of Pepa, who comments, agrees and disagrees.

a First, students listen to the recording and read the picture story.

b ◑ Students decide whether the pairs of words are opposites or not.

✚ An open-ended activity in which students describe the picture story characters in their own words.

Answers:　◑ *1 – no; 2 – sí; 3 – sí; 4 – no; 5 – sí; 6 – sí.*

TOMÁS:	Normalmente, soy ... tímido.
PEPA:	¡Qué va! Eres extrovertido.
TOMÁS:	Normalmente soy ... antipático.
PEPA:	No, eres simpático.
TOMÁS:	Normalmente, soy serio.
PEPA:	Eres gracioso y alegre.
TOMÁS:	Normalmente, soy callado.
PEPA:	En tu dormitorio, eres hablador.
TOMÁS:	Normalmente soy trabajador.
PEPA:	Sí, pero en tu dormitorio, ¡eres perezoso!
TOMÁS:	Normalmente soy pesimista.
PEPA:	¡Qué va! Eres optimista ...

Gramática

A brief item here refers students to the grammar summary, section 6 on p.148, for further information on adjectives, and to Acción: lengua 4, on p.37 for activities on the grammar point.

2 **¿De acuerdo? ¡Qué va!**

A pairwork activity in which students describe people in their class.

Gramática

Students are referred to the grammar summary, section 11 on p.150 for the present tense of *ser*.

3 **Los corresponsales**

a ◑ A sequencing activity in which students reorder the jumbled sections of a letter to a set of clues given.

✚ Students read the letter again and join up the unfinished sentences to the appropriate adjective.

Answers:　◑ *a – 3; b – 6; c – 1; d – 2; e – 4; f – 7; g – 5.*
　　　　　 ✚ *1 – b; 2 – d; 3 – c; 4 – e; 5 – a; 6 – g.*
　　　　　 Surplus word is habladora.

¿Cómo se dicen en inglés?

This box sets out the qualifying phrases such as *un poco*, *bastante*, etc., for reference. Students look up their meanings in the bilingual vocabulary at the back of the Student's Book. They can then use the expressions to give opinions about celebrities, for example, in a whole-class oral activity, and then play a memory game to see who can remember what opinion was given about whom.

Answers:　*un poco – a bit / slightly; bastante – quite;*
　　　　　 muy – very; normalmente – normally;
　　　　　 a veces – sometimes.

b Students write a similar letter, using Guillermo's as a model and selecting qualifiers from the box as described above, as appropriate.

SUPPORT MATERIALS

Worksheet 4.2 Los corresponsales

 ◐ A support worksheet which provides a lead-in for less able students to Activity 3a on p.33 of the Student's Book. Students fill in the gaps with the appropriate family member.

Answers: **1** *a – madre; b – hermano; c – padrastro; d – yo; e – Paco.*
2 *– pájaros;* **3** *– llamo;* **4** *– perezoso;* **5** *– escríbeme;*
6 *– cumpleaños;* **7** *– tímida.*

Worksheet 4.3 Una carta

 ◐ This is another worksheet to help less able students and give them some support in taking in the material presented in the unit. The activity consists of an open-ended letter-completion task, with a removable English rubric at the bottom of the page for those who need it.

Worksheet 4.4 El carácter

 ◐ Students listen to five conversations which present various pieces of information, and pick the correct visual to match each one.

♣ In this additional activity students listen again and complete the five short sentences in Spanish.

Answers: ◐ *1 – B; 2 – D; 3 – A; 4 – C; 5 (distractor); 6 – E.*

♣ *A – hermanos; B – tres; C – un perro;*
D – quince; E – rojo.

A	
MADRE:	¿Juan?
JUAN:	¡Sí!
MADRE:	¡Allí estás!
JUAN:	¿Qué?
MADRE:	¡Qué perezoso eres, Juan!
JUAN:	¿Yo perezoso?
MADRE:	Sí – ¡tú! ¿Dónde está tu hermano?
JUAN:	¡Tengo dos hermanos, Mamá! ¿Buscas a Paco o a Felipe?
MADRE:	Felipe. Todavía no ha arreglado su cama ...

B	
CHICA:	¿Quién es ése?
CHICO:	Es Roberto.
CHICA:	¡Qué serio es!
CHICO:	Sí, es serio. Y muy trabajador. Hace tres horas de deberes cada noche.
CHICA:	¿Tres horas? ¡Huy, es mucho!

C	
ENTREVISTADOR:	De carácter, ¿cómo eres?
CHICA:	Soy alegre ... y graciosa.
ENTREVISTADOR:	¿Y tienes algún animal en casa?
CHICA:	Sí, tengo un perro.
ENTREVISTADOR:	¿Qué tipo de perro es?

D	
CHICO:	¿Cómo es?
CHICO:	De carácter, no es muy habladora. Es tímida.
CHICO:	¿Cuántos años tiene?
CHICO:	Tiene quince años.
CHICO:	Es mayor que tú, entonces.

E	
ENTREVISTADOR:	De carácter, ¿cómo eres?
CHICO:	Soy extrovertido, y optimista.
ENTREVISTADOR:	¿Tienes amigos aquí en el instituto?
CHICO:	Sí, tengo muchos amigos.
ENTREVISTADOR:	¿Y tu color favorito?
CHICO:	El rojo. ¡Es un color muy extrovertido también!

Objectives
Students learn – to describe their build and ask others
– to describe their hair and eye colour

Key language
¿cómo es tu físico?
¿cómo tienes el pelo?
¿cómo tienes los ojos?
de carácter, ¿cómo eres?
soy / eres / es ...
alto/a
bajo/a
delgado/a
gordito/a
pelirrojo/a
tengo / tienes / tiene ...
llevo / llevas / lleva ...
de talla / estatura media
el pelo negro / rubio / moreno / castaño
los ojos grises / azules / marrones / verdes
pecas
barba
gafas

Skills / Strategies
Students learn – to make adjectives agree

ICT opportunities
Students can – format foreground and background shading to create white text against a black background

Ways in
Physical description – OHT 4A; Student's Book, Activity 1

Assessment opportunities
AT1,3 Worksheet 4.5, Activity 1: students listen and decide which person each of the conversations refers to.
AT2,2 Student's Book, Activity 2: pairwork descriptions.
AT3,2 Student's Book, Activity 3: students work out who is speaking.
AT4,3 Worksheet 4.7, Activity 3: students write a brief description of a teenage girl.

STUDENT'S BOOK, pages 34–35

1 En broma

a First students listen to the recording of José Luis and Carlos buying wigs in the joke shop. You could then ask a few basic questions relating to this, to check comprehension of the eye and hair colour structures.

ESCUCHA A JOSÉ LUIS Y A CARLOS EN LA TIENDA.	
JOSÉ LUIS:	Soy alto ... Soy bajo ... Soy delgado ... Soy gordito ... ¡Soy de talla media! ¿Y tú, Carlos?
CARLOS:	Tengo el pelo negro ... Tengo el pelo rubio ... Tengo el pelo moreno ... Soy pelirrojo ...
JOSÉ LUIS:	Tengo los ojos grises.
CARLOS:	Tengo los ojos azules.
JOSÉ LUIS:	Tengo los ojos marrones.
CARLOS:	Tengo los ojos verdes.

b Students now listen to a recording of some descriptions on a telephone chat line, and pick the appropriate visuals for each of the three speakers.

Answers: *Cristóbal – 2, 4, 13, 8; Gema – 7, 11, 5, 3; Tere – 9, 10, 1, 4.*

CRISTÓBAL	
CHICA:	¡Hola! ¿Cómo te llamas?
CRISTÓBAL:	Me llamo Cristóbal. ¿Y tú?
CHICA:	Reyes. Oye, Cristóbal, ¿cómo eres? Imagino que eres alto.
CRISTÓBAL:	No, soy bajo.
CHICA:	¿Muy bajo?
CRISTÓBAL:	No, un poco. Soy gordito, pero tengo los ojos muy bonitos.
CHICA:	¿Sí? ¿Cómo tienes los ojos, entonces?
CRISTÓBAL:	Verdes. Muy verdes. ¡Muy románticos!
CHICA:	¡Qué bien! ¿Y cómo tienes el pelo?
CRISTÓBAL:	Tengo el pelo castaño.
CHICA:	¿Castaño? ¡Qué guapo!
CRISTÓBAL:	Oye, Reyes, te toca a ti ahora. ¿Cómo es tu físico?
GEMA	
CHICO:	Dime, Gema, ¿cómo tienes el pelo?
GEMA:	¡Adivina!
CHICO:	Te imagino con el pelo rubio ...
GEMA:	¡Sí, es verdad! Tengo el pelo rubio ...
CHICO:	¡Y los ojos azules!
GEMA:	Sí. ¡Tienes telepatía! ¿Y mi físico?

CHICO:	Mm ... ¿alta?
GEMA:	No, soy de talla media, y soy delgada.
CHICO:	¡Mm! ¡Delgada! Oye, Gema, no sé si te interesaría salir ...
TERE	
CHICO:	¿Cómo eres, Tere?
TERE:	Soy pelirroja ...
CHICO:	¿Pelirroja? ¡Me gustan mucho las pelirrojas! ¿Y tus ojos?
TERE:	Tengo los ojos grises.
CHICO:	¿Eres alta?
TERE:	Sí. Bastante. Soy un poco gordita.
CHICO:	¡Y qué! ¿Quieres saber algo de mí, Tere?

2 El teléfono de la amistad

A pairwork activity which sets up dialogues about appearance via picture and written prompts.

3 El físico

◐ Students read a series of brief descriptions and work out which of the people pictured in Activity 2 each one relates to.

◑ A gap-fill activity practising the description language introduced on this page.

Answers: **◐** *a – Jaime; b – Soo Wun; c – Beatriz; d – Ramona; e – Jaime; f – Ramona; g – Soo Wun.*
◑ *1 – nada; 2 – gordita; 3 – alta; 4 – moreno; 5 – verdes; 6 – extrovertida; 7 – tímida; 8 – gusta.*

SUPPORT MATERIALS
OHT 4C ¿Cómo es tu físico?

Presentation of hair and eye colour. You could play a variety of ID and guessing / memory games with the cards.

Worksheet 4.5 Así somos

1 Los amigos

◐ Students use the visuals on p.35 of the Student's Book (Activity 2) for this activity. They listen and decide which person each of the conversations refers to.

Answers: *1 – Soo Wun; 2 – Jaime; 3 – Ramona; 4 – Beatriz; 5 – Soo Wun; 6 – Ramona.*

1
CHICO: ¿Cómo es?
CHICA: Tiene el pelo negro y los ojos grises.

2
CHICA: ¿Es alto?
CHICO: No, es bajo. Y es delgado también.

3
CHICA: ¿Es pelirroja?
CHICO: Sí, es pelirroja.
CHICA: Ah, sí, la conozco.

4
CHICO: Es muy guapa. Es bastante alta ...
CHICA: ¿Es alta?
CHICO: No es muy alta, pero no es baja.
CHICA: De estatura media, entonces.
CHICO: Sí.

5
CHICA: ¿No le conoces? Es de estatura media y un poco gordito.
CHICO: Un poco gordito ... Ah, sí. Está en la clase de mi hermano.

6
CHICA: Me gustaría ser alta, como ella.
CHICO: ¿Es muy alta?
CHICA: Sí, y delgada también.

2 ¿Qué opinan?

 Students listen and fill in the speakers' opinions on the grid provided.

Answers: Beatriz ; Jaime ;

Soo Wun ; Ramona ;

BEATRIZ
CHICA: ¿Beatriz? Es una persona muy optimista.
CHICO: Y muy graciosa también.
CHICA: Sí, es verdad.

JAIME
CHICO: ¿Te gusta Jaime?
CHICA: En clase es perezoso.
CHICO: Y tonto también. Es imposible trabajar a veces.

SOO WUN
CHICA: ¿Y Soo Wun? Es muy hablador en clase.
CHICO: Sí, pero es alegre, y extrovertido.
CHICA: Y muy simpático.

RAMONA
CHICO: ¡Qué seria es Ramona!
CHICA: Sí, siempre. Muy seria y, para decir la verdad, antipática.

3 El intercambio

Students listen and tick the correct information on the form.

Answers: 15 años, ojos grises, pelo moreno, de estatura media, positivo.

PROFE. 1: Bueno, Javier Solano Velázquez.
PROFE. 2: Sí, aquí está. Vamos a ver ... ¿Cuántos años tiene?
PROFE. 1: Mmm ... quince.
PROFE. 2: Quince años. Bien. Ojos ... grises, ¿no?
PROFE. 1: Sí, creo que sí.
PROFE. 2: Pelo. Rubio, no. Pelirrojo, no. Más bien moreno, ¿no te parece?
PROFE. 1: Sí. ¿Es alto?
PROFE. 2: Mmm, no creo. Pero no es bajo. Personalidad.
PROFE. 1: En mi clase, es bastante callado. No habla mucho.
PROFE. 2: Sí. Pero es una persona alegre, y simpático, ¿no crees?
PROFE. 1: Sí, estoy de acuerdo. Lo va a pasar muy bien en el intercambio.

Worksheet 4.6 Mi hermano mayor

 a A multiple-choice activity which gives reading practice of the personal description vocabulary. Students underline the appropriate word(s) in each speech bubble.

Answers: *1 – Francisco; 2 – dieciocho; 3 – alto; 4 – gordito; 5 – largo, gris, liso; 6 – lleva gafas.*

b Students use the choice of words from Activity a to describe another person, adding a drawing if they wish.

Worksheet 4.7 Los desaparecidos

1 Jóvenes desaparecidos

Students listen to four interviews about missing people and match the name of each person being spoken about with the appropriate picture.

Answers: *1 – Bernardo; 2 – Dani; 3 (distractor); 4 – Carlos; 5 – Adriano.*

GUARDIA: ¿Cuántos años tiene Adriano?
MADRE: Catorce años.
GUARDIA: ¿Nos puede dar una descripción?
MADRE: Sí. Mmm ... Es bastante delgado, pero no es súper delgado. Tiene el pelo corto, rizado ...
GUARDIA: ¿De qué color?
MADRE: Negro.
GUARDIA: ¿Y es alto, su hijo?
MADRE: No, pero no es bajo tampoco. Es de estatura media.
GUARDIA: Vale, gracias, señora. Y si nos puede decir lo que llevaba cuando desapareció ...

CHICA: ¿Señora?
DEPENDIENTE: ¿Sí?
CHICA: ¿Me puede ayudar? Busco a mi hermano. Estaba aquí hace cinco minutos, pero no le veo.
DEPENDIENTE: ¿Cómo es?
CHICA: Es alto, y delgado.
DEPENDIENTE: ¿Es rubio o moreno?
CHICA: Moreno. Tiene el pelo corto y liso, un poco en estilo 'punk'.
DEPENDIENTE: Mira, allí. ¿Es tu hermano?
CHICA: ¡Ah sí! Vale, muchas gracias! ¡Bernardo! ¡Bernardo, espera!

PERIODISTA: ¿Y su hijo Carlos desapareció hace dos días?
PADRE: Sí. Estamos muy preocupados. Sólo tiene trece años.
PERIODISTA: ¿Y cómo es? ¿Puede dar una descripción?
PADRE: Sí. Es bastante bajo, y delgado. Tiene el pelo corto, liso ...
PERIODISTA: ¿Es moreno?
PADRE: No, rubio.
PERIODISTA: ¿Lleva gafas?
PADRE: No, no. Carlos, si estás escuchando, llámanos, por favor.

GUARDIA: Y tu hermano, ¿cómo es?
CHICO: Es mi hermano gemelo, así somos muy parecidos.
GUARDIA: Pelo corto, ondulado ...
CHICO: Sí.
GUARDIA: Rubio. De estatura media.
CHICO: Sí. Tiene más pecas que yo.
GUARDIA: ¿Qué llevaba? ¿Igual que tú?

2 Las descripciones

Students read a set of descriptions and pick the person from Activity 1 who best matches each description.

Answers: *Chico 1 – 3; Chico 2 – 5.*

3 Te toca a ti

Students write their own missing persons advert, using Activity 2 as a model.

Objectives

Grammar: *ser* – to be (plural);
adjectives (plural)

Key language

Plural of *ser*
(nosotros) somos
(vosotros) sois
(ellos, ellas, ustedes) son
Plurals of adjectives already encountered
serios / serias
alegres
optimistas
trabajadores / trabajadoras
tonto/a(s)
divertido/a(s)
molesto/a(s)
imposible(s)
majo/a(s)
pesado/a(s)
el cuervo

Skills / Strategies

Students learn – to use the verb *ser*, 'to be'
– to form plural adjectives

ICT opportunities

Students can – write illustrated descriptions of people using
computer-generated images or clip-art

Ways in

Student's Book, Activity 1

Assessment opportunities

AT1,2 Student's Book, Activity 3: students listen to discriminate
between singular and plural.
AT3,1 Student's Book, Activity 1b: a gap-fill activity focusing on
ser.
AT4,1 Student's Book, Activity 2b: students write opinions about
people.

STUDENT'S BOOK, page 36

1 **Kiko Cuervo y los primos**

a Students read the picture story about Kiko the Crow and
pick the correct three adjectives to complete each of the
two sentences given. The adjectives in their plural forms
are given beneath as a help.

Answers: *1 – antipáticos, tontos, molestos;*
2 – simpáticos, graciosos, divertidos.

Gramática

Students are directed to the grammar summary section 11
on p.150 for help with plural forms of the verb *ser*. There are
also practice activities on the Acción: lengua 4 page (p.37).

b A gap-fill conversation which presents and practises the
plural forms of *ser*.

Answers: *1 – son; 2 – sois; 3 – somos; 4 – somos; 5 – sois.*

2 **Los amigos**

a This activity involves reading a short text and then
copying and completing a table of adjective endings using
information gained from the text.

Students are referred to the grammar summary section 6,
p.148 and to Acción: lengua 4, p.37 for further information
and practice.

Answers: *seria; alegres; optimistas; trabajadoras.*

b An open-ended writing activity in which students write a
few sentences giving opinions about the characteristics of
their best and worst friends.

3 **¡Escucha bien!**

Six brief conversations which comprise an aural
discrimination activity. Students work out whether each
conversation relates to a boy, a girl, boys or girls.

Answers: *1 – (m)(s); 2 – (f)(pl); 3 – (f)(s); 4 – (m)(s); 5 – (m)(pl);*
6 – (f)(s).

| 1 | CHICA: | Es muy majo. Es comprensivo, amable, gracioso ... me gusta mucho. |
| 2 | CHICO: | ¡Son tontas! ¡Son habladoras, perezosas, y pesadas! |

3	SEÑORA:	Me gusta mucho. Es trabajadora, simpática ... un poco callada, a veces, pero muy maja.
4	CHICA:	Es encantador. Guapo, inteligente – un amigo ideal.
5	CHICA:	No me gustan mucho. Pueden ser amables, pero en general son antipáticos y a veces agresivos.
6	CHICO:	Es alegre, y sincera y generosa. Muy simpática.

SUPPORT MATERIALS

Worksheet 4.8 Tú y yo

An information-gap activity which practises the vocabulary and
structures of description via a cued role-play.

Acción: lengua 4, page 37

Ser (to be); adjectives

1 The first activity practises the verb *ser* (to be) in the
singular and plural forms.

○ A gap-fill activity in which students complete a text by
choosing the correct verb forms.

✛ A gap-fill activity in which students fill in the correct
form of the verb 'to be' in each gap.

Answers: ○ *soy; somos; es; son; es; soy; eres.*
✛ *1 – eres; 2 – somos; 3 – sois; 4 – es; 5 – son;*
6 – soy.

2 This activity provides practice of all the singular and plural
adjective forms.

○ Students read a list of items needed for a happy
return to school in September, and change the adjective
endings where necessary.

✛ Students provide the correct forms for the adjectives.

Answers: ○ *una mochila nueva; un monedero lleno; un
uniforme limpio; una clase simpática; una aula
agradable; un tutor amable; una directora buena;
un libro interesante; una amiga comprensiva; una
profesora simpática.*

✛ *alta; delgada; marrones; moreno; guapos;
alegres; mayor; pesada; simpáticos; baja; glotona.*

Objectives
Students learn – to talk about school subjects
　　　　　　– to say what they have on each day

Key language
¿qué tienes hoy / el (lunes)?
tengo ...
(el) deporte
(el) dibujo
(el) español / la lengua
(el) francés
(el) inglés
(la) biología
(la) música
(la) informática
(la) geografía
(la) historia
(la) física
(la) química
(la) tecnología
(las) ciencias
(las) matemáticas
(la) ética
tengo ..., ¿tienes ...?
es ... / son ...
(revision of likes and dislikes, and descriptions, e.g. *aburrido*)

el campo de deportes
el gimnasio
el patio
el salón de actos
la biblioteca
el comedor / la cantina
la enfermería
la piscina
la sala de ordenadores
despachos
laboratorios
pasillos
vestuarios
aulas
servicios
cocinas

Skills / Strategies
Students learn – to ask and respond to questions, and to contradict a wrong answer

ICT opportunities
Students can – use a graphics or word-processing package to produce a list of their subjects, decorated with clip-art symbolising their opinions

Ways in
OHT 5A
Picture story, Student's Book, page 38

Assessment opportunities
AT1,3　Worksheet 5.1, Activity 1b: students listen and pick the facilities at each school.
AT2,1　Student's Book, Activity 3: circulate and listen to pairs as they do the activity.
AT3,2　Worksheet 5.1, Activity 1a: a basic vocabulary-recognition reading activity.
AT4, 3/4　Student's Book, Activity 4: students adapt a model letter to produce their own version.

STUDENT'S BOOK, pages 38–39

1 ¿Qué tienes hoy?
Picture story

Tomás, in disorganised fashion, is getting ready for school, leaving a trail of havoc in his wake. Students listen to the recording and look at a series of visuals representing various subjects. They write down whether Tomás has each subject depicted or not.

Answers:　1 – sí; 2 – no; 3 – sí; 4 – sí; 5 – no; 6 – sí; 7 – no; 8 – no; 9 – no; 10 – no; 11 – sí; 12 – no.

TERESA:	Tu mochila – toma. ¿Qué tienes hoy? ¿Francés?
TOMÁS:	No. Inglés. Tengo geografía, pero no tengo historia ... Un momento – tengo dibujo.
TERESA:	¿Tienes matemáticas?
TOMÁS:	Mm ... sí. Y tecnología.
TERESA:	¿Tienes ciencias? ¿Física? ¿Química?
TOMÁS:	No ... y no tengo biología. Y no tengo música ... Hola, Pepa.
TERESA:	La ética – ¿qué es exactamente?
TOMÁS:	Es como el PSHE en Gran Bretaña – religión, educación social y personal ...
PEPA:	Pero hoy, no hay. ¿No tienes deporte?
TOMÁS:	¡Ah, sí! Adiós, Mamá.
TERESA:	¡Muchas gracias, Tomás!

2 Mi horario

○ A listening activity which uses the same visuals as Activity 1, but features five people talking about what subjects they have. Students note down the numbers of the subjects for each person.

♣ For this activity students listen to the recording and decide whether each person finds the day very good, awful or is not bothered either way.

Answers:　**○** Nieves – 1, 4, 10, 12; Bernal – 2, 8, 11, 3; Alicia – 6, 5, 12, 4, 7; Iñigo – 9, 1, 3, 8; Víctor – 3, 7, 11, 2, 6.

♣ Nieves – 😐; Bernal – 🙂; Alicia – 🙁; Iñigo – 🙁; Víctor – 🙂 .

NIEVES	
CHICO:	¿Qué tal tu horario este año, Nieves?
NIEVES:	Vamos a ver ... Hoy tengo inglés ...
CHICO:	Sí. Inglés, deporte ...
NIEVES:	Sí, luego biología, y ética ... No está mal.

BERNAL	
MAMÁ:	¿Bernal?
BERNAL:	Sí, ¡soy yo! ¡Hola, Mamá!
MAMÁ:	¿Qué tal hoy?
BERNAL:	Bien, en general. Primero, francés.
MAMÁ:	Te gusta el francés, ¿no?
BERNAL:	Sí. Después, física y ... vamos a ver ... la tecnología.
MAMÁ:	¡Uf!
BERNAL:	¡Luego, dos horas de dibujo!
MAMÁ:	Tu asignatura favorita.
BERNAL:	Sí. Y el miércoles es mi día favorito.

ALICIA	
CHICA:	Alicia, ¿qué tenemos hoy? No tengo mi agenda.
ALICIA:	Primero, geografía. Y luego, música. Espera ...
CHICA:	La ética, ¿no?
ALICIA:	Sí. Luego, ay no, ¡deporte! ¡No me gusta nada el deporte!
CHICA:	A mí, sí. ¿Y luego ...?
ALICIA:	Historia. ¡Qué desastre! Hoy es un día horrible ...

IÑIGO	
CHICA:	¡Iñigo!
IÑIGO:	¿Sí? Maite, ¡hola!
CHICA:	¡Espera! ¿No vas al instituto hoy?
IÑIGO:	Sí que voy.

CHICA:	¡Pero no tienes mochila!
IÑIGO:	¡Y qué! ¿Qué tenemos hoy?
CHICA:	Primero química. Y luego inglés.
IÑIGO:	¡Inglés – qué horror!
CHICA:	Y tenemos dibujo.
IÑIGO:	Me gusta el dibujo – pero se ma ha olvidado el estuche.
CHICA:	¿No tienes estuche? ¡Qué despistado eres, Iñigo!
IÑIGO:	Lo dice mi madre también – ¡Qué despistado eres, Iñigo! ¿Qué más?
CHICA:	Física.
IÑIGO:	¿Física? ¡Fatal, fatal, fatal!

VÍCTOR

VÍCTOR:	Vamos a ver ... dibujo ... historia ... tecnología ... francés – ¿dónde está mi diccionario? ¡Ah! Allí está. Y luego ... geografía.
PADRE:	¿Listo?
VÍCTOR:	Sí. El viernes es mi día favorito.
PADRE:	¿Por qué?
VÍCTOR:	¡Porque mañana es sábado y no tengo clase los sábados!

3 **¡Adivina el día!**

Quick pairwork: students use their own timetables to describe the subjects on a particular day, and their partner works out which day of the week is being referred to.

4 **La carta de Miguel**

○ Students read a letter about school subjects and then modify it using the symbol cues next to it.

◑ Students read the letter again and choose the option which is incorrect for each sentence.

Answers: ○   *1 – geografía; 2 – física; 3 – ética; 4 – historia; 5 – jueves; 6 – dibujo; 7 – matemáticas; 8 – biología.*
            ◑   *1 – b; 2 – b; 3 – c; 4 – c; 5 – a.*

SUPPORT MATERIALS

OHT 5A ¿Qué asignaturas estudias?

The school subjects are presented as cards and can be used for different games.

Worksheet 5.1 ¿Qué instalaciones tiene?

1 **Las instalaciones**

a Students read and listen to the names of the different facilities.

---

1 – un campo de deportes
2 – un gimnasio
3 – un patio
4 – un salón de actos
5 – una biblioteca
6 – un comedor
7 – una enfermería
8 – una piscina
9 – una sala de ordenadores
10 – despachos
11 – laboratorios
12 – pasillos
13 – vestuarios
14 – servicios
15 – aulas
16 – cocinas

b ○ Students listen to four young people talking about the facilities at their school, and pick three visuals for each.

Answers: *Dario – 6, 16, 5; Gema – 8, 1, 2; José – 14, 13, 15; Paula – 3, 10, 12.*

DARIO

ENTREVISTADOR:	¿Qué instalaciones tiene tu instituto, Dario?
DARIO:	Tiene un comedor ... y cocinas ...
ENTREVISTADOR:	¿Tiene una biblioteca?
DARIO:	Sí, biblioteca y además tenemos muchos ...

GEMA

GEMA:	Mi instituto tiene buenas instalaciones.
ENTREVISTADOR:	¿Sí? ¿Qué tiene?
GEMA:	Una piscina ...
ENTREVISTADOR:	¿Una piscina? ¡Qué suerte!
GEMA:	También un campo de deportes, y un gimnasio.
ENTREVISTADOR:	¿Te gusta el deporte, Gema?

JOSÉ

ENTREVISTADOR:	José, ¿qué instalaciones tiene tu instituto?
JOSÉ:	Lo normal: servicios ... vestuarios ...
ENTREVISTADOR:	¿Aulas?
JOSÉ:	Sí, ¡claro que tiene aulas! ... pero el problema es que no tiene muchas ...

PAULA

PAULA:	Mi instituto es un desastre.
ENTREVISTADOR:	¿Por qué?
PAULA:	No tiene muchas instalaciones. Hay un patio. Eso es todo.
ENTREVISTADOR:	¿No tiene salón de actos?
PAULA:	No. Tiene despachos ... y pasillos ... Eso es todo.

2 **Mi instituto tiene ...**

○ Students draw a plan of their school with the facilities shown on it, using the numbers and vocabulary from Activity 1.

◑ Students write a brief description of their school. A help box is given for those who need it.

Objectives

Students learn – to say whether they like subjects or not
– to give a reason for liking / disliking
– Grammar: *gustar* (to like); revision of plural adjectives

Key language

(no) me gusta (el inglés, el francés, etc.)
(no) me gustan (nada) (la historia y la música, etc.)
el / la … es (divertido / aburrido, etc.)
las / los (matemáticas, trabajos manuales, etc.) son …
el / la profe es …
divertido/a
aburrido/a
difícil
fácil
interesante
simpático/a
porque …
pero
aunque

Skills / Strategies

Students learn – to express more sophisticated opinions and back them up with reasons

ICT opportunities

Student's Book, Activity 5 (follow-up): word-process opinions on subjects

Ways in

Own opinions and experience, building on language from previous topic area; Picture story, Student's Book, page 40

Assessment opportunities

AT1,3/4 Student's Book, Activity 3: students hear a selection of opinions about school subjects.
AT2,3 Student's Book, Activity 1b: students work in pairs to give their opinions on subjects.
AT3,2 Worksheet 5.3, Activity 2: students identify to whom the quotes belong.
AT3,4 Worksheet 5.4, Activity 2: reading a letter.
AT4,2/3 Student's Book, Activity 5: students write their own opinions on the subjects.

STUDENT'S BOOK, pages 40–41

1 **¿Gusta o gustan?**

Picture story

 a José Luis is chatting up Isabel, and Pilar is not very pleased! Students read and listen to the text. The activity presents the language required for giving opinions about school subjects which were presented on the previous spread.

JOSÉ LUIS:	¿Te gustan las matemáticas, Isabel?
ISABEL:	Sí, me gustan mucho. ¿Y a ti?
JOSÉ LUIS:	Sí. Pero prefiero el deporte. ¿Te gusta?
ISABEL:	Sí, sobre todo el tenis.
JOSÉ LUIS:	¡A mí también! ¡Qué bien!
PILAR:	No es el deporte que te gusta, Isabel – es José Luis …

b Students work in pairs to give their opinion of their own subjects, using the structures encountered in Activity **a**.

Students talk about their subjects using the structures in Activity **a** and the help grid for more varied language.

2 **¿Qué asignatura prefieres?**

A listening activity which gives further practice of the language used to give opinions about subjects. Students select the favourite subject of each of the six speakers.

Answers: *1 – la tecnología; 2 – el francés; 3 – la historia; 4 – la biología; 5 – la literatura; 6 – el dibujo.*

1	CHICO 1:	¿Qué asignatura prefieres?
	CHICO 2:	Prefiero la tecnología.
2	PADRE:	¿Qué tal tus clases este año, Juan?
	JUAN:	Bien, Papá.
	PADRE:	¿Qué asignatura prefieres?
	JUAN:	Este año, prefiero el francés.
3	CHICA 1:	¿Prefieres la historia o la geografía, Marta?
	CHICA 2:	Prefiero la historia. ¿Y tú?
4	MADRE:	¿Te gustan las clases de ciencia este año?
	CHICA 1:	Sí. En general, sí. No me gusta mucho la física, pero la química no está mal. Pero prefiero la biología.

5	CHICA:	¿No te gustan las ciencias ni las matemáticas?
	CHICO:	No están mal. Pero prefiero la literatura.
6	CHICA:	¡Qué bien! Ahora tenemos deporte.
	CHICO:	No me gusta mucho. Prefiero la clase después – el dibujo.

3 **¿Qué opina Tomás?**

Students listen to Tomás talking about various subjects and giving his opinion. They match up the subjects listed with his opinions.

Answers: *1 – d; 2 – f; 3 – b; 4 – a; 5 – c; 6 – e.*

PEPA:	Tenemos inglés hoy – ¿te gusta?
TOMÁS:	Sí. Es fácil.
PEPA:	Para ti, sí, claro – pero para mí, no. Y no tenemos dibujo. ¡Qué bién!
TOMÁS:	El dibujo me gusta.
PEPA:	¿Por qué?
TOMÁS:	La profe es simpática.
PEPA:	¿Te gusta el francés?
TOMÁS:	No, es aburrido.
PEPA:	A mí me gusta bastante. Pero hoy tenemos deporte también. ¡Qué horror!
TOMÁS:	¡Pepa, el deporte es divertido! … Y tenemos historia también.
PEPA:	¿No te gusta la historia?
TOMÁS:	No mucho. Es difícil.
PEPA:	Y luego tenemos … la ética. ¡Qué desastre!
TOMÁS:	A mí, me gusta. Es interesante.
PEPA:	Bueno, ¡aquí estamos!

4 **¿Cómo son las asignaturas?**

a An activity revising the adjective endings as preparation for students giving their opinions about the subjects they learn. Students refer back to Acción: lengua 4 on p.37 and complete the endings in the table here.

Answers: *divertida;*
divertidos, interesantes, fáciles;
divertidas, interesantes, fáciles.

b Students complete six model opinions with the appropriate adjective ending.

Answers: *1 – aburrida; 2 – divertida; 3 – interesante;*
               4 – interesantes; 5 – difíciles; 6 – fáciles.

5 En mi opinión

○ Students adapt the sentences from Activity 4b in order to give their own opinions.

○ An open-ended activity in which students give opinions about five subjects in their own words.

6 Mis comentarios

Students look at Tomás's timetable and use it as a model to draw up their own school timetable, decorating it by expressing their own feelings about the subjects in the form of graffiti.

SUPPORT MATERIALS

Worksheet 5.2 Una encuesta

Students fill in their own subjects in the left-hand column of the sheet. They then conduct a survey in class, interviewing their classmates about the subjects they (dis)like and why, referring to the vocabulary box at the bottom of the page for support if necessary.

Worksheet 5.3 Los gustos

Note that this sheet has removable English rubrics at the bottom.

1 Me gusta mucho

○ **a** Students listen to the dialogues and fill in the correct letters of the subjects for each person.

Answers: *1 Miguel – C, D; 2 Esther – F, A; 3 Alberto – G, B.*

---

1 **MIGUEL**
   MIGUEL: Me gusta la geografía.
   ENTREVISTADOR: ¿La geografía? Bien. ¿Algo más?
   MIGUEL: Sí. La ética. Me gusta mucho la ética.

2 **ESTHER**
   ENTREVISTADOR: Esther, te gusta el deporte, ¿no?
   ESTHER: Sí, me gusta el deporte. Y también la informática.
   ENTREVISTADOR: La informática es interesante.

3 **ALBERTO**
   ALBERTO: A mí, me gusta mucho la física.
   ENTREVISTADOR: Te gusta la física y …
   ALBERTO: Y el dibujo. El dibujo es divertido.

---

b Students listen and decide whether the opinions expressed are negative or positive.

Answers: *1 – ✓; 2 – ✗; 3 – ✓; 4 – ✗; 5 – ✗; 6 – ✓.*

---

1 – ¿Las matemáticas? ¡Me gustan mucho!
2 – ¿Qué opino de estudiar la lengua española? No me gusta.
3 – ¿Te gusta la historia? Es interesante.
4 – La química – ¡uf! Es difícil.
5 – Para mí, la música es aburrida.
6 – El francés es fácil. Y el profesor es muy simpático.

---

2 Las ciencias y la tecnología

Students look at a series of visual cues and six quotes, and decide which of the people the quotes belong to.

Answers: *1 – Elisa; 2 – Juana; 3 – Gema; 4 – Paco; 5 – Darío;*
               6 – María.

3 Con tu pareja

A pairwork activity in which students use the stimulus from Activity 2 as the basis for a conversation about school subject likes and dislikes.

Worksheet 5.4 ¿Qué opinas?

1 En mi opinión

○ In this activity students listen to Spanish teenagers, Emilio and Rosario, talking to their tutor, and fill in a grid representing their opinions on the subjects studied.

Answers:

		Francés	Matemáticas	Biología	Deporte	Trabajos manuales
a	¿✓ o ✗?	✓	✗	✓	✗	✗
b	¿Por qué?	divertido	difíciles	interesante	aburrido	no son interesantes

---

TUTOR: Dime, Emilio, ¿qué asignatura prefieres?
EMILIO: Me gusta mucho el francés.
TUTOR: ¿El francés? ¿Por qué?
EMILIO: Bueno … es divertido.

TUTOR: ¿Te gustan las matemáticas este año?
EMILIO: ¡No me hable de las matemáticas! ¡No me gustan nada!
TUTOR: ¡No me digas! Pero tu profesora es simpática …
EMILIO: Ya lo sé – es que para mí, las matemáticas son muy difíciles. No entiendo nada de nada …

TUTOR: ¿Qué tal tu clase de biología este año?
ROSARIO: Muy bien. Me encanta.
TUTOR: ¿Sí? ¿Por qué?
ROSARIO: Bueno, es muy interesante.

TUTOR: ¿Y el deporte?
EMILIO: ¡Uf! El deporte …
TUTOR: ¿No te gusta?
EMILIO: Es que no me gusta el fútbol. Y el baloncesto es estúpido …
TUTOR: ¿No te gusta la gimnasia?
EMILIO: No – en mi opinión el deporte es muy aburrido.

TUTOR: ¿Qué tal los trabajos manuales?
EMILIO: Me gustan bastante, pero …
TUTOR: ¿Son difíciles?
EMILIO: No. Son fáciles. Pero no son muy interesantes.

---

2 La carta de María Ángeles

○ Students read a letter and decide whether the opinions about subjects written about in the letter are positive, negative or both.

Answers: *a – P; b – N; c – P+N; d – P; e – P+N; f – N.*

3 La respuesta

○ Students write a reply to María Ángeles' letter in Activity 2, using the cues given but adding details of their own as they wish.

Objectives
Students learn – to ask and give the time
– to say when and where they have a subject
– to say how many hours a week they study it

Key language
Times: *a las (diez) ...*
es la una ...
son las (diez) ...
en punto
y cinco
y diez
y cuarto
y veinte
y veinticinco
y media
menos veinticinco
menos veinte
menos cuarto
menos diez
menos cinco
la mañana
la tarde
el aula
el campo de deportes
el laboratorio
la sala de ordenadores
tengo ... horas la mañana / tarde
luego ...
¿qué tienes el ... por la mañana / tarde?
¿cuántas horas de ... tienes?
tengo ... horas de ... la mañana / tarde / lunes / a la semana (etc.)
¿cuándo tienes ...?

Skills / Strategies
Students learn – to ask and tell the time and use time phrases
confidently

ICT opportunities
Generating own timetable, ideal timetable, nightmare timetable,
etc.

Ways in
Clock in Student's Book, page 42; own timetables;
dream / nightmare timetables

Assessment opportunities
AT1,3 Student's Book, Activity 3a: listening for mistakes and
differences.
AT2,2/3 Student's Book, Activity 3b: questions and answers on
timetables.
AT3,2 Worksheet 5.5, Activity 2: true or false activity.
AT4,3 Student's Book, Activity 3d: expressing own opinions on
timetable by modifying a model text.

STUDENT'S BOOK, pages 42–43

1 **¿Qué hora es?**

a ◗ Introduction of the times (exact hours only).
Students listen to young people talking about their
timetables and note down the times mentioned.

☻ Students listen again and work out who has what
subject.

Answers: ◗ *Ali – 9.00; Eduardo – 1.00; Nuria – 12.00;*
Rogelio – 1.00; Pedro – 11.00.

☻ *Ali – geografía; Eduardo – historia; Nuria –*
matemáticas, Rogelio – inglés; Pedro – dibujo.

ALI	
PROFE:	Chicos, ¿no tenéis geografía?
ALI:	Sí. ¿Qué hora es?
PROFE:	Son las nueve.
ALI:	¿Las nueve?
PROFE:	Sí, ¡rápido! ¡A clase!

EDUARDO	
EDUARDO:	Oye, Ana, ¿qué hora es?
ANA:	Es la una.
EDUARDO:	¿La una? ¡Ay no, hasta luego!
ANA:	¿Adónde vas?
EDUARDO:	Tengo clase de historia. ¡Y el profe es severo!

NURIA	
NURIA:	¡Matemáticas – qué bien! ¿Qué hora es?
CHICO:	Son las doce.
NURIA:	¿Las doce? ¡No me digas! ¡Adiós!

ROGELIO	
ROGELIO:	Y creo que tengo inglés.
CHICA:	¿A la una?
ROGELIO:	Sí.
CHICA:	¡Pero es la una en punto!
ROGELIO:	¿De veras? ¡Uh-ho! ¡Me voy!

PEDRO	
PEDRO:	Carmen, ¿qué hora es?
CARMEN:	A ver ... son las once.
PEDRO:	¿Las once? ¡Tengo dibujo!
CARMEN:	Pues, ¡rápido!

b This activity introduces times with minutes past and to
the hour. Students listen to the recording and pick one of
the times given for each dialogue.

Answers: *1 – d; 2 – b; 3 – f; 4 – h; 5 – c; 6 – a; 7 – g.*
(e is the distractor)

1	HOMBRE:	Perdone, ¿qué hora es, por favor?
	MUJER:	Son ... las diez.
	HOMBRE:	¿Las diez? Gracias.
2	MADRE:	Oye, Jaime, ¿qué hora es?
	JAIME:	Son las cinco.
	MADRE:	¿Las cinco? Oh, tengo que ir a buscar a Felipe ...
3	CHICO:	Matilde ¿qué hora es, por favor?
	MATILDE:	Son las ocho y media.
	CHICO:	¿Ocho y media? Vamos a clase, entonces.
4	CHICO:	¡Psst! ¡Benjamín!
	BENJAMÍN:	¿Qué?
	CHICO:	¿Qué hora es?
	BENJAMÍN:	Son las nueve y cuarto.
	CHICO:	¿Nueve y cuarto? ¡Quince minutos más!
	PROFE :	Javi y Benjamín – ¡a trabajar!
5	PROFE:	¡Josefa! ¿Qué hora es?
	JOSEFA:	Son las dos.
	PROFE:	Son las dos y cinco.
	JOSEFA:	Siento mucho llegar tarde ...

6	CHICO:	Perdone, señor. ¿Qué hora es, por favor?
	SEÑOR:	Vamos a ver ... Son las cuatro menos cuarto.
	CHICO:	Cuatro menos cuarto. Gracias.
	SEÑOR:	De nada.
7	CHICA:	¡Rápido!
	CHICA:	¡No puedo más! ¿Qué hora es?
	CHICA:	Son las siete y ... veinticinco.
	CHICA:	¿Siete y veinticinco? Cinco minutos más, y nos vamos a los vestuarios, ¿vale?

3 El horario

a A mixed-skill activity which presents the timetable language and the language used for giving details of the duration, frequency and location of lessons. Students listen and correct the words in italics, using information gleaned from the recording. Additional support for less able students is provided on Worksheet 5.5, Activity 1.

Answers: *1 – lunes, física, matemáticas; 2 – inglés, miércoles a las doce, jueves a la una y media; 3 – geografía, aula quince; 4 – historia, dos.*

TERESA:	¿Qué tal tu horario, Pilar? ¿Qué tienes el lunes por la mañana?
PILAR:	¿El lunes por la mañana? Tengo física, y luego matemáticas.
TERESA:	¿Física y matemáticas? ¡Uf! ¿Cuándo tienes inglés, Isabel?
ISABEL:	Inglés. Vamos a ver ... El miércoles, creo. Sí, el miércoles a las doce, y también el ... jueves, sí, jueves, a la una y media.
TOMÁS:	Oye, Isabel, ¿en qué aula tienes geografía?
ISABEL:	¿Geografía? En el aula quince.
TOMÁS:	¡Yo también! ¡Es una aula horrible! Pero el aula de historia está bien.
TERESA:	¿Y cuántas horas de historia tienes, Tomás?
TOMÁS:	Tengo dos horas a la semana. No me gusta mucho la historia. Es difícil.

b A pairwork activity in which students question each other about a sample timetable given in their books, using the language encountered in the preceding activity.

c A text manipulation activity which entails reading a passage giving information about the school timetable (from the previous activity) and correcting the errors in it.

Answers: *seis, lengua / español, martes, deporte, once y media, cinco, tarde, doce y media.*

d Students describe their own timetables using the text from Activity c as a model.

SUPPORT MATERIALS
Worksheet 5.5 El horario

Note that removable English rubrics are given at the bottom of this sheet.

1 El horario

 This activity is designed to support less able students with listening Activity 3a (p.43 of the Student's Book) – see tapescript above.

Answers: *1 – lunes, física, matemáticas; 2 – inglés, miércoles, 1.30; 3 – geografía, quince; 4 – historia, dos.*

2 ¿Verdad o mentira?

a A reading activity which further exploits the timetable on p.43 of the Student's Book. This is a basic 'true or false' activity.

Answers: *1 – V; 2 – M; 3 – V; 4 – V; 5 – M; 6 – M.*

b Students look at the timetable again and fill in the blanks in sentences giving details about it.

Answers: *1 – once y media; 2 – miércoles; 3 – informática; 4 – nueve (en punto); 5 – biología; 6 – lunes.*

Worksheet 5.6 Por favor

A pairwork information-gap activity which concentrates on timetable information. Students have half the sheet each and have to find out the missing information from their partner.

Worksheet 5.7 El horario de Tomás
1 Los comentarios

Students look at the timetable and read Tomás's comments, making notes of what they understand. They can look up words they are unfamiliar with in the vocabulary at the back of the Student's Book. Students can use this timetable as a model to write their own.

2 Te toca a ti

Students draw up their own timetable, adding comments in the style of the preceding activity, or others as they wish.

Objectives
Students learn – further ways of expressing likes and dislikes
– Grammar: revision of *gustar*

Key language
Revision of language in the first three objectives of this unit

Skills / Strategies
Students learn – to recognise and use the present tense of *gustar* and *encantar*

ICT opportunities
Writing dialogues; could use clip-art to generate picture dialogues like those in Student's Book, page 44 and exchange them with a partner

Ways in
'Real life' opinions

Assessment opportunities
AT1,3   Student's Book, Activity 1: students listen and fill in the missing subjects.
AT2,3/4   Worksheet 5.8: students give a presentation on their opinions of subjects.
AT4,3/4   Worksheet 5.8: students write down the basis for their presentation.

STUDENT'S BOOK, page 44

1 **Los gustos**

This activity revises *gustar* and presents some other impersonal verbs and ways of expressing likes and dislikes. Students listen and fill in the missing subjects.

Answers: *a – la química; b – el francés; c – la lengua; d – el inglés; e – la ética; f – la literatura; g – el dibujo; h – las matemáticas; i – el francés.*

CHICA:	Me encanta la química. Me gusta mucho el francés.
CHICO:	No está mal la lengua. Y me gusta bastante el inglés.
CHICA:	No me gusta mucho la ética. Y no me interesa mucho la literatura.
CHICO:	No me gusta nada el dibujo. Odio las matemáticas, ¡y detesto el francés!

2 **¿Te interesa ...?**

This information-gap activity practices *gustar* and the other language presented on this page via a set of symbol cues.

SUPPORT MATERIALS

Worksheet 5.8 Una presentación

 Students prepare a presentation to give to the class, using the framework given on the worksheet, and giving as much information as possible about the school, timetable, etc.

Acción: lengua 5, page 45
Using *gustar* (to like)

1 This activity provides basic practice of *gustar* via a simple gap-fill activity.

An open-ended activity which gives practice of *gustar* and the other expressions met in Unit 5. Students write opinions using expressions of their choice, in response to symbol prompts.

Answers: 1 – *gusta*; 2 – *gustan*; 3 – *gusta*; 4 – *gusta*; 5 – *gustan*; 6 – *gustan*.

2 A gap-fill activity which practises the correct pronouns to be used with *gustar* in different circumstances.

A gap-fill activity giving practice of all the forms of the pronouns used with *gustar*.

Answers: *te; me; le; te; me; te.*

1 – *les*; 2 – *me*; 3 – *le*; 4 – *os*; 5 *nos.*
(te is the one left over)

3 Students match up the sentence halves correctly.

An extended writing activity, giving students further opportunity to practise placing *a mí, a ti, a él/ella*, etc. in front of the indirect object pronouns.

Answers: 1 – *c*; 2 – *d*; 3 – *a*; 4 – *f*; 5 – *b*; 6 – *e*.

– *A vosotros os gustan los idiomas ¿no?*
+ *A nosotros, sí nos gustan.*
– *A Ana y Javi no les gusta el inglés.*
+ *¡A ellos, no les gusta nada!*
– *¿A vosotros os gusta el nuevo director?*
+ *Sí, a nosotros nos gusta. Es simpático.*

¡Repaso! 1–5

This revision section takes a look back over the language studied in Units 1–5 and gives students an opportunity to take stock and reflect on their progress, and also to see if they have any unsuspected weak areas.

STUDENT'S BOOK, page 46

1 **¡Rompecabezas!**

a Students look at each sequence of four words or phrases and find the odd one out.

Answers: 1 – hermana; 2 – amigo; 3 – domingo; 4 – puerta; 5 – odio.

b In this activity students write the opposite of each underlined word.

Answers: 1 – pesimista; 2 – extrovertida; 3 – inteligente; 4 – interesante; 5 – callada.

2 **¿De qué hablan?**

a Students listen to the recording and write down the order in which the subjects are mentioned.

Answers:

Geografía	Historia	Lengua	Matemáticas	Física	Informática	Ética	Dibujo
3	1		5	2	7	4	6

1 CHICO: ¿Qué tenemos ahora?
CHICO: Historia.
CHICO: ¿Historia? ¡Ay no! ¡Se me ha olvidado traer los deberes!

2 CHICA: ¿Qué hora es, Marta?
CHICA: Son casi las diez.
CHICA: Tenemos una clase de física, ¿no?
CHICA: Sí, en dos minutos.

3 MADRE: ¿Qué asignatura prefieres este año, Cristina?
CHICA: Prefiero la geografía. Es muy interesante.

4 PROFESOR: ¿Chicos? ¡Rápido! ¡A clase! Tenéis ética, ¿no?
CHICO: La ética – ¡qué aburrido!

5 PADRE: ¿Qué tal los deberes?
CHICO: ¡Fatal!
PADRE: ¿Qué pasa?
CHICO: Tengo un examen de matemáticas mañana.

6 CHICA: ¿Por qué te gusta el dibujo?
CHICO: No sé. El dibujo es fácil, y el profesor es muy divertido.

7 MADRE: Carlos, ¿no quieres este libro? Tienes tecnología hoy, ¿no?
CHICO: ¡Ah, sí! Gracias, Mamá. Tenemos tecnología primero.

b Students listen to a boy who is going on an exchange trip to Great Britain giving his details, whilst his teacher fills in a form about him.

Answers: 1 – Nombre: Iñaki; 2 – Edad: 15; 3 – Cumpleaños: 12/05; 4 – Número de personas en la familia: 5; 5 – Animal(es) en casa: perro; 6 – Asignatura favorita: inglés.

PROFESORA:	Te llamas Iñaki, ¿no?
IÑAKI:	Sí. Se escribe I-ñ-a-k-i.
PROFESORA:	¿Cuántos años tienes?
IÑAKI:	Tengo quince años.
PROFESORA:	Y ¿cuándo es tu cumpleaños?
IÑAKI:	Es el doce de mayo.
PROFESORA:	Muy bien. ¿Tienes hermanos?
IÑAKI:	Sí, dos. Somos cinco personas en casa.
PROFESORA:	¿Tienes algún animal?
IÑAKI:	Sí, un perro.
PROFESORA:	¿Y cuál es tu asignatura favorita?
IÑAKI:	Me encanta el inglés.
PROFESORA:	¡Menos mal, si quieres pasar quince días en Gran Bretaña!

3 **¡Cuánto sabes!**

a Students fill in the missing question words in a series of personal information questions.

Answers: 1 – Cómo; 2 – Cómo; 3 – Cuántos; 4 – Cuándo; 5 – cómo; 6 – Cómo; 7 – Cuántas; 8 – Quiénes; 9 – Qué; 10 – Qué; 11 – Cuántas; 12 – Cuántas.

b Students now ask their partner the same 12 questions, using the vocabulary and structures from the previous activity, and recording their conversations if appropriate.

4 **A ser autor …**

a An open-ended writing activity in which students produce a small educative booklet, decorated with pictures if preferred, aimed at teaching vocabulary and phrases from topics covered in the previous units: i.e., colours, how to tell the time, the months of the year, days of the week, school subjects.

b This activity involves inventing an imaginary person and then writing an introduction about them, giving as much information as possible about their appearance, character, family, friends, school, etc.

STUDENT'S BOOK, page 47

5 **Las opiniones**

A short listening activity in which students listen to three people discussing their favourite and least favourite school subjects. They note down the opinions. The grid on Worksheet 5.9 can be used.

Answers: Auri – matemáticas ✓, dibujo ✗; César – física ✗, historia ✓; Reyes – ética ✓, geografía ✗.

EJEMPLO
VOZ 1: ¿Qué asignatura te gusta más?
VOZ 2: Me gusta mucho la tecnología.
VOZ 1: ¿Hay algún asignatura que no te gusta?
VOZ 2: ¡Odio la geografía!

AURI
VOZ: ¿Qué tal tu horario, Auri?
AURI: No está mal. Ahora tengo matemáticas, que me encantan. Pero después, hay una clase de dibujo, que no me gusta mucho.

CÉSAR
VOZ: ¿Te gustan las clases aquí en Gran Bretaña, César?
CÉSAR: La clase de historia es muy interesante. Pero odio la física – ¡y tenemos dos horas esta tarde!

REYES
VOZ: ¿Qué clase tienes ahora, Reyes?
REYES: Voy con mi amiga inglesa a una clase de ética. La profesora de ética es muy divertida. Luego, tenemos geografía, creo. Es bastante aburrida, la clase de geografía.

6 **La carta electrónica**

a Students read the e-mail and identify whether various topics are mentioned in the text.

Answers: *1 – no; 2 – sí; 3 – no; 4 – no; 5 – sí; 6 – no.*

---

b ♣ A set of true / false questions exploiting the same text as Activity 6a.

Answers: *1 – verdadera; 2 – verdadera; 3 – falsa;*
4 – verdadera; 5 – verdadera; 6 – falsa.

---

c Students join together the sentence halves without referring to a dictionary. One sentence is a distractor.

Answers: *1 – c; 2 – e; 3 – f; 4 – a; 5 – g; 6 – b.*
(d is the distractor)

---

d Students write out questions and answers in preparation for interviewing Fernando, whose details appear in the information box. If appropriate, they can add extra details about his appearance and character.

SUPPORT MATERIALS

Worksheet 5.9 Las opiniones

 ♣ This sheet provides a grid on which students can record their answers to Activity 5 on p.47 of the Student's Book.

Worksheet 5.10 El intercambio

 ♣ Students read an exchange programme itinerary and listen to the teacher announcing changes to the day's programme of events to a group of students. Students make a note of what changes have been made.

Answers: *a – martes, not miércoles; b – 9.15, not 9.00;*
c – García, not Garfía; d – Laboratorio 2, not 3;
e – meet in playground, not in canteen; f – groups
now 11–14 and 15–18, not 11–13 and 14–18;
g – Bus no. 27, not 26.

> PROFESORA: ¡Shhh! Callaos, por favor ... Gracias. Lo siento, pero hay algunos cambios en el programa. ¿Alguien no tiene boli? Bien. Escucha y apunta los cambios.
>
> Primero, debe decir 'Horario para el martes', no miércoles. Martes. ¿Vale? Luego, nos reunimos a las nueve y cuarto. Nueve y cuarto en la recepción.
>
> Después, a las diez, hay dos posibilidades. Si os gusta la historia, hay una introducción a la historia de Valencia con la profesora Ibarra Garfía – ¡ay no! Hay un error – no es Garfía, es García: G-A-R-C-I con acento– A. La sala está bien, sala quince.
>
> Si no os interesa la historia, hay una clase de español en el laboratorio de idiomas dos. ¿Dos o tres, Sr. Benjumea? Laboratorio dos. ¿Vale?
>
> Luego a las once, nos reunimos en el patio, no en la cantina. En el patio a las once. Hay muchos alumnos mayores que quieren hacer deporte. Entonces, hay dos grupos: de once a catorce años, y de quince a dieciocho. Repito: de once a catorce años, y de quince a dieciocho. Finalmente, por la tarde, vamos a hacer una excursión en autocar. Pero cuidado: el número del autocar es el veintisiete – veintisiete. Si no, vais a ir a Madrid, y no a la costa.

STUDENT'S BOOK, pages 48–49

Lectura

Two pages of material designed for independent reading. Students should use a dictionary to look up any words they do not understand. No activities accompany the texts since they are meant to be read for pleasure and information. You could encourage students to offer comments and reactions, which might stimulate oral or written follow-up.

a En el instituto Super VGA – a school for little robots.

b Leonora – has she a future?

c El color y la personalidad – which colours reflect different personality types.

d El rey optimista – a humorous and ironic picture story about a rather naïve king. Students could think up a similar story about a queen, a prime minister, a football manager or a dinner lady, for example.

STUDENT'S BOOK, page 50

Táctica: lengua

This page is designed to help students develop their language skills. The three items covered in this section are grammatical gender, listening strategies and word memorisation skills.

Masculino y femenino

This section explains that Spanish nouns have either a masculine or feminine gender and that this is indicated in the vocabulary section at the back of the Student's Book and in dictionaries by (m) or (f). There are six Spanish words and six English words for students to look up.

Answers: *Spanish section:*
pupitre (m) – desk; papelera (f) – wastepaper basket; fichero (m) – filing cabinet; despensa (f) – storeroom; librería (f) – bookcase / bookshop.

English section:
headset – auriculares (mpl); audífonos (mpl); microphone – micrófono (m); chalk – tiza (f); sink – fregadero (m); curtain – cortina (f); blind – persiana (f).

Vamos a escuchar

Basic advice on how students should prepare for listening activities. For practice, they should pay 100% attention, use the pictures to guide them, and study the example in order to work out what the teacher is saying to Ramón, Paquita and Mohammed.

Answers: *Ramón – 5, 3; Paquita – 1, 6; Mohammed – 4, 2.*

RAMÓN	
PROFESOR:	¡Ramón!
RAMÓN:	¿Sí?
PROFESOR:	Pon el libro en la mesa, por favor. Y saca tu cuaderno.

PAQUITA	
PROFESORA:	Paquita, ¿no tienes una hoja de papel?
PAQUITA:	No.
PROFESORA:	Toma. ¡A estudiar!
PAQUITA:	Ana, ¿tienes un sacapuntas?
ANA:	¿No tienes tú? Toma.

MOHAMMED	
MOHAMMED:	Curro, ¿tienes una regla?
CURRO:	Sí. Hay una allí en mi mochila.
MOHAMMED:	Vale.
CURRO:	Oye, cierra la puerta por favor. Hace frío aquí.
MOHAMMED:	Ya voy.

Cómo aprender palabras

Three tips to help students learn new words in Spanish, especially if they are finding them difficult.

a Write out the Spanish and English words on separate pieces of paper, then spread them all out and match them up correctly (e.g. *un hermano* = brother)

b Divide the words in two and write each part on a separate piece of paper, then spread them out and pair up the correct parts (e.g. *un cuad* + *erno* = *cuaderno*).

c With a partner, select the words you want to learn. Partner **A** says the beginning of the word and Partner **B** completes it. (e.g. *saca* and *puntas*). After a while, they could change roles.

STUDENT'S BOOK, page 51

Práctica: lengua

Some summative grammar practice tasks based on the grammar items encountered in the first five units. Before tackling this page, you may wish to remind students where each point was first presented and also refer them to the grammar summary at the back of the Student's Book.

1 ◗ Students fill in the correct form of the adjective in the zoo-keeper's replies to the visitors' queries.

Answers: *1 – verde; 2 – negra; 3 – roja; 4 – gracioso, agresiva; 5 – marrón; 6 – perezosa; 7 – morada, tímida; 8 – inteligente.*

2 ◗ **a** Practice of the definite article.

Answers: *los gatos; el perro de mi tío; las personas agresivas; las discotecas; la clase de español; los sábados; el cine; el instituto; los deberes; el negro.*

b Practice of *gustar*. Students use the picture cues to write a sentence for each of the words in Activity 2a, using the correct part of *gustar*.

Answers: *Me gustan los gatos; No me gusta el perro de mi tío; No me gustan las personas agresivas; Me gustan las discotecas; Me gusta la clase de español; Me gustan los sábados; No me gusta el cine; Me gusta el instituto; No me gustan los deberes; No me gusta el negro.*

3 ◗ A sentence-matching activity on the subject of Sra. Velasco's family.

Answers: *1 – c; 2 – g; 3 – a; 4 – e; 5 – b; 6 – d; 7 – f; 8 – h.*

4 ♣ Students pick the correct adjectives to complete a gapped text.

Answers: *1 – alto; 2 – baja; 3 – negro; 4 – pelirroja; 5 – verdes; 6 – mi; 7 – sus; 8 – tu.*

5 ♣ Practice of putting singular sentences into the plural.

Answers: *1 – No hay sillas en los pasillos; 2 – Las agendas no tienen lápices; 3 – No hay proyectores en las salas; 4 – Las mesas no tienen lámparas; 5 – Los tablones no tienen rotuladores; 6 – Las carpetas son azules, en vez de naranjas; 7 – ¡Los directores son exigentes! ¡A trabajar!*

6 ♣ Students put the infinitives into the correct forms in the conversation.

Answers: *me llamo; somos; tenéis; son; tengo; tienes; tiene; son; es; se llama; es.*

Objectives
Students learn – to say where they live and ask others

Key language
¿dónde vives / vive?   *el centro*
vivo / vive en …   *un barrio*
una ciudad   *las afueras*
una ciudad grande   *el campo*
un pueblo   *cerca de …*

Skills / Strategies
Students learn – how to attract someone's attention

ICT opportunities
Students can   – design a poster with a decorative border and
caption and a space to add a photograph or
postcard (Student's Book, Activity 3)
– present the results of their class survey as a
graph (Worksheet 6.1, Activity 2b)

Ways in
Places to live – OHT 6A; photographs on page 52 in Student's
Book; picture story in Student's Book; wall map of
Spain; poster, postcards, slides, photographs,
leaflets and brochures to give an idea of the variety
of landscape in Spain in general, and Seville and
Andalucía in particular

Assessment opportunities
AT1,1   Worksheet 6.1, Activity 1: students identify where the
people live.
AT2,2   Worksheet 6.1, Activity 2a: students state where they live
during the class survey.
AT3,2   Worksheet 6.2, Activity 1: students match up the speech
bubbles with the correct people.
AT4,2   Student's Book, Activity 3: students write about five places
on the map.
AT4,2/3   Worksheet 6.2, Activity 2: students write speech bubbles
for the characters they create.

STUDENT'S BOOK, pages 52–53

1 **¿Dónde vives?**

Picture story

b Isabel and Pilar are looking at the map of Seville when
José Luis arrives with his cousin and a friend. The friends
all say where they live.

◐ Students respond to the statements by answering *sí*
or *no*.

Answers: *1 – no; 2 – sí; 3 – sí; 4 – no; 5 – no; 6 – no.*

b ♣ Students correct the incorrect statements in
Activity 1a.

Answers: *1 – José Luis vive en un barrio en el centro;*
4 – Pepa vive en un barrio en las afueras;
5 – Guillermo vive en el campo cerca de Ronda;
6 – Merche vive en Ronda.

ISABEL:	¡Uf! Sevilla es una ciudad grande, ¿no?
PILAR:	José Luis – tengo aquí el plano de Sevilla.
JÓSE LUIS:	Mi prima Merche … y mi amigo Guillermo.
ISABEL:	José Luis, ¿dónde vives?
JÓSE LUIS:	Vivo en El Arenal, un barrio en el centro de Sevilla.
ISABEL:	Y tú, Pepa, ¿dónde vives?
PEPA:	Vivo en San Jerónimo – un barrio en las afueras.
ISABEL:	¿Dónde vives, Carlos?
CARLOS:	Vivo en Camas, un pueblo en las afueras.
PILAR:	Merche, ¿dónde vives?
MERCHE:	Vivo en Ronda, una ciudad.
PILAR:	Y tú, Guillermo, ¿vives en Ronda?
GUILLERMO:	No. Vivo en el campo, cerca de Ronda.

2 🗨 **¡Imagina!**

A pairwork activity. In secret, Partner **A** imagines living in
one of the *barrios* on the map of Seville or in a town or
village on the map of Andalucía. Partner **B** has to find out
which it is by asking questions, but Partner **A** can answer
only *sí* or *no*.

3 **¿Qué tipo de ciudad es?**

Reading and writing practice using the photos on p.52–53
and the maps which help to give a flavour of Andalucía.
Following the example given, students choose five places
(areas, towns or cities) from the maps and describe each one.

SUPPORT MATERIALS

OHT 6A Vivo en …

A map depicting parts of a town and the surrounding area.
This can be used to present the key language of the unit.
Figures can be placed in turn on different locations on the
map, along with the appropriate language shown below
the map.

Worksheet 6.1 Oye, ¿dónde vives?

1 💿 **En la clase de Isabel**

Isabel is conducting a survey of where the students in her
class live. Note that she uses the phrases *Oye* and *Díme* as
well as the students' names to attract their attention.

Students shade in or mark with a cross the squares which
correspond to each student's reply.

Answers:

	Ana	Jaime	Marta	Pepe	Carmen	Gari
un barrio en el centro	X				X	
un barrio en las afueras						X
un pueblo cercano		X		X		
una ciudad cercana						
el campo			X			

ISABEL:	¡Ana! Oye, ¿dónde vives?
ANA:	Vivo en un barrio en el centro.
ISABEL:	¿En el centro? Vale, gracias.
ISABEL:	Jaime, ¿dónde vives?
JAIME:	Vivo en Tomares.
ISABEL:	¿Es un pueblo?
JAIME:	Sí, un pueblo cercano.
ISABEL:	¡Marta! … ¡Marta!
MARTA:	¿Sí?
ISABEL:	¿Dónde vives?
MARTA:	Vivo en el campo.
ISABEL:	¿En el campo? Vale, gracias.
PEPE:	Hola, Isabel.
ISABEL:	Oye Pepe, ¿dónde vives?
PEPE:	Vivo en Carmona.
ISABEL:	¿Es un pueblo?
PEPE:	Sí, es un pueblo que está cerca de Sevilla.
ISABEL:	Dime, Carmen, ¿dónde vives?
CARMEN:	En Sevilla.
ISABEL:	¿En el centro?
CARMEN:	Sí – vivo en la Macarena. Es un barrio del centro.
ISABEL:	Gari, ¿dónde vives?
GARI:	Vivo en un barrio de las afueras.
ISABEL:	Un barrio de las afueras – vale, gracias.

6A

2 Una encuesta

a Students can now carry out a survey of where people live in their own class. Encourage them to use *Oye* and *Díme* as they interview their friends. They should shade in or mark with a cross the appropriate squares.

b Students fill in the totals from their survey in Activity 2a, and could present the results as a bar graph, possibly on the computer.

Worksheet 6.2 Tecnópolis

1 ¿Quién habla?

○ Students match the speech bubbles a–f with the numbered figures in the map appearing on the computer screen, using the key for support.

♣ Students could invent names for the three remaining figures and write similar speech bubbles for them.

Answers: ○ *a – 3; b – 9; c – 1; d – 7; e – 4; f – 5.*

♣ **Suggested answers:**

1 – Me llamo … y vivo en un barrio en el centro;
2 – Me llamo … y vivo en un barrio en las afueras;
3 – Me llamo … y vivo en un pueblo cerca (de Tecnópolis) con mi padre.

---

2 Mi tecnociudad

Students design their own technocity. This could be done on computer, using drawing or paintbrush software to create figures and speech bubbles, or by importing clip-art figures. It could equally be done by hand if students have artistic talent.

Homework opportunity

Since this unit focuses on Seville and the south of Spain, you might like to give students the task of finding out more information about these places. Perhaps in consultation with your school librarian, you could produce a list of suitable materials that students could consult. A task such as finding the names of a few famous places, sights, monuments, etc. might encourage students to find out more about the country whose language they are learning.

Extra

If you have maps of Seville and Andalucía, display them on the wall and ask students to find certain places on them. Give them the first and last letters of districts in the city, or small and large towns in the area to help them to focus on some of the more important ones. You could also build up a class library of resources, such as maps, booklets, leaflets, guide books, posters and postcards, obtained commercially, from the Spanish National Tourist Office in London, or direct from the Tourist Office in Seville. Students could help to mount a display and might enjoy writing titles and captions.

Objectives

Students learn – to describe where they live
- the points of the compass

Key language

¿dónde está?
está en …
el norte / el sur   Gales
el este / el oeste   Irlanda del Norte
el noreste / el sureste   Irlanda del Sur
el noroeste / el suroeste   España
las Islas Británicas   en la sierra
Escocia   en la costa
junto al río   en el centro de …

Skills / Strategies

Students learn – to give more detailed information about a
particular area, and to ask and answer
questions on this topic

ICT opportunities

Students can – design leaflets and posters to advertise the
town or area they live in, using different fonts,
colours, point sizes, dropped capitals, bullets,
Word Art, etc.

Ways in

Points of the compass – Student's Book, Activity 1
The British Isles – wall map of the British Isles; Student's
Book, Activity 1
Spain – wall map of Spain; Student's Book,
Activity 2

Assessment opportunities

AT2,2 Student's Book, Activity 3 ◐: students answer as many
questions as they can in a minute.

AT2,3 Student's Book, Activity 3 ♣: students play the roles of
the people featured in the preceding activity.

AT3,2 Student's Book, Activity 2 ◐: students match the pictures
with the phrases.

AT4,2 Student's Book, Activity 2 ♣: students answer the
questions.

STUDENT'S BOOK, pages 54–55

1 **Las Islas Británicas**

Presentation of the countries of the British Isles and the
points of the compass.

a Students write down the numbers of the speech bubbles
in the order they hear the statements.

Answers: 3; 5; 1; 4; 2.

VOZ ESPAÑOLA:	¿Dónde vives?
ACENTO GALÉS:	Vivo en Gales, en el norte.
VOZ ESPAÑOLA:	¿Dónde vives?
ACENTO INGLÉS (DEL SUR):	Vivo en Inglaterra, en el sur.
VOZ ESPAÑOLA:	¿Dónde vives?
ACENTO IRLANDÉS (DEL SUR):	Vivo en Irlanda del Sur, en el sur.
VOZ ESPAÑOLA:	¿Dónde vives?
ACENTO ESCOCÉS:	Vivo en Escocia, en el este.
VOZ ESPAÑOLA:	¿Dónde vives?
ACENTO IRLANDÉS (DEL NORTE):	Vivo en Irlanda del Norte, en el oeste.

b Students draw a compass like the one shown, and add the
names of all the points of the compass in the correct places.

Answers:

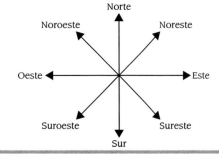

Norte
Noroeste   Noreste
Oeste   Este
Suroeste   Sureste
Sur

2 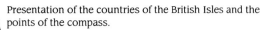 **¡Tu geografía está fatal!**

Picture story

The friends are discussing the location of Southport and
Seville. Tomás appears to miss Southport, and José Luis
shows an interest in Isabel.

◐ Students match up the phrases with the pictograms.

♣ Students write brief answers to the questions.

Answers: ◐ 1 – c; 2 – e; 3 – d; 4 – a; 5 – b.

♣ 1 – Está en el norte; 2 – Está en el sur;
3 – Se llamo el (río) Guadalquivir.
4 – Está en la costa; 5 – Está en el noroeste.

PEPA:	Isabel – en Inglaterra, vives en Liverpool, ¿no?
ISABEL:	Vivo cerca, en Southport. Está en la costa.
JOSÉ LUIS:	¿Dónde está exactamente – cerca de Londres?
ISABEL:	¡José Luis! Londres está en el sur …
PILAR:	¡… y Liverpool está en el norte!
CARLOS:	¿Está cerca de la sierra del Lake District?
TOMÁS:	Mm … sí.
CARLOS:	Liverpool está junto al río Mersey, ¿no?
TOMÁS:	Sí.
PEPA:	Sevilla está junto al río Guadalquivir.
TOMÁS:	Sí, pero Southport es fenomenal – y Sevilla …
ISABEL:	Oye, Tomás – ¡qué pesado eres!
CARMINA:	¡Pilar!
JOSÉ LUIS:	Isabel, tienes mi número de teléfono, ¿no?

3 **España**

Pairwork activity practising points of the compass, and
reinforcing some basic Spanish geography.

◐ Students use the map of Spain on p.55 to ask each
other where exactly the towns mentioned are.

♣ Partner **A** plays the part of one of the Spanish
youngsters pictured in Activity 2 and Partner **B** asks where
the person lives and where exactly that is in Spain.

SUPPORT MATERIALS

Worksheet 6.3 La geografía de España

1 **¿Qué tal tu geografía?**

This activity develops students' knowledge of Spain and
includes rivers and mountains as well as towns.

◐ Students read statements 1–8 and work out whether
they are true or false by consulting the map.

♣ Students read statements 9–16 and write the names
of the places (highlighted in bold) on the appropriate
dotted line on the map.

Answers: ◐ 1 – X; 2 – X; 3 – ✓; 4 – ✓; 5 – ✓; 6 – X; 7 – X;
8 – ✓.

Worksheet 6.4 Mi domicilio

1 Yo vivo en ...

Note that this sheet has removable English rubrics at the bottom.

 A listening activity offering more practice at a basic level for less able students. The activity entails listening to a selection of people saying where they live, and picking the appropriate symbols.

Answers: *a – 3; b – 1; c – 1; d – 2.*

a	ENTREVISTADOR:	Inés, ¿dónde vives?
	INÉS:	Vivo en el este de España.
	ENTREVISTADOR:	¿En el este?
	INÉS:	Sí.
b	ENTREVISTADOR:	Y, ¿dónde vives exactamente?
	INÉS:	Vivo en un pueblo junto al río Ebro.
	ENTREVISTADOR:	¿Junto al río? ¡Qué bien!
c	ENTREVISTADOR:	Y tú, Martín, ¿dónde vives?
	MARTÍN:	Vivo en el noroeste de España.
	ENTREVISTADOR:	Vives en el noroeste, en Galicia.
	MARTÍN:	Sí.
d	ENTREVISTADOR:	¿Vives en una ciudad grande?
	MARTÍN:	No, no me gustan las ciudades grandes. Vivo en un pueblo.
	ENTREVISTADOR:	Prefieres vivir en un pueblo.
	MARTÍN:	Sí.

2 El mapa

a An activity checking comprehension of various sentences giving information about the map of Spain on p.55 of the Student's Book.

Answers: *1 – h; 2 – d; 3 – b; 4 – f; 5 – a; 6 – g.*
(Surplus = c and e)

b Students complete the sentences giving the locations of Madrid, Seville and Barcelona.

Worksheet 6.5 El Hierro

1 La isla

This activity extends students' abilities to talk about where people live and introduces new vocabulary by means of a radio interview with Amaya, a girl who lives on the island of El Hierro. Students listen carefully in order to fill in the missing words. You may prefer to play the recording in sections rather than all in one go. As a follow-up, students could practise reading the interview in pairs.

Answers: *1 – España; 2 – cerca; 3 – campo; 4 – ciudades;*
5 – capital; 6 – qué; 7 – Hay.

PRESENTADOR:	¡Bienvenidos a todos! Hoy vamos a hablar can Amaya. Amaya, no vives en **España**, ¿verdad?
AMAYA:	No, vivo en las Islas Canarias, cerca de África.
PRESENTADOR:	¿Vives en la isla de Tenerife?
AMAYA:	No – vivo en una isla que se llama Hierro – está **cerca** de Gomera en el oeste.
PRESENTADOR:	¿Dónde vives exactamente?
AMAYA:	Bueno, vivo en el **campo**, en un valle, cerca de Frontera.
PRESENTADOR:	¿Hay **ciudades** en la isla?
AMAYA:	Bueno, hay ocho pueblos y la **capital** de Valverde, en el noreste.
PRESENTADOR:	¿Y **qué** más hay en la isla?
AMAYA:	Hay playas, bosques, y una montaña de 1500 metros de altura.
PRESENTADOR:	¿**Hay** un volcán, como en la isla de Tenerife?
AMAYA:	Sí hay volcanes – pero no hay peligro.
PRESENTADOR:	Bueno, muchas gracias, Amaya. Y si quieres escribir a Amaya, llama por teléfono al …

2 Diccionario

 Students should use the vocabulary at the back of the Student's Book or a dictionary to find out the meaning of the words marked with an asterisk in the dialogue in Activity 1. They then write the correct word under each pictogram, together with *un* or *una*, as in the example.

Answers: *1 – un volcán; 2 – una isla; 3 – una montaña;*
4 – un bosque; 5 – un valle; 6 – una playa.

3 Gomera

 An opportunity for creative oral work based on the area in which the students live, or on the island of Gomera. Using the interview with Amaya for support, students should prepare a similar interview with their partners and record it on tape.

Extra

Students can extend the language they know to add further captions to the display they started with Unit 6A including, for example, the points of the compass, but it might also be possible to display a map of your local town or area and add suitable labels in Spanish (e.g., *Vivo en un barrio de Londres que se llama Wood Green, Vivo en Bristol junto a un río, Whitby está en el noreste de Inglaterra en la costa …*)

Objectives
Students learn – to talk about what there is in their area

Key language
¿qué hay en tu barrio?	*un parque*
hay / no hay …	*un colegio*
… donde comer	*una discoteca*
… donde comprar	*una iglesia*
… lugares públicos	*un bar*
un supermercado	*un hotel*
una tienda	*un restaurante*
una panadería	*una cafetería*
un videoclub	*una piscina*
un cine	*un polideportivo*
un instituto	

Skills / Strategies
Students learn – how to write a letter using a model

ICT opportunities
Students can – write a letter about their town or area with computer-generated illustrations

Ways in
Places – Student's Book, page 56

Assessment opportunities
AT1,2 Student's Book, Activity 1 ◐: students identify the places.

AT1,2 Student's Book, Activity 1 ◑: students answer questions.

AT2,2 Student's Book, Activity 2 ◐: a rapid-fire pairwork activity. Circulate and listen to the pairs doing the activity.

AT2,3 Student's Book, Activity 2 ◑: true or false? Circulate and listen to the pairs doing the activity.

AT3,3 Student's Book, Activity 3: students read a letter.

AT4,3/4 Student's Book, Activity 4: students write about their own towns.

STUDENT'S BOOK, pages 56–57

1 En la calle
Presentation of places to be found near where people live. Students should follow the conversation between Isabel, Pilar and friends as each place is mentioned in the order presented in the Student's Book.

◐ Students identify small photo extracts from the larger photographs on the opposite page and write down the correct word for each one.

◑ Students work out whether each of the four statements is correct or not.

Answers: ◐ *a – 2; b – 8; c – 16; d – 3; e – 7; f – 4.*

◑ *1 – sí; 2 – no; 3 – sí; 4 – sí.*

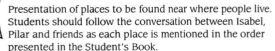

PEPA:	¿Qué hay en tu barrio, Pilar?
PILAR:	Hay mucho … Hay donde comprar … un supermercado, una tienda, una panadería, un videoclub…
	… Hay lugares públicos – un cine, un instituto, un parque, un colegio, una discoteca, una iglesia …
	… Hay donde comer … un bar, un hotel, un restaurante, una cafetería …
PEPA:	En tu barrio, ¿hay una piscina o un polideportivo?
PILAR:	En mi barrio, no.
TOMÁS:	¿Qué hay en tu barrio, Pepa?
PEPA:	No hay mucho: un bar, un parque, una tienda, una cafetería …
JOSÉ LUIS:	Una cafetería – ¡buena idea! Ven, Isabel …

2 ¡Al ataque!

◐ Quickfire pairwork. Partner **A** says a number and Partner **B** identifies the place on p.56 correctly. They can try to name them all within one minute, or time each other to see who is the fastest.

◐ More of a memory test to challenge students. Partner **A** gives a number and names a place. Without looking at the book, Partner **B** either says *¡verdad!* if it is true or *¡mentira!* if it is false. They could each try to get as many right as possible in one minute.

3 Una entrevista con Francisca
A reading and writing activity in which pictures appear in place of certain key words in a letter.

◐ Students complete the letter by substituting the correct word for each picture from the box underneath.

◑ By studying the text carefully students should work out which of the seven questions Francisca answers in her letter. Fast finishers can ask each other the seven questions.

Answers: ◐ *1 – pueblo; 2 – río; 3 – supermercados; 4 – cafeterías; 5 – hoteles; 6 – piscina; 7 – polideportivo.*

◑ *1 – sí; 2 – sí; 3 – sí; 4 – sí. 5 – no; 6 – sí; 7 – no.*

4 ¿Qué hay en tu ciudad?
An opportunity for students to write about their town or area in the form of a letter. Using Francisca's letter as an example they could simply start it with *¡Hola!* Note that students may need to refer to places in the plural, in which case you should draw their attention to Acción: lengua 6, p.59. If you wish to develop this more fully, the plurals are also dealt with in the grammar summary, section 4, p.148. The letter could be word-processed and illustrated with computer-generated clip-art or imported photos and artwork. Students could also add details of where they live and what amenities there are in the various neighbourhoods, onto the class database.

SUPPORT MATERIALS

Worksheet 6.6 Todo bajo el sol
Una canción
a b The song practises much of the language of the unit. By consulting the map on Worksheet 6.3, students will be able to fill in the missing words. The answers can be checked as they hear the song for the first time. They can then sing along as soon as they have the confidence to do so.

Answers: *1 – del Sol, de la Luz; 2 – Ebro; 3 – sur, Sierra.*

1 La Costa Cantábrica está en el norte
   La Costa **del Sol** está en el sur
   La Costa Brava está en el noreste
   Y la Costa **de la Luz** – en el suroeste.
   Norte, sur, este, oeste,
   Cada día parece una fiesta,
   ¡España tiene todo bajo el sol!

2 El río Duero está en el norte
   El Guadalquivir está en el sur
   El río **Ebro** en el noreste
   El río Tajo – en el oeste.
   Norte, sur, este, oeste
   Cada día parece una fiesta
   ¡España tiene todo bajo el sol!

3 ¿Los Picos de Europa? En el norte,
   La Sierra Nevada está en el **sur**
   ¿Los Pirineos? En el noreste,
   ¿La **Sierra** de Ronda? En el suroeste.
   Ciudades, ríos, costas, sierras
   Un país de muchas tierras –
   ¡España tiene todo bajo el sol!

c Students now write an extra verse about another city in Spain.

Worksheet 6.7 Tenerife

Tenerife ⬤

A reading activity. Students read information relating to the map and fill in a gapped text with the appropriate information using the picture cues.

Answers: *1 – ciudad; 2 – norte; 3 – bares; 4 – restaurantes; 5 – hoteles; 6 – parques; 7 – iglesias; 8 – piscina; 9 – polideportivo; 10 – tiendas.*

Objectives
Students learn – to talk about the weather and seasons

Key language
¿qué tiempo hace (en ...)
¿hace buen tiempo?
(sí,) hace buen tiempo
(no,) hace mal tiempo
el clima es ...
casi tropical
hace (mucho) calor
hace calor
hace frío
hace sol
hace viento
hay niebla
hay nieve
hay tormentas
llueve (mucho)

Skills / Strategies
Students learn – to understand phone-call structures and language

ICT opportunities
Students can – prepare a computer weather map and / or forecast

Ways in
Places – map on page 58; Student's Book Activity 1

Assessment opportunities
AT1,3 Worksheet 6.9, Activity 1: recorded weather forecast.
AT2,2/3 Worksheet 6.8: information-gap activity.
AT3,2 Worksheet 6.9, Activity 2: students match the places to the weather.
AT4,3 Worksheet 6.9, Activity 3: students write brief weather reports.

STUDENT'S BOOK, page 58

1 **¿Qué tiempo hace?**

a Presentation of the weather vocabulary items. Students should follow the conversation between Maite and Tomás and follow the visuals in the Student's Book on p.58 as they are mentioned.

b Students listen again and work out what the weather is like in Mexico and England in July and December respectively.

Answers: *Gran Bretaña en julio – 1, 6, 10. En diciembre – 5, 9, 4.*
México en julio – 3, 10. En diciembre – 1, 2, 8.

	NARRATOR:	Tomás habla por teléfono con su prima Maite, que vive en México.
a	MAITE:	¿Qué tiempo hace en Sevilla? ¿Hace buen tiempo?
	TOMÁS:	Sí, hace sol ... y hace calor.
	MAITE:	Pero en Gran Bretaña, hace mal tiempo, ¿no? Hace frío ... Hace viento ... Hay tormentas ... Hay niebla ... Hay nieve ... ¡y llueve mucho!
	TOMÁS:	¡No es verdad!
b	MAITE:	¿Qué tiempo hace en Gran Bretaña en julio?
	TOMÁS:	Hace buen tiempo ...
	MAITE:	¿Buen tiempo?
	TOMÁS:	Sí, en general. Pero a veces, hace viento.
	MAITE:	Llueve, ¿no?
	TOMÁS:	Sí, llueve.
	TOMÁS:	¿Qué tiempo hace en la ciudad de México en julio?
	MAITE:	Aquí en julio, hace calor. Mucho calor.
	TOMÁS:	El clima es casi tropical, ¿no?
	MAITE:	En la capital, sí. Y llueve mucho.
	MAITE:	¿Qué tiempo hace en Gran Bretaña en diciembre? Hace frío, ¿no?
	TOMÁS:	Sí. Hace frío, y hay nieve en la sierra. Hace mal tiempo. Y allí en México, ¿qué tiempo hace en diciembre?
	MAITE:	Hace buen tiempo, y hace sol.
	TOMÁS:	¡Qué bien!
	MAITE:	Pero a veces, hay niebla.

2 **España**

a This activity involves reading sentences about the weather in certain cities and identifying which city is being described in each by looking at the weather map.

Answers: *1 – Málaga; 2 – Santiago; 3 – Barcelona;*
4 – Valencia; 5 – Murcia; 6 – Madrid.

b Finally, students write sentences to describe the weather in the remaining two cities.

Answers: *Aquí en Bilbao, hay niebla.*
En Cáceres, hace mal tiempo y hay tormentas.

SUPPORT MATERIALS

Worksheet 6.8 ¿Qué tiempo hace?
A pairwork activity sheet where students ask each other questions based on the information contained in the grids. They must fill in the missing weather conditions for different locations.

Worksheet 6.9 El pronóstico

1 **México**

○ Students listen to radio weather forecasts for four Mexican cities and note down the appropriate city for the weather conditions pictured on the worksheet.

● Students underline the correct alternatives in the sentences.

Answers: ○ *1 – M, C; 2 – M; 3 – T, C; 4 – G; 5 – T; 6 – G; 7 – T; 8 – G; 9 – M; 10 – C.*

● *1 – llueve; 2 – 11; 3 – tropical; 4 – 22*

PRESENTADOR 1:	¿Qué tiempo hace hoy en las regiones? Vamos primero a Tijuana en el norte del país. ¿Qué tiempo hace en Tijuana?
PRESENTADOR 2:	¡Buenos días! Aquí en Tijuana hace viento. Hace sol también.
PRESENTADOR 1:	¿Llueve?
PRESENTADOR 2:	¡Hombre, no! ¡Esto es el desierto! Aquí no llueve mucho normalmente.
PRESENTADOR 1:	Buen tiempo, sol y viento entonces en Tijuana. Gracias.

PRESENTADOR 1:	Luego vamos a Guadalajara. ¿Qué tiempo hace hoy en Guadalajara?
PRESENTADOR 3:	Aquí, hace mal tiempo.
PRESENTADOR 1:	¿Mal tiempo?
PRESENTADOR 3:	Sí, hace frío. Sólo tenemos temperaturas de once grados.
PRESENTADOR 1:	No es mucho. ¿Y qué tal en la sierra?
PRESENTADOR 3:	En la sierra, hay nieve.
PRESENTADOR 1:	¿Nieve? ¡Qué horror!
PRESENTADOR 1:	Y ahora, Mérida. ¡Buenos días, Mérida!
PRESENTADOR 4:	¡Hola, allí en la capital! Aquí hace calor, mucho calor.
PRESENTADOR 1:	¡Qué bien!
PRESENTADOR 4:	Bueno, llueve y hay tormentas también. Aquí el clima es tropical.
PRESENTADOR 1:	¡Ah, sí, es verdad! Gracias, Mérida.
PRESENTADOR 1:	Y aquí en la capital, hay niebla, como siempre. Hace buen tiempo, pero hay niebla. Hace calor también – hasta veintidós grados por la tarde. Y con este pronóstico del tiempo, terminamos nuestro programa del noticias ...

2 Hoy

Students read some weather information and select the places where various weather conditions are to be found.

Answers: *1 – a, c; 2 – e, f; 3 – f; 4 – b.*

3 ¡Ideal!

Students describe the ideal weather conditions for a variety of activities. Any weather conditions should be accepted as long as students can justify their choice and have expressed it correctly.

Acción: lengua 6, page 59
Using *(no) hay / hace* with weather expressions; More plurals

Students learn to use the verb forms *(no) hay* and *hace* with weather expressions, and there is also a brief item presenting some more plural forms.

1 ◆ A simple activity which entails using cues to say what there is or isn't in a village.

♣ An activity which practises using or omitting the indefinite article as necessary with *hay* and *no hay*.

Answers: ◆ *Hay un supermercado; Hay dos o tres tiendas; No hay jardines; Hay un colegio; Hay iglesias; No hay polideportivo; Hay una piscina; No hay discoteca.*

♣ *una tienda; una iglesia; un colegio; un videoclub; cine; jardines; polideportivo; tiendas; un centro comercial.*

2 ◆ ♣ A gap-fill activity in which students fill in the correct form of *hay* or *hace.*

Answers: *1 – hace; 2 – hace; 3 – hay; 4 – hace; 5 – hace; 6 – hace; 7 – hay.*

More plural endings

This brief item presents further practice of the plural forms. Students can refer to the grammar summary, section 4, p.148 for additional support if necessary.

3 ◆ Students put the underlined words into the plural.

♣ Students translate the short text into Spanish.

Answers: ◆ *tiendas, hoteles, barrios, club(e)s, calles, mercados, jardines, museos, pub(e)s, instalaciones, chabolas.*

♣ *Hay monos, osos, tigres, leones, leopardos, elefantes, focas, tiburones, delfines, pero no hay balenas.*

Objectives

Students learn – to describe where they live
                 – to say where they would like to live
                 – to give their opinion and ask others

Key language

¿qué te parece?	feo
me parece …	ruidoso
moderno	aburrido
turístico	sucio
bonito	¡de acuerdo!
tranquilo	¡qué va!
divertido	no sé
limpio	¿dónde te gustaría vivir?
antiguo	me gustaría vivir en …
industrial	a (X) le gustaría vivir en …

Skills / Strategies

Students learn – to express their opinions, to agree and to disagree
                 – to give their preferences
                 – to cope with redundant language in listening comprehension

ICT opportunities

Students can – design a wordsearch on computer for their friends to solve

Ways in

Adjectives – OHT 7A; Student's Book, Activity 1: photos and recording

Assessment opportunities

AT1,2/3   Worksheet 7.1, Activity 1: students match the pictures to the descriptions.

AT2,2   Worksheet 7.3, Activity 2: target some students as they interview each other.

AT3,2   Student's Book, Activity 4: students match photos to texts.

AT4,2/3   Student's Book, Activity 5: students write their opinions about where they would like to live.

STUDENT'S BOOK, pages 60–61

1 **Sevilla**

Presentation of adjectives describing towns. Isabel uses positive ones, but Tomás uses negative ones. The new vocabulary can also be introduced using OHT 7A on which the adjectives are presented as contrasting pairs. The recording gives students time to relate the adjective to the photo.

〇 Students work out who gives each opinion – Tomás or Isabel.

✚ An opportunity for students to give their own opinions about certain places. You can point out that there are no right or wrong answers here, only personal opinions.

Answers: **〇** 1 – Tomás; 2 – Isabel; 3 – Tomás; 4 – Tomás; 5 – Isabel.

PILAR:	¡Sevilla es fenomenal!
ISABEL:	¡De acuerdo! El centro me parece … moderno … turístico … bonito … tranquilo … divertido … limpio.
TOMÁS:	¡Qué va! Es … antiguo … industrial … feo … ruidoso … aburrido … sucio.

2 **¿De acuerdo? ¡Qué va!**

A speaking activity which reinforces the key vocabulary and enables students to exchange simple opinions.

〇 Partner **A** says one of the adjectives and Partner **B** has to say the opposite.

✚ Partner **A** asks what Partner **B** thinks about local towns and villages. After Partner **B** responds, Partner **A** can agree using the phrase ¡de acuerdo! or disagree by saying ¡qué va! and then saying the opposite.

3 **¿Dónde te gustaría vivir?**

This activity develops students' ability to say what they want (quiero) into saying what they would like (me gustaría). The singular of the conditional of gustar is presented for all students, and the point could be introduced with the aid of the food and drink flashcards. For example: ¿Te gustaría café? If you wish to exploit the verb in the present tense further, see the grammar summary, section 15, p.151.

In this listening activity, Teresa, Isabel and Tomás are considering which part of Seville they would prefer to live in, since they cannot stay permanently with Carmina's family.

a Students match up each statement with the appropriate person.

Answers: 1 – Isabel; 2 – Isabel; 3 – Tomás; 4 – Teresa.

b The four phrases are to be completed with the pronoun which goes with the appropriate part of gustaría.

Answers: 1 – te; 2 – me; 3 – te; 4 – le.

TERESA:	Isabel – ¿dónde te gustaría vivir en Sevilla?
ISABEL:	Aquí, con la tía Carmina.
TERESA:	No es posible, Isabel con el bebé …
ISABEL:	Bueno, me gustaría vivir en el centro, en un barrio antiguo, divertido …
TOMÁS:	Yo no.
TERESA:	¿Te gustaría un barrio moderno? ¿O un pueblo bonito en las afueras?
TOMÁS:	No.
TERESA:	Pero ¿dónde te gustaría vivir, Tomás?
ISABEL:	¡A Tomás le gustaría vivir en una ciudad aburrida como Southport!
TOMÁS:	¡Southport no es una ciudad aburrida!
CARMINA:	¿Y tú Teresa? – ¿dónde te gustaría vivir?
TERESA:	Con Michael …

4 **Quiero vivir …**

Reading activities which consolidate and extend students' knowledge of adjectives.

〇 Five short texts in which people mention where they would like to live. Students choose which photo goes with which text.

✚ In order to answer the questions on Amaya's letter, students will need to look up the adjectives marked with an asterisk in the vocabulary at the back of the Student's Book. Three are synonyms and two are antonyms of key adjectives used in the questions.

Answers: **〇** 1 – c; 2 – b; 3 – e; 4 – d; 5 – a.

              ✚ 1 – sí (antiguo = viejo); 2 – sí (bonita = preciosa);
              3 – sí (sucio = descuidado);
              4 – no (aburrido ≠ interesante);
              5 – no (tranquilo ≠ animado).

5 **¿Mi opinión?**

Using the texts in the previous activity as models, students can now write their own opinion about where they would like to live. You should point out that to describe a large town (*ciudad*) the ending of the adjective may have to change. If you wish to exploit it further at this stage, you could also refer back to Acción: lengua 4, p.37 and the grammar summary, section 6, p.148.

SUPPORT MATERIALS

OHT 7A ¿Cómo es?

Presentation of adjectives describing towns in contrasting pairs (*moderno - antiguo, turístico - industrial*, etc.)

Worksheet 7.1 Ibiza

Note that this worksheet has removable English rubrics at the bottom.

1 **La Isla**

○ A listening activity in which students sequence a series of visuals.

Answers:	**1** *La ciudad de Ibiza – b, d;* **2** *Sant Antoni Abad – a, e;* **3** *Santa Eulalia – f, g;* **4** *Punta Arabí – a, c;* **5** *Portinatx – b, f;* **6** *Cala Llonga – e, c.*

LA CIUDAD DE IBIZA
VOZ 1: Vives en la capital de la isla, ¿no?
VOZ 2: Sí.
VOZ 1: ¿Cómo es?
VOZ 2: Es antigua, muy antigua.
VOZ 1: ¿Te gusta vivir allí?
VOZ 2: Sí, es muy bonito.

SANT ANTONI ABAD
VOZ 3: Yo vivo en Sant Antoni, pero no me gusta mucho.
VOZ 1: ¿No? ¿Por qué?
VOZ 3: Es turístico, pero es ruidoso también.

SANTA EULALIA
VOZ 1: ¿Qué opinas de vivir en Santa Eulalia?
VOZ 4: Vivo junto al río. Allí, es tranquilo.
VOZ 1: Viene mucha gente. ¿Es sucia, la ciudad?
VOZ 4: No, mi barrio es muy limpio.

PUNTA AARABÍ
VOZ 5: Vivo en Punta Arabí, en el noreste de la isla.
VOZ 1: ¿Cómo es?
VOZ 5: Es muy turístico. Hay un mercado grande, y por eso es bastante sucio también.
VOZ 1: Turístico, pero sucio.
VOZ 5: Sí.

PORTINATX
VOZ 1: Tus abuelos viven en Portinatx, ¿no?
VOZ 2: Sí. Les visito cada semana. El pueblo es muy antiguo.
VOZ 1: ¿Les gusta vivir allí?
VOZ 2: Sí. En invierno, es muy tranquilo.

CALA LLONGA
VOZ 1: ¿Qué opinas de Cala Llonga?
VOZ 3: No me gusta nada. En verano, es ruidoso.
VOZ 1: Y sucio.
VOZ 3: Sí, ruidoso y sucio. Prefiero el norte de la isla.

2 **Mahón**

○ Students read a series of opinions and decide whether each is positive, negative, or both.

Answers:	*Positivo: a, c, e; Negativo: d, f; Positivo + Negativo: b.*

3 **Lo contrario**

○ Students modify sentences by changing the underlined words to reverse the sense of the sentence.

Answers:	*Felipe: Mi barrio es limpio y moderno;* *Paloma: Vivo en un pueblo bonito;* *Emilio: No me gusta mi barrio porque es tranquilo;* *Vanesa: Mi ciudad es muy aburrido y antiguo;* *Rosario: Vivo en el centro de una ciudad grande. Es muy pesado/aburrido.*

Worksheet 7.2 Opiniones

1 **¿Cómo es Mallorca?**

An activity to encourage a positive attitude to listening. Some Spanish teenagers are being asked what they think of the island of Mallorca. The interviews contain some redundant language and the aim is to encourage students to listen out for words they recognise without being overwhelmed by the quantity of Spanish they hear or any of the unnecessary words.

○ Students tick the boxes on the grid when they hear the words mentioned.

♣ Students try to identify cognates and note these down. More able students could try the activity without the support of the grid, and see how many words they can pick out altogether. It might be interesting for the students to see how many more words they can identify after the second hearing. This should encourage them to persevere. (It might also be worth pointing out 'false friends' such as *coche*, which doesn't mean 'coach'!)

Answers:	○			
	Abi	**David**	**Mireia**	**Joaquín**
aburrido	✓			
antiguo				✓
bonito		✓		
divertido			✓	
feo				✓
industrial				✓
limpio		✓		
moderno		✓		
ruidoso			✓	
sucio				
tranquilo	✓	✓		
turístico			✓	

Suggested answers:	♣ *tourists / turistas; capital / capital; apartments / apartamentos; contamination / contaminación; centre / centro; buses / autobuses; traffic / tráfico; music / música.*

ABI
ENTREVISTADOR: ¡Hola! ¿Cómo te llamas?
ABI: Me llamo Abi
ENTREVISTADOR: ¿Y cómo es la Isla de Mallorca?
ABI: Bueno – yo vivo en el norte de la isla. Aquí, es muy **aburrido** para los jóvenes porque no hay mucha diversión. Hay muchas atracciones turísticas, pero nada para los jóvenes. Es muy **tranquilo**. Prefiero vivir en la capital, en Palma.

DAVID

ENTREVISTADOR:	Y tú, ¿cómo te llamas?
DAVID:	Me llamo David, y vivo en Puerto de Alcudia, en el noreste de Mallorca.
ENTREVISTADOR:	¿Y cómo es?
DAVID:	Es muy **bonito**. Donde vivo, es **moderno** con muchos apartamentos nuevos y hoteles.
ENTREVISTADOR:	¿Te gusta, entonces?
DAVID:	Sí, me gusta mucho. Lo bueno es que es **limpio** – no hay contaminación. Y es muy **tranquilo** ...

MIREIA

ENTREVISTADOR:	¡Hola!
MIREIA:	Hola.
ENTREVISTADOR:	¿Cómo te llamas?
MIREIA:	Me llamo Mireia.
ENTREVISTADOR:	¿Y cómo es la Isla de Mallorca en tu opinión?
MIREIA:	Bueno, vivo aquí en la capital, Palma. Me gusta mucho vivir aquí porque es **divertido**.
ENTREVISTADOR:	¿Hay algo negativo?
MIREIA:	Sí – lo malo es que es **turístico**. Hay muchos coches, autobuses ... en el centro, con todo el tráfico, es muy **ruidoso**.

JOAQUÍN

ENTREVISTADOR:	Hola. ¿Cómo te llamas?
JOAQUÍN:	Soy Joaquín, y vivo aquí en Palma.
ENTREVISTADOR:	¿Te gusta?
JOAQUÍN:	No me gusta mucho. El centro es **antiguo** e interesante y hay mucha movida, pero en las afueras es **feo**. De noche hay mucho jaleo, gente que va a discotecas, mucha música ... Prefiero el pueblo donde viven mi tío y mi tía.
ENTREVISTADOR:	¿Por qué?
JOAQUÍN:	La zona donde vivo es **industrial**. Prefiero vivir en el campo.

2   ¿Y o pero?

a An activity to practise the appropriate use of *y* and *pero*. By reading each of the descriptions on the map, students should be able to work out whether the additional information adds to or contradicts what has gone before. They then insert the more suitable conjunction.

Answers: *1 – pero; 2 – pero; 3 – y, y; 4 – pero; 5 – y; 6 – pero; 7 – y.*

b With the help of a simple illustration of the area in which they live, students can describe some of their local towns and villages. Encourage them to consider the positive as well as the negative sides, and to use *y* and *pero* appropriately.

Worksheet 7.3 Tu pueblo o ciudad

1   Parejas

a Students join together the two halves of each of a series of split words, all on the theme of describing towns and villages.

Answers: *limpia; bonita; industrial; tranquila; antigua; aburrida.*

b Students decide if each word is positive or negative, then place words of opposite meanings in the spaces provided in the grid for Activity 2 – positive words on the left-hand side and negative underneath. Encourage students to use the words to write a short description of their home town or nearby town.

2   ¿Cómo es tu ciudad?

Students ask 10 of their classmates to give three opinions of their town, and put ticks against the three adjectives they have each chosen. They can then add up the total number of positive and negative comments to see what the general consensus is.

Objectives

Students learn – to talk about the good and bad points of where
they live

Key language

¿te gusta?	*porque …*
me gusta	*hay mucha movida*
me gusta mucho	*hay mucha diversión*
no me gusta	*hay mucha cultura*
no me gusta nada	*hay mucho tráfico*
no está mal	*hay mucho turismo*
lo bueno es que …	*tiene mucha historia*
lo malo es que …	*tengo muchos amigos*
¿por qué?	

Skills / Strategies

Students learn – to give balanced reasons, both positive and
negative. (Student's Book, Activities 2 and 3)

ICT opportunities

Students can – use desktop software to produce a page for a
Spanish class magazine, creating newspaper
style columns. (Student's Book, Activity 4)
– produce survey results as bar graphs or charts

Ways in

Likes and dislikes – Student's Book, Activity 1; cards with
smiley / sad faces on them.

Assessment opportunities

AT1,2/3 Student's Book, Activity 2: students match two
comments to each person.
AT2,2/3 Student's Book, Activity 3b: students interview each
other.
AT3,2/3 Worksheet 7.4, Activity 2: students identify the errors.
AT4,2/3 Student's Book, Activity 4: students write their opinions
about their own town or region.

STUDENT'S BOOK, pages 62–63

1 **¿Te gusta?**

Before tackling the presentation in the Student's Book, you
might like to introduce the key phrases *me gusta, no me
gusta* and *¿te gusta?,* first and to link them with *me gustaría*
which was presented in the previous objective. You could
also use OHT 7B to present the positive and negative
characteristics of towns with two smiley / sad faces drawn
on card, for example. The language of the previous objective
could be recycled and extended to emphasise the contrast
with the reality (*me gusta*) and the ideal (*me gustaría*).

In the Student's Book, the key language is presented
in numerical order. Photos 3, 4 and 5 illustrate the
comments made by José Luis, and photos 8, 9 and 10
illustrate the comments made by Carlos. Students have to
match the photos with the opinions of Pepa and Tomás as
expressed in statements 12 and 13.

Picture story

The friends say whether they like the area they live in
or not.

Answers: Pepa – 8 and 5; Tomás – 3, 4 and 10.

José Luis ☺ ; Carlos ☹ ; Tomás 😐 ;

Pepa 😐 .

ISABEL:	¿Te gusta tu barrio, José Luis?
JOSÉ LUIS:	Sí, me gusta … Hay mucha diversión … Hay mucha movida … Tengo muchos amigos.
PEPA:	Carlos, ¿te gusta tu pueblo?
CARLOS:	No, no me gusta. No hay mucha diversión … No hay mucha movida … No tengo muchos amigos.
ISABEL:	Pepa, ¿te gusta tu barrio?
PEPA:	Bueno – no está mal. No hay mucha diversión, pero tengo muchos amigos.
TOMÁS:	En Sevilla, hay mucha diversión y mucha movida, pero no tengo amigos …

2 **¿Qué te parece Londres?**

This activity looks at some of the reasons for liking and
disliking a place. Before tackling it you could present the
six contrasting pictures on OHT 7B and remind students of
the comments made by the youngsters in Seville in
Activity 1. The recording introduces the phrases *lo bueno*
and *lo malo,* and each person offers a good and a bad
point about London. These are listed in two columns in the
Student's Book: good points 1–5 on the left and bad points
6–10 on the right.

Students listen to the comments and link one positive
phrase and one negative phrase with each of the
characters.

Written follow-up. Students write a speech bubble for
each person based on the answers to the first part of the
activity and using the example as a model.

Answers: Pilar – 2 & 10; Isabel – 3 & 6; Carlos – 5 & 9;
José Luis – 1 & 7; Pepa – 4 & 8.

TOMÁS:	Pilar, ¿qué te parece Londres? ¿Te gusta?
PILAR:	Mm, lo bueno es que hay mucha movida, pero lo malo es que es sucio. ¿A ti te gusta Londres, no, Isabel?
ISABEL:	¡Claro! Lo bueno es que hay clubs y discotecas, pero lo malo es que es feo. ¡Prefiero Sevilla! ¿Y tú, Carlos? ¿Conoces Londres?
CARLOS:	Sí, para mí, lo bueno de Londres es que hay mucha cultura, pero lo malo, es que es ruidoso. ¿Qué opinas tú, José Luis?
JOSÉ LUIS:	Pues, igual. Lo bueno es que tiene mucha historia, pero, claro, lo malo es que hay mucho tráfico. Pepa, ¿tú conoces Londres?
PEPA:	Sí, a mí me encanta Londres. Lo bueno para mí, es que hay mucha diversión pero – y es natural – lo malo es que hay mucho turismo.
JOSÉ LUIS:	¿No te gusta porque hay mucho turismo? ¡Pero, tú estabas allí en plan turístico también!

3 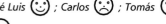 **La República Dominicana**

a A further listening activity practising the opinion-giving
structures and *lo bueno / malo es que …*

Students listen to the recording and look at the grid
containing cues, and work out who expresses each of the
opinions depicted.

Students listen again and read some slightly longer
quotations from the recording. Students work out the
identity of each speaker.

Answers: 1 – Alonso; 2 – Rafael; 3 – Bernardo;
4 – Alonso; 5 – Rafael; 6 – Bernardo; 7 – Rafael.

1 – Bernardo; 2 – Alonso; 3 – Bernardo;
4 – Rafael; 5 – Alonso; 6 – Rafael.

1	ENTREVISTADOR:	Y ¿dónde vives?
	ALONSO:	Vivo en el suroeste, en un pueblo. No me gusta mucho. Es feo.
2	ENTREVISTADOR:	¿Qué hay en tu ciudad?
	RAFAEL:	Hay muchos restaurantes, y un mercado, que es muy bonito.
3	ENTREVISTADOR:	¿Dónde vives en la isla?
	BERNARDO:	Vivo en la capital. Es una ciudad grande en el sur.
4	ENTREVISTADOR:	¿Te gusta vivir aquí?
	ALONSO:	Sí. Lo bueno es que es muy tranquilo.
	ENTREVISTADOR:	¿Y qué es lo malo?
	ALONSO:	Lo malo es que no hay mucha diversión.
5	ENTREVISTADOR:	¿Qué es lo malo de vivir aquí?
	RAFAEL:	Lo malo, es que no hay mucha movida, sobre todo por la noche. No hay muchos turistas. Es aburrido.
6	ENTREVISTADOR:	¿Qué hay en tu barrio?
	BERNARDO:	Es un barrio moderno y residencial. Es muy bonito, junto al río Ozama.
	ENTREVISTADOR:	¿Qué es lo bueno de vivir en tu ciudad?
	BERNARDO:	Lo bueno es que hay mucha cultura. Pero lo malo es el tráfico. ¡Es horroroso!
7	ENTREVISTADOR:	¿Qué es lo bueno de tu ciudad?
	RAFAEL:	Me gusta principalmente porque tengo muchos amigos allí. Y también porque está en la sierra, y por eso hace bastante frío por la noche, lo que es muy agradable.

b This pairwork activity practises the language used in talking about the area in which one lives by asking students to adopt the roles of speakers from the preceding activity, and to have a dialogue using the same kind of language and structures.

4 En mi opinión

Students write their opinions about their own town or region. The key phrases are given in the language support box, but vocabulary from the previous objective could also be used.

SUPPORT MATERIALS

OHT 7B Lo bueno y lo malo

This OHT offers opportunities for discusssing the good and bad points of things via the symbols presented on it.

Worksheet 7.4 La República Dominicana

The first three activities on this sheet refer to the people featured on p.63 of the Student's Book.

1 Bernardo

A gap-fill activity in which students complete sentences about where Bernardo lives.

Answers: *a* – ciudad; *b* – sur; *c* – parque; *d* – iglesia; *e* – cultura; *f* – tráfico.

2 Alonso

Students correct five errors in Alonso's description.

Answers: ciudad – pueblo; sureste – suroeste; bar – hotel; bonito – tranquilo; turístico – industrial.

3 Rafael

Students answer the six closed questions about Rafael.

Answers: *a* – Me llamo Rafael; *b* – Vivo en Constanza; *c* – Está en la sierra; *d* – Hay un mercado y unos restaurantes; *e* – Lo bueno es que tengo muchos amigos allí; *f* – Lo malo es que no hay mucha movida.

4 ¿Y tú?

Students use a model text as the basis for a description of their own town or village, changing the appropriate underlined words.

5 Con tu pareja

Students take it in turns to ask their partner the questions from Activity 3.

6 Un poema

A reading activity in which students fill in the gaps in a poem, using words selected from the menu beneath.

Answers: *a* – malo; *b* – diversión; *c* – ciudad; *d* – mucha; *e* – fea; *f* – fatal.

Worksheet 7.5 Madrid

1 Lo bueno y lo malo

a This extension worksheet looks at some of the good and bad points about Madrid. In preparation for the listening activity that follows, students should use a dictionary to work out the meanings of phrases a–j, and then match them with the appropriate picture.

Answers: *1* – c; *2* – h; *3* – j; *4* – b; *5* – g; *6* – i; *7* – f; *8* – d; *9* – e; *10* – a.

b Two young Spaniards, Pablo and Tere, are asked to give their views on Madrid for the radio programme *¿Qué te parece a ti?* In their interviews they will use some of the phrases a–j, so students should tick each box if they hear the phrase mentioned.

Answers:

		Pablo	Tere	Rafa	Inma
a	hay gente con dinero	✓			
b	hay mucho turismo	✓			✓
c	hay mucha movida	✓			
d	hay mucha cultura			✓	
e	hay mucha diversión		✓	✓	
f	hay mucho jaleo		✓		
g	hay mucho tráfico	✓	✓	✓	✓
h	hay mucha basura	✓	✓	✓	✓
i	hay mucha contaminación			✓	✓
j	hay mucha pintada	✓			

PRESENTADOR:	Buenos días y bienvenidos al programa para jóvenes ¿Qué te parece a ti? Hoy, el tema es Madrid, y el primer oyente se llama Pablo. ¡Hola Pablo!
PABLO:	¡Hola a todos!
PRESENTADOR:	Pablo, ¿dónde vives en Madrid?
PABLO:	Vivo en las afueras en Casa de Campo.
PRESENTADOR:	¿Y qué te parece Madrid?
PABLO:	Bueno, lo positivo es que Madrid es una ciudad bonita. Hay mucho turismo – en el centro, siempre hay turistas de Europa, de América. Y esta gente es gente con dinero, lo que es bueno para el comercio y las tiendas … Madrid no es aburrido, porque hay siempre mucha movida …
PRESENTADOR:	¿Y lo negativo?
PABLO:	Mm – no me gusta el tráfico. Hay mucho. Además, el centro es muy ruidoso y sucio. Y la pintada – hay mucha pintada en los parques, y esto no me gusta tampoco.
PRESENTADOR:	Bueno, muchas gracias Pablo, por tu opinión – en un momento, escuchamos otra.
PRESENTADOR:	En línea dos, tenemos otro oyente – ¿cómo te llamas?
TERE:	Hola – me llamo Tere.
PRESENTADOR:	¿Y dónde vives, Tere?
TERE:	Vivo en el centro en el barrio de la Encarnación.

PRESENTADOR:	¿Y qué te parece Madrid?
TERE:	Bueno, estoy bastante negativa. Yo creo que Madrid es una ciudad muy ruidoso. De día, hay mucho tráfico y luego de noche, hay mucho jaleo en los parques. Y es muy sucia, también – hay mucha basura por todas partes.
PRESENTADOR:	¿Qué es lo bueno de Madrid para ti, Tere?
TERE:	Lo bueno, es que hay cines, discotecas, clubs de noche … hay mucha diversión para los jóvenes.
PRESENTADOR:	Vale, muchas gracias, Tere … Y escuchamos al oyente número tres dentro de poco …

2 En la revista

Rafa and Inma have written letters to a magazine outlining their views on Madrid. In their letters they use some of the phrases a–j, and students should tick the relevant boxes.

Answers: *See grid with Activity 1b answers.*

---

3 Radio Gran Bretaña

Using the phrases in the language support box, students can now prepare a similar interview to the ones in Activity 1b. They should discuss their own or another local town. Encourage them to give as fair and balanced a view as possible.

Objectives

Students learn – to say what there is to do in their town or area
       – to say what they like doing
       – Grammar: *al* ('to the')

Key language

¿qué se puede hacer?	*ir de excursión*
se puede …	*ir de paseo en bici*
ir al cine	*ir de pesca*
ir al polideportivo	*salir con amigos*
ir a la bolera	*nadar*
ir a la playa	*visitar los pueblos típicos*
ir a las salas de juegos	
ir a los partidos de fútbol	
ir de compras	

Skills / Strategies

Students learn – how to say 'to the' (*Acción: lengua 7*)

ICT opportunities

Students can – use painting or drawing software to design a poster about their town (Student's Book, Activity 4)

Ways in

Things to do – Student's Book, Activity 1

Assessment opportunities

AT1,2   Worksheet 7.6, Activity 1: students work out the correct order of the pictures.

AT1,3   Worksheet 7.6, Activity 2: students work out which activities can be done in which place.

AT2,2   Student's Book, Activity 2b: say what can and can't be done.

AT3,3   Worksheet 7.7, Activity 1: students pair up the questions and answers correctly.

AT4,3/4   Student's Book, Activity 4: students write some publicity material about their town.

STUDENT'S BOOK, pages 64–65

1 ¿Qué se puede hacer?

Before tackling the presentation in the Student's Book, you could use OHTs 7C1 and 7C2 to introduce the different activities, which are the same as the ones Isabel and Tomás would like in their ideal city. The difference in character between them shows through, as Isabel mentions the five on the left (odd numbers), and Tomás mentions the five on the right (even numbers). The presentation is accompanied by appropriate sound effects.

a Students listen to Isabel and Tomás.

b ◐ After the initial presentation on the recording, eight of the sound effects are played in a different order. Students have to match the correct activity to each sound a–h.

♣ Students work out who says each of the phrases.

Answers: ◐ *a – 9; b – 4; c – 3; d – 1; e – 6; f – 2; g – 7; h – 8.*

♣ *1 – Tomás; 2 – Isabel; 3 – Tomás; 4 – Isabel.*

ISABEL:	En mi ciudad ideal se puede …
	… ir al cine [sound of wild west film]
TOMÁS:	… ir al polideportivo [sound of sports centre]
ISABEL:	… ir a la bolera [sound of bowls knocking over tenpins]
TOMÁS:	… ir a la playa [sound of waves and seagulls]
ISABEL:	… ir a las salas de juegos [sound of fruit machines]
TOMÁS:	… ir a los partidos de fútbol [sound of football crowd]
ISABEL:	… ir de compras [sound of cash till]
TOMÁS:	… ir de excursión [sound of bus]
ISABEL:	… ir de paseo en bici [sound of bike path]
TOMÁS:	… ir de pesca [sound of stream running]

ESCUCHA OTRA VEZ.
a [sound of bike]
b [sound of beach]
c [sound of bowling alley]
d [sound of cinema]
e [sound of football match]
f [sound of sports centre]
g [sound of shopping]
h [sound of bus excursions]

Gramática

A brief item here deals with the issue of the preposition *a* and the definite article *el* combining to form *al*. Students who need a more detailed explanation are referred to the grammar summary section 5, p.148. Further practice of this point is also available in *Acción: lengua 7*, p.67.

2 ¿Se puede …?

a Students read each of the activity phrases and decide where each can be done, listing the appropriate number from the list of places 1–5.

Answers: *ir de excursión en barco: 1, 3; ir al centro comercial: 2; ir al club de jóvenes: 2, 5; ir al estadio de fútbol: 2, 5; ir al parque de atracciones: 2, 5; ir a la pista de hielo: 2, 5; ir a la playa: 1; dar una vuelta: 1, 2, 4; hacer deporte: 4, 5; hacer deportes acuáticos: 1, 3; salir con amigos: 1, 2, 3, 4, 5; visitar museos / cuevas: 2, 4; visitar monumentos históricos: 1, 2, 4; visitar pueblos típicos: 1, 2, 4.*

b A pairwork activity in which students pick an activity from Activity 2a, make statements about what can be done where, and their partner answers the statements saying whether the suggestion is possible or not.

3 Isabel, Tomás y Teresa

Consolidation of the phrase *se puede*, with other activities which are introduced in Activity 2. Also, revision of *me gustaría*.

The family are discussing the advantages and disadvantages of living in the centre or outskirts of Seville, but find it hard to agree.

◐ Students listen to the recording to see who says which activity could be done and where. They select one of the locations from Activity 2a to finish each sentence.

♣ Students answer a set of closed questions in Spanish.

Answers: ◐ *a – 2; b – 5; c – 3; d – 4; e – 1.*

♣ *1 – A Tomás no le gusta el centro; 2 – Porque es ruidoso y sucio; 3 – Es aburrido; 4 – En un barrio en el centro; 5 – Un apartamento antiguo; 6 – Un apartamento moderno.*

TOMÁS:	No me gustaría vivir en el centro, Isabel – es ruidoso y sucio.
ISABEL:	En un pueblo en las afueras, ¡es aburrido!
TERESA:	Tomás, aquí en el centro se puede salir con amigos …
TERESA:	Se puede hacer deporte en el polideportivo.
ISABEL:	También se pueden hacer deportes acuáticos en el río Guadalquivir.
TERESA:	El fin de semana, se puede visitar los pueblos típicos de la sierra …
ISABEL:	¡… o ir a la playa en la Costa de la Luz!

TOMÁS:	Bueno …
TERESA:	¿Un barrio en el centro, entonces?
TOMÁS:	Vale. Pero me gustaría vivir en un apartamento antiguo.
ISABEL:	¡No me gustan los apartamentos antiguos! ¡Mamá! ¡A mí, me gustaría vivir en un apartamento moderno!
TERESA:	Por favor, niños, dejadme en paz …

4 **Un póster**

Students design a poster for the town or area they live in. You might need to supply some specific vocabulary to enable them to refer to local places of interest, but you could also encourage them to look up the words they need in a dictionary.

SUPPORT MATERIALS

OHTs 7C1 and 7C2

These sheets provide the stimulus for saying what can be done in the students' own area, and may be used to practise question and answer strategies with students prior to their taking part in the formal activities on the other worksheets.

Worksheet 7.6 ¡Qué maravilla!

1 **Sevilla y Andalucía**

A song which practises the key language. Students have to work out the correct order of the pictures as they hear and read the words of the song. After they have heard it once or twice they should join in and sing along.

Answers: *3, 4, 7, 5, 8, 1, 6, 2, 8.*

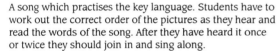

¿EN LA CIUDAD …?
Se puede ir de compras,
en la calle de Sierpes,
Visitar la cafetería
en el famoso Corte Inglés.
Se puede ir a la bolera
o al polideportivo –
¡Sevilla, que maravilla!
Tiene mucho de atractivo.

¿Y EN EL CAMPO?
Se puede ir de paseo en bici
o al campo en autobús.
Y visitar la playa
en la Costa de la Luz.
Ir de pesca en los ríos
o ir de excursión –
¡Andalucía, que maravilla!
Es la mejor región.

2 **El País Vasco**

An interview with Arantxa who lives in Zarauz near San Sebastián in the north of Spain.

 Students listen to the recording and decide whether the activities pictured can be done in Zarauz or San Sebastián. They need only write Z or SS as appropriate.

a At the end of the interview, Arantxa mentions other things to do in the area. Students have to name two of them.

b Finally, students complete the two speech bubbles to give Arantxa's opinions, both good and bad, about where she lives.

Answers: *1 – Zarauz; 2 – San Sebastián; 3 – San Sebastián; 4 – San Sebastián; 5 – Zarauz; 6 – Zarauz.*

a Any two of the following: ir a la montaña; hacer alpinismo; ir de excursión; subir al monte en autobús; dar un paseo en el campo.

SEÑOR:	Hablemos un poco de tu región, Arantxa. ¿Dónde vives?
ARANTXA:	Vivo en el País Vasco, en el norte de España.
SEÑOR:	¿Vives en una ciudad o un pueblo?
ARANTXA:	Vivo en un pueblo en la costa, que se llama Zarauz.
SEÑOR:	¿Y qué se puede hacer en Zarauz?
ARANTXA:	Zarauz tiene una playa. Se puede pasar el día en la playa, tomando el sol … Y luego hay unas tiendas bonitas – se puede ir de compras en las boutiques. Y como está en la costa, se puede ir de paseo en bici …
SEÑOR:	¿Vas mucho a San Sebastián?
ARANTXA:	Sí, normalmente voy con mis amigos el fin de semana.
SEÑOR:	¿Qué se puede hacer allí?
ARANTXA:	Se puede ir al polideportivo – hay uno muy grande en las afueras – o a la bolera. Y luego pues … hay dos o tres cines – se puede ir al cine.
SEÑOR:	¿Hay otras cosas que se puede hacer en la región?
ARANTXA:	Sí. Una actividad muy popular entre los jóvenes, es ir a la montaña y hacer alpinismo. Y también se puede ir de excursión a muchos sitios muy bonitos. A mí me gusta mucho subir al monte en autobús y pasar todo el día paseando en el campo … es muy bonito.
SEÑOR:	¿Te gusta vivir en Zarauz?
ARANTXA:	Mm … lo bueno es que tengo muchos amigos aquí, y hay mucha movida en verano en la playa. Pero, lo malo es que no hay mucha diversión.
SEÑOR:	¿Prefierías vivir en San Sebastián?
ARANTXA:	No sé … me parece que no. Al fin y al cabo, me gusta Zarauz.

Worksheet 7.7 La colonia espacial

1 **El año 2500**

 The text of an interview with a resident of a space colony on Mars in the year 2500.

Students have to match up the questions and answers correctly.

Answers: *1 – d; 2 – c; 3 – b; 4 – f; 5 – a; 6 – e.*

2 **¿Cómo es vivir allí?**

Students read an e-mail and answer the 10 true / false / impossible to tell questions.

Answers: *1 – verdad; 2 – verdad; 3 – no dice; 4 – mentira; 5 – mentira; 6 – mentira; 7 – no dice; 8 – verdad; 9 – verdad; 10 – mentira.*

7D ¿Qué deportes te gusta hacer?   Unidad 7 ¿Cómo es donde vives?

Objectives
Students learn – to talk about which sports they like to play or do
– to say which sports they would like to play or do

Key language
hacer los deportes acuáticos
hacer atletismo
jugar al hockey
hacer alpinismo
jugar al voleibol
hacer ciclismo
hacer piragüismo
hacer deportes
jugar al fútbol
jugar al squash
hacer esquí
hacer alpinismo
hacer footing
hacer vela
hacer atletismo y ciclismo

Skills / Strategies
Students learn – some more dictionary skills

ICT opportunities
Students can – produce a small computer profile about what sports they like, illustrated with clip-art if wished

Ways in
Sports – OHT 7D; students' own interests; dictionary discovery activity

Assessment opportunities
AT1,2   Worksheet 7.8, Activity 1: students listen and write each number under the appropriate symbol.
AT3,1   Student's Book, Acción: lengua 7, Activity 4 ◖: students join the sentence halves.
AT4,3/4 Student's Book, Activity 3b: students write a paragraph about the sports that can be done in their village or town.

STUDENT'S BOOK, page 66

1 **Me gusta ...**

This activity presents the new sporting activities being presented in this objective. Using a dictionary if necessary, students match a set of visuals to the appropriate sport.

Answers: *1 – a; 2 – c; 3 – d; 4 – g; 5 – e; 6 – k; 7 – j; 8 – h; 9 – i; 10 – l; 11 – b; 12 – f.*

2 **¿Qué deportes te gusta hacer?**

A listening activity in which students hear young people talking about the sports they like to do, and note down who mentions what.

◖ Students note down what the people like doing.

♣ This activity is similar to the diamond activity, but practises the conditional of *gustar, me gustaría*. Instead of noting what people <u>like</u>, students note down what they <u>would like</u> to do.

Answers: ◖ *Ricardo – 1, 5; Gloria – 6, 4; Javier – 3, 7; Silvia – 1, 2; Manuel – 9, 12.*

♣ *Ricardo – 11, 12; Gloria – 10, 8; Javier – 11, 12; Silvia – 8, 10; Manuel – 6, 7.*

GLORIA:	Oye, Ricardo, ¿qué deportes te gusta hacer?
RICARDO:	Me gusta jugar al fútbol, y también me gusta mucho jugar al rugby.
GLORIA:	¿Sí? Fútbol y rugby – ¡qué bien! Y ¿hay algún deporte que te gustaría hacer?
RICARDO:	Me gustaría hacer piragüismo. ¡Lo malo es que mi pueblo no está junto al río! Y me gustaría hacer vela también.
GLORIA:	Te gustan los deportes acuáticos, entonces.
RICARDO:	Sí, mucho.
JAVIER:	Y tú, Gloria, ¿qué deportes te gusta hacer?
GLORIA:	Me gusta mucho hacer atletismo.
JAVIER:	¿Atletismo? No lo sabía.
GLORIA:	También juego al hockey.
JAVIER:	¿Hay algún deporte que te gustaría hacer?
GLORIA:	Sí. Me gustaría mucho hacer alpinismo y esquí. Me encanta la sierra.

JAVIER:	¡El problema con el esquí es que hace mucho frío!
GLORIA:	Sí, ya lo sé. ¡Y no me gusta mucho el frío!
SILVIA:	Javier, ¿a ti te gusta el alpinismo?
JAVIER:	¡No! Me gusta jugar al voleibol.
SILVIA:	Jugar al voleibol es muy divertido.
JAVIER:	También me encanta hacer ciclismo.
SILVIA:	¿Qué te gustaría hacer?
JAVIER:	Me gustaría hacer piragüismo. Lo malo es que no vivo cerca de la costa. También me gustaría hacer vela.
RICARDO:	¿Y tú, Silvia, ¿qué deportes te gusta hacer?
SILVIA:	Bueno, me gusta jugar al fútbol ...
RICARDO:	¿Al fútbol?
SILVIA:	¿Por qué no? ¡Arriba las chicas y el fútbol!
RICARDO:	Bueno, vale. ¿Qué más?
SILVIA:	Me gusta jugar al squash también.
RICARDO:	Es muy rápido, el squash.
SILVIA:	Por eso me gusta. Pero me gustaría hacer esquí y también alpinismo.
GLORIA:	Manuel, ¿qué deportes te gusta a ti hacer?
MANUEL:	Me gusta hacer footing.
GLORIA:	¿Sí? ¿No es aburrido, hacer footing?
MANUEL:	No, ¡qué va! A mí me gusta. También me gusta hacer vela en la costa.
GLORIA:	¡Qué suerte! ¿Hay algún deporte que te gustaría hacer?
MANUEL:	Sí. Me gustaría hacer atletismo y ciclismo.
GLORIA:	¿Atletismo y ciclismo? ¿Por qué?
MANUEL:	Porque es buen ejercicio.

3 **En mi pueblo**

a A reading and basic writing activity in which students fill in the missing words in a text about activities possible in someone's town.

Answers: *1 – polideportivo; 2 – deportes; 3 – piscina; 4 – puede; 5 – vela; 6 – voleibol; 7 – aburrido; 8 – gustaría.*

b An open-ended writing activity which asks students to write a paragraph about the sporting possibilities in their town or village.

SUPPORT MATERIALS

OHT 7D Juego ... / Practico ...

Presentation of the different sports.

Worksheet 7.8 Los deportes 〇

Note that this worksheet has removable English rubrics at the bottom.

1 **¿Qué te gusta hacer?**

〇 Students listen to people describing the activities they do, and sequence a set of visuals. There is one remaining picture.

Answers:	1–e; 2–g; 3–c; 4–b; 5–a; 6–d (extra picture = jogging)

1	HOMBRE:	¿El deporte que más me gusta? El rugby. Me gusta mucho jugar al rugby.
2	CHICO:	Mi deporte favorito es la natación. Me gusta mucho hacer natación.
3	CHICA:	Me gusta hacer ciclismo. Es un deporte que me encanta, el ciclismo.
4	CHICO:	¿Qué deporte prefiero? Mm ... creo que es el squash. Me gusta mucho jugar al squash.
5	CHICA:	A mí, me gusta mucho jugar al fútbol. ¡El fútbol es estupendo!
6	CHICO:	Me gusta mucho hacer vela. Es algo que me gusta mucho, la vela.

2 **¿Dónde?**

〇 Students join the sentence halves.

Answers:	1–g; 2–d; 3–g; 4–c; 5–a; 6–b; 7–e.

3 **¿Por qué?**

〇 Students write sentences in Spanish in response to the given cues.

Answers:	1 – Me gusta jugar al fútbol porque es divertido; 2 – Me gustaría hacer vela porque es interesante; 3 – ¿Por qué no me gusta hacer atletismo? Porque es difícil; 4 – Me gusta jugar al voleibol – en mi opinión es fácil; 5 – ¿No te gusta hacer piragüismo porque es aburrido o porque no tienes amigos en el club?

Worksheet 7.9 El deporte en mi ciudad

1 **Los gustos**

♣ A listening activity in which students listen to find out what can or can't be done in four young people's cities.

Answers:

MELINDA		
CHICA:	¿Qué deportes te gustan, Melinda?	
MELINDA:	Me gusta jugar al squash, y también me gusta hacer ciclismo.	
CHICA:	¿Qué deporte no te gusta?	
MELINDA:	No me gusta mucho el fútbol. No es muy interesante.	

JORGE		
CHICO:	Jorge, a ti te gusta hacer vela, ¿no?	
JORGE:	Sí, me gusta mucho. Y el piragüismo me gusta también.	
CHICO:	Los deportes acuáticos, entonces.	
JORGE:	Sí, me gustan mucho.	
CHICO:	¿Quieres jugar al voleibol con nosotros mañana?	
JORGE:	Lo siento, no me gusta nada el voleibol.	

TERE		
CHICO:	Tere, ¿qué deportes te gustan?	
TERE:	Me gusta jugar al hockey.	
CHICO:	Y en invierno, te gusta hacer esquí, ¿verdad?	
TERE:	Sí, me gusta mucho.	
CHICO:	¿Qué deporte no te gusta?	
TERE:	No me gusta hacer footing. ¡Qué aburrido!	

GARI		
CHICA:	Gari, ¿por qué no te gusta jugar al hockey?	
GARI:	No sé. Es un poco aburrido, el hockey. Pero me gustan otros deportes. Me gusta jugar al fútbol, por ejemplo.	
CHICA:	Y te gusta hacer alpinismo, ¿no?	
GARI:	Sí, mucho.	

2 **Mi ciudad**

a ⊕ A listening activity which takes the form of a radio interview in which students have to work out which of a variety of topics are mentioned.

Answers:	1–✓; 2–✗; 3–✓; 4–✓; 5–✗; 6–✓.

ENTREVISTADOR:	¡Bienvenidos! Hoy continuamos nuestra investigación sobre los jóvenes y el deporte. Y vamos a charlar ahora con Carla. Carla, ¿dónde vives?
CARLA:	Yo vivo en la ciudad de Cuevamoros, en el norte de la provincia.
ENTREVISTADOR:	Y eres alumna aquí del instituto de Santo Domingo.
CARLA:	Sí.
ENTREVISTADOR:	Y ¿qué deportes te gusta hacer?
CARLA:	Me gusta jugar al baloncesto y al voleibol, pero me gustaría hacer otros deportes también.
ENTREVISTADOR:	Por ejemplo ...
CARLA:	Por ejemplo, el piragüismo. Me gustaría mucho hace piragüismo, pero el problema es que no hay río.
ENTREVISTADOR:	Es difícil si no hay río.
CARLA:	Sí. Hay clases de piragüismo en la piscina, pero después de cierto tiempo, es aburrido. No hay excursiones a un río o a la costa donde se puede practicarlo.
ENTREVISTADOR:	Mencionas una piscina. ¿Qué otras oportunidades hay para hacer deporte?
CARLA:	No muchas. Hay un polideportivo, pero es muy antiguo. Y no es muy grande.
ENTREVISTADOR:	¿La piscina está bien?
CARLA:	No. Está sucia. No me gusta nadar en agua sucia.
ENTREVISTADOR:	Lo malo de la ciudad es que no hay muchos lugares para hacer deporte.
CARLA:	Sí. El problema que tiene la ciudad, es que no hay instalaciones modernas. Es una ciudad turística, pero ...
ENTREVISTADOR:	Ideal si eres turista, pero no si eres joven ...

b Students listen again and list the problems connected with each topic mentioned in the grid.

Answers: *1 – No hay río; 2 – El polideportivo es muy antiguo y no es muy grande; 3 – La piscina está sucia; 4 – No hay instalaciones modernas.*

3 La entrevista

a Students complete the interview with the appropriate words.

Answers: *1 – nadar; 2 – montar a caballo; 3 – divertido; 4 – piscina; 5 – jugar al voleibol; 6 – al fútbol; 7 – hacer vela.*

b Now students write their own interview, talking about their own town and the activities they like to do and / or would like to do

Acción: lengua 7, page 67

Infinitives

This item presents and explains the various forms of infinitive ending and provides simple drill activities to practise them.

1 Students use their dictionaries to find the Spanish for a variety of new infinitives.

Answers: *1 – vivir; 2 – leer; 3 – escuchar; 4 – ver; 5 – escribir; 6 – trabajar; 7 – charlar; 8 – aprender.*

2 An open-ended activity in which students look back through everything they have studied so far and list all the infinitive forms they can find.

3 Students test a friend on the verbs.

4 A matching activity which practises *al, a la*, etc.

A slightly harder gap-fill activity to practise *al, a la*, etc.

Answers: 1 – c; 2 – e; 3 – d; 4 – a; 5 – b.

1 – a los; 2 – a las; 3 – al; 4 – a la; 5 – a; 6 – al.

Objectives
Students learn – to say what kind of house or flat they live in
– to explain how near or far away it is
– to say where it is in relation to other places
– Grammar: *del*

Key language
una casa	*en …*
una casa doble	*la calle*
una casa adosada	*la plaza*
un chalé	*está …*
un piso	*cerca (de)*
un bloque nuevo	*lejos (de)*
un bloque antiguo	*a unos cinco minutos andando*
una torre	*a tres kilómetros*
una finca	

Prepositions: *delante (de); detrás (de); al lado (de); encima (de); debajo (de); enfrente (de); entre*

Skills / Strategies
Students learn – how to say something is near or far away

ICT opportunities
Students can – write about their house and where it is situated, adding a map designed on computer or hand-drawn and scanned

Ways in
Student's Book, Activity 1 – photos and recording

Assessment opportunities
AT1,2 Student's Book, Activity 3: students sequence the visuals.
AT2,2 Worksheet 8.1, Activity 2: students discuss whether places are near or far away.
AT3,2 Student's Book, Activity 4 ◐ : students read some true / false sentences.
AT3,3 Student's Book, Activity 4 ◑ : students read and fill in the gaps.

STUDENT'S BOOK, pages 68–69

1 **¿Una casa o un piso?**

Presentation of types of house and flat. Before tackling this activity, you could introduce the different types of home with OHT 8A as well as the visuals on p.68. After listening to the recording, students then match the visuals to Teresa's reactions a–h.

Answers: *1 – d; 2 – g; 3 – c; 4 – h; 5 – e; 6 – b; 7 – a; 8 – f.*

ISABEL:	¿Te gustaría vivir en una casa o un piso, Mamá?
TERESA:	Mm … no sé.
ISABEL:	¿Una finca?
TERESA:	¿En el campo? ¡No!
ISABEL:	¿Una casa?
TERESA:	Es grande.
ISABEL:	¿Una casa doble?
TERESA:	Es bonita.
ISABEL:	¿Una casa adosada?
TERESA:	Mm, no está mal.
ISABEL:	¿Un piso en un bloque nuevo?
TERESA:	No sé …
ISABEL:	¿Un piso en un bloque antiguo?
TERESA:	Sí, me gusta.
ISABEL:	¿Un piso en una torre?
TERESA:	Es muy moderno.
ISABEL:	¿Un chalé?
TERESA:	¡Uf! Es mucho dinero – doscientos mil euros.

2 **¿Lejos o cerca?**

This activity presents ways of saying how near or far away a place is.

◐ This activity presents the structures for giving information about distance and proximity. Students listen to the recording and fill in the appropriate gap with how far away each place mentioned is.

◑ A gap-fill activity in which students select one of two alternative words in the sentences on the basis of the other information given in the listening text. A help box underneath contains the necessary information.

Answers: ◐ *1 – 3 km; 2 – 20 minutos; 3 – 10 minutos; 4 – 100 metros.*
◑ *1 – cerca; 2 – cerca; 3 – bonita; 4 – tranquila.*

TOMÁS:	Mamá, hay un piso en la calle Alberto Listo.
JUAN:	¡Uf! Está a tres kilómetros.
TERESA:	Me gustaría vivir cerca de Carmina, en Cristo del Burgos.
TOMÁS:	Hay un piso en la calle San Andrés.
TERESA:	Juan, ¿está cerca?
JUAN:	¡Qué va! Está lejos – a unos veinte minutos andando.
TOMÁS:	Pero está cerca del instituto. Hay un piso en la Plaza de la Encarnación. Está a diez minutos andando.
JUAN:	Hay mucho tráfico allí. ¿Me dejas ver? Hay un piso en la Plaza de la Alfalfa.
TERESA:	¿Sí? ¡Está cerca!
JUAN:	¡A cien metros!
TERESA:	Y es muy bonita, esta plaza.
JUAN:	Está a unos dos minutos andando. Y no hay mucha movida allí.
TERESA:	¡Perfecto!

Gramática

Students are reminded of the structure *de + el = del* and referred to the grammar summary section 5, p.148 and to *Acción: lengua 8*, p.75 for more information.

3 **¿Dónde está el pájaro de Pepa?**

A further listening activity which introduces the prepositions taught in this objective. The recording uses the context of Pepa and Tomás trying to catch Pepa's pet bird. Students must identify the prepositions used as the bird flies around the room and is finally recaught.

Answers: *6, 5, 3, 4, 2, 7, 1.*

PEPA:	¡Tomás! ¿Dónde está mi pájaro? ¿Lo ves?
TOMÁS:	Sí. Debajo de la mesa.
PEPA:	¡Ay! No está.
TOMÁS:	¡Mira! Allí – encima del armario. Voy yo … ¡No! Se ha escapado.
PEPA:	Tomás – cuidado. Está detrás de la puerta … ¡Uf! ¡No!
TOMÁS:	¡Pepa! ¡está al lado!
PEPA:	¿Dónde? No lo veo.
TOMÁS:	Está delante de la puerta … ¡No, no está! Se ha escapado otra vez.
PEPA:	Tomás, rápido. ¡Está enfrente del gato!
TOMÁS:	¡Voy yo! ¡Ah! Sí. ¡Lo tengo entre mis manos!
PEPA:	¡Gracias, Tomás!

4 El piso de José Luis

a ◐ Further presentation of the prepositions, in the form of an activity in which students answer a series of true / false questions about the positions of buildings on the basis of information given on the street plan.

b ♣ A higher-level follow-up activity, which provides semi-productive practice of the prepositions via a gap-fill activity.

Answers:
◐ *1 – verdad; 2 – verdad; 3 – mentira; 4 – mentira; 5 – mentira; 6 – mentira.*

♣ *1 – enfrente; 2 – debajo; 3 – entre; 4 – al lado; 5 – encima; 6 – enfrente.*

5 ◯ Por favor ...

A pairwork practice activity in which students quiz each other about where places in their area are situated.

SUPPORT MATERIALS

OHT 8A Viviendas

Presentation of types of house and flat. The pictures correspond to the photos presented in the Student's Book, p.68.

Worksheet 8.1 Casas, pisos

1 ¿Dónde está?

A listening activity which presents further practice of the concept of near or far.

◐ Students listen to the five short dialogues and write down whether the places in question are *cerca* or *lejos*.

♣ Students listen again and this time identify how far away the places are, either in kilometres or the time it would take to walk there.

Answers:
◐ *1 – cerca; 2 – lejos; 3 – lejos; 4 – lejos; 5 – cerca.*

♣ *1 – a unos dos minutos andando; 2 – a cuatro kilómetros; 3 – a tres kilómetros; 4 – a unos cinco o seis kilómetros; 5 – a unos cinco minutos andando.*

1	CHICO:	Oye, Paco, ¿dónde está el supermercado?
	CHICO:	En la Calle Aragón.
	CHICO:	¿Está cerca?
	CHICO:	Sí – a unos dos minutos andando.
2	CHICA:	¿Está muy lejos el polideportivo?
	SEÑORA:	Bueno sí, está lejos – a cuatro kilómetros.
	CHICA:	¡Uf! Cuatro kilómetros ...
3	SEÑOR:	Ana, por favor, ¿dónde está el instituto Bécquer?
	SEÑORA:	¿El instituto Bécquer? Está en el centro.
	SEÑOR:	¿Está cerca?
	SEÑORA:	No – está a tres kilómetros.
4	SEÑORA:	¡Oye, por favor! ¿Dónde está la piscina?
	CHICO:	¡Uf! ¡Está lejos!
	SEÑORA:	¿Sí?
	CHICO:	Está a unos cinco o seis kilómetros. Hay que seguir todo recto ...
5	NIÑO:	Mamá, ¿el parque está lejos?
	MUJER:	No, Miguel – está cerca. A unos cinco minutos andando.

2 ◯ ¿Cerca o lejos?

Pairwork activity in which students discuss the location of facilities in their own town, using the model dialogues for support.

◐ Students ask each other where the six places listed are in relation to their home, eliciting *está cerca / lejos* in response.

♣ Students ask each other where the six places are in relation to their school, this time eliciting more complex structures of distance in kilometres or time it takes to walk there.

3 Sacromonte

◐ Students read the text describing where Rosario lives with her gypsy family. From the text, they elicit the information needed to fill in Rosario's details on the form.

♣ Students refer to the same text and construct whole sentences by pairing up parts 1–7 with a–g.

Answers:
◐ *Nombre: Rosario   Apellido: Piquer*
Ciudad: Granada   Barrio: Sacromonte
Edad: 14   Familia: Padre, 3 hermanos
Tipo de vivienda: cueva

♣ *1 – e; 2 – c; 3 – g; 4 – f; 5 – a; 6 – d; 7 – b.*

Objectives
Students learn – to name the rooms in their house and say what
facilities there are

Key language
hay / tiene …
una entrada
una cocina
un salón
con balcón
un comedor
un cuarto de baño
un aseo
escaleras
un dormitorio
una terraza
un lavadero
un porche
un sótano
un jardín
un garaje
un desván

Skills / Strategies
Students learn – to ask what words mean in another language

ICT opportunities
Students can   – design a 'house to let' advertisement using some
language as a watermark (an imported graphic)
behind the main text (Student's Book, Activity 4)

Ways in
Students' (or teacher's) own houses; Student's Book, Activity 1

Assessment opportunities
AT2,2   Student's Book, Activity 2 ◖ : a miming and guessing
activity; eavesdrop on pairs at work!
AT3,2   Student's Book, Activity 1: students read house adverts.
AT4,2/3   Student's Book, Activity 4: students write a 'to let'
advertisement for their own home.

STUDENT'S BOOK, pages 70–71

1 **¿Qué hay en el piso?**

Presentation of rooms and interior of a flat. OHT 8B can
also be used to present the new language.

Picture story
Teresa is being shown round a flat she is interested in
renting.

◖ Students read the four advertisements for flats and
work out which one fits the one that Teresa is looking at.

Answers: *Piso número 3*

AGENTE:	Buenos días. Soy Ángela Martínez, de la Agencia Fincasur.
TERESA:	Señora Willoughby. Encantada.
AGENTE:	Hay una entrada … una cocina … un salón con balcón … un comedor … un cuarto de baño … un aseo … un dormitorio … hay tres en total. Hay unas escaleras para subir a una terraza … y un lavadero. ¿Qué le parece? ¿Le gusta?
TERESA:	Sí, está bien.
AGENTE:	¿Le gustaría ver el piso otra vez?
TERESA:	Sí, con Isabel y Tomás.

2 ◗ **Las habitaciones**

Speaking practice to consolidate the names of the rooms
in the house.

◖ Partner **A** invents a sound and mimes an action, and
Partner **B** has to say which room it is.

♣ After carefully studying Teresa's guided visit of the flat
again, students should try to memorise the order in which
she was shown the various rooms. Partner **A** then tests
Partner **B** who is not allowed to look at the Student's Book
page. The roles are then reversed, and the winner is the
person who needs least prompting or correcting. This
could be practised two or three times in order to improve.

3 **La casa de Tomás**

Presentation of additional vocabulary.

Picture story
Tomás shows Omar photos of his house in England.

◖ Students copy the picture of the house and label the
five parts of it correctly.

♣ Students ask each other how to say the new Spanish
words in English, or the English words in Spanish.

Answers: ◖ *1 – un jardín; 2 – un garaje; 3 – un desván;*
4 – un porche; 5 – un sótano.

♣ *1 – garden; 2 – garage; 3 – attic; 4 – porch;*
5 – cellar.

OMAR:	¿Es tu casa de Inglaterra, Tomás?
TOMÁS:	Sí – hay un porche, un garaje, un jardín …
OMAR:	¿Hay un desván?
TOMÁS:	Sí.
OMAR:	¿Y un sótano?
TOMÁS:	Sí. Me gusta mucho mi casa de Inglaterra.

4 **Se alquila …**

An opportunity for students to write about the features of
their own house. They might imagine that it is to be let or
rented out, and should prepare a simple advertisement for
insertion in a Spanish magazine. The language support box
offers some phrases to make it sound attractive, and the
four adverts on p.70 can also serve as examples. Students
who wish to design their adverts on computer could use one
of the key phrases (e.g., *¡piso magnífico!*) as a watermark
diagonally across the page behind the main text.

SUPPORT MATERIALS
OHT 8B En casa
Presentation of the different rooms and features in a house.

Worksheet 8.2 ¡Vacaciones en la Costa de la Luz!
1 **Matalascañas**

Listening for details about flats to let. There are three
separate telephone conversations with sufficient repetition
of information for students to pick out what they need to
hear and be able to ignore redundant language.

◖ Students fill in the missing details with a tick, a cross,
a number or the word *balcón* or *terraza*, as appropriate.

♣ Pupils write down the advantages and disadvantages
of each flat.

Answers:

	Piso 1	Piso 2	Piso 3
cocina amueblada	✓	✓	✓
salón-comedor	✓	✓	✓
cuarto de baño	✓	✓	✓
otro aseo	✗	✓	✓
número de dormitorios	3	4	3
aire acondicionado	✓	✓	✓
balcón / terraza	balcón	terraza	balcones

Suggested answers: 1 – 3 dormitorios; sólo un aseo;
2 – tiene terraza bonita, encima de un
supermercado;
3 – hay una piscina, está a 20 minutos
andando de la playa.

PISO NÚMERO UNO

PADRE:	Vamos a ver ... Piso número uno.
SEÑORA:	¿Dígame?
PADRE:	¿Usted alquila un piso?
SEÑORA:	Sí – está en la costa, en Mazagón.
PADRE:	¿Y qué tiene el piso, exactamente?
SEÑORA:	Bueno, hay una cocina amueblada, un salón-comedor, un cuarto de baño ...
PADRE:	¿Hay otro aseo?
SEÑORA:	No, sólo un aseo.
PADRE:	¿Y cuántos dormitorios tiene?
SEÑORA:	Tiene tres. Y también hay aire acondicionado ...
PADRE:	¿Tiene terraza?
SEÑORA:	Mm, no – terraza no hay, pero el salón tiene un balcón. Allí por la tarde, se está muy bien.
PADRE:	¿Y está en la playa?
SEÑORA:	Muy cerca de la playa.
PADRE:	Vale, muchas gracias.
SEÑORA:	Vale, adiós.
JOSÉ LUIS:	Lo bueno es que tiene tres dormitorios, pero el problema es que sólo hay un aseo. Con toda la familia ...

PISO NÚMERO DOS

MADRE:	Bueno, llamamos al piso número dos de la lista.
SEÑOR:	¿Dígame?
MADRE:	¿Usted alquila un piso en Matalascañas en la calle Balmes?
SEÑOR:	Sí.
MADRE:	¿Qué tiene el piso?
SEÑOR:	Cocina, salón-comedor, cuarto de baño, claro, y ...

MADRE:	¿Tiene otro aseo?
SEÑOR:	Sí – hay otro aseo al lado de la entrada. Y tiene cuatro dormitorios en total, aire acondicionado ...
MADRE:	¿Tiene balcón o terraza?
SEÑOR:	Terraza. Tiene una terraza espléndida, con plantas, flores y de todo.
MADRE:	Pues, me parece estupendo. ¿Dónde está exactamente en la calle Balmes?
SEÑOR:	Está en el primer piso, encima del supermercado.
MADRE:	Bueno, vale, adiós ...
JOSÉ LUIS:	Lo positivo es que tiene una terraza bonita, Mamá.
MADRE:	Sí. Pero está encima de un supermercado. No es ideal.

PISO NÚMERO TRES

PADRE:	Bueno, vamos a intentarlo otra vez. Piso número tres.
SEÑOR:	¿Diga?
PADRE:	Oiga, le llamo por lo del anuncio en el periódico. ¿Usted alquila un piso en Matalascañas en agosto?
SEÑOR:	Sí.
PADRE:	¿Qué tiene?
SEÑOR:	Pues, todo nuevo. Tiene una magnífica cocina amueblada, salón, comedor, aire acondicionado, cuarto de baño y además hay otro aseo.
PADRE:	¿Y cuántos dormitorios tiene?
SEÑOR:	Tiene tres: uno doble y dos individuales.
PADRE:	¿Y tiene terraza?
SEÑOR:	Terraza, no – pero todos los dormitorios tienen balcones, con unas vistas preciosas al mar ...
PADRE:	¿Está cerca de la playa?
SEÑOR:	Es un piso en uno de esos bloques nuevos, enfrente del parque. Lo bueno es que tiene piscina detrás. La piscina es para la comunidad – no es una piscina pública.
PADRE:	Pues, me parece perfecto. ¿Le puedo volver a llamar dentro de quince minutos?
SEÑOR:	Hombre, claro.
PADRE:	Vale, gracias, hasta luego.
SEÑOR:	Adiós.
JOSÉ LUIS:	¿Tiene piscina? ¡Qué bien!
MADRE:	Sí. Pero lo malo es que está a veinte minutos andando de la playa.
PADRE:	¿No te parece que vale la pena verlo ...?

2 **El alojamiento ideal**

A coupon to be filled in for the 'Wanted' section of a local
newspaper in Seville. Students write a small advertisement
for the holiday accommodation of their dreams using the
example as a model. They should describe it, list its
features, say where they want it to be situated and when
they would want it.

Objectives
Students learn – to say where rooms are in their home

Key language
¿cuántas plantas tiene …?
¿cuántas habitaciones tiene?
¿cuántos dormitorios tiene?
en la planta baja
en la primera planta
en la segunda planta
arriba
abajo
a la derecha
a la izquierda
al final

Skills / Strategies
Students learn – to recognise Spanish handwriting (Worksheet 8.5, Activity 2)

ICT opportunities
Students can — use design or drawing software to draw and label a plan of their house or flat

Ways in
Phrases of position — Student's Book, Activity 1

Assessment opportunities
AT2,2/3 Student's Book, Activity 3b: students prepare an interview about their homes.
AT3,2/3 Student's Book, Activity 2a: students identify the rooms in the house.
AT4,1 Student's Book, Activity 2b ◐ : students write the names of the rooms.
AT4,2/3 Student's Book, Activity 2b ♣ : students write about the rooms in their own house.

STUDENT'S BOOK, pages 72–73

1 **En el piso**
As you play the recording you can emphasise each phrase giving position with an appropriate gesture.

Picture story
Teresa returns to the flat with Tomás and Isabel.

a ◐ Students listen and read, and note down what is on each storey of the building.

♣ Four comprehension questions requiring numbers for answers.

Answers: ◐ *PB – tiendas; 1° – oficinas; 2° – cuatro pisos; 3° – terraza / lavadero.*

♣ *1 – cuatro plantas; 2 – dos plantas; 3 – 7 habitaciones (+ terraza); 4 – tres dormitorios.*

TOMÁS:	¿Cuántas plantas tiene el bloque?
TERESA:	En total, cuatro. En la planta baja, hay tiendas. En la primera planta hay oficinas. En la segunda planta, hay cuatro pisos.
ISABEL:	¿Cuántas habitaciones tiene el piso en total?
TERESA:	Abajo tiene siete …
ISABEL:	¿Cuántos dormitorios tiene?
TERESA:	Tiene tres. A la izquierda hay un sálon y un comedor … A la derecha hay una cocina …
TOMÁS:	¡Al final hay unas escaleras! ¿Qué hay arriba?
TERESA:	Arriba, hay una terraza y un lavadero. ¿Te gusta, Tomás?
TOMÁS:	¡Estupendo!

b Students match up the correct pictogram with each phrase.

Answers: *1 – b; 2 – d; 3 – e; 4 – a; 5 – c.*

c A simple pairwork activity involving gestures. Partner **A** mimes one of the new phrases and Partner **B** says what it is in Spanish.

2 **La carta de Teresa**
a An extract from Teresa's letter to her sister in Mexico telling her all about the flat she is planning to move into. Students read it and identify on the plan the rooms mentioned.

Answers: *1 – entrada; 2 – salón con balcón; 3 – comedor; 4 – dormitorio grande; 5 – escaleras; 6 – dormitorio; 7 – dormitorio; 8 – aseo; 9 – cuarto de baño; 10 – cocina; 11 – lavadero; 12 – terraza.*

b ◐ In this activity students draw a plan of one floor of their own house and write the name of each room.

♣ Students describe their own house, using Teresa's letter as a model.

3 **Tomás el curioso**
Listening practice to consolidate the new language. Tomás asks Pepa a lot of questions about her home, and she feels he is being rather inquisitive.

a Students listen to Pepa's replies and note down her answers.

Answers: *1 – una casa adosada; 2 – dos plantas; 3 – ocho habitaciones; 4 – un salón, una cocina, un comedor, un dormitorio, un aseo y unas escaleras; 5 – dos dormitorios y un cuarto de baño; 6 – sí.*

b Students prepare a similar interview based on the same six questions.

TOMÁS:	¿Vives en una casa o en un piso?
PEPA:	Vivo en una casa adosada.
TOMÁS:	¿Cuántas plantas tiene?
PEPA:	Tiene dos.
TOMÁS:	¿Cuántas habitaciones tiene?
PEPA:	En total, tiene ocho.
TOMÁS:	¿Qué hay abajo?
PEPA:	¿Abajo? ¡Qué curioso eres, Tomás! A la izquierda, hay un sálon y una cocina y a la derecha hay un comedor y un dormitorio, y al final hay un aseo y unas escaleras.
TOMÁS:	¿Qué hay arriba?
PEPA:	Hay dos dormitorios y un cuarto de baño.
TOMÁS:	¿Tiene jardín?
PEPA:	Sí, tiene jardín, pero no es muy grande.
TOMÁS:	¿Te gusta?
PEPA:	Sí, me gusta, porque es bonito. ¿Ya has terminado con todas tus preguntas?¡Qué curioso eres!

SUPPORT MATERIALS

Worksheet 8.3 El piso

 A pairwork activity which will work best if the worksheet is cut in half and / or supporting vocabulary is written on the board for reference. Partner **A** fills in the names of the rooms on an imaginary flat on his / her blank plan in secret. Partner **B** has to find out what rooms are in the flat and where they are located in relation to each other. Students could repeat the activity with Partner **A** eliciting the information from Partner **B** and the winner is the person with the least mistakes!

Worksheet 8.4 Las habitaciones

1 **¡Qué raro!**

A simple listening activity which practises vocabulary associated with a building.

Answers:	Basement – 5; Ground floor – 4; 1st floor – 1, 3; 2nd floor – 7, 2; Attic – 6.

SEÑOR:	¿Cómo es tu nuevo piso, Matilde?
SEÑORA:	Me gusta mucho, pero es un poco raro.
SEÑOR:	¿Por qué?
SEÑORA:	En la planta baja, sabes que hay una tienda.
SEÑOR:	Sí. Es bastante normal, ¿no?, una tienda en la planta baja.
SEÑORA:	Luego, en la primera planta hay un dormitorio.
SEÑOR:	¿El dormitorio?
SEÑORA:	Pero es muy tranquilo. Allí también está el cuarto de baño.
SEÑOR:	¿Dónde está el salón?
SEÑORA:	Está en el desván, al lado de la terraza.
SEÑOR:	¡Qué bien! ¿A que tienes vistas estupendas?
SEÑORA:	Sí, es verdad. Me gusta el salón arriba en el desván. Luego, en la segunda planta está la cocina.
SEÑOR:	¿Tienes comedor?
SEÑORA:	Sí, hay un comedor al lado de la cocina en la segunda planta.
SEÑOR:	¿Hay un lavadero en la terraza?
SEÑORA:	No, esto es lo malo. El lavadero está en el sótano.
SEÑOR:	¿El sótano? ¡Qué faena, tener que subir toda la ropa mojada a la terraza …!

2 **¡En bici!**

Consolidation of the phrases of position.

a Students pair up the pieces of paper to make five phrases or words.

b Students match up the words / phrases from Activity 2a to the pictures of the cyclist.

Answers:	a la izquierda – a; arriba – b; abajo – c; al final – d; a la derecha – e.

3 **Mis lugares favoritos**

a Students read people's opinions about various parts of the house and pick two of the visuals from Activity 1 for each text for parts that they say they like.

Answers:	Señora Morales – 1, 6; Nuria – 2, 7; Paco – 3, 1; Señor Velázquez – 6, 2.

b Students now write brief opinions about the rooms in their own house or flat.

Worksheet 8.5 La casa de los abuelos

1 **El piso de José Luis**

Students listen and identify the rooms, writing the word for each in Spanish.

Answers:	1 – cocina; 2 – aseo; 3 – lavadero; 4 – salón-comedor; 5 – terraza; 6 – dormitorio de José Luis; 7 – dormitorio de su hermano; 8 – dormitorio de sus padres; 9 – cuarto de baño; 10 – dormitorio de su hermana.

ISABEL:	Oye, José Luis, ¿vives en una casa o en un piso?
JOSÉ LUIS:	Vivo en un piso dúplex – tiene dos plantas.
ISABEL:	¿Dos plantas? ¿Qué hay en la planta baja?
JOSÉ LUIS:	Primero, una entrada.
ISABEL:	Hm … mm.
JOSÉ LUIS:	Luego a la izquierda, una cocina.
ISABEL:	Una cocina …
JOSÉ LUIS:	Y a la derecha, un aseo.
ISABEL:	Un aseo a la derecha …
JOSÉ LUIS:	Sí. Y al lado del aseo hay unas escaleras …
ISABEL:	¿Tienes lavadero?
JOSÉ LUIS:	Sí – hay un lavadero al lado de las escaleras.
ISABEL:	¿No tienes salón?
JOSÉ LUIS:	Sí – al final hay un salón-comedor grande, con terraza. Es muy bonita, eh, con flores, y plantas …
ISABEL:	Y arriba, ¿qué hay arriba?
JOSÉ LUIS:	Bueno, a la izquierda de las escaleras está mi dormitorio.
ISABEL:	¿Y luego …?
JOSÉ LUIS:	Luego, a la izquierda está el dormitorio de mi hermano.
ISABEL:	¿Y el dormitorio de tus padres?
JOSÉ LUIS:	Está al final. El dormitorio de mis padres está al final.
ISABEL:	¿Tiene terraza también?
JOSÉ LUIS:	No, pero tiene dos balcones. A la derecha está el cuarto de baño.
ISABEL:	No es muy grande …
JOSÉ LUIS:	No, el cuarto de baño es pequeño. Y luego está el dormitorio de mi hermana, con un balcón.
ISABEL:	¿Tiene balcón, tu hermana? Ay, qué bien …
JOSÉ LUIS:	¿Y tu piso nuevo, ¿cómo es?
ISABEL:	Bueno, si me dejas el boli, te lo dibujo ….

2 **La carta de Isabel**

Students read Isabel's letter and then fill in the gaps in the summary.

Answers:	8 (grande); 2 (cuatro); 3 (dormitorios); 7 (aseos); 1 (garaje); 4 (detrás); 5 (gusta); 6 (salones) is a distractor.

Objectives

Students learn – to say what there is in their bedroom
            – to explain where things are

Key language

el dormitorio
grande
pequeño
no está mal ...
la cama
la mesilla de noche
la lámpara
el armario
el guardarropa
el pupitre
la butaca
la cómoda
la alfombra
la estantería

Skills / Strategies

Students learn – to make descriptions and explanations

ICT opportunities

Students can   – use design or drawing software to draw and label a plan of their room (follow-up to Student's Book, Activity 2b)

Ways in

Students' / teacher's own rooms; plan accompanying Activity 1, Worksheet 8.6

Assessment opportunities

AT1,2   Student's Book, Activity 1b: students write the number of the appropriate furniture item.

AT4,1/2   Student's Book, Activity 2b ◐ : students list the things in their room.

AT4,3   Student's Book, Activity 2b ◑ : students write a brief description of their room.

STUDENT'S BOOK, page 74

1   El nuevo dormitorio de Tomás

a Presentation of the furniture items. Students listen and look at the pictures of the furniture which Tomás has in his room. Before playing the recording, you could give some information about a (real or imaginary) room and then elicit information about it from students in a memory activity. More able students might also be able to give some information about their own rooms.

TOMÁS:	Este es mi dormitorio, Pepa.
PEPA:	No es muy grande.
TOMÁS:	No. Es pequeño.
PEPA:	No está mal ...
TOMÁS:	Una cama: ¡Mmm ...!
PEPA:	Una mesilla de noche con una lámpara.
TOMÁS:	Un armario. Bien. Y un guardarropa.
PEPA:	Un pupitre.
TOMÁS:	¡Y una butaca! ¡Qué bien!
PEPA:	Una cómoda.
TOMÁS:	Una alfombra.
PEPA:	Una estantería ...
TOMÁS:	... para mis libros.
	No está mal, pero es un poco aburrido.
PEPA:	Y muy convencional ...

b Tomás decides to rearrange the furniture in his room in a most unconventional way! He is giving instructions regarding where he would like each piece to be placed. Students listen and complete the sentences in the book. It would be a good idea briefly to revise the prepositions taught earlier, before moving on to the recorded activity.

Answers: *a – 6; b – 4; c – 1; d – 10; e – 7; f – 2; g – 9; h – 3.*

PEPA:	Tu dormitorio no es grande.
TOMÁS:	Vamos a hacer unos cambios.
PEPA:	¿El pupitre y la silla?
TOMÁS:	Delante de la ventana.
PEPA:	¿El armario?
TOMÁS:	Detrás de la puerta.
PEPA:	¿La cama?
TOMÁS:	¡Encima del armario!
PEPA:	¡Cómo pesa! ¿La estantería?
TOMÁS:	¡Debajo de la cama!

PEPA:	¿La butaca?
TOMÁS:	Enfrente de la puerta.
PEPA:	¿La mesilla?
TOMÁS:	Al lado de la butaca.
PEPA:	¿La alfombra?
TOMÁS:	Entre la cama y el pupitre.
PEPA:	¿Y la lámpara? ¿En la mesilla?
TOMÁS:	No, en el pupitre. ¡Perfecto!
TERESA:	¡Ay no! Rápido, Tomás – pon los muebles bien. ¡El agente está aquí!

2 ¿Cómo tienes el dormitorio?

a Students write an 'ideal bedroom' list, naming things they would like to have in their room. Briefly revise *me gustaría* before doing the activity.

b ◐ A simple list-writing activity in which students list the furniture and other items in their bedroom.

◑ A longer writing activity in which students produce a piece of prose describing their own room. Students can refer to the vocabulary box for support.

SUPPORT MATERIALS

Worksheet 8.6 El dormitorio desordenado

This worksheet has removable English rubrics at the bottom.

1   La madre

a ◐ Students look at the plan and complete each sentence with the correct Spanish word.

Answers: *1 – mesilla; 2 – pupitre; 3 – puerta; 4 – armario; 5 – estantería; 6 – cama.*

---

b ◐ Students now write five more sentences with instructions for the positioning of the other items in the room.

2 Mi habitación

◐ Students write seven sentences describing their bedroom, selecting the most appropriate words for their own situation from the model given.

Acción: lengua 8, page 75

Practice of *estar* (to be) and *de* (of / from)

Estar (to be)

1 ◐ A basic drill activity on *estar*, which involves picking the correct form of *estar* from the choice of two in each sentence.

♣ A gap-fill activity practising *estar*.

Answers: ◐ *1 – estoy; 2 – están; 3 – está; 4 – está; 5 – está; 6 – estás.*

♣ *1 – estás; 2 – está; 3 – estoy; 4 – están; 5 – estamos; 6 – están.*

De (of / from the ...)

2 ◐ Students pick the correct word from a list of alternatives, to follow on from various forms of *de / del*, etc.

♣ A gap-fill activity practising *del*, *de la*, *de los* and *de las*.

Answers: ◐ *1 – cine; 2 – jardines; 3 – tiendas; 4 – ciudad; 5 – España.*

♣ *1 – del; 2 – de la; 3 – de los; 4 – el; 5 – de las; 6 – de la.*

Objectives

Students learn – to say how they are feeling and ask others
– to say what they want to do and ask others
– Grammar: *querer* (to want to)

Key language

estoy, estás, está …
cansado/a
contento/a
decepcionado/a
deprimido/a
egoísta
enfadado/a
estresado/a
extrovertido/a
harto/a (de)
ilusionado/a
optimista
preocupado/a
triste
querer (quiero, quieres, etc.)

Skills / Strategies

Students learn – to attract people's attention and make suggestions

ICT opportunities

Students can – Use a word-processing package to create a cloze activity based on the dialogues encountered in this topic area

Ways in

OHT 9A
Recorded presentation in Student's Book, page 76

Assessment opportunities

AT1,3   Student's Book, Activity 1b ◗ : students note the characters' moods.
AT1,4   Student's Book, Activity 1b ✚ : students do a supplementary multiple-choice activity.
AT2,3   Student's Book, Activity 3: students practise giving invitations and responding.
AT3,3   Student's Book, Activity 4: students draw the appropriate symbol for each message.
AT4,2   Worksheet 9.2, ◗ : students write the emotions for various situations.
AT4,3/4   Worksheet 9.2, ✚ : students write the emotions for various situations and add reasons.

STUDENT'S BOOK, pages 76–77

1 ¿Qué tal están?

Use OHT 9A or mime and photos of people selected at random (from your own or other people's photo albums, colour supplements, etc.) to present the adjectives describing moods.

a Students listen and follow the presentation. You may like to point out the masculine and feminine endings at this point, and see if students can establish the pattern.

> 1 – Estoy contento.
> 2 – Estoy triste.
> 3 – Estoy harto.
> 4 – Estoy cansada.
> 5 – Estoy deprimido.
> 6 – Estoy estresada.
> 7 – Estoy enfadado.
> 8 – Estoy preocupada.
> 9 – Estoy decepcionado.
> 10 – Estoy ilusionada.

b Before starting the second part of the activity, get students to agree on a gesture or posture for each mood – they can listen again to the initial presentation, and accompany it silently with the agreed gesture. In part b, the characters explain how they feel about each other.

◗ Students jot down the number of the appropriate emotion for each person. To simplify the activity, put a list of the emotions on the board or OHP in the wrong order, and ask students to identify the name of the person who is talking.

✚ Students listen again and complete a simple multiple-choice mixed skill reading and listening activity.

Answers: ◗ *José Luis – 1; Carlos – 9; Juan – 10; Tomás – 3; Isabel – 5; Pilar – 2; Teresa – 4; Carmina – 6, 7.*

✚ *1 – Isabel; 2 – egoísta; 3 – ilusionado; 4 – enfadada; 5 – a ver a su marido; 6 – de Isabel.*

JOSÉ LUIS:	Estoy contento – Isabel es guapa, inteligente, divertida. La quiero mucho …
CARLOS:	Estoy decepcionado – José Luis es mi amigo pero es muy egoísta.
JUAN:	¡Estoy ilusionado! La familia Willoughby tiene un nuevo piso. Vivir con Tomás es difícil – no le gusta Sevilla, pero a mí me gusta mucho.
TOMÁS:	¡Estoy harto! Papá no está aquí, y Mamá no está bien. Lo bueno es que tenemos un piso nuevo.
ISABEL:	Estoy deprimida … no sé qué hacer. Me gusta mucho José Luis, pero Pilar es mi prima y mi amiga …
PILAR:	Estoy triste – José Luis es mi amigo especial. ¡Pero Isabel! … ¡Isabel es increíble a veces!
TERESA:	Estoy cansada – está el nuevo piso, el bebé … y quiero ver a Michael …
CARMINA:	Estoy estresada – tengo mucho trabajo en el hospital … y estoy muy enfadada con Isabel …

2 Quiero ir … ¿Quieres venir?

◗ Students listen to six dialogues and work out where each person wants to go and at what time of day. Students can fill in the details on the ready-made grid provided on Worksheet 9.1

✚ Students note down how each person's companion is feeling.

Answers:

		1	2	3	4	5	6
◗	¿Dónde?	al cine	al parque de atracciones	al estadio de fútbol	a la discoteca	al centro comercial	al club de jóvenes
◗	¿Cuándo?	T	M	N	N	T	N
✚	¿Qué tal?	harto	decepcionado	ilusionado	deprimida	estresada	preocupada

1 ESTEBAN: ¿Diga?

PILI: Oye, Esteban, ¿quieres venir al cine conmigo?

ESTEBAN: ¿Cuándo, Pili?

PILI: Esta tarde.

ESTEBAN: Gracias Pili por la invitación, pero no quiero salir hoy.

PILI: ¿Qué te pasa?

ESTEBAN: No sé. Estoy harto.

PILI: ¿Harto de qué?

ESTEBAN: Hay muchos problemas aquí en casa, Pili ...

2 MARTA: ¡Álvaro!

ÁLVARO: ¡Marta! ¡Hola! ¿Qué tal?

MARTA: ¡Bien! Escucha, mañana es mi cumpleaños y quiero ir al parque de atracciones. ¿Quieres venir?

ÁLVARO: ¿Cuándo? ¿Por la tarde?

MARTA: No, por la mañana.

ÁLVARO: Ay, lo siento mucho, Marta, pero mi padre quiere ir a Huelva para ver a mi abuela y quiero ir con él. No está muy bien, la abuelita.

MARTA: ¡Ah, qué pena!

ÁLVARO: Sí, yo estoy muy decepcionado también. Pero espero que lo pases muy bien, Marta ...

3 RAFA: ¡Adivina adónde voy yo esta noche, Papá!

PAPÁ: No sé, Rafa. ¡Ni idea! ¡Pero estás muy ilusionado!

RAFA: ¡Voy al estadio de fútbol!

PAPÁ: ¿Al partido del Real Betis y Sevilla Fútbol Club?

RAFA: ¡Sí!

PAPÁ: ¿Esta noche?

RAFA: ¡Sí!

PAPÁ: ¡Qué suerte!

RAFA: El padre de Carlos tiene dos entradas, pero en el último momento él no pudo ir ...

4 ROSARIO: ¿Diga?

CURRO: ¡Oye! ¡Soy Curro!

ROSARIO: ¡Hola, Curro! ¿Qué tal?

CURRO: Muy bien. Oye, Rosario, ¿quieres venir conmigo a la discoteca esta noche?

ROSARIO: ¿Esta noche? Mmm ... no, lo siento, Curro.

CURRO: ¿No? ¿Qué te pasa? Normalmente te encanta la idea de ir a la discoteca.

ROSARIO: No sé ... Estoy un poco deprimida. No quiero salir. Quiero quedarme en casa.

CURRO: Bueno, vale. Pero si cambias de opinión, llámame.

5 MAMÁ: ¡Inma! ¡Inma!

INMA: ¿Sí?

MAMÁ: Inma, ¿quieres ir al centro comercial conmigo? ¿Esta tarde?

INMA: Mm, no sé ... No, no tengo tiempo.

MAMÁ: ¡Pero a ti te gusta mucho ir de compras! ¿Qué te pasa?

INMA: ¡Estoy estresada, Mamá! ¡Tengo exámenes el lunes, tengo una clase de guitarra a las doce y un montón de deberes que hacer! ¡Así que no!

MAMÁ: ¡Uf! ¡Inma está de mal humor!

6 PAPÁ: ¿Dónde está Conchita?

MAMÁ: En su dormitorio. Oye, Conchita quiere ir al club de jóvenes esta noche, y ...

PAPÁ: ¿El club de jóvenes en el centro?

MAMÁ: Sí, ése. Estoy un poco preocupada, porque está bastante lejos y tiene mala fama.

PAPÁ: Sí, estoy de acuerdo. ¿Conchita quiere ir con su grupo de amigos o va sola?

3 **Quiero quedarme en casa**

A pairwork activity which practises the language used for giving invitations and responding. Students invite each other, using the words in the help box if necessary.

Gramática

This brief note sets out the verb *querer* and refers students to the grammar summary section 12, p.150 for further explanation, and to Acción: lengua 9, p.83.

4 **Los mensajes electrónicos**

A reading activity in which students read a series of short messages and then draw symbols to express the moods of the messages.

Answers: *Débora –* *; Juan –* ☹ *; Manolo –* ☺ *;*

Marisa – ☹ *;* ☺ *; Ana –* ☹ *;*

Sohora – *;* ☹ *; Pablo –* ☹ *.*

SUPPORT MATERIALS

OHT 9A ¿Qué tal estás?

This OHT presents the following feelings: *triste, enfadado/a, estresado/a, preocupado/a, deprimido/a, harto/a, cansado/a, ilusionado/a, decepcionado/a.*

It can be used for presentation or for follow-up games on the OHP. It can be photocopied onto card, and used for matching games.

Worksheet 9.1 Quiero ir ... ¿quieres venir?

This sheet is designed to accompany listening Activity 2 on p.77 of the Student's Book.

Worksheet 9.2 Las emociones

◐ Students write how they feel in various circumstances and at various times. The activity is semi-open-ended in that they can write any emotion as long as it makes sense and they could justify it if asked.

◓ A similar activity, except that students add a reason for their emotion. There are 10 scenarios offered for students to respond to.

Objectives
Students learn – to say where they're going and ask others
– to ask if someone is free and reply
– to say they can't, and give excuses
– Grammar: the verbs *ir* (to go) and *poder* (to be able to)

Key language
¿quieres ir / venir ...?	*a la bolera*
voy / vas / va	*a la pista de hielo*
al cine	*a la piscina*
al polideportivo	*por la mañana*
al parque de atracciones	*por la tarde*
al club de jóvenes	*por la noche*
al estadio de fútbol	*vale, gracias*
al centro comercial	*(lo siento), (el problema) es que ...*
no tengo mucho tiempo	*no tengo ganas*
no tengo mucho dinero	*tengo un montón de deberes*
no puedo ... porque ...	*no quiero ... porque ...*

Skills / Strategies
Students learn – to say where they go / are going, and ask others
– to accept and decline invitations

ICT opportunities
Students can – word-process and decorate with clip-art any raps they or others produce (Student's Book, Activity 2)

Ways in
Excuses – OHT 9B; Student's Book, presentation

Assessment opportunities
AT1,1/2 Student's Book, Activity 1a ◑: students work out who is going where, and with whom.
AT2,3 Student's Book, Activity 3: students invite each other out and give excuses.
AT4,2 Student's Book, Activity 3 ◑: students modify the dialogues in the book to produce their own.
AT4,3/4 Student's Book, Activity 3 ◐: students invent other conversations.

STUDENT'S BOOK, pages 78–79

1 **La invitación**

a Presentation of excuses. You might like to use OHT 9B to teach and practise these in the context of the now familiar key language. It could be done in the context of days of the week (*el sábado voy al centro comercial ... / y tú (Claire), ¿vas al polideportivo el viernes?*).

Picture story

Pilar wants to invite José Luis and Carlos to the swimming pool, but they have other plans. She is hurt to discover that José Luis has invited Isabel to go to Granada with him and his family.

◑ Students listen and read in order to match both parts of the statements correctly and identify who is saying them.

◐ Students fill in the gaps in a brief text saying who is doing what and with whom.

Answers: ◑ *1 + b: Carlos; 2 + d: Juan; 3 + a: Pilar;
4 + c: José Luis.*

◐ *1 – va; 2 – sábado; 3 – ilusionada; 4 – triste;
5 – preocupada.*

PILAR:	José Luis – voy a ir a la piscina con Isabel el sábado. ¿Quieres venir?
JOSÉ LUIS:	Es que ... voy a Granada con mi familia.
PILAR:	Carlos – el sábado voy a la piscina con Isabel. ¿Quieres venir?
CARLOS:	Es que ... voy al estadio de fútbol con Miguel.
CARMINA:	¿No vas a la piscina con José Luis y Carlos?
PILAR:	No, José Luis va a Granada, y Carlos va al estadio de fútbol.
JOSÉ LUIS:	Isabel, ¿quieres venir a Granada con mi familia?
ISABEL:	¡Estupendo! ¿Por la mañana o por la tarde?
JOSÉ LUIS:	El sábado por la mañana.
ISABEL:	Sí, fenomenal ...
JUAN:	¡Mamá! Voy al centro con Papá ...
CARMINA:	¿Qué te pasa, Pilar?
PILAR:	Isabel va a Granada con José Luis el sábado ...

b Students listen to a follow-up to the previous activity, and sequence excuses in the order in which they appear.

Answers: *3, 2, 1, 4.*

PILAR:	¿Dígame?
JOSÉ LUIS:	¡Oye! ¿Pilar?
PILAR:	¡José Luis!
JOSÉ LUIS:	Pilar, voy al cine el viernes por la noche – ¿quieres venir?
PILAR:	Mm, lo siento ... no tengo mucho dinero.
JOSÉ LUIS:	Bueno, ¿el sábado por la tarde, quieres ir a la piscina?
PILAR:	No sé ..., la piscina ... lo siento, no tengo ganas.
JOSÉ LUIS:	O por la noche, ¿quieres ir a la discoteca?
PILAR:	Lo siento, pero no tengo tiempo.
JOSÉ LUIS:	¿Y el domingo?
PILAR:	Lo siento, pero tengo un montón de deberes.
JOSÉ LUIS:	Pero, ¿qué pasa Pilar? ¿No quieres salir conmigo?
PILAR:	José Luis, no puedo. Lo siento. Adiós ...
JOSÉ LUIS:	Bueno, adiós, Pilar ...

2 **El rap**

A listening, speaking and singing activity to reinforce the present singular forms of *ir*. It is a variation of the 'Cookie Jar' rap, and students may be familiar with the rhythm and principle.

a Students listen to the rap and fill in the gaps with *voy*, *vas* or *va*.

Answers: *1 – va; 2 – vas; 3 – voy; 4 – va; 5 – va.*

b Students take part in the rap. It works like a chain, involves everyone in the group responses, and gives each person the chance to speak individually. You will need to choose a student's name to start it off. To make sure everyone is included, students could stand until their name is mentioned, then sit down. You might prefer to let shyer students stay seated and join in with the group responses until they gain enough confidence to stand up and speak individually.

VOZ 1:	Conchita va a Alcalá.
CONCHITA:	¿Quién? ¿Yo?
TODOS:	¡Sí, tú! **Vas** con tu mamá.
CONCHITA:	¡Yo no **voy** con mi mamá!
TODOS:	¿Quién **va** entonces a Alcalá?
CONCHITA:	Felipe **va** a Alcalá.
FELIPE:	¿Quién? – ¿Yo?
TODOS:	¡Sí, tú! Vas con tu mamá.
FELIPE:	Yo no voy con mi mamá.
TODOS:	¿Quién va entonces a Alcalá?

Gramática

This brief grammar item sets out the verb *ir* and refers students to the grammar summary section 11, p.149 and to *Acción: lengua* 9, p.83 if they need further explanation and / or practice.

3 **¿Estás libre?**

A pairwork activity which involves using substitution boxes to modify a model dialogue. Students read the original conversation with their partner and then invent four more.

Students invent two more conversations and record them if they wish.

SUPPORT MATERIALS

OHT 9B ¿Estás libre?

The nine images present the key phrases for asking if someone is free, and offering excuses. They can be used before, and in conjunction with, the recorded presentation in the Student's Book.

Worksheet 9.3 Excusas

An information-gap activity for pairwork. Cut the worksheet in half and cut off the language support box below each diary page if you feel your students can cope without it. The activity involves students inviting each other out. They must mention the place they want to go to, the day, and the time of day. If they both agree, they should enter the details in their diary. They should take it in turns to ask the questions and give the responses. Encourage some positive reactions as well.

Worksheet 9.4 Práctica: lengua – *poder* (to be able to)

A grammar sheet offering some practice activities with *poder*.

Students pick the correct one of two alternative verb forms each time to complete the letter.

Students fill in the correct forms of *poder* in the gaps in the dialogue.

Answers: *puedo; puede; puedes; puedo.*

            1 – puedes; 2 – puedo; 3 – puedes;
            4 – podemos; 5 – podéis; 6 – puede; 7 – pueden.

El alumno perezoso

Students fill in the gaps in the song with words chosen from the menu.

Answers: *1 – estudiar; 2 – ir; 3 – clase; 4 – enfermería;*
            5 – ventana; 6 – trabajar; 7 – puedo; 8 – tres.

> ¿Puedo abrir la ventana?
> (¡porque no quiero **estudiar**!)
> ¿Puedo **ir** a los servicios?
> (¡porque no quiero trabajar!)
>
> ¿Puedo ir a mi **clase** de trompeta?
> (porque me gusta la música)
> ¿Puedo ir a la **enfermería**?
> No estoy muy bien (¡ja! ¡ja!)
>
> ¿Puedo cerrar la **ventana**, señor?
> (¡No es justo decir que no!)
> ¿Puedo **trabajar** con Juan?
> (¡Porque es más perezoso que yo!)
>
> ¿**Puedo** quitarme el jersey?
> (¡psst! ¡Oye! Dime – ¿qué pasa?)
> ¿Son las **tres** y media ya?
> ¡Ay, qué bien – puedo ir a casa!

Worksheet 9.5 Excusas

1 **El agenda**

A reading activity to consolidate the language of invitations.

Students read the five messages and enter the information into the diary pages for Saturday and Sunday.

Answers: *Sábado*
            Mañana: ¿piscina? ¿pista de hielo?
            Tarde: ¿centro comercial?
            Noche: ¿club de jóvenes?

            Domingo
            Mañana: ¿polideportivo?
            Tarde: ¿cine?

2 **La respuesta**

Since two of the invitations in Activity 1 are for the same time, students have to decline one, filling in a pro forma letter doing so.

Worksheet 9.6 El amigo triste

 Students read carefully a selection of things said in one side of a telephone conversation and write the other person's possible responses. This is an open-ended activity and there are various possibilities.

Objectives
Students learn – to arrange where and when to meet
            – Grammar: revision of prepositions (place)

Key language
¿estás libre?
(no) estoy libre
¿dónde nos vemos?
¿cuándo nos vemos?
¿a qué hora nos vemos?
a la una / a las (dos)
¡estupendo!
hasta luego
adiós

Skills / Strategies
Students learn – how to make arrangements to meet

ICT opportunities
Students can   – draft and format an invitation

Ways in
Excuses   – recorded introduction in Student's Book

Assessment opportunities
AT1,3   Student's Book, Activity 4: students note down the times and places.

AT2,3   Worksheet 9.7, Activity 3: students have a conversation about proposed meetings.

AT3,3   Worksheet 9.7, Activity 2: a multiple-choice comprehension activity.

AT4,2   Student's Book, Activity 6: students fill in the gaps in a letter.

STUDENT'S BOOK, pages 80–81

1   **¡Repaso!**

This activity revises the prepositions introduced in Unit 8. Students are referred back to p.69, Activity 3, and have to join together the two halves of various prepositions.

Answers: *delante; entre; al lado; encima; detrás; enfrente; debajo.*

2   **Pepa llama a Tomás por teléfono**

Presentation of the structures for making suggestions. Students listen to Tomás' questions and match Pepa's answers to each one.

Answers: *1–d; 2–e; 3–a; 4–b; 5–c.*

PEPA:	¿Tomás?
TOMÁS:	Sí, soy yo.
PEPA:	¿Estás libre esta tarde?
TOMÁS:	Mm … sí, estoy libre. ¿Por qué?
PEPA:	¿Quieres dar una vuelta en moto?
TOMÁS:	Sí – ¡qué bien! ¿Pero tú tienes una moto?
PEPA:	Mi primo Quique tiene una. ¿Dónde nos vemos?
TOMÁS:	Delante de mi casa.
PEPA:	¿A qué hora nos vemos?
TOMÁS:	¿A las ocho?
PEPA:	¡Estupendo!
TOMÁS:	Hasta luego, adiós.
PEPA:	Adiós …

3   **¿Dónde nos vemos? ¿A qué hora?**

a Students read a series of suggestions and match each to the appropriate visual on the town plan.

Answers: *1–c; 2–e; 3–a; 4–b; 5–d; 6–f.*

b Students use the town plan to invent conversations with their partners.

4   **¡Los micrófonos ocultos!**

These are meant to be spoof 'secret agents' arranging meetings. All conversations are on a phone or a walkie talkie. Students listen to the clandestine rendezvous as they are arranged, and note down the place and time of the meetings mentioned.

Answers: *1 – delante del cine, 7.30; 2 – al lado de la cafetería, 10.15; 3 – enfrente de la piscina – 7.50; 4 – detrás del supermercado, 5.25; 5 – en la terraza encima del bar, 11.15.*

1   AGENTE 2:   ¿Diga?
      AGENTA 1:   Número uno aquí. ¿Dónde nos vemos?
      AGENTE 2:   Nos vemos delante del cine Rex.
      AGENTA 1:   Vale. ¿A qué hora?
      AGENTE 2:   A las siete y media.
      AGENTA 1:   Perfecto. Adiós.

2   AGENTE 2:   Número 2 aquí. ¿Me oye?
      AGENTA 3:   Sí. ¿A qué hora nos vemos?
      AGENTE 2:   A las diez y cuarto.
      AGENTA 3:   ¿A las diez y cuarto? Muy bien. ¿Pero dónde nos vemos?
      AGENTE 2:   Al lado de la cafetería.
      AGENTA 3:   ¿La cafetería Sol?
      AGENTE 2:   Correcto. ¡Cambio y corto!

3   AGENTA 1:   ¿Dígame?
      AGENTE 3:   ¡Oiga! Número tres aquí. ¿A qué hora nos vemos?
      AGENTA 1:   A las ocho menos diez.
      AGENTE 3:   Ocho menos diez. Bien. Pero, ¿dónde?
      AGENTA 1:   Nos vemos enfrente de la piscina.
      AGENTE 3:   Perfecto, adiós …

4   AGENTE 3:   ¡Número cuatro! ¡Número cuatro!
      AGENTE 4:   ¡Diga!
      AGENTE 3:   ¿A qué hora nos vemos?
      AGENTE 4:   A las cinco y veinticinco.
      AGENTE 3:   ¿Y dónde nos vemos?
      AGENTE 4:   Detrás del supermercado.
      AGENTE 3:   Muy bien. Hasta las cinco y veinticinco, detrás del mercado.
      AGENTE 4:   ¡No dije 'mercado', estúpido! ¡Detrás del supermercado!
      AGENTE 3:   ¡Ay, perdón! Vale, adiós.

5   AGENTE 4:   ¿Diga?
      AGENTA 5:   Número cinco aquí. Nos vemos a las once y cuarto, encima del bar. Adiós.
      AGENTE 4:   ¡Espera! ¡Un momento! ¿Dónde está mi boli? Mi boli … mi boli.
      AGENTA 5:   ¡No debes escribir NADA! ¡Apréndelo de memoria! Repite: 'a las once y cuarto' …
      AGENTE 4:   A las once y cuarto …
      AGENTA 5:   … encima del bar.
      AGENTE 4:   Encima del bar. … ¿Encima del bar?
      AGENTA 5:   ¡Claro! Hay unas escaleras detrás que suben a una terraza.
      AGENTE 4:   Muy bien. Gracias.
      AGENTA 5:   ¡Adiós!
      AGENTE 4:   En la terraza del bar, a las once y cuarto – ¿o a las once menos cuarto?… y cuarto, menos cuarto, yo qué sé … detesto ser espía …

5 **Vamos a salir**

A pairwork activity in which students have conversations with each other suggesting going out to do things. Help boxes and linked, numbered cues are given to provide some guidance.

Students move on to invent some completely different conversations and practise these with their partner.

6 **La invitación**

A mixed-skill reading and copywriting activity in which students fill in gaps in a postcard inviting someone out.

Answers:	*1 – viernes; 2 – noche; 3 – pista de hielo; 4 – discoteca; 5 – siete y media; 6 – bar; 7 – restaurante; 8 – dinero.*

SUPPORT MATERIALS

Worksheet 9.7 ¿Dónde? y ¿cuándo?

1 **Nos vemos ...**

Students listen and write down the appropriate letter of the place of each appointment, and the time.

Answers:	*1 – F, 7:30; 2 – H, 8:00; 3 – C, 12:30; 4 – A, 6:45; 5 – G, 7:10; 6 – D, 9:15.*

1	CHICA:	Manolo, ¿dónde nos vemos?
	CHICO:	¿Nos vemos al lado de la panadería?
	CHICA:	¿La panadería? Vale. ¿A qué hora?
	CHICO:	A las siete y media.
	CHICA:	Vale.

2	CHICO:	¡Pablo! ¿Dónde nos vemos más tarde?
	CHICO:	Detrás del restaurante.
	CHICO:	Y ¿a qué hora?
	CHICO:	¿Nos vemos a las ocho?
	CHICO:	A las ocho – vale. ¡Hasta luego!

3	CHICA:	¿Nos vemos en la cafetería?
	CHICO:	Vale. En la cafetería, a las doce y media.
	CHICA:	¿Las doce y media? Perfecto.

4	SEÑOR:	Anita, ¿a qué hora nos vemos?
	SEÑORA:	¿A las siete menos cuarto?
	SEÑOR:	Vale. Las siete menos cuarto ... ¿dónde?
	SEÑORA:	Enfrente del videoclub.
	SEÑOR:	Muy bien. Hasta luego.

5	CHICO:	¿Dónde nos vemos, Carmen?
	CHICA:	¿Detrás de la cafetería?
	CHICO:	Vale. Detrás de la cafetería a las siete y diez.
	CHICA:	Vale. Nos vemos a las siete y diez.

6	CHICA:	Antonio, ¿a qué hora nos vemos?
	CHICO:	¿A las nueve y cuarto?
	CHICA:	Sí, las nueve y cuarto está bien. ¿Dónde?
	CHICO:	¿Al lado de la discoteca?
	CHICA:	Muy bien. Hasta luego, Antonio.

2 **La conversación**

Students read a conversation and then do a multiple-choice activity which involves picking the best of three words to fill each gap.

Answers:	*1 – tarde; 2 – hacer; 3 – a la discoteca; 4 – dinero; 5 – el parque; 6 – hora; 7 – delante.*

3 **Con tu pareja**

A speaking activity which sets up appointment dialogues via picture prompts.

Objectives

Students learn – to say what they're going to do
– to say where they're going and with whom
– Grammar: simple future

Key language

voy / vas (etc.) a ...
¿con quién ...?
¿adónde vas a ...?
¿cuándo vas a ...?
¿qué vas a hacer?
voy a ...
quedarse

Skills / Strategies

Students learn – how to ask and answer questions and use the
simple future

ICT opportunities

Students can – draft and format a diary or timetable of proposed
activities for a set period

Ways in

Recorded introduction in Student's Book

Assessment opportunities

AT1,3 Student's Book, Activity 2a: students work out who is
talking.
AT2,3/4 Student's Book, Activity 2b: students perform a cued
dialogue using words from a help box.
AT4,2 Worksheet 9.9 (Práctica: lengua): students write in the
appropriate time expressions.

STUDENT'S BOOK, page 82

1 **¿Qué piensa Isabel?**

This activity presents the simple future structures using
ir a + the infinitive. Before beginning, you could present
the language being taught by talking briefly about your
own (alleged!) near-future plans and then eliciting answers
from students in similar terms. Then play the recording
and do the activity. Students listen and fill in the gaps in
the sentences.

Answers: *1 – Granada; 2 – sábado; 3 – días; 4 – ciudad;*
5 – monumentos; 6 – ir.

OMAR:	Vas a ir a Granada el fin de semana, Isabel, ¿no?
ISABEL:	Sí. Voy a salir el sábado con José Luis y su familia.
OMAR:	Tú vas a visitar la ciudad también, ¿no, Pilar?
PILAR:	¿Yo? No. Voy a quedarme en casa.
OMAR:	¿Pilar no va a ir, pero Isabel sí? ¿Qué pasa?
CARMINA:	Es complicado ... Isabel va a quedarse dos días solamente. Va a ver los monumentos importantes, hacer turismo ...
OMAR:	E Isabel no va a ir con Pilar ... ¡Pilar no está muy contenta!
CARMINA:	No. Yo tampoco. Pero ¿qué se puede hacer?

2 **¿Adónde? ¿Qué? ¿Con quién?**

a An activity which presents the other structures being
taught here (further details about where one is going and
with whom). In this activity students listen and read
simultaneously, and work out who is speaking each time.

Answers: *1 – Federico; 2 – Joaquín; 3 – Federico; 4 – Pedro;*
5 – Joaquín; 6 – Pedro.

1 CHICA:	¿Adónde vas a ir el fin de semana?
FEDERICO:	Voy a ir a la costa con mi familia.
2 FEDERICO:	¿Adónde vas a ir el fin de semana?
JOAQUÍN:	Voy a ir de compras en Londres.
FEDERICO:	¡Londres – qué bien!
3 CHICA:	¿Qué vas a hacer?
FEDERICO:	Voy a hacer natación, y hacer vela también, si es posible.
4 CHICA:	¿Adónde vas el fin de semana?
PEDRO:	No voy a salir el fin de semana. Voy a salir el miércoles.

CHICA:	¿Con quién vas a ir?
PEDRO:	Voy a ir con mis padres.
CHICA:	¿Y qué vas a hacer?
PEDRO:	Voy a hacer alpinismo.
5 FEDERICO:	¿Cuánto tiempo vas a quedarte?
JOAQUÍN:	Voy a quedarme tres días, y voy a salir el sábado en avión.
FEDERICO:	¿Qué vas a hacer allí?
JOAQUÍN:	Voy a ver los monumentos históricos, hacer una excursión al castillo de Windsor ...
6 CHICA:	¿Qué otras cosas vas a hacer?
PEDRO:	Voy a hacer piragüismo en el río, si puedo. Me gusta mucho la sierra.
CHICA:	¿Cuánto tiempo vas a quedarte?
PEDRO:	Voy a quedarme cinco días en total.
CHICA:	¡Qué suerte! A mí, me gustaría mucho ir a la sierra ...

b Students invent similar conversations with their partners,
using the questions and answers in the help box on p.82.

SUPPORT MATERIALS

Worksheet 9.8 ¡Qué cara!

¡Qué cara!

 The letter is a humorous 'sick note' giving excuses for not
going to school.

 a A gap-fill activity. Students complete the text of the
letter, choosing from the list of options given.

Answers: *1 – venir; 2 – ir; 3 – quedarme; 4 – estar; 5 – dar;*
6 – hacer; 7 – visitar.

 b Using Mariana's letter as an example, students write a
similar 'sick note' for their own class teacher. This could
be created on computer and formatted appropriately with
both the sender's and recipient's addresses, a suitable
introduction and ending, and perhaps a formal letter
heading complete with clip-art logo.

Worksheet 9.9 Práctica: lengua – expressions of time

Practice of time expressions. Students fill in an appropriate
expression of time in each sentence.

Answers: *1 – El viernes; 2 – Esta mañana; 3 – Esta tarde;*
4 – El miércoles; 5 – El jueves; 6 – El fin de semana;
7 – El lunes que viene.

Acción: lengua 9, page 83

querer (to like, want) and *ir* (to go)

The verb *querer* (to like, want)

○ A gap-fill activity practising *querer*.

Answers: *1 – quiero; 2 – quiere; 3 – quieres; 4 – quiero;*
5 – quiere; 6 – quieres.

♣ Students construct new sentences on the basis of given prompts.

Answers: *1 – ¿Qué queréis hacer vosotros? 2 – Julio y Miguel
quieren ir al cine; 3 – Papá y yo queremos visitar el
nuevo museo; 4 – Y Amaya y Belén, ¿qué quieren
hacer ellas? 5 – Los abuelos quieren venir a las seis;
6 – ¿Qué queremos hacer? ¡Ni idea!*

The verb *ir* (to go)

○ An activity entailing distinguishing between present and future sentences in Spanish.

Answers: *1 – the present; 2 – the present; 3 – the future;
4 – the future; 5 – the present; 6 – the future.*

♣ This activity involves putting an e-mail into the immediate future tense.

Answers: *va a cumplir; va a querer; va a ser; voy a tener;
vamos a tener; van a estar; va a ser; vas a ir.*

Objectives

Students learn – to say what they have to do at home and ask others
– Grammar: *tener que* (to have to); expressions of frequency

Key language

¿qué tienes que hacer?
(no) tengo, tienes, tiene que …
ayudar
hacer la / mi cama
lavar los platos
compartir
quitar la mesa
quitar el polvo
pasar la aspiradora
planchar
lavar la ropa
limpiar el cuarto de baño

preparar la comida
poner la mesa
recoger mi dormitorio
sacar la basura
todos los días
el fin de semana
de vez en cuando
nunca
la pocilga

Skills / Strategies

Students learn – to spot negatives (Worksheet 10.2, Activity 2)

ICT opportunities

Students can – present the results of the survey activity (Worksheet 10.1) on the computer, using appropriate software to make graphs, etc.

Ways in

OHT 10A
Picture story in Student's Book, page 84

Assessment opportunities

AT1,2   Worksheet 10.2, Activity 1: students put the pictures in order.

AT2,3   Student's Book, Activity 2: students exchange information on household chores.

AT3,2   Student's Book, Activity 1: students match the pictures to the new language.

AT4,2   Student's Book, Activity 5 ◐: students write about who does what to help in their family.

AT4,2   Student's Book, Activity 5 ◑: students use Pilar's letter as a model to write some information about chores.

STUDENT'S BOOK, pages 84–85

Picture story

Tensions are mounting within the household, as Isabel is discovered to be out enjoying herself, while everyone else helps out at home.

1 Tengo que …

Students listen to the recording and list who does each task mentioned.

Answers: *Tomás – d, a, j, h; Juan – i; Pilar – c, e, g; Papá – b; Teresa – f.*

TERESA:	¡Un momento, Tomás! Tienes que quitar la mesa y lavar los platos … pasar la aspiradora y poner la mesa.
OMAR:	¡Juan! Tienes que recoger tu dormitorio. ¡Es una pocilga!
JUAN:	El problema es que tengo que compartirlo con Tomás … Y tú – ¿qué tienes que hacer?
PILAR:	Tengo que hacer la cama … quitar el polvo y sacar la basura. Y Papá tiene que planchar.
JUAN:	¿Y la tía Teresa?
PILAR:	La tía Teresa no está muy bien. Va a preparar la comida. Todo el mundo tiene que ayudar en casa, Juan, – ¡es normal!
JUAN:	¿Sí? Entonces, ¿dónde está Isabel?

2 ◓ ¿Cuándo tienes que ayudar en casa?

◐ A pairwork activity in which one partner asks the other when he / she does various tasks, using the visuals from Activity 1 as a stimulus.

◑ Students interview each other about which household chores they do, and add an opinion about each task mentioned.

3 La encuesta

A listening activity in which students listen to the eight people being interviewed and identify how often they each have to help at home. Students choose their answers from one of the time phrases a–d in Activity 2.

Answers: *1 – b; 2 – c; 3 – a; 4 – d; 5 – b; 6 – c; 7 – b; 8 – a.*

PRESENTADORA:	Número uno es Celia: ¿tienes que ayudar en casa?
CELIA:	Mm … sí – el fin de semana.
PRESENTADORA:	Número dos es Fernando: ¿tienes que ayudar en casa?
FERNANDO:	Sí, de vez en cuando.
PRESENTADORA:	Número tres: ¿tienes que ayudar en casa?
CHICA:	Sí, claro – todos los días.
PRESENTADORA:	Número cuatro es Amalia: ¿tienes que ayudar en casa, Amalia?
AMALIA:	No, nunca.
PRESENTADORA:	¿Nunca? ¡Qué bien! Número cinco: ¿tienes que ayudar en casa, Manolo?
MANOLO:	Bueno, mm, normalmente el fin de semana.
PRESENTADORA:	Número seis es Yolanda: ¿tienes que ayudar en casa, Yolanda?
YOLANDA:	Depende … de vez en cuando.
PRESENTADORA:	Número siete es Elena: ¿tienes que ayudar en casa, Elena?
ELENA:	Sí. Ayudo el fin de semana.
PRESENTADORA:	Número ocho es Raúl: dime, ¿tienes que ayudar en casa?
RAÚL:	Somos ocho en mi familia, así que tengo que ayudar todos los días.

4 Pilar escribe a su prima, Maite

An extract from a letter written by Pilar to her cousin, in which she mentions a lot of household chores. Students read the letter and fill in the gaps with words from the selection given.

Answers: *1 – tiempo; 2 – cama; 3 – sacar; 4 – lavar; 5 – pasar; 6 – recoger; 7 – hermano; 8 – preparar.*

5 ◓ Te toca a ti

◐ A straightforward writing activity in which students write a sentence about the chores done by each member of their family. A little leniency could be extended to students who have exceptionally large families.

◑ An activity which involves writing a short text about who does what chore in the family, how often they do it and whether they like or dislike doing it. Students can use Pilar's letter for support or as a template if necessary.

Gramática

Tener que in the singular is presented here and students are referred to the grammar summary, section 11, p.149 for more information.

SUPPORT MATERIALS

OHT 10A ¿Qué tienes que hacer?

This can be used for presentation before looking at the Student's Book or as a memory-jogger in a subsequent lesson. Those who find writing difficult can use it to complete Activity 5 in the Student's Book with a minimum of writing. It can be photocopied onto card and cut up into squares to use in speaking and reading games (see introduction: Games with small cards).

Worksheet 10.1 ¿Qué tienes que hacer en casa?

This is a survey sheet to find out who does what at home. If you work in a single sex school, simply white out either the *chicas* or the *chicos* in the heading and in the conclusions. If you want to make it more challenging with a more able group, white out the *chicos / chicas* headings, divide the vertical columns again to give four, and write in *todos los días, el fin de semana, de vez en cuando, nunca,* and alter the sample speech bubbles to *¿Tienes que hacer tu cama?* / *Sí, todos los días.*

Worksheet 10.2 Los quehaceres

1 **La llamada de Pepa**

Pepa telephones Tomás.

◐ Students listen for the excuses, and note the number of the picture.

♣ More able students do this multiple-choice activity.

Answers:	◐ 4; 7; 8; 6; 3.
	♣ 1–b; 2–c; 3–c; 4–c; 5–b.

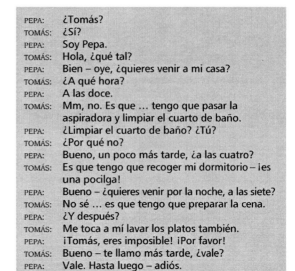

PEPA:	¿Tomás?
TOMÁS:	¿Sí?
PEPA:	Soy Pepa.
TOMÁS:	Hola, ¿qué tal?
PEPA:	Bien – oye, ¿quieres venir a mi casa?
TOMÁS:	¿A qué hora?
PEPA:	A las doce.
TOMÁS:	Mm, no. Es que … tengo que pasar la aspiradora y limpiar el cuarto de baño.
PEPA:	¿Limpiar el cuarto de baño? ¿Tú?
TOMÁS:	¿Por qué no?
PEPA:	Bueno, un poco más tarde, ¿a las cuatro?
TOMÁS:	Es que tengo que recoger mi dormitorio – ies una pocilga!
PEPA:	Bueno – ¿quieres venir por la noche, a las siete?
TOMÁS:	No sé … es que tengo que preparar la cena.
PEPA:	¿Y después?
TOMÁS:	Me toca a mí lavar los platos también.
PEPA:	¡Tomás, eres imposible! ¡Por favor!
TOMÁS:	Bueno – te llamo más tarde, ¿vale?
PEPA:	Vale. Hasta luego – adiós.

2 **La rutina de Ana**

A longer reading activity about Ana, who works in a hotel in Mallorca.

a ◐ This activity encourages students to read for meaning and check the sentence for negatives, rather than simply spotting the key language.

Answers:	1–sí; 2–no; 3–no; 4–sí; 5–sí; 6–no; 7–sí; 8–sí.

b ◐ This activity encourages reading for detail, and using the context and similarity of English words to Spanish to work out the meaning.

Answers:	dormitorios – 20; cuartos de baño – 30; salones – 4; clientes – 200; mesas – 100; camas – 50.

3 **¿Qué te gusta hacer?**

An opportunity for students to recycle the language of likes and dislikes with household chores.

Objectives
Students learn – to say what they have to do as part of their daily routine

Key language

cenar	escuchar
ir a la cama	leer
trabajar mucho	escribir
cenar con …	volver a casa
coger el autobús	comer
desayunar	ir al instituto (andando)
estudiar	ir al polideportivo
hacer los deberes	llegar a tiempo
hay que …	salir un rato
hoy	temprano
ir al instituto	tener exámenes
llegar a tiempo	ver la tele (un poco)
pronto	volver a casa

Skills / Strategies
Students learn – to talk about daily routine

ICT opportunities
Students can   – word-process a list of helpful phrases for display

Ways in
OHT 10B
Picture story in Student's Book, page 86

Assessment opportunities
AT1,3   Worksheet 10.3, Activity 1: students listen and sequence the visuals.

AT2,4   Worksheet 10.3, Activity 2: students do cued dialogues with their partners.

AT3,3   Student's Book, Activity 2 ◐: students read and insert the missing words.

AT3,3   Student's Book, Activity 2 ◓: students read and comment via smiley / sad faces on the opinions given.

AT4,2   Student's Book, Activity 3 ◐: students copy or word-process short phrases.

AT4,3/4   Student's Book, Activity 3 ◓: students write phrases about chores, adding some unfamiliar ones or ones from other topic areas.

STUDENT'S BOOK, pages 86–87

1 **Hay que …**

Picture story

Pepa and Tomás are feeling gloomy about the humdrum routine they endure. The dog agrees …

a Students initially just listen to the recording and look at the sequence of pictures.

PEPA:	¡Qué aburrido! Todos los días, hay que …
TOMÁS:	desayunar
PEPA:	coger el autobús
TOMÁS:	ir al instituto
PEPA:	llegar a tiempo
TOMÁS:	escuchar
PEPA:	leer
TOMÁS:	escribir
PEPA:	volver a casa
TOMÁS:	comer
PEPA:	estudiar y hacer los deberes
TOMÁS:	salir un rato
PEPA:	ver la tele un poco
TOMÁS:	cenar
PEPA:	ir a la cama
AMBOS:	¡Hay que trabajar mucho! ¡Es una vida de perros!

b ◐ Students now listen to the recording and note down the numbers of the activities in the sequence in which they are mentioned for each person.

◓ This activity entails answering a set of closed questions with the name of the appropriate person.

Answers: ◐ *Auri – 2, 4, 8; David – 1, 3, 10; Jazmina – 5, 7, 14; Lorenzo – 2, 9, 11; Montse – 10, 13, 14.*

◓ *a – Auri; b – Lorenzo; c – Jazmina; d – David; e – Jazmina; f – Montse.*

AURI
MAMÁ:	¡Auri! ¡Rápido! ¡Son las ocho menos cuarto!
AURI:	¿Hay que coger el autobús hoy?
MAMÁ:	Sí, no tengo coche.
AURI:	Vale, ¡me voy! ¡Con el nuevo director, hay que llegar a tiempo!
MAMÁ:	¡Menos mal! Y tienes que volver a casa temprano.

AURI:	¿Volver a casa temprano? ¿Por qué?
MAMÁ:	¡Porque tu dormitorio es una pocilga! Bueno, ¡rápido, o vas a perder el autobús!

DAVID
PAPÁ:	David, ¿no quieres cereales?
DAVID:	No, gracias.
PAPÁ:	¿Café?
DAVID:	No.
PAPÁ:	Pero ¡hay que desayunar algo!
DAVID:	No tengo tiempo, Papá. Hay que ir al instituto andando, y está lejos.
PAPÁ:	¿Vas al polideportivo hoy, después de las clases?
DAVID:	No, hay que estudiar y hacer los deberes. Tenemos exámenes pronto. Bueno, ya está. Bueno, me voy. ¡Adiós!

JAZMINA
PROFE.:	¡Jazmina!
JAZMINA:	¿Sí?
PROFE.:	¿Estás escuchando? ¡Hay que escuchar!
JAZMINA:	Vale.
PROFE.:	¿Me dejas ver tu trabajo? ¡Pero no has escrito nada! ¡Hay que escribir más!
JAZMINA:	Bueno, es que no tengo mucha energía hoy.
PROFE.:	¡Y hay que ir a la cama temprano! No vas a poder estudiar si no duermes bastante por la noche …

LORENZO
MAMÁ:	Lorenzo, hay que coger el autobús hoy …
LORENZO:	Vale.
MAMÁ:	Y hay que comer en casa de los abuelos hoy.
LORENZO:	¿Hay que comer con los abuelos? ¿Por qué?
MAMÁ:	¡Porque yo no estoy aquí!
LORENZO:	Ah, sí, es verdad. Pero tengo que salir un rato.
MAMÁ:	¿Tienes que salir? ¿Adónde vas?
LORENZO:	A la piscina – tengo clase. ¿Se te ha olvidado?
MAMÁ:	Sí, completamente. Explícaselo a tu abuela – seguro que lo va a entender.

MONTSE
MONTSE:	¿Diga? … ¡Miguel! ¿Qué tal? … Bien. Bueno, bastante bien … No, lo siento, no puedo … ¡Porque hay que estudiar y hacer los deberes! Tengo un montón … No, tengo que cenar aquí con mis padres … ¡Hay que cenar con mi familia de vez en cuando! … No, no quiero salir, es demasiado tarde … ¡Sí, hay que ir a la cama temprano! No … no … bueno, adiós Miguel, ¡adiós!

2 **La rutina del campamento**

○ Students read eight young people's opinions on the daily routine in a school / activity camp and pick one of two alternatives to fill in each gap.

♣ For this activity students read the text and decide whether each opinion given is positive, negative or not obvious either way.

Answers: ○ *Muriela – desayunar; Dani – llegar; Olivia – escribir; Nando – volver; Azahara – comer; Julio – ver; Paloma – hacer; Victor – leer; Montse – ir.*

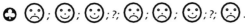

3 **Mi rutina ideal**

○ Students write lists of the activities which feature and do not feature in their ideal daily routine, using *hay que* and *no hay que*.

♣ This activity involves writing sentences from Unit 10A or 7C/D about their ideal routine. Students can use a dictionary if necessary.

SUPPORT MATERIALS

OHT 10B La rutina diaria

This sheet can be used for presentation of the daily routine vocabulary. It can be used for a variety of speaking or memory games (see Introduction, p.6).

Worksheet 10.3 La rutina

1 🖉 **Esteban y su padre**

a Students listen and sequence the activities mentioned by Esteban on the recording.

Answers: *1 – c; 2 – a; 3 – b; 4 – e; 5 – d.*

b Then they listen again and sequence the order in which Esteban's father says he should do the activities.

Answers: *1 – d; 2 – g; 3 – e; 4 – a; 5 – f.*

ESTEBAN

PADRE: ¿Qué vas a hacer esta tarde, Esteban?

ESTEBAN: Primero, tengo que salir un rato. Segundo, voy a cenar a casa de mi amigo Javier. Allí, voy a ver la tele con Javier – el partido de fútbol del Real Betis – Manchester United es esta tarde. Después, voy a volver a casa a las nueve.

PADRE: ¿Y cuándo vas a estudiar y hacer los deberes?

ESTEBAN: Después. A las diez.

SU PADRE

PADRE: Bueno, escucha, Esteban. Eres muy perezoso. ¡Esto es lo que vas a hacer! Primero tienes que estudiar. Tienes que hacer tus deberes ahora hasta las ocho y media. Segundo, tienes que hacer media hora de footing conmigo.

ESTEBAN: ¿Footing? ¡Odio el footing!

PADRE: Me da igual. Después, vamos a volver a casa. Luego vamos a cenar en la cocina con tu mamá. Y después, tienes que ir a la cama.

ESTEBAN: ¿A la cama? ¿A las nueve y media?

PADRE: Lo siento, pero si tú no tienes auto-disciplina, tenemos que ayudarte ...

---

2 **Los padres estrictos y permisivos**

Speaking practice, in which students play the role of parents of varying strictness. Students take it in turns to ask each other five questions, using the pictures as prompts for both their questions and answers. The vocabulary box offers support if necessary.

Objectives

Students learn – to describe what they do
              – Grammar: the present tense (part 1)

Key language

Verbs in the present tense, including:
me levanto (temprano)
desayuno (zumo de naranja)
cojo (el autobús)
voy (al instituto)
llego (a tiempo)
escucho (a los profesores)
escribo (en mi carpeta)
trabajo (mucho)
vuelvo (a casa)
como (con la familia)
salgo (con mis amigos)
juego (al tenis)
veo (la televisión)
leo (una revista)
hago (mis deberes)
ceno (en la cocina)
voy (a la cama)

Skills / Strategies

Students learn – the 1st person form of the present tense (regular verbs)

ICT opportunities

Students can   – word-process daily routine sentences
                  (Worksheet 10.5, Activity 3)

Ways in

Recorded presentation in Student's Book, page 88

Assessment opportunities

AT1,3   Student's Book, Activity 1: students underline the correct alternatives.
AT2,3/4   Student's Book, Activity 2: students give a presentation.
AT 4,2   Worksheet 10.5, Activity 3: students write sentences about daily routine.
AT 4,3   Worksheet 10.6, Activity 2: students complete a gapped text.

STUDENT'S BOOK, pages 88–89

1 Isabel

Isabel is talking to her father on the phone. Students look at the text in the Student's Book and on Worksheet 10.4. They listen to the recording and read the text. Each time a verb is mentioned they note down the correct ending, underlining the correct one of the three alternative endings to each sentence.

Answers: *temprano, desayuno, zumo de naranja, el autobús, sola, llego, a tiempo, escucho, a los profesores, escribo, en mi carpeta, trabajo, mucho, a las tres, como, en casa con la familia, con mis amigos, al tenis, veo, la televisión, leo, una revista, mis deberes, ceno, en la cocina, a la cama a las diez y media.*

MICHAEL:	¿Qué tal la rutina en Sevilla, Isabel? ¿Todo está bien?
ISABEL:	Sí, Papá, está bien. Por la mañana, me levanto temprano y desayuno zumo de naranja, y luego ... cojo el autobús y voy al instituto sola.
MICHAEL:	¿Sola? ¿No vas con Pilar?
ISABEL:	No, voy sola. Llego a tiempo, y ... no sé, escucho a los profesores, y ... escribo en mi carpeta ... trabajo mucho.
MICHAEL:	¿Trabajas mucho? ¡Me alegro! ¿Qué haces por la tarde?
ISABEL:	Por la tarde, vuelvo a las tres, y como en casa con la familia. A veces, salgo con mis amigos ...
MICHAEL:	¿Tus amigos?
ISABEL:	Sí, bueno, con mi amigo José Luis. Juego al tenis con él. Y luego por la noche veo la televisión, o ... leo una revista ... hago mis deberes, ceno en la cocina y voy a la cama a las diez y media. Y ya está ...

2 Prepara un ejercicio oral

Students note down details of their own daily routine in abbreviated form and then make a brief oral presentation in front of the class and / or teacher.

3 Beltrán, monje medieval

Students read a letter from a medieval monk to his mother and sequence the visuals according to the order in which they are mentioned in the letter.

A multiple-choice activity in which students read three possible alternative endings for a series of sentences relating to the letter, and decide which ending is incorrect.

Answers: ⭕ *3, 6, 5, 1, 7, 2, 4.*

                ⊕ *1 – A es falsa; 2 – B es falsa; 3 – B es falsa; 4 – B es falsa; 5 – A es falsa.*

4 Imagina ...

An open-ended writing activity which entails writing the daily routine of an historical person, an imaginary person or a person from the future.

Gramática

This brief item directs students to the grammar summary, section 11, p.149 and to Acción: lengua 10, p.93 for more information on *ar*, *er* and *ir* verbs. Worksheets 10.5 and 10.6 provide further practice of this point.

SUPPORT MATERIALS

Worksheet 10.4 Isabel

⭕ This worksheet accompanies Activity 1 on p.88 of the Student's Book. There are removable English rubrics at the bottom of the sheet.

Worksheet 10.5 El fin de semana

This sheet has removable English rubrics at the bottom.

1 ¿Cuándo?

⭕ Students listen and write the correct letter in each box. There is one letter left over.

Answers:

	Mañana	Tarde	Noche
Sábado	e	g	b
Domingo	d	c	a

f = distractor

ENTREVISTADOR:	¿Qué haces el sábado, Jesús?	
JESÚS:	Por la mañana, me levanto temprano.	
ENTREVISTADOR:	¿Temprano?	
JESÚS:	Sí, porque voy a la piscina.	
ENTREVISTADOR:	Y ¿el sábado por la tarde?	
JESÚS:	Depende. Pero muchas veces veo la tele.	
ENTREVISTADOR:	¿Qué ves en la tele?	
JESÚS:	El deporte – me gusta ver los partidos de fútbol.	
ENTREVISTADOR:	¿Sales por la noche?	
JESÚS:	Sí. Salgo con mis amigos. Voy a la discoteca o al cine. Tengo un grupo grande de amigos y es divertido.	
ENTREVISTADOR:	El domingo por la mañana, ¿qué haces?	
JESÚS:	Trabajo en casa. Tengo que pasar la aspiradora, recoger mi dormitorio ... lo normal.	
ENTREVISTADOR:	¿Y por la tarde?	
JESÚS:	Normalmente, salgo un rato al parque, o por ahí.	
ENTREVISTADOR:	No mencionas los deberes. ¿No tienes que estudiar?	
JESÚS:	Sí, claro. Estudio el domingo por la noche.	

c   CHICA: Voy a salir a las ocho de casa y voy a llegar a Barcelona a las once. Primero, voy a ir de compras – las tiendas allí en la Diagonal son estupendas.

d   CHICO: No sé todavía lo que voy a hacer por la mañana. Por la tarde, voy a jugar al fútbol, y luego voy a coger el autobús al centro.

e   CHICA: Ceno con mi familia a las nueve, y después veo la tele un rato. Me voy a la cama a eso de las once.

f   CHICO: Vuelvo a casa en autobús con mis amigos. De vez en cuando voy a la cafetería de enfrente, pero en general hago mis deberes primero.

g   SEÑORA: Voy a ir a la playa la semana que viene. Voy a quedarme en un hotel de cuatro estrellas. No voy a trabajar, no voy a estudiar – voy a leer libros, tomar el sol, y cenar fuera por la noche.

h   SEÑOR: Prefiero comer en casa con la familia, pero a veces no puedo. Entonces, como algo en la oficina, trabajo hasta las siete, y vuelvo a casa.

2 El sábado por la mañana

A sentence-matching activity practising the daily routine vocabulary.

Answers: *1–c; 2–e; 3–h; 4–a; 5–f; 6–d; 7–g; 8–b.*

3 Un sábado o domingo típico

Students complete a schedule giving details of their own daily routine.

Worksheet 10.6 Lo normal

1 ¿Normalmente o en el futuro?

A listening activity in which students decide whether the activities mentioned are done normally (present tense) or will be done at the weekend (future tense).

Answers: *a – N; b – N; c – F; d – F; e – N; f – N; g – F; h – N.*

a	CHICA:	Me levanto bastante temprano a las siete, pero no tengo mucho tiempo para desayunar. Desayuno fruta y café.
b	CHICO:	Me gusta bastante mi instituto, pero la rutina es un poco aburrida. Todos los días voy a clase, escucho a mis profesores, escribo, aprendo, leo ... ¡es una vida de perros!

2 Alicia

Students read a letter about daily routine and replace the symbols with words. The activity is open-ended in that students can choose the details of what they insert, as long as it is the correct sort of information as classified on the symbols menu.

Worksheet 10.7 Práctica: lengua – el presente y el futuro

A practice sheet giving drills on the present and future tenses.

Students say whether each sentence is in the present or the future tense.

Answers: *1 – Present; 2 – Future; 3 – Present; 4 – Future; 5 – Future; 6 – Present.*

Students rewrite the sentences in the immediate future tense.

Answers: *1 – Voy a desayunar cereales y un zumo de fruta; 2 – Después, voy a salir de casa; 3 – Voy a ir andando al instituto; 4 – Voy a volver a las cuatro de la tarde; 5 – Voy a hacer mis deberes en el salón; 6 – Voy a escuchar música o leer un poco.*

Objectives
Students learn – to ask questions about daily routine
                – Grammar: present tense (*tú*)

Key language
Question forms, including the following:
¿qué desayunas?
¿cómo vas al instituto?
¿a qué hora llegas?
¿dónde comes al mediodía?
¿sales mucho con tus amigos?
¿cuántas horas de deberes haces?
¿qué desayunas en Gran Bretaña?
¿vuelves a casa?
¿a qué hora te levantas?
¿tienes tiempo para desayunar?
¿vas al instituto andando?
¿qué haces en el recreo?
¿llevas un bocadillo para comer?
¿y después de las clases?
¿haces algún deporte?
¿ves mucho la tele?

Skills / Strategies
Students learn – to ask and answer questions

ICT opportunities
Students can   – word-process a 'questions bank' or database as a
                   follow-up activity (Worksheet 10.8)

Ways in
Recorded presentation in Student's Book, page 90

Assessment opportunities
AT1,2   Student's Book, Activity 1c: students identify Tomás'
          answers.
AT3,2   Student's Book, Activity 2a: a gap-fill activity practising
          verb forms.
AT4,2   Worksheet 10.8, Activity b: students write as many
          questions as they can.

STUDENT'S BOOK, pages 90–91

1 Interrogativos

a Students listen to questions posed by Tomas' classmates. No activity is set initially, but students can listen to the recording and follow the questions in the Student's Book.

PROFESOR:	Háblanos de tu rutina en Gran Bretaña, Tomás.
ESTUDIANTE:	¿Qué desayunas, por ejemplo?
ESTUDIANTE:	¿Cómo vas al instituto?
ESTUDIANTE:	¿A qué hora llegas?
ESTUDIANTE:	¿Dónde comes al mediodía?
ESTUDIANTE:	¿Sales mucho con tus amigos?
ESTUDIANTE:	¿Cuántas horas de deberes haces?

b This revision activity asks students to work out the English for the question forms in the green box which form the core teaching point of the objective.

Answers: *At what time (When)? When? What? Where? How? How much / many?*

c Students listen to Tomás being questioned about his daily routine, and note down his answers.

Answers: *1 – cereales, té; 2 – en autobús; 3 – 8.45 a.m.; 4 – comedor; 5 – no mucho entresemana; 6 – una hora y media.*

1	CHICA:	Tomás, ¿qué desayunas en Gran Bretaña? ¿Beicon?
	TOMÁS:	¡No! Desayuno cereales, un té ...
2	CHICO:	¿Y cómo vas al instituto?
	TOMÁS:	Voy en autobús, normalmente.
3	CHICA:	¿A qué hora llegas?
	TOMÁS:	Llego a las nueve menos cuarto.
4	CHICO:	¿Dónde comes al mediodía? ¿Vuelves a casa?
	TOMÁS:	No. Como en el comedor del instituto.
5	CHICA:	¿Sales mucho con tus amigos?
	TOMÁS:	No, entresemana no salgo mucho.
6	CHICA:	¿Cuántas horas de deberes haces?
	TOMÁS:	Depende. Una hora y media ...
	CHICA:	¿Una hora y media? ¡Qué poco! ¡Aquí, tenemos dos o tres horas de trabajo que hacer!

2 Los verbos

a A verb practice activity. Students look at a help box giving the verb forms needed, and then complete a series of questions correctly.

Answers: *1 – levantas; 2 – desayunas; 3 – vas; 4 – llegas; 5 – Trabajas; 6 – comes; 7 – vuelves; 8 – cenas; 9 – haces; 10 – Ves; 11 – Sales; 12 – vas.*

Gramática

Students are directed here to the grammar summary, sections 10 and 12, p.149 and p.150 for more information on verbs, and to Acción: lengua 10 on p.93 for further practice.

b Students now match up the 12 answers to the 12 questions in Activity 2a.

Answers: *1 – h; 2 – l; 3 – a; 4 – j; 5 – c; 6 – k; 7 – d; 8 – b; 9 – g; 10 – e; 11 – f; 12 – i.*

c Students now write the verb form for each of the answers to a–i in Activity 2b.

Answers: *a – Voy andando; b – Ceno; c – Trabajo; d – Vuelvo; e – Veo; f – Salgo; g – Hago; h – Me levanto; i – Me voy; j – Llego; k – Como; l – Desayuno.*

3 Con tu pareja

A pairwork activity in which students use the 12 questions from Activity 2a (p.90) and adapt the answers from Activity 2b to their own circumstances.

4 La rutina de Santi

Students listen to Santi being interviewed about his rather unhealthy daily routine and answer whether each phrase is true or false.

Answers: *1 – F; 2 – V; 3 – V; 4 – F; 5 – F; 6 – V.*

ENTREVISTADOR:	Tu rutina no es muy sana, ¿verdad, Santi?
SANTI:	¡Me dicen que no!
ENTREVISTADOR:	¿A qué hora te levantas?
SANTI:	A las ocho y media.

ENTREVISTADOR:	¡No muy temprano!
SANTI:	No. El instituto está cerca pero muchas veces llego tarde.
ENTREVISTADOR:	¿Tienes tiempo para desayunar?
SANTI:	¡Sí! Siempre desayuno! Cereales, un huevo, tostadas, zumo de fruta, un yogur ...
ENTREVISTADOR:	¡Uf! ¿Vas al instituto andando?
SANTI:	Sí.
ENTREVISTADOR:	¿Qué haces en el recreo? ¿Llevas un bocadillo para comer?
SANTI:	No. Voy a la cafetería de enfrente, y tomo una pizza y una hamburguesa.
ENTREVISTADOR:	¿Y después de las clases? ¿Haces algún deporte?
SANTI:	No. Odio el deporte. Vuelvo a casa y veo la tele.
ENTREVISTADOR:	¿Ves mucho la tele?
SANTI:	Mm ... cuatro o cinco horas al día.

5 Una vida sana

Santi wishes to adopt an altogether healthier lifestyle as shown by his plans in the green box on p.91 of the Student's Book. This is a cued writing activity in which students invent an interview with Santi about his daily routine and supply the details in their own words from the information given. Worksheet 10.9 can be used either as a support template for the activity or as an additional gap-fill activity.

An activity which entails developing the previous activity and adding further details, using language encountered in other units.

SUPPORT MATERIALS

Worksheet 10.8 ¡Aún más preguntas!

a Students fill in the blank spaces in the box in English by translating the Spanish words. All of these words are listed in the Spanish–English vocabulary section at the back of the Student's Book.

Answers: *¿Qué? – What? ¿Cuándo? – When? ¿A qué hora? – At what time? ¿Dónde? – Where? ¿Adónde? – Where to? ¿Cómo? – How? ¿Cuántos? – How many? (mpl); ¿Cuántas? – How many? (fpl).*

b Students write as many different questions as they can, using the stimuli given on the sheet.

Worksheet 10.9 La rutina de Santi

This sheet has removable English rubrics at the bottom.

1 Una vida sana

Students fill in the details of Santi's routine (see Student's Book, p.91) with the appropriate verbs.

Answers: *A – te levantas, desayunas, vas; B – trabajas, vuelves; C – cenas, ves; D – sales; E – comes, vas.*

2 Los dibujos

Students read sections A–E in Activity 1 again and pick a visual to match each.

Answers: *1 – D; 2 – E; 3 – B; (4 is the distractor); 5 – A; 6 – C.*

Worksheet 10.10 Práctica: lengua – reflexive verbs

A worksheet explaining and giving practice of reflexive verbs.

Students fill in the correct reflexive pronouns.

Answers: *1 – te; 2 – me; 3 – te; 4 – me; 5 – me; 6 – me; 7 – te; 8 – se.*

Students fill in the correct form of the verbs.

Answers: *me arreglo; se relaja; se lavan; se ducha; se lava; nos quedamos; se levantan.*

Objectives
Students learn – to talk about what other people do
– Grammar: present tense (*él, ella, usted*)

Key language
Verbs in the third person singular, including:
ies un desastre!
se levanta tarde
no desayuna
no llega a tiempo
no estudia en clase
no escribe los deberes
sale con Pepa al parque
vuelve a casa a las diez
va a la cama a las once de la noche
come una tostada y es todo
llega tarde también
estudia nueve asignaturas
no escribe nada en sus cuadernos
ve cuatro horas de tele cada noche

Skills / Strategies
Students learn – to transfer sentences into the third person form

ICT opportunities
Students can – word-process a daily diary in the third person

Ways in
Recorded presentation in Student's Book, page 92

Assessment opportunities
AT1,3   Student's Book, Activity 1 ◑: students sequence the visuals.
AT1,4   Student's Book, Activity 1 ◓: students add details of the conversation.
AT3,2   Student's Book, Activity 2: students work out who each sentence refers to.

STUDENT'S BOOK, page 92

1 **Teresa y Carmina**
Picture story
Teresa is complaining to her sister Carmina about Tomás over coffee at the kitchen table.

◑ Students read and listen to the first part of the conversation and pick the appropriate picture for each of the numbered sentences in the picture.

◓ Students listen to the whole conversation and fill in the gaps in the six sentences summarising the conversation between Carmina and Teresa.

Answers:
◑ *1 – d; 2 – b; 3 – g; 4 – a; 5 – e; 6 – c; 7 – f.*

◓ *1 – a la cama, once; 2 – una tostada; 3 – tarde; 4 – nueve asignaturas; 5 – en sus cuadernos; 6 – cuatro horas.*

TERESA:	¿Tomás? iEs un desastre! Se levanta tarde ... No desayuna ... No llega a tiempo al instituto ... No estudia en clase ... No apunta los deberes en su agenda ... Sale con Pepa al parque ... y vuelve a casa a las diez ...
TERESA:	¿Tomás? iEs un desastre! Se levanta tarde ...
CARMINA:	¡Juan es igual, Teresa! Va a la cama a las once de la noche.
TERESA:	Tomás no desayuna.
CARMINA:	Juan come una tostada y es todo.
TERESA:	Tomás no llega a tiempo al instituto ...
CARMINA:	Y Juan llega tarde también.
TERESA:	Tomás no estudia en clase ...
CARMINA:	¡Juan estudia nueve asignaturas!
TERESA:	Tomás no escribe los deberes en su agenda ...
CARMINA:	Y Juan no escribe nada en sus cuadernos.
TERESA:	Tomás sale con Pepa y vuelve a casa a las diez ...
CARMINA:	¡Y Juan ve cuatro horas de tele cada noche!
LAS DOS:	¡Qué difíciles son los niños!

2 **Ana y Daniela**
Students read the sentences and decide whether they apply to Ana Angelita, who does all the right things, or to Daniela Desastre, who does all the wrong things.

Answers:
1 – Ana Angelita; 2 – Daniela Desastre; 3 – Daniela Desastre; 4 – Ana Angelita; 5 – Daniela Desastre; 6 – Ana Angelita; 7 – Daniela Desastre; 8 – Daniela Desastre.

Gramática
The brief help box refers students to the grammar summary, sections 10 and 12, p. 149 and p.150 and to Acción: lengua 10, p.93 if help is needed with the third person forms.

SUPPORT MATERIALS
Worksheet 10.11 Práctica: lengua – stem-changing verbs
◑ ◓ Practice of stem-changing verbs. Students fill in the missing letters.

Answers:
*vuelvo, vuelves, vuelve, volvemos, volvéis, vuelven
meriendo, meriendas, merienda, merendamos, merendáis, meriendan
repito, repites, repite, repetimos, repetís, repiten*

	acostarse (ue) (to go to bed)	despertarse (ie) (to wake up)	vestirse (i) (to get dressed)
yo	me acuesto	me despierto	me visto
tú	te acuestas	te despiertas	te vistes
él, ella, usted	se acuesta	se despierta	se viste
nosotros	nos acostamos	nos despertamos	nos vestimos
vosotros	os acostáis	os despertáis	os vestís
ellos, ellas, ustedes	se acuestan	se despiertan	se visten

Acción: lengua 10, page 93 The present tense
Presents activities and drills to practise the present tense.

1 ◑ Students put the verbs into the first person singular form.

◓ Students match up the sentence halves.

Answers:
◑ *1 – lavo; 2 – preparo; 3 – saco; 4 – pongo; 5 – recojo; 6 – salgo; 7 – leo.*

◓ *1 – e; 2 – f; 3 – b; 4 – c; 5 – a; 6 – d.*

2 ◑ Students choose the correct form of the verbs.

◓ Students put the verbs into the correct form in the present tense.

Answers:
◑ *hago; ayudo; pasa; plancha; recojo; salgo; como; juego; hago.*

◓ *1 – hacéis; 2 – comen; 3 – bebemos; 4 – cenáis; 5 – juegan; 6 – vemos; 7 – salís.*

¡Repaso! 6–10

A review and revision section concentrating on Units 6–10. As with the first of these sections, it may be used for ongoing assessment and analysis of students' progress.

STUDENT'S BOOK, pages 94–95

1 ¿De qué hablan?

a Students listen and pick the correct visual for each fragment of conversation.

Answers: *1–e; 2–b; 3–d; 4–g; 5–a; 6–f; 7–c.*

b Students listen again and decide whether each reply is positive or negative.

Answers: *1–✓; 2–✗; 3–✓; 4–✓; 5–✗; 6–✗; 7–✓.*

1	CHICO	¡Hola, Margarita! Oye, ¿quieres venir a la cafetería?
	CHICA	¡Qué bien! Sí, me gustaría mucho.
2	CHICO	Dime, Hugo, ¿qué tal la vela? Haces vela, ¿no?
	CHICO	Sí, los sábados. Pero es muy aburrido.
3	CHICA	¿Me dejas ver tu dormitorio?
	CHICA	Sí, pasa, pasa.
	CHICA	¡Qué bien! Recién pintado ... Oh, ¡me gusta mucho la cómoda!
	CHICA	Sí, a mí también. Es muy bonito, el azul y el blanco.
4	CHICO	¿Te gustaría ir a la bolera?
	CHICA	Sí, me gustaría mucho. ¿A qué hora?
	CHICO	¿Si nos vemos a las seis?
	CHICA	Vale.
5	SEÑOR	¿Qué tal tu piso nuevo, Inma? Está en la costa, ¿no?
	SEÑORA	Sí, pero la costa allí es fea. Es industrial y sucia.
6	CHICA	Vamos todos a la discoteca, Irene. ¿Quieres venir?
	CHICA	¿A qué hora salís?
	CHICA	A las siete.
	CHICA	No, lo siento. A las siete, no. Voy al centro con Marta.
7	CHICA	¿Quieres ir al cine, Rafa?
	CHICO	¡Sí! Y te invito a cenar después.
	CHICA	¡Muchas gracias! ¡Qué generoso!
	CHICO	¡Es que tengo mucho dinero esta semana! ¡Hay que aprovechar!

2 Julio

Students read what Julio says and fill in the letters of the visuals which represent his opinions.

Answers: 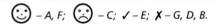 ☺ – A, F; ☹ – C; ✓ – E; ✗ – G, D, B.

3 La verdad

Students read an estate agent's truthful description of a house in the style of a 'For sale' advert. They then attempt to do the same for an imaginary house / flat, using the example given as a model.

4 Nancy ✪

a Reading comprehension activity. Students read Nancy's e-mail and identify those topics mentioned in it.

Answers: *1–sí; 2–sí; 3–no; 4–no; 5–sí; 6–no; 7–sí; 8–sí; 9–sí.*

b Students read the e-mail again and identify italicised words from it which match the six definitions given.

Answers: *1–el diseño; 2–las noticias; 3–el senderismo; 4–agotada; 5–limpiar el cuarto de baño; 6–la pandilla.*

c Students look at the visuals and decide when Nancy does each thing – on a regular basis (N) or at some point in the future (F).

Answers: *1–N; 2–N; 3–F; 4–N; 5–F; 6–N.*

d Students write a reply to Nancy's letter, answering the questions she has posed and including additional information if appropriate.

5 ¿Cuánto sabes?

✪ Students prepare their own answers to a set of 10 interview questions, referring to the sections of the Student's Book given in brackets for additional support. In pairs, students practise asking and answering the questions.

SUPPORT MATERIALS

Worksheet 10.12 La agenda

 ✪ Reading activity practising the third person verb formation and daily routine. Students read the itinerary for the day and fill in the correct times for each activity mentioned.

Answers: *a–9.30; b–11.00; c–17.00; d–10.00; e–12.00; f–10.30; g–19.00; h–13.30.*

Worksheet 10.13 Nancy en Sevilla

1 **Las vacaciones**

✪ Students listen to Nancy discussing her holidays – both what she normally does and her future holiday plans. They tick the grid to show whether each activity mentioned forms part of her normal routine (N), is something she is planning to do in future (F), or both.

Answers:

	Rutina normal	Futuro
1 ir a Inglaterra	✓	✓
2 ir de compras	✓	
3 hacer natación	✓	
4 visitar los pueblos típicos		✓
5 ir de paseo		✓
6 hacer footing	✓	

ENTREVISTADOR:	¿Vuelves a Gran Bretaña?
NANCY:	Sí. El mes de junio, voy normalmente con mi familia a Londres y me quedo allí hasta septiembre.
ENTREVISTADOR:	¿Vas a ir este verano también?
NANCY:	Sí. Este año voy a ir a Londres en primer lugar, para quedarme con una amiga.
ENTREVISTADOR:	¿Qué quieres hacer en Londres? ¿Visitar los monumentos y las tiendas?

NANCY:	Mm ..., prefiero ir de compras en Sevilla. Los sábados por la mañana, voy al centro con mi hermana. Londres es demasiado grande.
ENTREVISTADOR:	¿Qué otras cosas te gusta hacer en Sevilla?
NANCY:	Voy a la piscina dos o tres veces a la semana, pero prefiero nadar en el mar.
ENTREVISTADOR:	¿Y los fines de semana?
NANCY:	Depende. Este fin de semana, el sábado, voy a ir con la familia a Ronda, en la sierra.
ENTREVISTADOR:	¿Para ...?
NANCY:	No sé exactamente. Vamos a visitar los pueblos blancos, típicos de allí y, si tenemos tiempo, ir a la costa.
ENTREVISTADOR:	¿Te gusta la sierra?
NANCY:	Sí, mucho. Si puedo, voy a ir de paseo por la sierra el domingo. ¡En Sevilla, hago footing todos los días para prepararme!

2 El tiempo libre

🔵 An extended writing activity in which students write a short piece of prose about their free time. They can refer to Julio's letter as a model (p.94 in the Student's Book) and use the accompanying information box for support.

STUDENT'S BOOK, pages 96–97

Lectura

A variety of texts to read for information or fun. Students read them on their own, using a dictionary if necessary.

a Adiós – Picture story. Isabel and her family move out, on an unhappy note. The letter presents *está* to describe other people's feelings. Students could write a list of the main protagonists and attribute a mood to each of them.

b Amor – a short poem.

c El 'ping' – a short cartoon.

d ¿Qué tipo de persona eres? – A personality quiz. After choosing their answers, students add up the points they have scored and read what it says about their personality. Students could also jot down the answers they think their partners might give and compare them to see whether they agree.

STUDENT'S BOOK, page 98

Táctica: lengua

Three learning strategies designed to help students to develop their language skills. The activities cover language dictionary skills, language production strategies and writing skills. A brief sentence-joining activity is set at the bottom of the page.

Problemas de diccionario / Dictionary problems

The first dictionary problem students may have is not being able to find the word they are looking for – it apparently doesn't exist. Three pieces of advice are offered here to help them avoid this frustration.

Firstly, they need to check the spelling of the word, and remember the order of the letters in the alphabet, not forgetting that *ñ* comes after *n* in Spanish.

Secondly, they should try removing the plural *–s* or *–es* and look for the singular form of the word. Thirdly, they should try changing the feminine *–a* ending and look for the masculine *–o* ending. Six words are suggested to practise these points.

Answers: *mañana – morning, tomorrow (accent, ñ comes after n); deprimida – depressed (see: deprimido); pimientos – peppers (see: pimiento); países – countries (see: país); cansada – tired (see: cansado); platos – plates, dishes (see: plato).*

Tomando apuntes / Taking notes

Students are advised to devise their own note-taking techniques and abbreviations.

They then attempt to identify the meanings of a list of abbreviations used in the house-buying process.

Answers: *casa doble, afueras, cocina, comedor, salón, cuarto de baño, 3 dormitorios, terraza, jardín.*

Students then listen to a short interview with Pedro who describes the rooms of his house in extensive detail. They take down the main information in abbreviated form.

Answers: **1 Familia** *– 3 personas, madre, padrastro y Pedro – hijo único;*
2 Pontevedra *– bonita, muchos atractivos, antigua, histórica, en la costa;*
3 Piso *– entrada grande, cocina, salón, comedor, 2 balcones, 4 dormitorios, 2 cuartos de baño.*

ENTREVISTADOR:	Dime Pedro – ¿Cuántas personas hay en tu familia?
PEDRO:	Somos tres, mi madre, mi padrastro y yo.
ENTREVISTADOR:	Así que, hermanos no tienes.
PEDRO:	No, soy hijo único – pero tengo muchos amigos, así que siempre hay alguien con quien jugar o salir.
ENTREVISTADOR:	¿No te gustaría tener un hermano o una hermana?
PEDRO:	No sé, como nunca he tenido ...
ENTREVISTADOR:	Y ¿Vives aquí en Pontevedra?
PEDRO:	Sí – vivo en el centro.
ENTREVISTADOR:	¿Te gusta?
PEDRO:	Sí, me encanta, porque es una ciudad muy bonita ... Tiene muchos atractivos. Es antigua e histórica también y eso me gusta.
ENTREVISTADOR:	¿Y te gusta el hecho de que este en la costa?
PEDRO:	Claro – la costa por aquí es preciosa.
ENTREVISTADOR:	Me dices que vives en el centro – ¿vives en un piso o en una casa?
PEDRO:	En un piso. Es grande y muy moderno dentro, aunque fuera, tiene una fachada antigua, como todas las otras casas en la calle ...
ENTREVISTADOR:	¿Y cuántas habitaciones hay?
PEDRO:	Bueno, hay una entrada ... una entrada grande. Y luego hay una cocina y un salón ...
ENTREVISTADOR:	¿Es un salón-comedor?
PEDRO:	No, hay un salón y luego un comedor aparte, con dos balcones que dan a la calle abajo.
ENTREVISTADOR:	¿Cuántos dormitorios tiene?
PEDRO:	¿Dormitorios? Tiene cuatro en total: uno para mis padres, otro para mí, y luego dos para ... huéspedes o amigos, si vienen a pasar la noche ... Y hay dos cuartos de baño también.
ENTREVISTADOR:	¿Dos?
PEDRO:	Sí – un cuarto de baño para mis padres y otro para mí.
ENTREVISTADOR:	¡Qué bien vives hijo!

Escribir mejor / **Improving your writing**

Suggestions to develop greater written fluency. Instead of writing a long series of short sentences, students can join them up together with words such as *que*, *y*, *pero* and *porque* to make longer and more fluent sentences. In the example, six short sentences are converted into two longer sentences. Students should use the same words to make Matthew's letter read more smoothly.

Suggested answers:	*Me llamo Matthew **y** vivo en Sheffield **que** es una ciudad industrial. Es grande **pero** me gusta **porque** tengo muchos amigos. Hay mucha diversión **porque** hay una piscina, una bolera y dos o tres cines.*

STUDENT'S BOOK, page 99

Práctica: lengua

Some summative grammar practice activities based on the grammar items encountered in Units 6–10.

1 ◗ An activity in which students answer the questions in the negative.

Answers:	*1 – No me levanto temprano; 2 – No desayuno bien; 3 – No hago deporte; 4 – No voy mucho al polideportivo; 5 – No tengo energía todo el día; 6 – No quiero cambiar de rutina.*

2 ◗ A matching activity which gives practice of prepositions and direction-giving phrases.

Answers:	*1 – c 2 – e; 3 – a; 4 – f; 5 – b; 6 – d.*

3 ◗ A gap-fill activity giving practice of *a, al, a la, a los* and *a las*.

Answers:	*1 – a la; 2 – a; 3 – a la; 4 – a la; 5 – al; 6 – al; 7 – a las; 8 – a los; 9 – a.*

4 ◗ A gap-fill activity. Students choose the correct form of the verb from the alternatives given to fill in the blanks in the text.

Answers:	*voy; va; vamos; vais; voy.*

5 ✿ Students put the present-tense sentences into the future tense.

Answers:	*1 – Toñi, vas a ayudar en casa cada día; 2 – Tu hermana va a hacer su cama por la mañana; 3 – Los chicos van a volver a casa a tiempo; 4 – Papá va a recoger el salón cada noche; 5 – Nosotros vamos a tener una casa limpia por fin; 6 – ¿Y yo? voy a leer novelas en el sofá todo el día.*

6 ✿ A gap-fill activity entailing filling in the correct verbs in an e-mail from a menu of three options for each.

Answers:	*1 – estoy; 2 – está; 3 – quiere; 4 – puedo; 5 – escucha; 6 – es; 7 – su; 8 – ayuda; 9 – hace; 10 – recogemos; 11 – vuelves.*

7 ✿ Students choose the correct form of the verb to fill in blanks in a text.

Answers:	*se llama; somos; está; quiere; soy; estoy; tengo.*

Objectives

Students learn – to order a hot or cold drink
– to ask others what they want to drink

Key language

¿qué quieres?	*con hielo*
quiero …	*un granizado*
una bebida caliente / fría	*un batido de chocolate*
algo frío / caliente	*un batido de fresa*
un agua mineral	*camarero / camarera*
un café con leche	*cliente*
un café solo	*¡oiga camarero!*
un té solo	*dígame*
un té con leche	*¿algo más?*
un té con limón	*sí, por favor*
un chocolate	*no, gracias*
una limonada	*nada más*
una naranjada	*es todo*
una Coca-cola	*en seguida*
un zumo de naranja	*¿cuánto cuesta …?*
con gas / sin gas	

Skills / Strategies

Students learn – to exchange information orally

ICT opportunities

Students can – design a café menu of drinks and prices, formatting it as a table

Ways in

OHT 11A
Student's Book, Activity 1

Assessment opportunities

AT1,1/2   Worksheet 11.2, Activity 1: students listen and check prices.
AT2,1/2   Worksheet 11.1: students exchange information in pairs.
AT4,2   Student's Book, Activity 3: students invent horrible drinks and juices.

STUDENT'S BOOK, pages 100–101

1 **¿Sí, señora?**

Picture story

 The friends meet up for a drink in a café. They overhear the conversation at the next table.

🔵 Students note down which drinks the four people order.

🟢 Students identify the other drinks in the photos, using the list given with Activity 2 as support.

Answers:

🔵 *Elvira – b, j; Santi – d; Javi – g; Carlos – e.*

🟢 *a – un chocolate; b – un agua mineral sin gas; c – un batido de fresa; d – un café solo; e – una limonada; f – una naranjada; g – una coca; h – un agua mineral con gas; i – un té con limón; j – un café con leche.*

JOSÉ LUIS:	Isabel – ¡aquí!
CARLOS:	Quiero una limonada …
PILAR:	Carlos, mira …
SANTI:	Elvira, ¿qué quieres?
JAVI:	Papá, yo quiero …
SANTI:	Javi, un momentito. ¿Elvira?
ELVIRA:	Yo … un café con leche y un agua mineral.
SANTI:	¿Con gas, o sin gas?
ELVIRA:	Sin gas. ¿Y tú, Santi?
SANTI:	Mm … un café sólo.
	¿Javi quiere algo frío? ¿Una limonada?
ELVIRA:	Sí.
JAVI:	¡No!
ELVIRA:	¿Quieres algo caliente, Javi? ¿Un chocolate?
JAVI:	¡No!
SANTI:	¿Quieres una coca?
JAVI:	¡Quiero DOS cocas!
ELVIRA:	¡Oiga, camarero!
	UNA coca.
JAVI:	Quiero dos …
CAMARERO:	¿Sí, señora?

2 **¿Quieres algo frío / caliente?**

A pairwork guessing game. Partner **A** thinks of a drink and Partner **B** has to ask questions to find out what it is, but Partner **A** can only answer *sí* or *no*. Students can grade their attempts using the suggested ratings. The aim here is to practise *¿quieres?, quiero,* and *¿cuánto cuesta?* You may like to prepare the activity with the whole class first in order to reinforce the phrases and numbers.

3 **Bebidas**

An opportunity for students to use their imagination.

🔵 By mixing up some of the vocabulary in the unit, students create 'horrible' drinks.

🟢 Students look up words in the dictionary and invent new fruit juices, different from the ones encountered on the drinks board in Activity 2.

4 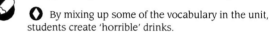 **¿Qué quieres beber?**

a The four friends give their order to the waiter. With the support of the speech bubble, students listen to the conversation and fill in the gaps by working out which drink each person wants.

Answers: *José Luis – una limonada; Isabel – un té con leche; Carlos – una naranjada; Pilar – un café solo.*

JOSÉ LUIS:	¡Oiga camarero!
CAMARERO:	Sí, ¿dígame?
JOSÉ LUIS:	Quiero una limonada.
ISABEL:	Y yo, un té con leche.
CARLOS:	Yo quiero una naranjada. Pilar, ¿qué quieres beber?
PILAR:	Algo caliente – un café solo.
CAMARERO:	¿Algo más?
PILAR:	No, nada más. Es todo.
CAMARERO:	Muy bien, en seguida.

b 🔵 Students practise the same conversation in groups of five – changing the orders, but still keeping with the context.

🟢 Students invent other conversations in the café, using the material on this spread as a stimulus if necessary.

SUPPORT MATERIALS

OHT 11A ¿Qué quieres beber?

This can be used to present the vocabulary items associated with restaurants and cafés. Possibilities for use of this OHT include memory games, dressing up as a waiter and doing impromptu offers of service to class members (only a tea towel over the forearm is necessary to become an 'instant waiter/-tress'), etc.

Worksheet 11.1 Los nuevos camareros

 An information-gap activity which practises the names of drinks and prices. The new waiters are checking how much the drinks cost, but their lists are incomplete. Cut the worksheet in two and distribute a different half to each student in a pair. They should then take it in turns to ask each other the price of the drinks they don't know. Prices are expressed in euros and should need little explanation, although it might be worth explaining the Spanish ways of talking about euro cents (*céntimos*).

Worksheet 11.2 Las bebidas

1 **¡Qué memoria!**

A senior waitress is checking that the junior waiter knows the correct prices of the drinks.

a Students look at the correct list of prices and listen to the junior waiter's answers. They tick the ones he gets right and cross the ones he gets wrong.

Answers: *1–✗; 2–✓; 3–✗; 4–✓; 5–✓; 6–✗; 7–✓.*

b There are two extra drinks not on the price list, but which are mentioned on the recording. Students have to listen out for their prices.

Answers: *un batido – un euro diez;*
un granizado de naranja – un euro treinta.

DUEÑA:	Bueno, ¿sabes los precios de memoria ya?
CAMARERO:	Mm … sí.
DUEÑA:	¿Cuánto cuesta un café solo?
CAMARERO:	Sesenta y cinco céntimos.
DUEÑA:	¿Un té?
CAMARERO:	Ah … cincuenta y cinco.
DUEÑA:	¿Cuánto cuesta una naranjada?
CAMARERO:	Mm … setenta y tres.
DUEÑA:	¿Y un chocolate?
CAMARERO:	Ochenta y cinco.
DUEÑA:	¿Un zumo de naranja? ¿Cuánto cuesta?
CAMARERO:	Mm … setenta y cinco.
DUEÑA:	¿Agua mineral?
CAMARERO:	Sesenta … no, sesenta y dos.
DUEÑA:	¿Una Coca-Cola?
CAMARERO:	Noventa.
DUEÑA:	Muy bien. Y un batido – ¿cuánto es?
CAMARERO:	Un batido … Un euro diez.
DUEÑA:	¿Y un granizado de naranja?
CAMARERO:	Un euro treinta.
DUEÑA:	No lo tienes perfecto, pero en fin … ¡No está mal!

2 **El crucigrama**

a Students complete the grid by filling in the names of the drinks pictured on the sheet. There is no visual clue for number 6, which they should be able to work out after doing the others. The letters in the shaded areas can be arranged to spell a seventh drink.

Answers:

b Students write a speech bubble ordering each drink 1–7 in Activity 2a.

Extra

Students could make their own *Lista de bebidas*. It could either be poster-sized for classroom display, or designed on computer and printed as a hand-sized menu. Students could create a table on screen, giving headings to the columns (e.g. *Bebidas, Precio – barra: Precio – mesa*) and number each row, for example. They could then practise entering data in the appropriate cells before formatting the table, adding the names and addresses of an imaginary café and decorating it with clip-art or borders.

Worksheet 11.3 Típico de España

1 **El granizado**

Students replace pictures of various items in the *granizado* recipe with the appropriate words.

Answers: *1 – naranja; 2 – café; 3 – hielo; 4 – limón;*
5 – manzana; 6 – cafeterías; 7 – calor.

2 **La horchata**

Students read a description of the drink *horchata* and answer a series of true or false questions on it.

Answers: *1–✓; 2–✓; 3–✗; 4–✓; 5–✗; 6–✓; 7–✗; 8–✓.*

Objectives

Students learn – how to order something to eat
              – other ways of saying what they'd like
              – to ask what there is for vegetarians
              – Grammar: *para mí, ti, él, ella*, etc.

Key language

¿para quién es?	*un cruasán / bocadillo de chorizo*
para mí / él / ella	*una tortilla española*
para mi amigo/a	*calamares*
¿quieres probar …?	*patatas fritas*
¿hay algo para vegetarianos?	*pescado frito*
soy vegetariano/a	*churros*
una hamburguesa	*aceitunas*
un perrito caliente	
un bocadillo de jamón York	**Extension language**
un cruasán de queso	*¿tienes hambre / sed?*
un cruasán vegetal	*(no) tengo hambre / sed*

Skills / Strategies

Students learn – to improve their ability to memorise words

ICT opportunities

Students can – design a café menu of snacks and prices, similar to the drinks menu, if one was created in the previous spread

Ways in

Student's Book, Activity 1; visuals on page 102

Assessment opportunities

AT1,1	Student's Book, Activity 3: students match the snacks with the four people.
AT2,2	Worksheet 11.4, Activity 2: students identify the snacks the customers want.
AT2,2/3	Student's Book, Activity 5: students say which snacks they want.
AT4,3	Worksheet 11.5, Activity 3: students write their own dialogues.

STUDENT'S BOOK, pages 102–103

1 **¡Rápido!**

a The snacks are presented on the recording for students to listen to and repeat.

b As follow-up practice, students test each other orally in threes. Partner **A** says a number between 1 and 12, and Partners **B** and **C** compete to name the snack. Award a point to the one who gets it right first and find out who has the fastest reactions.

> 1 – una hamburguesa
> 2 – un perrito caliente
> 3 – un bocadillo de jamón York
> 4 – un cruasán de queso
> 5 – un cruasán vegetal
> 6 – un cruasán de chorizo
> 7 – una tortilla española
> 8 – calamares
> 9 – patatas fritas
> 10 – pescado frito
> 11 – churros
> 12 – aceitunas

2 **¿Para quién es?**

Picture story

The friends decide what snack to have. Isabel is vegetarian.

⭕ Students match up the snack with the person who orders it.

✚ Students decide whether the statements are true or false and write *sí* or *no* accordingly.

Answers: ⭕ *José Luis – 3; Isabel – 2; Pepa – 4; Tomás – 1.*

         ✚ *1 – no; 2 – no; 3 – no; 4 – sí.*

JOSÉ LUIS:	Para mí, pescado frito. Y ¿para ti, Isabel? ¿Qué quieres comer?
ISABEL:	Es que … soy vegetariana.
JOSÉ LUIS:	¿Sí? Y tú, Tomás – ¿eres vegetariano también?
TOMÁS:	¿Yo? ¡No! Quisiera una hamburguesa.
JOSÉ LUIS:	¿Para ti, Pepa?
PEPA:	Un perrito caliente.
ISABEL:	¿Hay algo para vegetarianos?
JOSÉ LUIS:	Bueno, hay cruasanes de queso, y tortilla …
NARRADOR:	15 minutos más tarde …
CAMARERO:	¿Para quién es?
JOSÉ LUIS:	La tortilla de patatas es para ella.
ISABEL:	¿Pescado frito? ¡Es para él! Eugh …

3 **El resto de la conversación**

The conversation continues when four other friends arrive. Students write down the number of the snack at the top of p.102 that each person orders.

Answers: *Carlos – 11 (churros); Pilar – 4 (cruasán de queso); Merche – 6 (bocadillo de chorizo); Guillermo – 3 (bocadillo de jamón York).*

JOSÉ LUIS:	Oye, Carlos, ¿qué quieres?
CARLOS:	Quiero churros.
JOSÉ LUIS:	Carlos – churros. Pilar, ¿quieres churros también?
PILAR:	No – para mí, un cruasán de queso.
JOSÉ LUIS:	Vale – Pilar … queso. ¿Merche?
MERCHE:	Bueno, para mí un bocadillo de chorizo y para Guillermo …
JOSÉ LUIS:	Un momento, Merche – bocadillo de chorizo …¿Y para Guillermo?
MERCHE:	Para él, un bocadillo de jamón.
JOSÉ LUIS:	Jamón York. Vale, gracias …

4 **¿Para vegetarianos o no?**

⭕ Students read a brief passage about snacks on sale in Spain, and divide them into two lists: vegetarian and non-vegetarian items. Items containing fish have been classified as non-vegetarian here; if some students are the 'non-strict' kind of vegetarian who do eat fish, then the classification of fish items as vegetarian should be accepted.

✚ Students answer the six true or false questions based on the same text.

Answers: ⭕

Para vegetarianos:	No para vegetarianos:
sandwiches tostados de queso y tomate	bocadillos de chorizo
almendras fritas	bocadillos de salchichón
croquetas de patatas	bocadillos de atún y mayonesa
champiñones al ajillo	bocadillos de jamón serrano
	ensaladilla rusa

         ✚ *1 – verdad; 2 – verdad; 3 – mentira; 4 – verdad; 5 – verdad; 6 – mentira.*

5 **Para comer y beber**

A groupwork activity in which students first read a model conversation in groups of three, and subsequently modify it using information from the spread, to produce their own versions. A help box at the bottom of p.103 gives support to students who need it.

Gramática

Students are referred to the grammar summary, section 18 on p.151 for further information on disjunctive pronouns, and to Acción: lengua 11, p.107.

SUPPORT MATERIALS

Worksheet 11.4 ¡Qué rico!

1 **El camarero automático no funciona**

The automatic snack vending machine with the robotic voice is not working properly: the name of each snack it announces is incomplete.

◖ Students write down the number of the snack each customer wants.

◗ Students decide how each customer reacts to the machine and draw an appropriate smiley / sad face.

Answers: ◖ *a – 2; b – 4; c – 6; d – 3; e – 5; f – 1.*

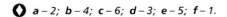

a	MÁQUINA:	Un perrito cal ... un perrito cal ...
	SEÑOR:	Oye, Luisa – ven y escucha – ¡no funciona bien!
b	MÁQUINA:	Un cruas ... un cruas ...
	NIÑO:	¿Qué pasa, Papá?
	PAPÁ:	No sé. No funciona.
c	MÁQUINA:	Patatas fri ... patatas fri ...
	SEÑORA:	Oye, ¿qué pasa aquí? ¿No funciona bien?
d	MÁQUINA:	Un bocadillo de ja ... un bocadillo de ja ...
	CHICA:	¿Qué dice?
	CHICO:	*Un bocadillo de ja ...*
e	MÁQUINA:	Una tort ... una tort ...
	SEÑOR:	¿Cómo? ¿Qué pasa aquí? Esta máquina no funciona – oye, ¡no parece posible!
f	MÁQUINA:	Una hambur ... una hambur ...
	CHICA:	No funciona – ¡qué raro! Bueno, vamos a la cafetería entonces.

2 **¡Termina la frase!**

Pairwork to practise and consolidate vocabulary. Partner **A** gives the beginning of a snack or drink and Partner **B** completes it by adding the correct ending.

3 **En la cafetería**

◖ Students work together in pairs to play the two dialogues.

◗ Students invent other dialogues using these as a model, but changing the food, drink and price details.

Worksheet 11.5 Tengo hambre y sed ...

1 **En la cocina**

Picture story

This presents the extension language which enables students to say they are hungry or thirsty. Students follow the text and listen to the recording in order to fill in the gaps.

Answers: *1 – Tengo; 2 – quieres; 3 – hay; 4 – tengo; 5 – Tienes.*

PADRE:	¡Hola! ¿Qué tal?
HIJA:	¡Uf! **Tengo** sed.
PADRE:	¿Qué **quieres** beber?
HIJA:	¿Hay limonada?
PADRE:	No, pero **hay** naranjada.
HIJA:	Vale.
PADRE:	¿Qué quieres comer?
HIJA:	Nada, gracias – no **tengo** hambre.
HIJO:	Yo, sí, tengo hambre.
PADRE:	**Tienes** hambre todo el día, Miguel – ¡eres imposible!

2 **¿Tienes hambre?**

Reading comprehension to reinforce the key phrases presented in the picture story. Students match up each statement with the correct picture.

Answers: *d – 1; a – 2; c – 3; e – 4; f – 5; b – 6.*

3 **¡Te toca a ti!**

With the help of the language support box, students can now make up simple dialogues of their own in which they ask each other whether they are hungry or thirsty and what they would like to eat or drink.

Extra

Students could make a *Lista de platos* similar to the *Lista de bebidas* in Unit 11A. If the drinks menu was created and saved on computer, students could open the document, use the Edit command to Select All, then Copy and Paste it on to a new document in order to save formatting time. Alternatively, the original document could be opened, copied and renamed using the Save As ... facility. The original data could then be deleted and replaced with the names and prices of the snacks.

Objectives

Students learn – to ask how much something is
– how to pay the bill
– numbers from 100 to 1000

Key language

Numbers from 100 to 1000   *una moneda*
la cuenta, por favor   *un duro*
¿cuánto es en total?   *sólo tengo*
un billete   *no tengo cambio*

Skills / Strategies

Students learn – how to say what they want (*querer*)

ICT opportunities

Students can – design a café bill which automatically calculates
the total cost using a formula in a spreadsheet

Ways in

Numbers – introductory recording in Student's Book, Activity 1
Money – real euros!

Assessment opportunities

AT1,1   Student's Book, Activity 1: students fill in the blanks.

AT2,3/4   Student's Book, Activity 5: students generate open-
ended dialogues using the menu as a stimulus.

AT3,2   Student's Book, Activity 4: a sentence-matching activity.

AT4,2   Worksheet 11.6, Activity 2 ◆: students decide whether
the waiter or the client said the phrases.

AT4,3   Worksheet 11.6, Activity 2 ♣: students sequence the
dialogue correctly.

STUDENT'S BOOK, pages 104–105

1 Números grandes

a Students listen to the larger numbers being read out,
and fill in the gaps.

Answers: *200 **dos**cientos; 300 **tres**cientos; 400 **cuatro**cientos;
600 **seis**cientos; 800 **ocho**cientos.*

cien	seiscientos
doscientos	setecientos
trescientos	ochocientos
cuatrocientos	novecientos
quinientos	mil

b A differentiated pairwork guessing game.

◆ Using the numbers from Activity 1a, students think of
a number, which their partner has to guess.

♣ Students do the same as for the diamond activity, but
using more complicated numbers.

2 El dinero español

Picture story ◆

As the friends are paying their bill, they are interrupted by
a biker and his friend, the latter who turns out to be Pepa's
cousin. Students listen to the recording and read the text.
They then do the simple gap-fill activity to practise
numbers and money vocabulary.

Answers: *Hay billetes de: 5 euros, 20 euros
Hay monedas de: 2 céntimos, 5 céntimos,
20 céntimos, 1 euro, 2 euros.*

JOSÉ LUIS:	¡Oiga, camarera! La cuenta, por favor.
PILAR:	¿Cuánto es en total?
JOSÉ LUIS:	Doce euros, setenta y cuatro céntimos. Guillermo ...
GUILLERMO:	Sólo tengo un billete de cinco euros. Pilar – ¿tienes cambio?
PILAR:	No sé – un minuto ...
GAMBERRO:	¿Qué hay aquí? Un billete de veinte euros, y monedas de ... un euro, dos euros ... veinte, cinco, y dos céntimos. Bueno, el billete para mí, y las monedas para ti.
PILAR:	¡Oye!
PEPA:	¡Quique!
QUIQUE:	Lo siento, toma.
PEPA:	¡Quique es mi prima!

3 Aquí tiene

◆ Students listen to a conversation between the friends
and pick the appropriate bill for each person.

♣ Students answer three straightforward closed
questions based on the listening material.

Answers: ◆ *Isabel – 1.56; Pilar – 1.49; Carlos – 1.65;
Merche – 1.68; Guillermo – 1.52; José Luis – 1.74.*
♣ *1 **Tomás** – 1.64; 2 **Pepa** – 1.59; 3 – No tiene
(bastante) dinero.*

JOSÉ LUIS:	Isabel, tu tortilla española y el té con leche cuestan ... un euro, cincuenta y seis céntimos.
ISABEL:	Vale. Un euro, cincuenta y seis.
JOSÉ LUIS:	¿Pilar?
PILAR:	¿Sí?
JOSÉ LUIS:	Para ti, es un euro cuarenta y nueve céntimos.
PILAR:	Vale – un momento. ¿Un euro cuarenta y nueve? Toma ...
JOSÉ LUIS:	Carlos, para ti es un euro sesenta y cinco.
CARLOS:	Vale – toma. Un euro sesenta y cinco.
JOSÉ LUIS:	Gracias. ¿Merche?
MERCHE:	¿Sí?
JOSÉ LUIS:	Quiero un euro sesenta y ocho, por favor.
MERCHE:	¿Un euro, sesenta y ocho? Un minuto.
JOSÉ LUIS:	Y para ti, Guillermo, es ... mm ... un euro, cincuenta y dos.
GUILLERMO:	Bueno, espera. No sé si tengo un euro, cincuenta y dos ...
ISABEL:	¿Y para ti, José Luis? ¿Cuánto es?
JOSÉ LUIS:	Para mí, es ... un euro setenta y cuatro.
ISABEL:	¿Un euro setenta y cuatro? No está mal.
JOSÉ LUIS:	¿Pepa y Tomás?
TOMÁS:	¿Qué?
JOSÉ LUIS:	Pepa – el perrito caliente y la naranjada cuestan ... un euro, cincuenta y nueve.
PEPA:	Vale – toma. Un euro, cincuenta y nueve.
JOSÉ LUIS:	Gracias. Tomás – quiero un euro, sesenta y cuatro.
TOMÁS:	¡Ay! Bueno, no sé ... es que no tengo un euro, sesenta y cuatro.
JOSÉ LUIS:	Tomás – ¡eres imposible! ¡Isabel! ¡Isabel!

4 En la cafetería

A reading activity involving matching up sentences said by
the client and the waiter / waitress.

Answers: *1 – f; 2 – g; 3 – e; 4 – d; 5 – a; 6 – b; 7 – c.*

5 **En la cafetería con un grupo de amigos**

Students use the structures from Activity 4 and Activity 5 of Unit 11B to make up their own group dialogues.

SUPPORT MATERIALS

Worksheet 11.6 ¡Oiga, camarero!

1 **Quique y Manolo**

A short picture story. Students read the text and fill in the gaps.

Answers: *1 – ¿Dígame?; 2 – Quiero; 3 – mí; 4 – Oiga;*
5 – cuenta; 6 – Cuánto; 7 – cambio.

2 **¿Camarero o cliente?**

A conversation between a waiter and a customer in which all the phrases are jumbled up. The first eight phrases involve ordering and the last six involve paying.

◗ Students identify who says each phrase: the waiter or the customer.

◗ Students rewrite the conversation with all the phrases in the correct order.

Answers: ◖ *1, 2 , 4, 6, 9, 10, 11 – camarero;*
3, 5, 7, 8, 12, 13, 14 – cliente.

Suggested answers: ◖
3 ¡Oiga, camarero!
2 Sí. ¿Dígame?
8 Para mí, un batido de chocolate. Y un café para mi amiga.
1 ¿Algo más?
7 Sí. ¿Hay churros?
4 Lo siento, no hay churros.
5 Quiero algo caliente … patatas fritas, y una hamburguesa por favor.
6 Muy bien, en seguida.
12 ¡La cuenta, por favor!
11 Muy bien.
14 ¿Cuánto es en total?
10 Cuatro euros, treinta y cinco céntimos.
13 Sólo tengo un billete de cincuenta euros.
9 No hay problema.

3 **Un poco de teatro**

Using all the vocabulary and phrases from the unit, and following the pattern of the dialogue on this worksheet, students could invent their own conversation involving different drinks, snacks and prices. They might like to record it on tape.

Extra

Since most tills calculate bills automatically, students could design on computer their own bill for a Spanish café. Using spreadsheet software they could enter a formula in the final cell of the column in which the waiter would normally note down the prices, so that the total sum payable is calculated instantly. The activity could be made more authentic if one student is given the task of working on the 'till' (the classroom computer) while other students are preparing their conversations in the café (Student's Book, Activity 5). As soon as a waiter or waitress takes an order, the till operator enters the items and prices, so that when the bill is required it can be printed off and presented to the customers. More able students could also enter a formula to calculate an additional 10% service charge. Extra credit could be given for the addition of suitable language on the bill such as *Gracias por su visita* or *Bienvenidos otra vez.*

Objectives
Students learn – how to order a three-course meal
– Grammar: the verb *preferir* (to prefer)

Key language
¿nos trae más pan, por favor?
¿qué van a tomar de postre?
¿qué van a tomar?
¿y de segundo?
¿y para beber?
buenas tardes
de primero
filete de ternera / cerdo
flan
fruta (del tiempo)
gambas al ajillo
helados
para mí
pisto manchego
prefiero fruta
quisiera
sopa de verduras
tortilla de champiñones
trucha con almendras
una botella de agua mineral con / sin gas
una botella de vino blanco / tinto / rosado
voy a tomar
helado de fresa
helado de vainilla
zumo de naranja / piña

Skills / Strategies
Students learn – to use the verb *preferir* and some discourse strategies

ICT opportunities
Students can – design a restaurant menu

Ways in
Student's Book, Activity 1; menu on page 106

Assessment opportunities
AT1,3   Student's Book, Activity 2: students listen and fill in the gaps.
AT2,3   Student's Book, Activity 3: students take part in a restaurant role-play.
AT3,2   Worksheet 11.8, Activity 2: students read and fill in the waiter's notepad.

STUDENT'S BOOK, page 106

1 **El menú**
Presentation and revision of the food items. Students look at a Spanish menu and write a list of items they would or would not like.

2 **En el restaurante**
Students listen to the recording and read the dialogue, and each time there is a missing item they note down the appropriate food / drink item from the menu.

Answers: *A – 2; B – 1; C – 3; D – 4; E – 6; F – 5; G – 10; H – 11; I – 8; J – 7; K – 9.*

CAMARERO:	Buenas tardes.
TODOS:	Buenas tardes.
CAMARERO:	¿Qué van a tomar?
CARMINA:	De primero, gambas al ajillo.
OMAR:	Para mí, sopa de verduras.
TERESA:	Quisiera pisto manchego, por favor.
CAMARERO:	¿Y de segundo?
OMAR:	Yo, filete de ternera.
TERESA:	Quisiera tortilla de champiñones.
CARMINA:	Para mí, trucha con almendras.
CAMARERO:	¿Y para beber?
OMAR:	Una botella de vino blanco.
TERESA:	Y una botella de agua mineral sin gas.
CAMARERO:	Muy bien. ¿Algo más?
OMAR:	¿Nos trae más pan, por favor?
CAMARERO:	Muy bien, en seguida.
CAMARERO:	¿Qué van a tomar de postre?
OMAR:	¿Qué hay?
CAMARERO:	Hay flan, fruta, helados ...
CARMINA:	Prefiero fruta.
OMAR:	Para mí, flan. ¿Qué prefieres, Teresa?
TERESA:	Voy a tomar un helado de vainilla.
CAMARERO:	Muy bien, señores.

3 **¿Qué prefieres tú?**
a Students work in pairs and take it in turns to ask what their partner wants for starter, main course, dessert, etc.

b A group activity in which students read the script from Activity 2 and modify it to produce their own versions.

Gramática
Students are referred to the grammar summary, section 12, p.150 for more information on stem-changing verbs such as *preferir*. There is also practice of these verbs in Acción: lengua 11, p.107.

SUPPORT MATERIALS
Worksheet 11.7 Para mí ...
This sheet has removable English rubrics at the bottom.

1 **¡Oiga!**
Students listen and choose the correct main course and dessert for each speaker.

Answers: *Alonso – c, f; Catalina – d, h; Federico – b, h; Josefa – a, e.*

ALONSO	
CHICA:	¿Qué vas a tomar, Alonso?
ALONSO:	Para mí, sopa. Sopa y ... flan.
CHICA:	Vale. Sopa y flan para Alonso.
CATALINA	
CHICA:	Catalina, ¿qué quieres?
CATALINA:	Quisiera la tortilla con patatas fritas y ...
CHICA:	Espera ... Tortilla con patatas fritas. Y luego ...
CATALINA:	De postre, un helado.
CHICA:	Postre – helado. Vale.

FEDERICO

CHICA:	Federico, te toca a ti. ¿Qué vas a tomar?
FEDERICO:	Para mí, el pescado con ensalada.
CHICA:	La trucha, ¿no?
FEDERICO:	Sí. La trucha con ensalada.
CHICA:	¿Y de postre?
FEDERICO:	Un helado de fresa.
CHICA:	Un helado. Muy bien.

JOSEFA

CHICA:	Josefa, ¿qué quieres tomar tú?
JOSEFA:	¿Yo? Filete de cerdo, con champiñones.
CHICA:	Filete de ternera con champiñones ...
JOSEFA:	Y de postre ... no sé.
CHICA:	La piña está muy buena aquí.
JOSEFA:	Sí, me gusta la fruta. Vale, la piña entonces.

2 ¿Correcto o no?

○ Students read what the waiter has brought for the customers and compare with what the customers ordered. They note the discrepancies.

Answers:

	Plato principal	Postre
Cliente 1:	a ✓	✗ e
Cliente 2:	d ✓	h ✓
Cliente 3:	✗ b	g ✓
Cliente 4:	c ✓	f ✓

Worksheet 11.8 Vamos a comer fuera

1 ¿Qué piden?

○ Students listen to a dialogue in a restaurant and choose the correct words to complete the sentences which summarise the dialogue.

Answers: *a* – 5 (caliente); *b* – 4 (pescado); *c* – 7 (fruta); *d* – 9 (helado); *e* – 1 (vino); *f* – 8 (agua).

CAMARERO:	Buenas tardes, señores.
ANA:	¡Hola!
PEDRO:	Buenas tardes. Ana, ¿qué vas a tomar de primero? ¿Tortilla? ¿Una ensalada?
ANA:	No, no quiero nada frío. Me gustaría un plato caliente. Vamos a ver ... La sopa de champiñones, y un filete con patatas fritas, por favor.
CAMARERO:	Muy bien. ¿Y usted, señor?

ANA:	¿Te gustaría probar las gambas, Pedro? ¿O las sardinas? La trucha está muy buena aquí.
PEDRO:	No, no me gustan. Voy a tomar una tortilla y un pisto manchego.
CAMARERO:	¿Y de postre?
PEDRO:	¿Hay helados de fresa o chocolate?
CAMARERO:	Sí, hay.
PEDRO:	Uno de chocolate para mí, entonces. ¿Ana?
CAMARERO:	La piña fresca está buena hoy. Y tenemos unas naranjas muy buenas también.
ANA:	Perfecto.
CAMARERO:	¿Y para beber?
PEDRO:	Mejor tinto o rosado, ¿no?
ANA:	Sí. Tinto de la casa.
CAMARERO:	Muy bien.
ANA:	¿Y nos trae más agua por favor?
CAMARERO:	Claro, señora, en seguida.

2 Decisiones ...

♣ Students read the thoughts of some customers and write down the waiter's notes using the menu on p.106 of the Student's Book. Accept any reasonable answers.

Acción: lengua 11, page 107

Practice of *preferir* (to prefer) and *para mí, ti*, etc.

1 ○ Students fill in the blanks with the correct present tense singular forms of *preferir*.

♣ Students complete a dialogue with the correct forms of *preferir*.

Answers: ○ *1* – prefieres; *2* – Prefiero; *3* – prefiere; *4* – Prefieres; *5* – Prefiero.

♣ Prefieres; Prefiero; Prefiere; Prefieren; preferís.

Practice of *para mí, para ti*, etc.

2 ○ Students select the appropriate form from two alternatives.

♣ Students paraphrase the six sentences.

Answers: ○ para mí; para él; para ella; para mí; para ella; para ti.

♣ *1* – Para Enrique; *2* – Para mí; *3* – Para ti; *4* – Para nosotros; *5* – Para ellos; *6* – Para vosotros.

Objectives

Students learn – the names of different types of shops
              – the names for different types of items to buy

Key language

el tomate	*los pasteles*
el azúcar	*el ajo*
el pan	*las patatas*
la mantequilla	*el café*
la aspirina	*la harina*
el limón	*los pimientos*
el filete de cerdo	*la leche*
la revista	*la naranja*
las patatas fritas	*el vino*
la cebolla	*la limonada*
los pañuelos	*las sardinas frescas*
la carne picada	*la tortilla*
el gazpacho	*el barrio*
los huevos	*la ropa*
la comida	*el supermercado*
el periódico	*los antibióticos*
el hipermercado	*el champú*
el detergente	*el almacén*
la pasta de dientes	*la tienda*
el zumo de fruta	*la pescadería*
la panadería	*la pastelería*
la droguería	*la tienda de alimentación*
la carnicería	*el quiosco*
la frutería	*el mercado*
la farmacia	

Skills / Strategies

Students learn – the passive form of the verb *comprar* – both
              singular and plural (*se compra / se compran*)

ICT opportunities

Students can – generate computer-based shopping lists and
             decorate them with clip-art if wished

Ways in

Food items – OHT 12A;
Spanish shops – presentation in the Student's Book; visuals on
page 108

Assessment opportunities

AT1,2/3 Worksheet 12.2, Activity 1: students answer the true or
           false questions.

AT2,2   Student's Book, Activity 2b: students ask each other
           what is bought where.

AT3,3   Student's Book, Activity 3 ◐: students read the text
           and sequence the visuals.

AT3,3   Student's Book, Activity 3 ✢: students select the
           appropriate word to fill in the gapped sentences.

AT4,2   Worksheet 12.1, Activity 3: students write a shopping list
           for a picnic.

STUDENT'S BOOK, pages 108–109

1 **Las tiendas**

a Teresa and Tomás have decided to throw a surprise
birthday party for Pilar, and are preparing their shopping
list before beginning the expedition to the shops. Students
initially just listen and read.

NARRADOR:	Teresa y Tomás deciden hacer una fiesta sorpresa para celebrar el cumpleaños de Pilar. Teresa hace una lista de compras antes de visitar las tiendas del barrio.
TERESA:	Hay que ir a … la panadería …
TOMÁS:	La pastelería …
TERESA:	La frutería …
TOMÁS:	La pescadería …
TERESA:	La carnicería …
TOMÁS:	El quiosco … La droguería …
TERESA:	La tienda de alimentación …
TOMÁS:	Y la farmacia.
TERESA:	¿La farmacia?
TOMÁS:	Sí, ¡para las aspirinas!

b ◐ Students listen and write down the order in which
Tomás and Teresa visit the shops.

✢ Students listen and identify four particular shops.

Answers: ◐ *D, E, A, I, C, G, F, B, H.*

          ✢ *1 – E; 2 – I; 3 – G; 4 – B.*

TOMÁS:	¿Adónde vamos primero, Mamá?
TERESA:	¿Por qué no vamos a la pescadería …
TOMÁS:	… y luego a la carnicería? La que está cerca de casa.
TERESA:	Sí, esa carnicería es buena. Después, a la panadería.
TOMÁS:	Y luego a la farmacia. Es la única farmacia del barrio, ¿no?

TERESA:	Sí. Luego vamos a la frutería, y después a la droguería.
TOMÁS:	¡Está lejos, Mamá!
TERESA:	Ya lo sé, pero no hay más remedio. Después al quiosco.
TOMÁS:	Sí, ¡para mi copia de Superpop!
TERESA:	Y luego a la pastelería Mango.
TOMÁS:	¡Estupendo! Me gusta mucho esa pastelería.
TERESA:	Y finalmente, a la tienda de alimentación.
TOMÁS:	¡Uf! ¡Estoy cansado ya!
TERESA:	¡Ánimo, Tomás! ¡Vámonos!

2 **La lista de compras de Teresa**

a Students look at the shopping list and write down what
is bought in each shop.

Answers: *la panadería – 5; la pastelería – 2; la frutería –1, 11,
17, (4, 6, 13, 20); la pescadería – 24; la carnicería –
14, 23; el quiosco – 16; la droguería – 22; la tienda
de alimentación – 3, 7, 8, 10, 12, 15, 18, 19, 21 (4,
6, 13, 17, 20); la farmacia – 9.*

b Students ask and answer questions in pairs about where
things are bought. The help box shows the passive use of
the verb *comprar* (to buy) with one item or more, i.e.
'Where can it / they be bought?'

3 **Las tiendas españolas**

◐ A matching activity in which students read a text
about shops and select the correct word for each picture.

✢ Students pick the appropriate word to complete each
of the sentences.

Answers: ◐ *1 – mercado; 2 – el detergente; 3 – ropa;
4 – el champú; 5 – pasta de dientes; 6 – periódicos.*

          ✢ *1 – tiendas; 2 – mercado; 3 – hipermercados;
4 – el fin de semana; 5 – medicina; 6 – almacenes.*

SUPPORT MATERIALS

OHT 12A De compras

A sheet of 15 images representing the shopping items which can be used to present the vocabulary taught in this topic area via memory games, guessing games, true or false and other activities (see also Introduction for more details).

Worksheet 12.1 Vamos de compras

This sheet has removable English rubrics at the bottom.

1 **¿Adónde van?**

Students listen and identify which shops the people wish to visit.

Answers: 1–f; 2–a; 3–g; 4–d; 5–b; 6–e; (Distractor = c).

1	CHICO:	¿Adónde vas, Papá?
	PADRE:	Voy al quiosco. ¿Quieres venir?
2	CHICA:	¿Vas a casa ahora, Marta?
	CHICA:	No. Voy primero a la pescadería. Mamá quiere sardinas.
3	MADRE:	Julio, ¿vas a pasar por la calle Mayor?
	JULIO:	Sí, ¿por qué?
	MADRE:	¿Puedes ir a la carnicería? Necesito carne picada para la comida.
4	CHICO:	¡Tengo hambre!
	CHICO:	Pues, mira – hay una pastelería allí.
5	SEÑORA:	Íñigo, ¿me puedes traer más naranjas y limones?
	SEÑOR:	Naranjas y limones, vale.
6	MADRE:	Ana, ¿te importa bajar a la calle, y traerme un par de cosas?
	ANA:	Vale. ¿Qué quieres, Mamá?
	MADRE:	Café, té, azúcar y harina.
	ANA:	Café, té, azúcar y harina. ¿Algo más?

2 **¿Dónde se compra ...?**

Students match phrases indicating what shopping is needed with the appropriate responses.

Answers: 1–d; 2–g; 3–a; 4–f; 5–b; 6–h; 7–c; (Distractor = e).

3 **La lista**

Students write a list of items they need to buy to prepare a picnic.

Worksheet 12.2 Más tiendas

1 **Se hace con ...**

Students listen to Teresa explaining to Tomás the ingredients of various Spanish dishes and indicate whether the sentences are true or false.

Answers: 1–✓; 2–✓; 3–✗; 4–✓; 5–✗; 6–✓.

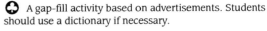

TOMÁS:	El gazpacho, Mamá, ¿se hace con ...?
TERESA:	El gazpacho se hace con tomates, pimientos y pan.
TOMÁS:	¿Es una sopa?
TERESA:	Sí, es una sopa fría.
TOMÁS:	¿Se puede tomar caliente?
TERESA:	No, no.
TOMÁS:	La tortilla española, ¿con qué se hace?
TERESA:	Se llama también la tortilla de patatas, porque se hace con patatas, cebolla y huevos.
TOMÁS:	¿Pones ajo también?
TERESA:	No, nunca. Se toma caliente o fría.
TOMÁS:	¿La sangría se hace con vino, no?
TERESA:	Sí – normalmente tiene alcohol. Se hace con vino, zumo, limonada.
TOMÁS:	Para la fiesta de Pilar, no se hace con vino ...
TERESA:	No, voy a preparar una sangría sin vino.
TOMÁS:	¿Qué más contiene?
TERESA:	Un poco de azúcar, y además naranjas, a veces limones ... es muy refrescante.

2 **Los anuncios**

A gap-fill activity based on advertisements. Students should use a dictionary if necessary.

Answers: 1–la bombonería; 2–el estanco; 3–la librería; 4–la papelería; 5–la tienda de moda; 6–la zapatería.

3 **De tiendas en Sevilla**

A multiple-choice activity based on reading texts about the shopping opportunities in Seville.

Answers: 1–c; 2–b; 3–c; 4–a.

Objectives

Students learn – to ask for and give directions
             – Grammar: positive commands: *tú, usted*

Key language

perdone, ¿por dónde se va a ...?
tome la primera / segunda (calle) a la izquierda / derecha
cruce la plaza
baje la calle
suba la calle
coja la segunda a la derecha
siga todo recto
está al final
está allí
hasta los semáforos
tuerza a la izquierda en el cruce

Skills / Strategies

Students learn – to process map information and give directions
                   based on it

ICT opportunities

Students could use Internet map services such as Mapblast! to generate maps and directions, and then write or speak directions based on them

Ways in

Directions – picture story presentation, map in the Student's Book, page 111

Assessment opportunities

AT1,3/4   Student's Book, Activity 1b: students listen and answer true or false questions.

AT2,3/4   Worksheet 12.3: students ask and say where shops are, in an information-gap activity.

AT3,4   Student's Book, Activity 3b ◐ : students read and process the directions.

AT4,3   Student's Book, Activity 3b ♣ : students produce directions for their partner.

STUDENT'S BOOK, pages 110–111

1   **¿Por dónde se va?**

a This introduces the directions structures for passive recognition. You could also practise these briefly via flashcards and / or giving directions to known places in the local town. Initially, students listen and follow the conversation between Isabel, Tomás and the man.

SEÑOR:	Perdone, ¿por dónde se va a la Cafetería Caracol?
ISABEL:	Tome la primera a la izquierda.
TOMÁS:	Cruce la plaza.
ISABEL:	Baje la calle.
TOMÁS:	¡No! Suba la calle.
ISABEL:	Coja la segunda a la derecha.
TOMÁS:	No, siga todo recto.
ISABEL:	Tome la segunda a la izquierda.
TOMÁS:	No, tuerza a la izquierda.
ISABEL:	Está al final.
SEÑOR:	Vale, gracias. ¡Adiós!

b Students listen and decide whether the picture for each conversation is correct or not.

Answers: *1 – ✓; 2 – ✗; 3 – ✗; 4 – ✓; 5 – ✗; 6 – ✗.*

1	VOZ:	Perdone, señor, ¿por dónde se va a la pastelería?
	SEÑOR:	¿A la pastelería? Vamos a ver ... Cruce la plaza, y suba la calle. Está allí.
	VOZ:	Vale, muchas gracias.
2	VOZ:	¿Señora? Perdone, pero ¿por dónde se va a la panadería?
	SEÑORA:	Suba la calle hasta los semáforos ... y luego tome la primera calle a la derecha.
	VOZ:	La primera a la derecha. Vale, gracias.
3	VOZ:	Perdone, señor, ¿por dónde se va a la pescadería?
	SEÑOR:	Mm ... Tuerza a la izquierda en el cruce, y siga todo recto.
	VOZ:	A la izquierda en el cruce ...
	SEÑOR:	Y todo recto.
	VOZ:	Vale, gracias.
4	VOZ:	Señora, perdone.
	SEÑORA:	¿Sí?
	VOZ:	¿Por dónde se va a la frutería?

	SEÑORA:	La frutería ... Tome la primera calle a la izquierda en la rotonda.
	VOZ:	Primera a la izquierda.
	SEÑORA:	Sí. Luego, coge la segunda calle a la derecha.
	VOZ:	Y la segunda a la derecha.
	SEÑORA:	Eso es.
	VOZ:	Vale, muchas gracias.
5	VOZ:	Perdone, señora, ¿por dónde se va a la farmacia?
	SEÑORA:	Tuerza a la izquierda en los semáforos, y luego suba la calle.
	VOZ:	A la izquierda en los semáforos ...
	SEÑORA:	Y suba la calle.
6	VOZ:	¿Señor?
	SEÑOR:	¿Sí?
	VOZ:	Perdone, pero ¿por dónde se va a la carnicería?
	SEÑOR:	La carnicería ... Tome la primera a la izquierda y cruce la plaza.
	VOZ:	La primera a la izquierda ...
	SEÑOR:	Y cruce la plaza. Está allí.
	VOZ:	Vale, gracias.

c Students now use the visuals from Activity 1b to create their own six conversations giving directions of their own with a partner.

3   **Los clientes**

a A brief revision activity in which students are asked for the English for a selection of Spanish prepositions.

Answers: *al lado – next to / beside; entre – between; al final – at the end; lejos – far; enfrente – opposite; en – in.*

b Students now read sets of directions from the Hotel los Álamos to various places in the town, and follow these on a map to work out the final destination.

♣ This activity involves using the map as a stimulus, and writing three sets of directions for other people. A help box with all the second and third person forms is provided.

Answers: ◐ *1 – el restaurante; 2 – el cine; 3 – la droguería; 4 – la farmacia; 5 – la pastelería; 6 – el mercado.*

Gramática

Students are referred to the grammar summary, section 22, p.152 for further information on positive commands, and to Acción: lengua 12, p.117 for further practice.

SUPPORT MATERIALS

Worksheet 12.3 Perdone …

An information-gap activity. Cut the sheet in half and distribute one half each to students in pairs. Each partner has a slightly different map, but certain points of reference are common to both: *la Plaza Mayor, el Bar Manolo, el Hotel Marina, la piscina, el Instituto San Juan*. Students have to take it in turns to ask each other *¿dónde está …?* in order to find the location of the five places listed at the top of their sheet. As they progress through the activity they should find at least one correct statement to give in answer to their partner's question, and should be able to fill in the gaps in their own plan. Partner **A** has to locate: *el quiosco, la panadería, la frutería, la pastelería* and *el videoclub*, and Partner **B** has to find *la farmacia, la pescadería, la droguería, la cafetería* and *la tienda de alimentación*. After completing the activity, students can check their own answers.

Worksheet 12.4 ¿Me puede ayudar?

1 **Las instrucciones**

Students listen and work out the locations of six places in town.

Answers:	1–F; 2–C; 3–A; 4–D; 5–B; 6–E; (G is the distractor).

1	SEÑOR:	Por favor, ¿por dónde se va a la panadería?
	SEÑORA:	Siga todo recto.
	SEÑOR:	Todo recto …
	SEÑORA:	Cruce la plaza …
	SEÑOR:	Hay que cruzar la plaza …
	SEÑORA:	Y está directamente enfrente.
	SEÑOR:	Directamente enfrente. Vale, gracias.
2	CHICA:	Oye, ¿sabes dónde está la pescadería?
	CHICO:	Sí. Sigue todo recto, y toma la primera a la izquierda.
	CHICA:	Todo recto, la primera a la izquierda.
	CHICO:	La pescadería está a la derecha.
	CHICA:	A la derecha. Gracias.

3	CHICO:	Perdone, señor – ¿por dónde se va a la droguería?
	SEÑOR:	¿La droguería? Está aquí mismo, a la izquierda.
	CHICO:	A la izquierda …
	SEÑOR:	Sí, en la esquina. ¿La ves?
	CHICO:	Ah, sí. Gracias.
4	SEÑORA:	Perdone, ¿sabe dónde está la farmacia?
	CHICA:	Sí. Siga todo recto, y tome la segunda a la derecha.
	SEÑORA:	Todo recto, y la segunda a la derecha.
	CHICA:	Sí. Y está a la derecha, un poco más abajo.
	SEÑORA:	Vale, gracias.
5	CHICO:	Oye, ¿Por dónde se va al supermercado?
	CHICA:	En el cruce, toma la primera a la derecha.
	CHICO:	Hasta el cruce, y luego la primera a la derecha.
	CHICA:	Sí, eso es. El supermercado está a la derecha.
	CHICO:	Estupendo.
6	CHICA:	Señora, ¿me puede ayudar? Busco un estanco.
	SEÑORA:	El estanco. Bueno, siga todo recto, y tome la segunda a la izquierda.
	CHICA:	La segunda a la izquierda.
	SEÑORA:	Sí. Está al final, enfrente.
	CHICA:	Muchas gracias.

2 **Repaso**

Gap-fill activity. Students read directions a–f and study the map in Activity 1. They write down the correct option from a choice of three in brackets.

Answers:	a – Calle Sol; b – al lado; c – a la derecha; d – al lado; e – primera; f – la esquina.

3 **Los verbos**

a A gap-fill activity which involves filling in the appropriate verb forms.

Answers:	1 – Siga, cruce; 2 – Tome; 3 – Suba; 4 – siga; 5 – tuerza; 6 – Baje.

b Students put the answers to Activity 3a into the *tú* form.

Answers:	1 – Sigue, cruza; 2 – Toma; 3 – Sube; 4 – sigue; 5 – tuerce; 6 – Baja.

Objectives
Students learn – to buy groceries
               – to talk about quantities and containers

Key language
¿qué desea?	*un tubo de*
quisiera ...	*una bolsa de*
un kilo de	*un paquete de*
un litro de	*una barra de*
medio kilo de	*tomates*
medio litro de	*mermelada*
cien gramos de	*pañuelos*
un bote de	*vino*
una caja de	*sardinas*
una botella de	*pasta de dientes*
una lata de	*bombones*

Revision of: *naranjas; limonada; leche; queso; café; pan; ¿algo más?; nada más; ¿cuánto es? en total, son ...; aquí tiene; ¿tiene ...?*

Skills / Strategies
Students learn – to develop their transactional skills in shops
               (Student's Book, Activity 6; Worksheet 12.6,
               Activity 2)

ICT opportunities
Students can   – draft and redraft a scene in a supermarket on
                  word-processor; See Extra

Ways in
Shopping items, quantities and containers – presentation Activity 1 in the Student's Book

Assessment opportunities
AT1,3	Student's Book, Activity 5 ◑: students listen and match up the questions and answers.
AT1,3	Student's Book, Activity 5 ◒: students listen and answer closed questions.
AT2,3	Worksheet 12.6, Activity 2: students act out their shopping dialogues.
AT2,4	Student's Book, Activity 6: students take part in a structured conversation, substituting words and phrases.
AT4,3/4	Worksheet 12.6, Activity 2: students write shopping dialogues in response to cues.

STUDENT'S BOOK, pages 112–113

1 La compra
Presentation of shopping items and expressions of quantity.

◑ Students listen to Pilar as she unpacks her grocery shopping bags. They complete each of the quantity phrases (1–11) on her list with the correct item. You may wish to run through some abbreviations of the food items listed in the box on the board to give students more confidence before starting this activity.

◒ Students write down what item Pilar has forgotten and who is going to go and get it: Pilar or Carmina.

Answers: ◑ *1 – naranjas; 2 – tomates; 3 – queso; 4 – limonada; 5 – leche; 6 – bombones; 7 – vino; 8 – sardinas; 9 – mermelada; 10 – pasta de dientes; 11 – pañuelos.*

            ◒ *el pan; Carmina.*

CARMINA:	Hola, Pilar – ¿lo tienes todo?
PILAR:	Sí, vamos a ver ... un kilo de naranjas ... sí; medio kilo de tomates ... sí; cien gramos de ... queso ... un litro de limonada. Mmm ... medio litro de leche ... una bolsa de bombones ... una botella de vino ... una lata de sardinas ... un bote de mermelada ... un tubo de pasta de dientes ... ¡ah! una caja de pañuelos. ¿Pero dónde está la barra de pan? ... ay, Mamá – ¡se me ha olvidado el pan!
CARMINA:	Bueno – voy yo. Si tú recoges todo, voy a la tienda de abajo. A ver si tengo cambio ... Sí, tengo. Bueno, ahora vuelvo, eh.
PILAR:	Vale. Adiós ...

2 ¿Cuál es?
Students match up the numbered phrases 1–11 in Activity 1 with the items a–k in the photo.

Answers: *1 – h; 2 – e; 3 – i; 4 – a; 5 – c; 6 – k; 7 – b; 8 – d; 9 – g; 10 – j; 11 – f.*

3 ¡Improbable!
Speaking practice to consolidate the new vocabulary. Students invent different combinations of quantities or containers and shopping items, and their partners state whether they are probable or improbable.

4 Recipientes
A fun activity: students invent new and imaginary containers by combining some of the new phrases.

5 ¿Qué desea?
A model conversation in a grocer's shop. This introduces two more expressions of quantity: *una barra de ...* and *un paquete de ...* and recycles transactional language first introduced in the context of cafés.

Picture story
When Carmina goes to buy the bread, she meets Tomás and Isabel who discover to their horror that Pilar is not going to be in Seville for her birthday.

◑ Students match up the questions and the answers.

◒ Students work out why Tomás is worried, and put a tick or a cross for each reason.

Answers: ◑ *¿Qué tal? – Bien. ¿Qué desea? – Quisiera ... ¿Algo más? – No, nada más. ¿Cuánto es? – En total, son (2,46) euros.*

            ◒ *1 – ✗; 2 – ✓; 3 – ✗; 4 – ✓.*

CARMINA:	Buenos días.
DEPENDIENTE:	Buenos días, señora. ¿Qué desea?
CARMINA:	Quisiera una barra de pan, por favor.
DEPENDIENTE:	¿Algo más?
CARMINA:	¿Tiene café descafeinado?
DEPENDIENTE:	Sí ...
CARMINA:	Un paquete.
DEPENDIENTE:	¿Algo más?
CARMINA:	No, nada más, gracias. ¿Cuánto es?
DEPENDIENTE:	En total son dos euros cuarenta y seis céntimos.
CARMINA:	Aquí tiene ... Gracias, adiós.
DEPENDIENTE:	Adiós.
TOMÁS:	¡Tía Carmina!
CARMINA:	¡Hola! ¿Qué tal?

ISABEL:	Bien ... ¿y Pilar?
CARMINA:	Bien, muy ilusionada.
TOMÁS:	¿Por qué?
CARMINA:	Porque el día de su cumpleaños, ¡vamos a Madrid!
ISABEL:	¡A Madrid!
TOMÁS:	¿Y la fiesta sorpresa?
CARMINA:	¿Qué fiesta? No te entiendo ...

6 En la tienda

Speaking practice. Using the model conversation from Activity 5, students replace each of the phrases in bold with alternative items, quantities and prices. The new conversation could be recorded on tape or learnt off by heart.

SUPPORT MATERIALS

Worksheet 12.5 ¿Cuánto quiere?

1 ¿Cuánto?

Students listen to four conversations and write down the quantities bought by each person in the appropriate column.

Answers:

	oranges	tomatoes	cheese	strawberry jam	toothpaste	milk	sweets
Cliente 1		1 kilo			1 tubo		
Cliente 2	1/2 kilo			2 botes		1 litro	
Cliente 3			250 gramos		2 tubos		una caja
Cliente 4		1 lata	100 gramos			1/2 litro	

1	DEPENDIENTE:	Buenos días, ¿qué desea?
	SEÑORA:	Quisiera un kilo de tomates.
	DEPENDIENTE:	Un kilo de tomates, muy bien. ¿Algo más?
	SEÑORA:	Sí. Un tubo de pasta de dientes.
	DEPENDIENTE:	Muy bien. ¿Es todo?
	SEÑORA:	Sí, es todo. ¿Cuánto le debo?
2	DEPENDIENTE:	Buenos días, señor.
	SEÑOR:	Buenos días.
	DEPENDIENTE:	¿Qué desea?
	SEÑOR:	Quisiera medio kilo de naranjas.
	DEPENDIENTE:	Medio kilo de naranjas, muy bien. ¿Algo más?
	SEÑOR:	Sí. Mermelada de fresa. Dos botes, por favor.
	DEPENDIENTE:	Aquí tiene. ¿Es todo?
	SEÑOR:	No, necesito un litro de leche.
	DEPENDIENTE:	Y un litro de leche.
	SEÑOR:	Gracias. ¿Cuánto es en total?
3	DEPENDIENTE:	Buenos días, Laura. ¿Qué tal estás?
	LAURA:	Bien gracias.
	DEPENDIENTE:	¿Qué quieres hoy?
	LAURA:	Queso manchego.
	DEPENDIENTE:	Queso manchego. ¿Cuánto quieres?
	LAURA:	Doscientos cincuenta gramos.
	DEPENDIENTE:	Doscientos cincuenta. Muy bien. ¿Algo más?

	LAURA:	Sí. Una caja de bombones.
	DEPENDIENTE:	¿Una caja de bombones, eh? ¿Ésta está bien?
	LAURA:	Sí. Perfecto.
	DEPENDIENTE:	¿Es todo?
	LAURA:	No. Dos tubos de pasta de dientes.
	DEPENDIENTE:	¿DOS tubos? Bueno, ¡si vas a comer una caja entera de bombones de chocolate, los vas a necesitar!
4	DEPENDIENTE:	Buenos días, señora.
	SEÑORA:	Buenos días.
	DEPENDIENTE:	¿Qué desea?
	SEÑORA:	Una lata de tomates, por favor.
	DEPENDIENTE:	Una lata de tomates, muy bien. ¿Algo más?
	SEÑORA:	Sí. ¿Tiene leche fresca?
	DEPENDIENTE:	Sí. ¿Quiere un litro?
	SEÑORA:	No, medio litro. Y también, cien gramos de queso de cabra.
	DEPENDIENTE:	Cien gramos de queso. Muy bien. Aquí tiene. ¿Es todo?
	SEÑORA:	Sí. Es todo por hoy. Gracias. ¿Cuánto le debo?

Worksheet 12.6 En la tienda de alimentación

1 Ayuda al dependiente

Students read the list of prices and write each price in the correct place on the shop fronts.

Answers:

Fruit and vegetables
1 kg pears 1.95 euros
1 kg oranges 1.60 euros
1 kg peppers 2.15 euros
1 kg tomatoes 1.45 euros

Drinks
1L mineral water 0.38 euros
2L Coca-Cola 2.50 euros
2L lemonade 1.66 euros
2L orange juice 1.66 euros
1L fruit juice 0.85 euros

General items
coffee 2.45 euros
jam 1.29 euros
crisps 0.85 euros
tea 2.60 euros

Toiletries
tissues 1.50 euros
aspirins 1.65 euros
toothpaste 1.70 euros
shampoo 1.25 euros

Refrigerated foods
100g York ham 1.80 euros
100g Serrano ham 2.80 euros
100g Cheese 1.75 euros

Bread and sweet things
chocolate 0.75 euros
bread 0.45 euros

2 Dependiente y cliente

Using the prices and items from Activity 1, students write a dialogue and practise it with their partner.

Objectives

Students learn – to buy a present
 – to say whether it's a little, very or too expensive, large, etc.
 – Grammar: revision of agreement of adjectives

Key language

¿cuánto es?
¿qué te parece este plato?
aburrido
barato
caro
enorme
grande
muy
pequeño
un compact disc
un jersey
un poco
un reloj
un vale-regalo
una caja de turrón

¿qué desea?
¿tiene algo más barato?
algo de cerámica
bonito
demasiado caro
gracias
lo dejo, gracias
oiga, por favor
un cinturón
un estéreo personal
una pegatina / un pegatín
un póster
un tarro
un videojuego
una camiseta

Skills / Strategies

Students learn – to express their opinion on gift items on sale
 (Student's Book, Activity 4)

ICT opportunities

Students can – word-process a gift or wants list

Ways in

Presentation Activity 1 in the Student's Book

Assessment opportunities

AT1,3   Student's Book, Activity 5: students listen and sequence the gifts.
AT2,3   Student's Book, Activity 6: students take part in a gift shop role-play.
AT3,3   Worksheet 12.8, Activity 2: students read and complete a letter.
AT4,3/4 Student's Book, Activity 4: students write their opinion on various items.

STUDENT'S BOOK, pages 114–115

1 Un regalo para Pilar

Picture story

While Tomás and Pepa are looking for a birthday present for Pilar, they are spotted by Roberto. Presentation of the nouns, and the characteristics and other adjectives and qualifiers associated with the buying of gifts.

○ Students pick the appropriate adjective to fill each blank.

● Students complete the longer sentences with the appropriate word.

Answers: ○ *1 – caro; 2 – pequeña; 3 – barato; 4 – aburrido; 5 – grande; 6 – ideal.*

● *1 – caro; 2 – barato; 3 – ideal; 4 – grande; 5 – pequeña; 6 – aburrido.*

TOMÁS:	¿Una camiseta? ¡Es un poco pequeña!
PEPA:	¡Ojo!, Roberto.
ROBERTO:	¿Un jersey? Es grande, Pepa.
PEPA:	Es ideal para ti, Roberto.
TOMÁS:	¿Un reloj? ¡Uf! Es caro.
PEPA:	¿Un póster? Es barato.
TOMÁS:	Sí, pero no me gusta.
DEPENDIENTE:	¿Qué desea?
TOMÁS:	Quisiera comprar un regalo para mi prima.
DEPENDIENTE:	¿Un compact disc? Son veinte euros. ¿O un videojuego?
TOMÁS:	Mmm ... es demasiado caro. ¿Tiene algo más barato?
DEPENDIENTE:	¿Un cinturón? Ocho euros.
TOMÁS:	Mmm ... es un poco aburrido. ¿Tiene vale-regalos?
DEPENDIENTE:	Sí.
TOMÁS:	¡Ideal! Pues, un vale-regalo de quince euros.
TOMÁS:	Un estéreo personal – ¡Pepa, no! ¡Qué estúpida!
PEPA:	Perdón ...

2 ¿Qué hay en el paquete?

A pairwork activity in which students imagine what is inside a mystery packet and their partner guesses what it might be.

3 Yo quisiera

○ A basic open-ended writing activity in which students list gifts in order of personal preference.

● Students use the dictionary (or the services of their teacher!) to find out the names of other presents to list.

4 ¿Qué te parece?

A slightly more challenging activity in which students give their opinion about a selection of pictured gift items, saying whether the items shown are suitable or not.

Answers: *1 – El cinturón es demasiado grande / El problema es que es demasiado grande; 4 – El jersey es demasiado grande; 6 – La camiseta es demasiado pequeña; Other answers are open-ended.*

5 En la tienda de recuerdos

Further practice of the gift-selection and description vocabulary, with the addition of some more language on the theme of money and prices.

○ Students listen and pick the appropriate gift for each dialogue and add the price accordingly.

● Students add the appropriate adjective(s) describing the items being discussed.

Answers: ○ *1 – un plato: 50 euros; 2 – una bufanda: 15 euros; 3 – un tarro: 45 euros; 4 – una caja de turrón: 7 euros; 5 – un pegatín: 1 euro; 6 – una camiseta: no price given.*

● *1 – muy caro; 2 – no muy caro; 3 – bonito; 4 – muy típico; 5 – barato; 6 – muy pequeña / enorme / no le gusta el color.*

1	CHICA:	¿Qué te parece este plato?
	CHICA:	Sí ... ¿Cuánto es?
	CHICA:	Cincuenta euros.
	CHICA:	¡Ay, no! Es muy caro. Lo dejo, gracias.
2	CHICO:	¡Mira la bufanda!
	CHICO:	¿Cuánto es?
	CHICO:	Son ... no sé ... ¡Oiga, por favor! ¿Cuánto es la bufanda de Real Betis?

DEPENDIENTE:	Quince euros.
CHICO:	¿Quince? No es muy caro.
CHICO:	Vale, está bien.

3 MUJER: Quisiera comprar un regalo para mi hermana.
DEPENDIENTE: ¿Algo de cerámica? ¿Un tarro?
MUJER: Es bonito. ¿Cuánto es?
DEPENDIENTE: Cuarenta y cinco euros.
MUJER: ¿Cuarenta y cinco? Mm ... Bueno, lo dejo, gracias.

4 DEPENDIENTE: ¿Qué desea?
CHICO: Quisiera comprar un regalo para mi amigo inglés.
DEPENDIENTE: ¿Un cinturón? ¿Un póster de Sevilla?
CHICO: Mm, no sé ...
DEPENDIENTE: ¿O una caja de turrón? El turrón es muy típico ...
CHICO: ¿Cuánto es?
DEPENDIENTE: Siete euros.
CHICO: Siete euros ... Bueno, vale – está bien. Una caja de turrón entonces.

5 DEPENDIENTE: ¿Qué desea?
PADRE: Dile ... ¿Qué quieres?
NIÑO: Un pegatín.
DEPENDIENTE: ¿Un pegatín? ¿Del Sevilla Fútbol Club o del Real Betis?
NIÑO: Real Betis.
DEPENDIENTE: ¿Te gusta el fútbol?
PADRE: Es que es un poco tímido. ¿Cuánto es?
DEPENDIENTE: Es un euro.
PADRE: Un euro – ¡qué barato! Toma ... Vale, gracias. Adiós.
DEPENDIENTE: Adiós.
NIÑO: Adiós.

6 DEPENDIENTE: ¿Qué desea?
MADRE: Bueno, Raquel quiere una camiseta.
DEPENDIENTE: ¿Una camiseta? Mm ... ¿Te gusta ésta?
RAQUEL: Es muy pequeña.
DEPENDIENTE: ¿O prefieres esta camiseta?
RAQUEL: Es muy grande. ¡Es enorme!
DEPENDIENTE: Ésta es muy bonita.
RAQUEL: No me gusta el color.
MADRE: Bueno, lo dejo, gracias. Ven, Raquel. ¡Eres absolutamente imposible! Es la última vez que te llevo a comprar algo ...

6 **De compras**

Students work in pairs to practise gift-buying dialogues, one partner playing the role of the shop assistant and the other the role of the purchaser.

SUPPORT MATERIALS

Worksheet 12.7 ¿Qué prefieres de regalo?
¿Qué prefieres?

 A listening activity to consolidate the language of the objective. The radio station, Radio Sol, has interviewed six young people about the kind of present they would like to receive for their birthday.

◑ Pupils put a tick in the boxes of the birthday presents mentioned by each person on the recording.

♣ Students listen again and this time answer six questions in Spanish – one question for each of the people speaking.

Answers: ◑

	un CD	un Walkman	un póster	una camiseta	un jersey	un reloj	un cinturón	un vale-regalo
1		✓		✓				
2						✓		✓
3	✓		✓					
4		✓				✓		
5				✓	✓		✓	
6	✓							✓

♣ *1 – un libro; 2 – una bicicleta; 3 – le encanta la música; 4 – son regalos caros; 5 – una nueva agenda; 6 – un televisor – para ver la televisión en su dormitorio.*

1 CHICO: Bueno, yo ... quisiera un Walkman, y una camiseta ... No quiero un libro. ¡Odio leer!
2 CHICA: Quisiera un reloj – es que no tengo – y un vale-regalos. ¡Lo mejor sería una bicicleta!
3 CHICA: Mm ... un compact disc, ... ah, un póster de mi grupo favorito ... me gustan estos regalos porque me encanta la música.
4 CHICO: Pues yo quisiera un Walkman o una radio, y un reloj ... El problema es que son regalos caros. Cuestan mucho.
5 CHICA: ¿Regalos de cumpleaños? Quisiera un jersey, y una camiseta ... un cinturón ... y una agenda. He perdido mi agenda, y una nueva sería ideal.
6 CHICO: Quisiera un compact disc, o un vale-regalos. Me encantaría un televisor – ¡podría ver la televisión en mi dormitorio!

Worksheet 12.8 Los regalos
1 **¿Positivo o no?**
a ◑ Students read comments relating to gifts and match up each with the corresponding picture.

Answers: ◑ *1 – d; 2 – e; 3 – g; 4 – h; 5 – a; 6 – j; 7 – b; 8 – i; 9 – c; 10 – f.*

b ♣ Students decide whether each comment is positive (P) or negative (N).

Answers: ♣ *1 – N; 2 – P; 3 – N; 4 – P; 5 – P; 6 – N; 7 – P; 8 – P; 9 – N; 10 – N.*

2 **La carta de Gema**
a ◑ Students fill in the missing words in a letter about gifts. The numbers refer to the pictures in Activity 1.

Answers: *boli; reloj; videojuego; libro; camiseta; jersey.*

b ♣ Students read a summary of the letter and complete a simple multiple-choice activity.

Answers: *Sevilla; hermano; lejos; popular; salir con amigos; estudiar; perezosa.*

Objectives
Students learn – to say what they don't eat, and why
– Grammar: direct object pronouns

Key language
¿hay algo que no comes / tomas?
¿no te / me gusta(n)?
(soy) alérgico(a) a la / al …
el queso
el trigo
la leche
la miel
las nueces
los mariscos
los productos (con) …
los productos lácteos
los yogures
porque es …
no como / tomo
vegetariana (estricta)

Skills / Strategies
Students learn – to express negative opinions and impart negative information

ICT opportunities
Students can – research food habits on the Internet and summarise dietary requirements via word-processor

Ways in
Students' and teacher's own habits; presentation Activity 1 in the Student's Book

Assessment opportunities
AT1,3 Worksheet 12.10, Activity 1: students listen and answer a series of closed questions.
AT3,3 Student's Book, Activity 2: students read and summarise dietary information.
AT4,3/4 Worksheet 12.10, Activity 2: students summarise people's dietary requirements in response to given cues.

STUDENT'S BOOK, page 116

1 **¿Hay algo que no comes?**

✥ Students listen to the dialogues in which each person mentions something they don't eat, and note down the issue mentioned (i.e. vegetarianism – V, an allergy – A or simple taste – X).

Answers: *1 – A; 2 – V; 3 – X; 4 – A; 5 – X.*

1 ENTREVISTADOR:	¿Hay algo que no comes?
LUIS:	Sí, no como el trigo o los productos con trigo.
ENTREVISTADOR:	¿No? ¿Por qué?
LUIS:	Es que soy alérgico al trigo. Y no me siento bien si lo como.
2 ENTREVISTADOR:	¿Y tú, Gabriela? ¿Hay algo que no comes?
GABRIELA:	No tomo la miel.
ENTREVISTADOR:	¿La miel? ¿No te gusta?
GABRIELA:	Es que soy vegetariana estricta. No tomo la miel porque es un producto de un animal.
3 ENTREVISTADOR:	Curro, háblanos de lo que comes, o no comes. ¿Hay algo que no tomas?
CURRO:	No tomo los mariscos.
ENTREVISTADOR:	¿Eres alérgico?
CURRO:	No, es simplemente que no me gustan.
4 ENTREVISTADOR:	Cecilia, ¿hay algo que tú no tomas?
CECILIA:	No tomo los productos lácteos.
ENTREVISTADOR:	Quieres decir, la leche.
CECILIA:	La leche, el queso, los yogures.
ENTREVISTADOR:	¿Por qué?
CECILIA:	Soy alérgica a los productos lácteos. Es una lástima, porque me gustan.
5 ENTREVISTADOR:	Reme, ¿es verdad que no tomas las nueces?
REME:	Sí. No las como.
ENTREVISTADOR:	¿Eres alérgica a las nueces?
REME:	No, es simplemente que no me gustan. ¡Y ya está!

2 **Los jóvenes**

 ✥ Students read some information about what people don't eat, and fill in a grid with the appropriate names.

Answers:

	Productos lácteos	Pescados y mariscos	Nueces	Cereales	Carnes
Hay algo de estos grupos de alimentos que no toma	Charo, Úrsula (el queso) Paco (el queso)	Nina (gambas) Paco	Darío	Úrsula	Paco

3 **Los pronombres**

✥ Presentation and practice of the direct object pronouns. Students read the texts about food tastes again and then select the correct pronouns for the items in the grid. You could ask students to make a new four-column grid with the columns headed: *el, la, los* and *las,* under which they list the items in their singular and plural forms.

SUPPORT MATERIALS
Worksheet 12.9 Los alimentos

1 **¿Te gusta?**

◯ Miguel asks Joss if he likes various things to eat. Students fill in the boxes with two ticks for things he likes a lot, one tick for things he just likes, and a cross for things he dislikes.

Answers: *1 – los pimientos ✓; 2 – el zumo de fruta ✓✓; 3 – el chocolate ✗; 4 – el pan ✓✓; 5 – la carne ✗; 6 – el pescado ✓; 7 – el queso ✓; 8 – los huevos ✗; 9 – los tomates ✗; 10 – las patatas fritas ✓✓.*

MIGUEL:	Joss, ¿te gusta el pan?
JOSS:	Sí, me gusta mucho.
MIGUEL:	¿Te gusta el zumo de fruta?
JOSS:	Sí, mucho.
MIGUEL:	¿Te gusta el chocolate?
JOSS:	No – no me gusta mucho el chocolate.
MIGUEL:	¿No te gusta el chocolate? ¡Uf! ¡Qué raro! ¿Te gusta el queso?
JOSS:	Sí, me gusta.
MIGUEL:	¿Te gusta la carne?
JOSS:	Mm … es que … no me gusta mucho la carne.
MIGUEL:	¿Te gusta el pescado?
JOSS:	El pescado, sí me gusta.
MIGUEL:	¿Te gustan los pimientos?
JOSS:	¿Pimientos? Sí, me gustan.
MIGUEL:	¿Te gustan los tomates?
JOSS:	No mucho, no.
MIGUEL:	¿Te gustan los huevos?
JOSS:	No, lo siento, pero no …
MIGUEL:	¿Te gustan las patatas fritas?
JOSS:	¡Mmm! ¡Sí, me encantan!

2 **Mi pareja**

◐ A pairwork activity in which students take it in turns to give their opinion on the food items mentioned in Activity 1.

3 **¿Qué opinas tú?**

◐ Using a dictionary if necessary, students write a list of their opinions on various drinks and food items.

Worksheet 12.10 ¿Comer o no comer?

1 **¿Qué dicen?**

Students listen to three people giving details of what they do and don't eat. They write the appropriate person's initials by each sentence.

Answers: *1 – N; 2 – C; 3 – V; 4 – C; 5 – C; 6 – V.*

NURIA:	Carlos, ¿quieres un poco de pan?
CARLOS:	No, gracias. No puedo tomar pan.
VERÓNICA:	¿No puedes tomar pan, Carlos? ¿Qué pasa? ¿Eres alérgico al trigo?
CARLOS:	A la mayoría de los cereales, sí. Si tienen gluten, no los tomo.
VERÓNICA:	Pues, no lo sabía, Carlos. Y tú, Nuria, no tomas carne, ¿verdad?
NURIA:	Sí, es verdad. Y no tomo pescado tampoco.
CARLOS:	¡No sé cómo puedes vivir sin comer carne, Nuria! Yo la tomo de cualquier forma – chuletas, filetes, … todo me encanta.
VERÓNICA:	A mí, me gusta bastante. Pero yo no tomo leche.
CARLOS:	¿No tomas leche, Verónica?
VERÓNICA:	No. Ni leche, ni quesos, ni yogures … Si tiene leche, no lo tomo.
CARLOS:	Yo no tomo gambas. Me ponen malo. Gambas, mejillones …, no los puedo tomar. ¿Hay otras cosas que tú no tomas, Verónica?
VERÓNICA:	Las almendras, los cacahuetes … no me gustan nada.

2 **Paloma y Patricio**

Students produce a cued piece of writing about Paloma and Patricio based on visual information about what they do and don't eat.

3 **Lo que tú comes – ¡o no!**

Finally, students write a brief paragraph about what they themselves do and don't eat, justifying their argument with reasons.

Acción: lengua 12, page 117

Practice of positive commands in both the *tú* and *usted* forms. Students also learn how to use the direct object pronouns *lo / la / los / las*.

1   ◐ Students decide whether the commands are in the *tú* or the *usted* form.

✚ Students generate instructions for healthy living.

Answers: ◐ *a – usted; b – tú; c – tú; d – usted; e – tú; f – usted.*

✚ *bebe; come; estudia; escucha; recoge. cene; lave; planche; beba; lea.*

2   Practice of the direct object pronouns.

◐ Students fill in the correct words for 'it / them' in the blanks.

✚ Students fill in the gaps with the correct form of the direct object pronouns.

Answers: ◐ *1 – lo; 2 – las; 3 – la; 4 – los; 5 – la; 6 – lo.*

✚ *1 – lo; 2 – los; 3 – la; 4 – las; 5 – los.*

Objectives

Students learn – to say they don't feel well and where it hurts
– to name the parts of the body
– Grammar: revision of *me, te, le*, etc.; the verb *doler* (to hurt)

Key language

¿qué te pasa?
no me siento bien
me duele el / la …
me duelen los / las …
el brazo
el estómago
el oído
el ojo
el pecho
el pie
la boca
la cabeza
la espalda
la garganta
la mano
la muela
la nariz
la pierna

Skills / Strategies

Giving excuses (in the classroom)

ICT opportunities

Use a word-processing package to create a cloze activity based on the dialogues encountered in this topic area

Ways in

Picture story, Student's Book, page 118
Parts of the body, Student's Book, Activity 2
'Simon says' games / cardboard skeleton for parts of the body

Assessment opportunities

AT1,2/4 Worksheet 13.1, Activity 1: students decide whether pictures and speech bubbles match what is said.

AT1,4 Worksheet 13.2, Activity 1 ♦ : students listen and fill in the missing details.

AT2,3 Student's Book, Activity 3b: students have 'illness' conversations.

AT3,2 Student's Book, Activity 3a ♦ : students match the pictures to the complaints.

AT4,4 Worksheet 13.2, Activity 2 ♦ : students invent excuses.

STUDENT'S BOOK, pages 118–119

1 No me siento bien

Picture story

Pilar arrives at the party, and finds that Isabel is ill in bed – there is a tentative 'making up' between them.

♦ Students fill in blanks in sentences taken from the picture story: this highlights the core language and the structures *me duele* and *me duelen*.

♦ Students read between the lines and decide if they think the statements are true or false: encourage them to use the vocabulary section at the back of the Student's Book for words they have forgotten.

Answers: ♦ *1 – me; 2 – te; 3 – estómago; 4 – cabeza; 5 – oídos.*

♦ *1 – verdad; 2 – verdad; 3 – mentira; 4 – verdad; 5 – verdad; 6 – mentira.*

TODOS:	¡Feliz cumpleaños, Pilar!
PILAR:	¡Qué sorpresa! ¿Dónde está Isabel?
TOMÁS:	En su dormitorio.
PILAR:	¿Isabel? ¿Qué te pasa?
ISABEL:	No me siento muy bien. Me duele la cabeza … y me duele el estómago también.
PILAR:	¿No quieres venir a la fiesta? José Luis está aquí …
ISABEL:	José Luis ya no me interesa.
PILAR:	¿De verdad?
ISABEL:	Sí, de verdad. ¡Ahora me duelen los oídos!
PILAR:	Bueno … hasta luego.

2 El robot no funciona bien

Presentation of other parts of the body. Students listen to the doctor quizzing the robot as to which bits of him hurt. The first time round students could simply listen and follow the parts of the body mentioned; the second time, they note which parts of the robot hurt by writing or

indicating with ticks or a cross: *mucho* (two ticks), *un poco* (one tick) or *no* (a cross).

As a follow-up speaking activity, to practise the key language with written support, students could read Activity 2 taking the roles of the doctor and the robot in pairs, with the robot (in a 'robotic' voice), answering *mucho, un poco, no* as he / she chooses.

Answers: *1 – mucho; 2 – mucho; 3 – un poco; 4 – mucho; 5 – no; 6 – mucho; 7 – un poco; 8 – no; 9 – mucho; 10 – no; 11 – no; 12 – un poco; 13 – no; 14 – mucho.*

MÉDICA:	¿Qué tal el cuerpo? Uno. ¿te duele … la cabeza?
ROBOT:	Mucho.
MÉDICA:	Dos. ¿El ojo?
ROBOT:	Mucho.
MÉDICA:	Tres. ¿La nariz?
ROBOT:	Un poco.
MÉDICA:	Cuatro. ¿El oído?
ROBOT:	Mucho.
MÉDICA:	Cinco. ¿La boca?
ROBOT:	No.
MÉDICA:	Seis. ¿La muela?
ROBOT:	Mucho.
MÉDICA:	Siete. ¿La garganta?
ROBOT:	Un poco.
MÉDICA:	Ocho. ¿La espalda?
ROBOT:	No.
MÉDICA:	Nueve. ¿El pecho?
ROBOT:	Mucho.
MÉDICA:	Diez. ¿El brazo?
ROBOT:	No. Está bien.
MÉDICA:	Once. ¿La mano?
ROBOT:	No.
MÉDICA:	Doce. ¿El estómago?
ROBOT:	Un poco.
MÉDICA:	Trece. ¿La pierna?
ROBOT:	No.
MÉDICA:	Catorce. ¿El pie?
ROBOT:	Mucho.
MÉDICA:	¡Mi pobre robot! Vamos a ver si podemos repararte …

3 **¿Quién habla?**

Reading practice, highlighting *me duelen*.

a ◐ Students match up the statements 1–5 to the correct pictures a–g.

♣ Students write speech bubbles for the pictures not used in the diamond activity. The new language box will offer support.

Answers: ◐ *1 – c; 2 – e; 3 – d; 4 – a; 5 – b.*

♣ *f – Me duelen las manos;*
g – Me duelen las muelas;
h – Me duele la garganta / Tengo dolor de garganta.

b Students use the visuals from Activity 3a as the stimulus for pairwork dialogues on the same topic.

Gramática

Students are referred to the grammar summary, section 17, p.151 for more information on indirect object pronouns.

SUPPORT MATERIALS

Worksheet 13.1 ¡Ay!

1 **¿Qué te pasa?**

◐ Students listen to the conversations and read the speech bubbles, deciding if they match what is said by each sick student on the recording.

Answers: *Pedro – ✓; Rosario – ✗; Joaquín – ✗; Ana – ✓;*
Paco – ✗; Marta – ✓.

1	CHICA:	¿Qué te pasa, Pedro?
	PEDRO:	No me siento bien. Me duele el estómago.
2	CHICO:	¡Hola, Rosario! Pero, ¿qué pasa?
	ROSARIO:	Me duele la cabeza. Es terrible.
3	JOAQUÍN:	No me siento muy bien.
	CHICO:	¿No? ¿Qué te pasa, Joaquín?
	JOAQUÍN:	Me duele la garganta.
4	CHICA:	Ana, ¿qué te pasa?
	ANA:	Me duele la muela. ¡Odio el dolor de muelas!
5	CHICO:	¿Qué tal, Paco?
	PACO:	¡Mal!
	CHICO:	¿Mal? ¿Por qué?
	PACO:	Tengo dolor de oídos.
6	CHICA:	¿Marta? ¡Marta! ¿Qué te pasa? ¿No ves bien?
	MARTA:	No. Me duele el ojo izquierdo.
	CHICA:	¿El ojo izquierdo? ¿Me dejas ver?

2 **Los anuncios**

◐ Students write the correct number for each advert.

Answers: *A – 1; B – 3; C – 5; D – 8; E – 4; F – 2.*

3 **¡Los pobres profes!**

◐ This activity gives further practice in the language of the objective.

Students imagine what each teacher is saying, and write a speech bubble for each cartoon. For less able students, put a variety of possible answers, including a few distractors, on the board in random order. They can match them up to the pictures and copy out the one they think fits best.

Answers: *1 – Me duele la cabeza; 2 – Me duelen los oídos;*
3 – Me duele la boca; 4 – Me duele el estómago;
5 – Me duele la mano.

Worksheet 13.2 Excusas

1 **En la enfermería**

♣ Students listen and fill in the boxes with the appropriate details about people's illnesses and excuses.

Answers: *Juan – Le duele la cabeza / Tiene matemáticas;*
Lali – Le duele la garganta / Le duele también la cabeza;
Martín – Le duele el estómago / No le gusta mucho el profesor;
Anita – Le duele una muela / Le gusta mucho el chocolate;
Paco – Le duele la garganta y la cabeza / Es el profe de geografía;
Susana – Le duele el ojo / Viene de una clase de química.

1	ENFERMERA:	¿Hola? ¿Eres Juan, no?
	JUAN:	Sí, Juan Moya. No me siento bien.
	ENFERMERA:	¿Qué te pasa, Juan?
	JUAN:	Me duele la cabeza.
	ENFERMERA:	¿Qué asignatura tienes ahora?
	JUAN:	Matemáticas. Me gustan las matemáticas, pero no puedo concentrarme.
	ENFERMERA:	¿Sí? ¿Dónde está el termómetro?
2	LALI:	¿Señora?
	ENFERMERA:	Hola.
	LALI:	Soy Lali. Lali Conde.
	ENFERMERA:	Y ¿qué te pasa, Lali?
	LALI:	Es que, mm, me duele la garganta.
	ENFERMERA:	¿La garganta? ¿Me dejas ver?
	ROSARIO:	Aaaghhh ...
	ENFERMERA:	Hmm ...
	ROSARIO:	Y me duele la cabeza mucho.
3	ENFERMERA:	¿Sí?
	MARTÍN:	No me siento muy bien.
	ENFERMERA:	¿Cómo te llamas?
	MARTÍN:	Martín Valdés. Me duele el estómago ...
	ENFERMERA:	¿Tienes deporte, no?
	MARTÍN:	Sí.
	ENFERMERA:	¿Te gusta el deporte?
	MARTÍN:	No está mal, pero no me gusta mucho el profesor.
	ENFERMERA:	Bueno, siéntate un momentito ...
4	ANITA:	No me siento bien.
	ENFERMERA:	Un momento, por favor. ¿Cómo te llamas?
	ANITA:	Soy Anita. Anita Lagares. Es que tengo una muela que me duele mucho ...
	ENFERMERA:	¿Una muela? ¿Me dejas ver? ¿Comes muchos bombones?
	ANITA:	No, no muchos. Pero me gusta mucho el chocolate.
	ENFERMERA:	Tendrás que ir al dentista, Anita. Yo no puedo hacer nada.
	ANITA:	¡Ay no! Odio ir al dentista ...
5	PACO:	¿Señora?
	ENFERMERA:	Dime.
	PACO:	Soy Paco Hernández. Es que no me siento bien.
	ENFERMERA:	¿Qué te pasa?
	PACO:	No se ... Me duele la garganta, me duele la cabeza ...
	ENFERMERA:	Siéntate un momento. ¿Cómo se llama tu profe?
	PACO:	Señor Roldán. Es profe de geografía.
	ENFERMERA:	Ah, sí. ¿Abres la boca?

6 SUSANA: ¡Ay! ¡Me duele el ojo!

ENFERMERA: Ven aquí, ¿me dejas ver?

SUSANA: ¡Ay! ¡Cómo me duele!

ENFERMERA: ¿Eres Susana, no? ¿Qué te ha pasado?

SUSANA: Sí. No sé exactamente. Estaba haciendo un experimento en química ...

ENFERMERA: ¿Química? Debemos lavar el ojo en seguida.

2 **Porque me duele(n) ...**

An open-ended writing activity in which students invent excuses for people.

3 **¡Qué pena!**

a Students join the sentence halves correctly.

Answers: *1 – c; 2 – e; 3 – a; 4 – f; 5 – d; 6 – b.*

b Students fill in the gaps with the correct pronouns.

Answers: *1 – me; 2 – te; 3 – le; 4 – le; 5 – me; 6 – le.*

Objectives
Students learn – to give further reasons for feeling unwell
– to say what's wrong with other people

Key language
tengo / tienes / tiene
fiebre
tos
un catarro
náuseas
la fiebre del heno
una picadura
una ampolla
le duele/n

Skills / Strategies
Students learn to recognise / use *le* to talk about other people

ICT opportunities
Students can word-process the memo to the doctor in Student's Book Activity 4

Ways in
OHT 13A
Presentation – Student's Book, Activity 1

Assessment opportunities
AT1,2   Student's Book, Activity 2 ◑: a 'who is it' activity.
AT2,3   Student's Book, Activity 3: students invent a dialogue about a sick football team.
AT3,2   Worksheet 13.4, Activity a: students unscramble words and insert them correctly in the song.
AT4,3   Student's Book, Activity 4: students write a memo.

STUDENT'S BOOK, pages 120–121

1 **Al médico**

a Presentation of the key language with *tengo*: the dwarves are miserable and can't go to work for a variety of reasons. Snow White sends them to see the doctor. Initially, students just read the speech bubbles and listen to the dwarves telling Snow White how they feel.

NARRADOR:	Son las ocho de la mañana en la casa de Blancanieves y los siete enanitos.
BLANCANIEVES:	¿Qué pasa aquí?
ENANITO 1:	Tengo fiebre.
ENANITO 2:	Tengo tos.
ENANITO 3:	Tengo náuseas.
ENANITO 4:	Tengo un catarro.
ENANITO 5:	Tengo la fiebre del heno.
ENANITO 6:	Tengo una picadura.
ENANITO 7:	Tengo una ampolla.
BLANCANIEVES:	Bueno, ¡al médico, todos!

b Students listen to the next part of the recording and note down whether the dwarves answer *sí* or *no* to the doctor's question as he tries to sort out who is who: his questions highlight *¿tienes...?*

Answers: *2 – sí; 4 – no; 6 – no; 1 – no; 5 – sí; 3 – no; 7 – no.*

MÉDICO:	Vamos a ver ... Número Dos, tienes tos, ¿no? Y número Cuatro ... tienes náuseas, ¿verdad? Número Seis ... una ampolla. Parece que tienes una ampolla. Número Uno, aquí dice que tienes una picadura. Enanito Número Cinco, ¿tienes la fiebre del heno? Número Tres ... mmm ... tienes fiebre, ¿no? Y finalmente Número Siete, tienes un catarro. ¿Sí?

2 **Teresa**
Picture story
Presentation of how to say what's the matter with someone else. Teresa, now very pregnant, falls and hurts herself at the party.

◑ Students work out who is being referred to in each of the sentences 1–5.

✚ Pilar rushes to Isabel's room to tell her what has happened. Students use the words in the box to complete Pilar's explanation.

Answers: ◑ *1 – Isabel; 2 – Isabel; 3 – Teresa; 4 – Isabel; 5 – Teresa.*

     ✚ *ven; está; Tiene; estómago; duelen; cabeza; bebé.*

JOSÉ LUIS:	¿Qué tal está Isabel?
PILAR:	Le duele la garganta ...
JOSÉ LUIS:	¿Tiene tos?
PILAR:	No, pero le duele el estómago también.
TOMÁS:	¡Pilar!
PILAR:	¡Tía Teresa! ¿Qué le pasa?
TOMÁS:	Tiene náuseas ... y le duele la espalda.
PILAR:	¡Mamá! ¡Rápido, ven!

3 **El equipo de fútbol**

An oral pairwork activity. Students use a model conversation and a substitution box to invent dialogues between the football team and their manager.

4 **¿Qué le pasa?**

Students write a memo to the director of the mines explaining why the dwarves can't come to work, using *tiene* and the new language. More able students can add in parts of the body as appropriate from the previous unit, including *le duele/n*.

SUPPORT MATERIALS

Worksheet 13.3 ¡Qué mal me siento!

1 **¿Qué tienes?**

Students match up the sentence halves, then match each sentence with the appropriate picture.

Answers: *1 – d, Ramón; 2 – c, Mercedes; 3 – e, Javier; 4 – f, Sara; 5 – a, Victoria; 6 – b, Oscar.*

2 **¡Qué desastre!**

This activity entails inventing dialogues with a partner about feeling unwell, explaining symptoms and eliciting a suitable remedy.

3 **Los mensajes de texto**

Students write excuses in response to text message invitations. The activity is open-ended in that they can write what they want as long as they fulfil the criteria set.

Worksheet 13.4 En las minas

En las minas

a Students use the visual and verbal clues to identify the words 1–8.

b A more able class can read the text of the song and work out where to insert the words before listening to check their answers and sing along. A group needing more support may find it easier to listen several times before writing the words in the correct places. The transcript below highlights the missing words in bold.

Answers: *1 – Qué; 2 – fiebre; 3 – tres; 4 – estómago; 5 – pasa; 6 – día; 7 – duele; 8 – cama.*

A las minas no podemos bajar,
En las minas no podemos cavar,
Para las minas no podemos trabajar,
¡Día de descanso en la cama!

¿Qué te **pasa**, número uno?
'Me duele la cabeza y tengo fiebre.'
Le duele la cabeza y tiene **fiebre** –
¡Día de descanso en la cama!

¿Qué te **pasa**, número dos?
'Me **duele** la garganta y tengo tos.'
Le duele la garganta y tiene tos –
¡Día de descanso en la **cama**!

A las minas no podemos bajar,
En las minas no podemos cavar,
Para las minas no podemos trabajar,
¡Día de descanso en la cama!

¿Qué te **pasa**, número **tres**?
'Me duele el estómago y tengo náuseas.'
Le duele el **estómago** y tiene náuseas –
¡Día de descanso en la cama!

¿**Qué** te pasa, número cuatro?
'Me duele la nariz y tengo un catarro.'
Le duele la nariz y tiene un catarro –
¡**Día** de descanso en la cama!

A las minas no podemos bajar,
En las minas no podemos cavar,
Para las minas no podemos trabajar,
¡Día de descanso en la cama!

Objectives

Students learn – to ask what they have to do and tell others
– to make suggestions
– Grammar: verb *deber* (to have to)

Key language

debo, debes, debe ...
tomar ...
una aspirina
una pastilla
un antibiótico
un poco de agua
un jarabe
poner(me/te) ...
una crema
una tirita
llamar / ir ...
al médico
al dentista
al hospital
a la cama
descansar

Skills / Strategies

Using the modal verb *deber*

ICT opportunities

A cloze-type activity practising *deber* (Student's Book, Activity 1) could be produced

Ways in

Picture story in Student's Book, page 122

Assessment opportunities

AT1,3   Student's Book, Activity 2: students note what should be done.

AT2,3   Student's Book, Activity 3: a hospital role-play.

AT3,2   Student's Book, Activity 2: students read and listen to texts to work out what each person should do ◗ and what exactly is wrong with them ✚.

AT4,2   Worksheet 13.5, Activity 2: a text-completion activity.

STUDENT'S BOOK, pages 122–123

1   La emergencia

Picture story

Carmina decides that Teresa must go to hospital. Isabel is ill and can't go with her. Pilar rings her uncle Michael (Teresa's husband) in London to ask him to come.

◗ Students match the new language with the pictures.

✚ More able students complete the sentences with the appropriate part of the verb *deber*.

Answers: ◗   *1 – d; 2 – b; 3 – f; 4 – c; 5 – e; 6 – a.*

✚   *1 – debo; 2 – debo; 3 – debes; 4 – debes; 5 – debe; 6 – debe.*

TOMÁS:	Mamá, debes tomar una aspirina y un poco de agua.
PILAR:	¿Me dejas? ¡Ay! Debes ponerte una crema, tía Teresa.
TERESA:	No, es que yo ... debo llamar a Michael en Londres.
CARMINA:	Tú debes descansar.
CARLOS:	¿No debes llamar al médico?
CARMINA:	¡Pero yo soy médica!
CARLOS:	¡Ay perdón, es verdad!
CARMINA:	Teresa debe ir al hospital – Pilar, llama a una ambulancia.
ISABEL:	¡Pero yo quiero ir al hospital con Mamá!
CARMINA:	No, Isabel, no estás bien. Pilar, llama a tu tío, por favor. Debe venir aquí a Sevilla.
PILAR:	Vale ...

2   Si no se mejora ...

Further presentation and listening practice; students read and listen to Carmina's recommendations to her young patients. On the first listening students could simply raise their hands when they hear the key language in the speech bubbles. On a second listening, they could note down what the problem is. This revises the language of the previous objectives of the unit. Put the expressions *tiene / le duele / le duelen* on the board before students listen, or when feeding back the answers, to help them to reply in the third person.

◗ Students pick the appropriate visual depicting what each person needs to do.

✚ Students write down what exactly is wrong with each person.

Answers: ◗ *Amalia – 2; Bernardo – 1; Celia – 3; David – 4; Eulalia – 6.*

✚ *Amalia tiene fiebre y le duele la cabeza; A Bernardo le duelen mucho las muelas; Celia tiene una ampolla (que le duele mucho); David tiene tos y le duele la garganta; A Eulalia le duele la boca.*

AMALIA	
CARMINA:	¿No te sientes bien?
AMALIA:	No. Es que tengo fiebre, y me duele la cabeza.
CARMINA:	Hmm ... Si no se mejora, debes ir a la cama.
BERNARDO	
CARMINA:	¿Qué te pasa?
BERNARDO:	Me duelen mucho las muelas.
CARMINA:	¿Me dejas ver? Hmm. Si no se mejora dentro de un día, debes ir al dentista.
CELIA	
CARMINA:	Hola, Celia. ¿Qué te pasa?
CELIA:	Tengo una ampolla aquí en el pie. Me duele mucho.
CARMINA:	Debes ponerte una tirita. Y si no se mejora, debes volver aquí para un antibiótico, por si acaso tienes una infección.
DAVID	
CARMINA:	¿No te sientes bien?
DAVID:	Es que tengo tos y ... me duele la garganta.
CARMINA:	¿Me dejas ver? Bueno. Creo que es un virus. Debes tomar un jarabe. Si no se mejora dentro de cuatro o cinco días, debes tomar un antibiótico.
EULALIA	
CARMINA:	¿Qué te pasa?
EULALIA:	No sé. Me duele la boca.
CARMINA:	¿La boca? Ábreme la boca, entonces. Hmm. Tienes una infección. Debes tomar unas pastillas.

3 **En la enfermería**

This speaking practice activity could take place with students in pairs role-playing either Carmina as a doctor or a male or female nurse in the school sick bay, and a student who is feeling unwell. Student **A** has a variety of complaints and Student **B** recommends something suitable. If you assume the role of an incompetent medic, this can be extended to whole-class practice: individual students come with complaints, you listen and make recommendations, and the rest of the class decide whether your suggested treatment is appropriate or not by a show of hands, or tick / cross on paper, or verbal feedback. This could then be done in groups.

Gramática

Students are referred to the grammar summary, section 23, p.152 and to Acción: lengua 13, p.125 for verbs of obligation, including *deber*.

SUPPORT MATERIALS

Worksheet 13.5 ¿Qué debo hacer?

1 **¿Grave o no?**

○ Students listen and find the correct illustration of the suggested remedy for each dialogue.

✚ Students note what is wrong with each person (revision from the previous objective). There is some redundant language, but much of it consists of cognates. If appropriate, you could encourage students to suggest words they thought they heard, so that you can confirm or elaborate and write new vocabulary on the board. This encourages students to regard listening as an opportunity to learn, rather than a test.

Answers:
○ *1 – e; 2 – c; 3 – a; 4 – f; 5 – b; 6 – d.*

✚ *1 – tiene una ampolla / le duele el pie – N;*
2 – tiene náuseas / le duele la cabeza / está vomitando – G;
3 – le duele la garganta – N;
4 – le duele la pierna – G;
5 – tiene una picadura / quizás un shock anafaláctico – G;
6 – le duele el estómago – N;

1	JAZMINA:	¡Ay, me duele el pie!
	ANA:	¿Qué te pasa?
	JAZMINA:	No sé – voy a quitarme la sandalia.
	ANA:	Tienes una ampolla – mira.
	JAZMINA:	Me duele mucho.
	ANA:	¡Nah! Necesita un poco de crema, nada más …
2	SECRETARIA:	Pero, ¿qué pasa?
	PROFE.:	Un accidente en el patio. Marta Velázquez se ha caído y le duele muchísimo la cabeza. Tiene náuseas también y está vomitando. Voy a llamar al médico.

3	DINO:	Mamá …
	MAMÁ:	¿Qué …?
	DINO:	Me duele la garganta.
	MAMÁ:	¿Me dejas ver? No veo nada. No es nada grave.
	DINO:	¿Debo tomar una aspirina?
	MAMÁ:	Buena idea. Tómate una aspirina o una pastilla – están en el cuarto de baño.
4	ALI:	¡Ay!
	GABI:	¿Qué te pasa?
	ALI:	No sé – me duele la pierna. No la puedo mover … ¡Ay!
	GABI:	Hm. Debes descansar un rato. Y luego veremos.
5	PROFE.:	¿Qué pasa aquí?
	IÑAKI:	Rosa tiene una picadura en la boca. Le ha picado un bicho, no sé …
	PROFE.:	Pero, esto es más que una picadura. ¡Rosa!
	ROSA:	Me duele la boca, y la garganta. Y no puedo hablar…
	PROFE.:	Esto puede ser un shock anafaláctico. ¡Rápido, Juan! Debemos llevarla directamente al hospital ¡Corre!
6	DANI:	Papá, no me siento bien.
	PAPÁ:	¿Qué te pasa?
	DANI:	Me duele el estómago …
	PAPÁ:	No es nada … ¿Has comido algo?
	DANI:	No quiero. Creo que es una apendicitis.
	PAPÁ:	¡No lo creo, Dani! Son las ocho de la mañana y tienes que ir al colegio – ¿no es eso?
	DANI:	Sí.
	PAPÁ:	Bueno, debes tomar un poco de agua y luego comer algo. ¿Te apetece un cruasán o un suizo?

2 **¿Qué debo hacer?**

A verb-completion activity practising *ir, tomar* and *ponerte*.

Answers:
1 – ponerte; 2 – tomar; 3 – ir; 4 – ponerte;
5 – tomar; 6 – ir; 7 – tomar; 8 – ir.

3 **Michael y Pilar**

✚ Students read the text of a telephone call between Michael and Pilar, and fill in the gaps.

Answers:
1 – tal; 2 – pasa; 3 – hospital; 4 – problemas;
5 – debo; 6 – cama; 7 – le; 8 – duelen; 9 – llamar;
10 – debes; 11 – debe; 12 – vale.

Objectives
Students learn – to say what they or others ought to do to be / stay healthy
           – Grammar revision of *hay que* (Unit 10B) and *tener que* (Unit 10A)

Key language
andar
correr
debes beber / comer / hacer (etc.)
decir 'no'
el azúcar
el chocolate
el ejercicio físico
el pescado
hacer … veces por semana / día
hacer deporte
hacer footing
hay que beber (etc.)
el agua
la carne
la fruta y verduras
la grasa
las cereales
las colas …
muchos contienen azúcar
las naranjadas
los colorantes artificiales
los dulces
los edulcorantes
los gaseosos
los pasteles
los productos lácteos
los refrescos
más
menos
practicar deporte
repite … veces
ver (demasiado) la tele

Skills / Strategies
Giving and understanding advice and the structures used for this

ICT opportunities
Students could word-process healthy living advice by cutting and pasting the advice structures in a word-processing application

Ways in
Visuals on page 124; mime

Assessment opportunities
AT1,2   Worksheet 13.6, Activity 1: students react to the recommendations they hear.
AT3,2   Worksheet 13.6, Activity 2: students evaluate health suggestions.
AT3,3   Worksheet 13.7, Activity 1a: students sequence the visuals.
AT4,3/4   Worksheet 13.7, Activity 2a: students paraphrase the recommendations from the previous activity.

STUDENT'S BOOK, page 124

1 **Tomás y Omar**
     a Tomás' uncle Omar is giving him unwelcome health advice. Initially students just listen and read.

     b Students listen again and match Omar's recommendations to the visuals in the Student's Book.

Answers: *5, 1, 3.*

TOMÁS:	No me siento muy bien.
OMAR:	¡Debes beber menos refrescos! ¡Debes comer menos chocolate! Y debes hacer más ejercicio físico …
TOMÁS:	¡Y tú no eres mi padre!

2 **¿Qué debes hacer?**
Radio interviews on the subject of healthy living. Students listen to the recording and decide which heading best suits each of the interviews.

Answers: *1–B; 2–A; 3–C; 4–A; 5–C; 6–B.*

1	VOZ 1:	Para una vida más sana …
	VOZ 2:	Y una piel más clara …
	VOZ 1:	Debe beber más agua.
	VOZ 2:	Agua mineral …
	VOZ 1:	Con gas o sin gas …
	VOZ 2:	O simplemente agua del grifo …
	VOZ 1:	¡Dos litros por día!
	VOZ 2:	Para una vida más sana.

2	VOZ 3:	¿Es verdad que los jóvenes ven demasiado la tele? ¿Es verdad que no practican deporte?
	VOZ 4:	Todos no, pero en general los jóvenes no hacen el ejercicio físico necesario.
	VOZ 3:	¿Qué quiere usted decir al joven que escucha este programa?
	VOZ 4:	Digo: escucha. Tú debes hacer media hora de deporte o media hora de ejercicio físico cada día. Más, si puedes.

3	VOZ 5:	¿Siempre estás intentando perder kilos? Las reglas son muy fáciles. Debes acostumbrarte a decir 'no' a los dulces, 'no' al chocolate, 'no' a los pasteles. ¡Y ya está!

4	VOZ 6:	¿Qué recomiendan nuestros jóvenes a un compañero …
	VOZ 1:	… o a una compañera?
	VOZ 2:	Debe hacer footing. Es lo mejor. Empieza haciendo quince minutos en el parque: dos minutos de andar, un minuto de correr. Repite el ciclo cinco veces. Debe hacerlo tres veces por semana al principio.

5	VOZ 4:	¡Los consejos que voy a dar no son nuevos! Hay que comer menos azúcar y grasa así vas a tomar menos calorías, y debes comer más fruta y verduras. Debes comer también algo de cereales, productos lácteos y carne o pescado, si quieres.

6	VOZ 3:	Los peores son los refrescos: los gaseosos, las naranjadas y las colas … Muchos contienen azúcar, edulcorantes, colorantes artificiales – aún los formulados especialmente para los deportistas.

3 **Receta para una vida más sana**

Finally, students write an advert for a healthy life, containing at least six recommendations. A help box gives suggestions, as do the preceding activities.

Gramática

Students are referred to the grammar summary, section 23, p.152. More comprehensive information and practice of verbs of obligation is provided in Acción: lengua 13, p.125 of the Student's book.

SUPPORT MATERIALS

Worksheet 13.6 ¿Buena idea o mala idea?

This worksheet has removable English rubrics at the bottom.

1 **¿Mas o menos?**

Students listen to six short dialogues where people are being advised about their lifestyle. Should they have more of certain foods and drinks (+) or should they have less to eat / drink (−), or is their lifestyle just right (✔)? Students put the appropriate symbol in each box.

Answers: *a −; b ✔; c +; d −; e −; f −.*

1	CHICA:	¿Haces footing todos los días?
	CHICO:	Sí, todos los días.
	CHICA:	Está bien.
2	CHICO:	Oye, Miguel, ¿cuántas tazas de café bebes al día?
	CHICO:	Cinco o seis.
	CHICO:	¡Es demasiado! Hay que beber menos café.
3	CHICA:	A mí, me encantan los huevos.
	CHICA:	¿Sí? ¿Cuántos huevos tomas a la semana?
	CHICA:	No sé. Con las tortillas ... ocho o nueve, supongo.
	CHICA:	Es mucho. Tres o cuatro huevos ya es suficiente.
4	CHICO:	Marta, bebes cuatro o cinco refrescos al día. Es demasiado.
	CHICA:	¿Debo beber menos?
	CHICO:	¡Claro!
5	MÉDICO:	¿Y cuántas raciones de fruta o verduras toma usted al día?
	SEÑORA:	Tomo cinco o seis, doctor. ¿No es suficiente?
	MÉDICO:	No, está bien. Puede tomar aún un poco más, si quiere.
6	CHICA:	¿Cuánta leche bebes por día?
	CHICO:	Un litro. Litro y medio.
	CHICA:	Oye, eso es mucho. Debes tomar menos.

2 **Para la vida sana**

Students read the pieces of advice and evaluate whether they are good or bad for a healthy life.

Answers: *1 − ✗; 2 − ✓; 3 − ✓; 4 − ✗; 5 − ✗; 6 − ✓; 7 − ✓; 8 − ✓.*

3 **¿Qué opinas tú?**

Students use prompts and cues to write their own pieces of health advice.

Worksheet 13.7 Para una buena salud

1 **Para una vida sana**

a Students read the 'healthy living' recommendations and match each with the appropriate picture.

Answers: *1 − d; 2 − c; 3 − e; 4 − b; 5 − f; 6 − a.*

b Students match up the titles with the pieces of advice in Activity 1a.

Answers: *1 − e; 2 − b; 3 − c; 4 − d; 5 − f; 6 − a.*

2 **Las recomendaciones**

a Students write the recommendations from Activity 1 in a different form, replacing the infinitive with an imperative. Students are directed to the necessary support pages in the grammar summary and Acción: lengua to help them.

b Students invent four further recommendations using the imperative.

Worksheet 13.8 ¿Qué debo hacer?

1 **El chico triste**

Students read the letter and fill in the blanks with words from the given menu.

Answers: *1 − preocupado; 2 − bastante; 3 − gordo; 4 − muchos; 5 − tengo; 6 − chica; 7 − hacer.*

2 **La respuesta de Corazón**

A multiple-choice activity in which students read Corazón's reply and pick two suitable responses for each phrase.

Answers: *1 − a + d; 2 − a + b; 3 − c + b; 4 − b + d.*

3 **¿Qué consejos das tú?**

a Students invent a person and write a problem letter to Corazón similar to the one in Activity 1.

b Students now exchange their letters with a partner and write Corazón's reply to the letter they now have.

Acción: lengua 13, page 125

Verbs of obligation 'must' / 'have to' / 'ought to'.

Practice of *deber*

Students fill in the appropriate form of *deber*.

Answers: *1 − debo; 2 − debes; 3 − debe; 4 − debemos; 5 − deben.*

Students create new sentences by replacing one verb of obligation with another, then translate the sentences into English.

Answers: *1 − debes: You ought to get to class on time;*
2 − hay que: You have to listen to the teachers;
3 − tienes: You have to eat in the canteen today;
4 − debes: You ought to do some sport every day;
5 − hay que: You ought to drink sugar-free drinks;
6 − debemos: We must go to the sports centre.

Objectives

Students learn – to say where they went, how, and with whom
– to say when, and how long for
– Grammar: the preterite tense of the verb *ir*

Key language

¿(por) cuánto tiempo fuiste?
¿adónde fuiste?
¿cómo fuiste?
¿con quién fuiste?
¿cuándo fuiste?
en autobús / en autocar / en coche / en avión / en tren / en barco /
a pie / en barco de vela / en aerodeslizador / en metro / en bicicleta /
en taxi / en globo / en ciclomotor / en motocicleta
fui a / en / con / por …
me quedé en casa

Skills / Strategies

Recognising and forming the preterite tense of *ir*

ICT opportunities

Students produce a word-processed diary of where they have been recently

Ways in

OHT 14A
Picture story in Student's Book, page 126

Assessment opportunities

AT1,3	Worksheet 14.3, Activity 1: students listen and complete the sentences.
AT2,3	Worksheet 14.2: a cued information-gap activity.
AT3,3	Worksheet 14.3, Activity 3b: students read the letter and answer the true or false questions.
AT4,1	Student's Book, Activity 4b ●: students fill in a gapped summary.
AT4,3/4	Student's Book, Activity 4c ●: students write a paragraph about where they went.

STUDENT'S BOOK, pages 126–127

1 **En el despacho del tutor**

This activity practises the question forms needed for this spread, and also the preterite forms *fui* and *fuiste*, for passive recognition. Students listen and read, and fill in the gaps in the sentences with the appropriate question forms. A help box explains that the question forms have a stress accent.

Answers: *1 – Adónde; 2 – quién; 3 – Cómo; 4 – cuánto;*
                  5 – Cuándo.

NARRADOR:	Problemas para Tomás con su tutor y Omar ...
TUTOR:	Tomás, ¿adónde fuiste el viernes?
TOMÁS:	Fui al centro.
OMAR:	¿Cuándo fuiste?
TOMÁS:	A las nueve.
TUTOR:	¿Cómo fuiste?
TOMÁS:	En autobús.
TUTOR:	¿Por cuánto tiempo fuiste?
TOMÁS:	Tres horas.
OMAR:	¿Con quién fuiste?
TOMÁS:	Fui solo.
OMAR:	¿Y por la tarde?
TOMÁS:	Me quedé en casa.

2 **¿Cuándo?, ¿cuánto tiempo?, ¿con quién?**

Practice of the question and answer forms. Students match up the questions and possible answers within a five minute time limit.

Answers: *1 – d, i; 2 – b, f, g; 3 – a, c, e, h.*

3 **¿Adónde fuiste de vacaciones?**

a Further practice of the question and answer forms with the preterite tense. Students listen to eight conversations and note down the name of the person concerned for each conversation.

Answers: *1 – Lali; 2 – Swemi; 3 – Débora; 4 – Swemi; 5 – Lali;*
                  6 – Swemi; 7 – Débora; 8 – Débora.

1	VOZ 1:	¿Adónde fuiste de vacaciones?
	LALI:	Fui a Italia.
	VOZ 1:	¿Cuándo fuiste?
	LALI:	Fui en agosto.
2	VOZ 2:	Dime, ¿cómo fuiste?
	SWEMI:	Fui en coche, con mi padre.
3	VOZ 3:	¿Cuándo fuiste de vacaciones?
	DÉBORA:	Fui en mayo.

	VOZ 3:	¿Por cuánto tiempo fuiste?
	DÉBORA:	Una semana.
4	VOZ 2:	¿Adónde fuiste tú de vacaciones?
	SWEMI:	Fui a Portugal.
	VOZ:	¿A Portugal? ¡Qué bien!
5	VOZ 1:	¿Fuiste en coche?
	LALI:	No, fui en autocar. No era mal.
	VOZ 1:	¿Cuánto tiempo fuiste?
	LALI:	Cinco días en total.
6	VOZ 3:	¿Cuándo fuiste de vacaciones? ¿En agosto?
	SWEMI:	No, en julio. Fuimos por quince días – ¡estupendo!
7	VOZ 2:	¿Con quién fuiste?
	DÉBORA:	Con mi madre y mi hermana.
8	VOZ 1:	¿Cómo fuiste – en avión?
	DÉBORA:	Sí. Escocia está demasiado lejos para ir en tren y en barco.

b A pairwork activity in which students use a list of cued questions, and the visuals from Activity 3, as the stimulus for a dialogue.

4 **Dime**

a ● A reading activity which further exploits the material presented in Activity 3. Students use the information they have about Débora to answer the true or false questions.

Answers: *1 – verdad; 2 – mentira; 3 – verdad; 4 – mentira;*
                  5 – verdad; 6 – mentira.

b ● A gap-fill activity based on Lali's account of her holidays.

Answers: *1 – llamo; 2 – fui; 3 – agosto; 4 – autocar;*
                  5 – madre; 6 – cinco.

c ● Students adopt Swemi's persona and use the gap-fill text in Activity 4b as a stimulus to write a brief account of Swemi's holiday.

Gramática

A brief reminder for students who need it that the preterite tense is covered in the grammar summary, section 21, p.152, with futher practice in Acción: lengua 14, p.133.

SUPPORT MATERIALS

OHT 14A Fui en ...

This OHT presents the vocabulary items for different means of transport. It can be used for initial presentation, or later revision.

Worksheet 14.1 Los países y el transporte

1 ¿Adónde? y ¿cómo?

Students listen to conversations about journeys and transport, and fill in the grid with the letters of the countries visited and the numbers of the transport mentioned.

Answers:

Diego	Montse	Imelda	Hugo	Ali	Bea	Adán
f 5	d 3	b 9	g 4	a 6	e 2	i 8

DIEGO
CHICO: ¿Adónde fuiste de vacaciones, Diego?
DIEGO: Fui a Portugal.
CHICO: ¡Qué bien! ¿Cómo fuiste?
DIEGO: Fui en bicicleta.
CHICO: ¡A Portugal en bicicleta!
DIEGO: Sí. No vivo muy lejos de la frontera.

MONTSE
CHICA: Montse, ¿es verdad que fuiste a la India?
MONTSE: Sí. Fui a la India para ver a mis primos. ¡Fue estupendo!
CHICA: Fuiste en avión, supongo.
MONTSE: Sí, fui en avión pero ¡qué aburrido! No me gustó nada ...

IMELDA
CHICO: ¿Adónde fuiste tú de vacaciones, Imelda?
IMELDA: Me quedé aquí en España. Pero fuimos a Madrid una semana.
CHICO: ¿Fuiste en el Ave?
IMELDA: No, fuimos en coche.

HUGO
CHICO: ¿Qué tal las vacaciones, Hugo?
HUGO: ¡Estupendas! Fui a Gran Bretaña.
CHICO: ¿A Gran Bretaña? ¿Te gustó?
HUGO: Sí. Fui en aerodeslizador por primera vez.
CHICO: ¿Qué tal, el aerodeslizador?
HUGO: ¡Fatal! Duró unos cuarenta minutos, pero me marée mucho ...

ALI
CHICA: Fuiste a Francia, Ali, ¿no?
ALI: Sí. Fui con mis padres.
CHICA: ¿Cómo fuiste?
ALI: Andando.
CHICA: ¡Andando! ¡A pie!
ALI: Sí. Cruzamos los Pirineos. Son sólo cincuenta kilómetros hasta la frontera ...

BEA
CHICA: ¿Adónde fuiste de vacaciones, Bea?
BEA: Fui a Alemania.
CHICA: ¿Qué tal Alemania? ¿Te gustó?
BEA: Sí, fuimos en tren y luego viajamos por el país en tren también.

ADÁN
CHICO: ¿Fuiste de vacaciones en tu barco, Adán?
ADÁN: Sí, fuimos en barco a Marruecos.
CHICO: ¡Qué bien! ¿Qué tal Marruecos? No he ido nunca.
ADÁN: Muy interesante. Es otro mundo allí en la costa norte de África ...

2 El fin de semana

A substitution activity entailing putting the correct words for the different modes of transport into a text.

Answers: 1 – a pie; 2 – en autocar; 3 – en ciclomotor; 4 – en tren; 5 – en barco de vela; 6 – en coche; 7 – en taxi.

3 En Madrid

Students use cues to write a description of their week.

Answers: El lunes, fui a Barcelona en avión, y luego fui al hotel en autobús.
El martes, fui al centro en metro.
El miércoles fui a la ciudad de Tarragona en tren.
El jueves, fui de excursión en globo.
El viernes, fui a la isla de Mallorca en barco de vela.
El sábado, fui al norte de la isla en ciclomotor.
El domingo, fui a Francia en barco.

Worksheet 14.2 De vacaciones

A pairwork information-gap activity in which students exchange information about holidays using the picture prompts. They need to elicit the following information: where did their partner go? how did he / she get there? how long did he / she stay? with whom? and when? (month). They then fill in the details gleaned in the blank boxes and compare their answers afterwards.

Worksheet 14.3 Mis viajes

1 Las vacaciones de Idaira

Students listen and complete each sentence in Spanish.

Answers: 1 – Portugal; 2 – julio; 3 – cinco días; 4 – tren; 5 – mi familia.

ISABEL: ¡Idaira! ¿Qué tal? ¿Adónde fuiste de vacaciones?
IDAIRA: ¿De vacaciones? Fui a Portugal.
ISABEL: Y ¿cuándo fuiste?
IDAIRA: Fui en julio.
ISABEL: ¿Por cuánto tiempo fuiste?
IDAIRA: Fui por cinco días.
ISABEL: ¿Cómo fuiste?
IDAIRA: Fui en tren.
ISABEL: ¿Con quién fuiste? ¿Con tu amiga?
IDAIRA: No, fui con mi familia – ¡qué aburrido!

2 ¡Poemas!

a Students fill in the gaps in the poem with the appropriate words.

Answers: 1 – a; 2 – en; 3 – por; 4 – con; 5 – a; 6 – por; 7 – en tren; 8 – con.

b Students identify the rhyming words.

Answers: ¡Fenomenal! / ¡Fatal!; ¡Qué ilusión! / ¡Qué decepción!; ¡Qué divertido! / ¡Qué aburrido!; ¡Estupendo! / ¡Tremendo!; ¡Qué susto! / ¡Qué disgusto!.

c Students now write their own poem, using the one in Activity 2a as an example.

3 Isabel

a A gap-fill activity in which students replace the pictures with appropriate words.

Answers: Italia; julio; autocar; avión; madre; cinco.

b Students then read the six sentences and decide whether they are true or false.

Answers: 1 – verdad; 2 – falsa; 3 – verdad; 4 – falsa; 5 – verdad; 6 – falsa.

Objectives

Students learn – to describe some of the things they did on holiday
or at the weekend
– Grammar: preterite tense of regular –er / –ir verbs

Key language

¿qué hiciste?
bebí (un refresco)
cogí (el autobús)
comí (algo en una cafetería)
conocí (a una chica inglesa)
di (una vuelta)
escribí (una postal)
leí (una revista)
salí (a las diez)
vi (una película)
volví (a casa)
me aburrí (un poco)
me divertí (mucho)

Skills / Strategies

Students learn to recognise and form the preterite tense of –er and
–ir verbs

ICT opportunities

Students could produce a (real or imaginary) holiday diary
illustrated with clip-art or imported photos

Ways in

OHT 14B; Presentation, Student's Book, page 128

Assessment opportunities

AT1,4/5 Student's Book, Activity 3: students listen to a
description of weekend activities and then either ◐
say whether it was positive or negative; or ◑
listen again and say what each person did.

AT2,4/5 Student's Book, Activity 2b: a pairwork activity in which
one student says a preterite tense phrase and the other
says whether it is possible or not.

AT3,5 Student's Book, Activity 4: students read a brief story in
the preterite tense and respond by sequencing the texts.

AT4,4/5 Student's Book, Activity 2a: students use a 'phrase
generator' to build up sentences in the preterite tense.

STUDENT'S BOOK, pages 128–129

1 El día de Tomás

Presentation of the preterite tense forms. Before playing
the recording you could say some model sentences
describing things from personal experience, and
contrasting between the present and the preterite. Then do
the Student's Book activity, in which students read and
listen to what Tomás says in explanation of his truancy,
and pick the correct word to fill in the blanks.

Answers: 1 – *Salí del instituto a las diez;*
2 – *En el centro di una vuelta;*
3 – *Fui al cine y vi una película;*
4 – *En El Corte Inglés, bebí un refresco;*
5 – *También, conocí a una chica inglesa;*
6 – *Escribí una postal a mi padre.*

> TUTOR: ¿Qué hiciste, exactamente, Tomás?
> TOMÁS: Salí a las diez. Di una vuelta por el centro.
> Comí algo en una cafetería, y bebí un
> refresco. Conocí a una chica inglesa. Leí una
> revista, escribí una postal a mi padre. Luego,
> vi una película en el cine. Después, cogí el
> autobús y volví a casa.

2 Una multitud de posibilidades

a Using a menu of three sets of words, students pick one
word from each set and invent 10 sentences, some of
which are impossible, others possible.

b Students take it in turns to read the sentences to their
partner, who in turn says whether the sentences are
possible or impossible.

3 ¿Qué tal el fin de semana?

◐ Students listen to five young people giving opinions
about what they did at the weekend, and note down the
appropriate symbol to show whether the opinions
expressed are positive or negative.

◑ Students listen again and add an activity for each
person.

Answers: ◐ 1 – ☹ ; 2 – ☺ ; 3 – ☺ ; 4 – ☹ ; 5 – ☺.

◑ 1 – ☹ , *vi una película;*

2 – ☺ , *salí al centro y fui de compras;*

3 – ☺ , *cogí el autocar a Granada;*

4 – ☹ , *leí un libro y escribí unos e-mails;*

5 – ☺ , *conocí a una chica italiana y salí a la discoteca.*

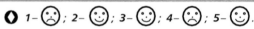

> **1** CHICO: ¿Qué tal el fin de semana? Bastante
> aburrido. Fui al cine, vi una película ... no era
> muy interesante. Me aburrí un poco.
> **2** CHICA: ¿El fin de semana? Me divertí mucho. Salí
> con mi amiga al centro y fui de compras.
> **3** CHICO: El sábado, cogí el autocar a Granada. La
> ciudad es muy bonita. Me divertí mucho.
> **4** CHICA: ¿Qué tal el fin de semana? Bueno ... no muy
> bien. Leí un libro, escribí unos e-mails ... Me
> aburrí bastante.
> **5** CHICO: El fin de semana, conocí a una chica italiana.
> Es muy simpática. Salí con ella por la tarde a
> la discoteca. Me divertí mucho, mucho.

4 Las vacaciones de Kiko

◐ Students read the excerpts from Kiko the crow's
return journey from Spain and compare them with the
route and picture shown, then put them in order.

Answers: *6, 3, 2, 1, 4, 5, 7.*

5 La amiga de Kiko pregunta

◐ Students copy out the verb box and fill in the missing
verb endings.

◑ Students use the examples given in the box to work
out the rest of the question forms and then complete the
questions 1–6. As an oral follow up, they could be asked to
work with their partner to produce a conversation in which
they ask each other about their holidays, including at least
four questions each.

Answers: ○ *cogiste; comiste; bebiste; escribiste; leíste; volviste; te aburriste; te divertiste.*

◐ *1 – comiste; 2 – Bebiste; 3 – escribiste; 4 – Leíste; 5 – Conociste; 6 – Te divertiste.*

Gramática

A reminder that a brief summary of the preterite tense can be found in the grammar summary, section 20, p.151 and further practice drills are provided in Acción: lengua 14, p.133.

SUPPORT MATERIALS

OHT 14B ¿Qué hiciste?

This OHT can be used to present the preterite forms. It may be used for a variety of text-completion activities, or for a simple guided presentation, possibly with students ultimately filling in the verb endings as they gain confidence.

Worksheet 14.4 Una multitud de posibilidades

Una multitud de posibilidades

a Students use the vocabulary box from Activity 2 on Student's Book p.128 and copy the appropriate word(s) under each picture on the sheet.

Answers: *1 – una postal; 2 – el autobús; 3 – una vuelta en bici; 4 – a un chico; 5 – una revista; 6 – un té; 7 – el tren; 8 – una carta; 9 – un libro; 10 – un perrito caliente; 11 – un grupo de jóvenes; 12 – una hamburguesa; 13 – la tele; 14 – a casa a las cuatro; 15 – una vuelta a pie; 16 – una naranjada.*

b Students complete each phrase 1–8 with an expression from Activity 1a. Hopefully at least some of them will produce humorous sentences.

Worksheet 14.5 De viaje

This worksheet has three activities graded in order of difficulty.

1 **Los sonidos del viaje**

○ In this activity students match the sounds and fragments of conversation they hear with the sentences a–j.

Answers: *a – 4; b – 2; c – 10; d – 5; e – 9; f – 6; g – 1; h – 8; i – 3; j – 7.*

1	(Sound of cathedral bells)
2	(Sound of whistle and train moving off)
3	(Boy unwrapping sandwich from wrapper and saying: ¿Jamón y tomate? ¡Qué bien!)
4	(Clock chiming 8 and noise of front door closing)
5	(Boy yawning and saying: ¡Qué aburrido!)
6	(Bird song, noise of footsteps crunching on gravel, ducks quacking)
7	(Pen scratching as if writing on postcard)
8	(Noise of someone drinking through straw at bottom of juice carton)
9	(Noise from inside train carriage and boy's voice saying: ¡Hola! ¿Vas a Madrid también?)
10	(Rustling of magazine pages)

2 **Ester y Jorge**

○ Students listen to the two accounts and write E (for Ester) or J (for Jorge) underneath the appropriate pictures: some will have two letters, others only one.

Answers: *a – J; b – E; c – J, E; d – E; e – J, E; f – E; g – E, J; h – J.*

JORGE	
ESTER:	Fuiste de vacaciones la semana pasada, ¿no?
JORGE:	Sí. Fui a Zaragoza para visitar a mis abuelos.
ESTER:	¿Cómo fuiste? ¿En autocar?
JORGE:	No, fui en tren.
ESTER:	¿Qué tal el viaje? ¡A que te aburriste!
JORGE:	Pues, sí, un poco. Salí a las ocho y cuarto de la mañana. Leí una revista ...
ESTER:	¿Qué leíste?
JORGE:	Una revista de Internet. Me interesa mucho. Y bebí una naranjada que compré en la estación.
ESTER:	¿Te gustó la ciudad?
JORGE:	Bastante, sí. Di una vuelta por la ciudad con mis abuelos.

ESTER	
JORGE:	¿Y tú, Ester? Fuiste al sur, ¿no?
ESTER:	Sí. Fui con mis padres en autocar a Málaga, pasando por Toledo.
JORGE:	¿Te gustó el viaje?
ESTER:	Sí, mucho. Leí una revista, pero luego me dormí un poco. Paramos en Toledo. ¿Conoces la ciudad?
JORGE:	No, pero dicen que es muy bonita.
ESTER:	Sí, es verdad. Di una vuelta por la ciudad antigua con Mamá.
JORGE:	¿Viste la catedral?
ESTER:	Sí, vi la catedral desde fuera. Luego bebí una naranjada en una cafetería cercana, y escribí unas postales.
JORGE:	¡No me escribiste a mí!
ESTER:	¡Ah, pobre Jorge! Te mando una postal la próxima vez ...

3 **Jaime**

◐ Students listen to Jaime's account of his holiday and fill in the details on the grid.

Answers:

	Jaime
Hora de salida	cuatro de la mañana
Transporte	avión muy grande
Duración del viaje	nueve horas
Actividades durante el viaje	leí, vi una película, dormí
Opinión del viaje	aburrido

JAIME	
ELENA:	¡Jaime! ¿Qué tal tu viaje en Nueva York?
JAIME:	Pues, bien. Lo único es que salimos súper temprano, ¡a las cuatro de la mañana!
ELENA:	¡Ay, madre qué horror! No me gusta levantarme temprano. ¿Y qué tal el avión?
JAIME:	Era un avión de esos muy grandes – no sé cuánta gente había.
ELENA:	¿El viaje duró cuántas horas en total?
JAIME:	Mmm ... nueve.
ELENA:	¡Nueve! Pero ¿qué hicisteis?
JAIME:	Pues, yo leí un poco, luego vimos una película, me dormí un poco ...
ELENA:	¡Qué emocionante!
JAIME:	¿El viaje en el avión? ¡Qué va! Me aburrí en el avión, pero era muy emocionante visitar los Estados Unidos. Nos divertimos un montón.
ELENA:	Pues, yo no he viajado nunca en avión y me haría mucha ilusión sabes ...

Objectives

Students learn – to talk about further holiday activities
     – to use time phrases ('yesterday', etc.)
     – Grammar: preterite tense of –ar verbs

Key language

¿qué compraste?
compré un regalo para Pilar
alquilé una bici ...
tomé el sol
visité ...
bailé en la discoteca
cené en un restaurante
compré recuerdos
conocí a un chico
el agua estaba muy fría
lo pasé fatal / bomba / muy bien
me aburrí mucho
monté a caballo
nadé (en la piscina)
no comí nada
no hubo nada
yo lo pasé fatal / muy bien
yo me quedé en el hotel
fuimos a ...
charlamos

Skills / Strategies

Students learn – to use time phrases such as 'yesterday', 'last
     weekend', etc.

ICT opportunities

Students can write a week's diary with dates and word-process a
brief summary of each day

Ways in

OHT 14C
Diary on Student's Book page 130

Assessment opportunities

AT1,5   Student's Book, Activity 1b: students select the
    appropriate opinion in response to the information on
    the recording.

AT2,5   Student's Book, Activity 3b: preterite tense pairwork
    activities at differentiated levels.

AT3,5   Student's Book, Activity 3a: a preterite tense gap-fill
    activity.

AT4,5   Worksheet 14.7, Activity 1: students fill in a diary in
    response to cues.

STUDENT'S BOOK, pages 130–131

1   **La agenda de Isabel**

a This activity presents more preterite tense verbs, initially
for recognition. Students listen to Isabel reading her
holiday diary.

> ISABEL: Tomé el sol en la playa – ¡pero con el jersey
> puesto!
> Nadé en la piscina climatizada.
> Alquilé una bici.
> Bailé en la discoteca por la noche.
> Visité un pueblo pesquero.
> Cené en un restaurante con la familia.
> Monté a caballo.
> Compré recuerdos. ¡Lo pasé bomba!

b Students listen to Isabel and Pilar and summarise Pilar's
opinion of each day mentioned with a tick, two ticks or a
cross.

Answers: *Día 1 – ✓; Día 2 – ✗; Día 3 – ✓✓; Día 4 – ✓; Día 5 – ✗
(fin de semana); Día 6 – ✗ (fin de semana); Día 7 – ✓;
Día 8 – ✓✓.*

> PILAR: ¿Qué tienes allí, Isabel?
> ISABEL: Mi agenda. Relleno los espacios – ¿me ayudas?
> PILAR: Sí, claro.
> ISABEL: Martes, día 1 – tomé el sol en la playa.
> PILAR: Sí, es verdad. Yo también lo pasé muy bien.
> Me gusta la playa.
> ¿El día dos?
> ISABEL: Miércoles, día dos, nadé en la piscina. ¿Te
> acuerdas?
> PILAR: Sí, ¡lo pasé fatal! Normalmente me gusta la
> natación, pero ese día el agua estaba muy fría.
> ISABEL: Bueno, el día tres alquilé una bici ...
> PILAR: ¡Ay, qué risa! ¿Te acuerdas? ¡Papá y Mamá en
> un tándem! ¡Lo pasé bomba!
> ISABEL: Y el día cuatro ...
> PILAR: La discoteca. ¡Lo pasé muy bien!
> ISABEL: El fin de semana fuimos al pueblo pesquero,
> ¿te acuerdas?
> PILAR: Y la fila de monumentos históricos en camino.

> ISABEL: Me aburrí mucho.
> PILAR: Yo también lo pasé fatal.
> ISABEL: El lunes, día siete, fuimos al restaurante. No
> comí nada.
> PILAR: Ah, sí, porque eres vegetariana ...
> ISABEL: y no hubo nada para mí en el menú.
> PILAR: Pues yo lo pasé muy bien esta tarde.
> ISABEL: Ayer, día ocho, monté a caballo. ¿Y tú ...?
> PILAR: Yo me quedé en el hotel, y conocí a un chico
> muy simpático.
> ISABEL: Ah, ¡un novio nuevo!
> PILAR: ¿Novio? ¡No! Fuimos a la playa, charlamos ...
> lo pasé bomba.
> ISABEL: ¿No quieres verle otra vez?

2   **Tomás y el estéreo personal**

a Students listen to Tomás being interviewed about his
truancy, and fill in the gaps with the appropriate verb.

Answers: *A – 6; B – 3; C – 4; D – 1; E – 5; F – 2.*

> OMAR: No dices toda la verdad, Tomás.
> TUTOR: Visitaste El Corte Inglés, ¿no?
> TOMÁS: Ah, sí. Visité El Corte Inglés por la mañana.
> TUTOR: Tomás, ¿qué compraste?
> TOMÁS: Compré un regalo para Pilar.
> OMAR: ¿Es todo?
> TOMÁS: Sí. ¿Por qué?
> TUTOR: Según Roberto, robaste un estéreo personal.
> TOMÁS: ¡No es verdad! ¡Yo no robé nada!

b Students copy out the help box and complete the
verbs.

Answers: *tomaste; nadaste; bailaste; visitaste; cenaste;
montaste.*

Gramática

Students are referred to the grammar summary, section 20,
p.151 for more information on the preterite, and to Acción:
lengua 14, p.133.

3 **¡Qué curioso eres!**

a A verb-completion gap-fill activity in which students fill in blanks in a set of questions and answers.

Answers: *1 – ¿Nadaste en la piscina del hotel? – No, nadé en el mar; 2 – ¿Tomaste el sol en la playa? – No, tomé el sol en la piscina. 3 – ¿Visitaste algún pueblo pesquero? – No, visité los pueblos típicos de la sierra. 4 – ¿Montaste a caballo? – Sí, monté a caballo en la finca de unos amigos. 5 – ¿Cenaste en un restaurante? – No, cené en casa con la familia. 6 – ¿Alquilaste una bici? – Sí, alquilé un tándem con mi hermana. 7 – ¿Bailaste en la discoteca del hotel? – No, bailé en un club de noche hasta muy tarde. 8 – ¿Compraste algún recuerdo? – Sí, compré regalos para mis amigas en el mercado.*

b A pairwork activity in which students ask and answer the questions from Activity 3a.

 Students try to do this activity without looking at their notes.

 Students substitute other vocabulary items if wished

SUPPORT MATERIALS

OHT 14C ¿Qué hiciste?

Presentation of the different activities, each with a preterite tense verb.

Worksheet 14.6 ¡Lo pasé bomba!

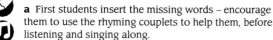 **¡Lo pasé bomba!**

This song reuses the core language of the unit.

a First students insert the missing words – encourage them to use the rhyming couplets to help them, before listening and singing along.

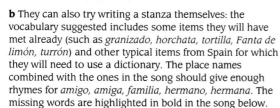 **b** They can also try writing a stanza themselves: the vocabulary suggested includes some items they will have met already (such as *granizado, horchata, tortilla, Fanta de limón, turrón*) and other typical items from Spain for which they will need to use a dictionary. The place names combined with the ones in the song should give enough rhymes for *amigo, amiga, familia, hermano, hermana*. The missing words are highlighted in bold in the song below.

> (Estribillo)
> ¿Adónde fuiste?
> ¿Qué hiciste?
> ¿Con quién saliste?
> ¡Cuéntame!
>
> **1** Fui a Sicilia,
> con mi **familia**,
> visité un **museo**,
> di un paseo,
> no salí, me **aburrí** –
> ¡lo **pasé fatal**!
> (Estribillo)
>
> **2** Fui a **Espinama**,
> con mi hermana,
> saqué fotos,
> alquilé **motos**,
> tomé el sol,
> jugué al fútbol –
> ¡lo pasé **muy** bien!
> (Estribillo)

> **3** Fui a Vigo
> con mi **amigo**,
> comí **pasteles**,
> bebí **cócteles**,
> cada noche salí,
> me **divertí** –
> ¡lo pasé bomba!
> (Estribillo)

Worksheet 14.7 Lo que hice ...

1 **El pasado y el futuro**

Students read a diary and fill in the appropriate details, based on the knowledge that 'today' is Wednesday the 17th.

Answers:

miércoles	10	el miércoles pasado
jueves	11	hace cinco días
viernes	12	hace cuatro días
sábado / domingo	13/14	el fin de semana pasado
lunes	15	anteayer
martes	16	ayer
miércoles	17	HOY
jueves	18	mañana
miércoles	19	pasado mañana

2 **El fin de semana pasado**

A pairwork cued dialogue activity.

Worksheet 14.8 Una postal

This sheet has removable English rubrics at the bottom.

1 **¿Vacaciones buenas o malas?**

 Students read the postcard and then reverse the sense of the text by replacing the underlined words with their opposites, selected from a menu given beneath the postcard.

Answers: *fatal; incómodo; feo; lejos; frío; a la sierra; aburrida; mal; mi habitación; decepción.*

2 **Te toca a ti**

 Now students use the sentence-starters to write a guided postcard in a similar fashion to the one in Activity 1.

Worksheet 14.9 El fin de semana

1 **Pilla al intruso**

a A 'find the odd one out' activity. Students pick which word or phrase from each group of four is the odd one out.

Answers: *1 – un helado; 2 – me aburrí; 3 – recuerdos; 4 – cené en un restaurante; 5 – ¡lo pasé bomba!; 6 – me quedé en casa.*

b Students now pick one of the words from each group in Activity 1a and write a sentence which includes it.

2 **El fin de semana**

An activity in which students add details to a rather plain, basic text, using prompts to do so.

Objectives
Students learn – to say what someone else did, or didn't do
       – Grammar: preterite tense of –ar, –er, –ir verbs (él, ella, usted)

Key language
¿adónde fue X?
¡X ha ido a Londres!
hizo
compró
comió
leyó
visitó
fue
robó
dio
cogió
vio
salió
insistió que ...
volvió

Skills / Strategies
Students learn to understand and use the preterite tense of –ar, –er and –ir verbs (él, ella, usted)

ICT opportunities
Students can   – use a word-processing package to write some faxes, using the ones in the Student's Book as a model

Ways in
Presentational texts on Student's Book page 132

Assessment opportunities
AT1,5   Student's Book, Activity 1 ◗ : students sequence the visuals.
AT1,5   Student's Book, Activity 1 ◆ : a gap-fill activity.
AT3,5   Student's Book Acción: lengua, Activity 3: a preterite tense sentence-completion activity.
AT4,5   Student's Book, Activity 2: a cued writing activity in the preterite tense.

STUDENT'S BOOK, page 132

1   **¿Dónde está Tomás?**

◗ Students listen and read and pick the most appropriate picture for each message or fax.

◆ Students fill in the gaps in the sentences with the appropriate preterite tense verb.

Answers: ◗ *1 – C; 2 – E; 3 – B; 4 – D; 5 – A.*

◆ *10.00 – robó; 10.30 – volvió; 11.00 – cogió; 13.30 – vio; 14.45 – compró; 16.00 – salió.*

1   NARRADOR: Son las cuatro de la tarde. Omar lee el mail de Carmina.
     OMAR: Las dieciséis horas. ¡Omar! ¿Sabes dónde está Tomás? No volvió del instituto para comer a las tres como normal. Estoy muy preocupada. Carmina.

2   NARRADOR: Son las cinco y media de la tarde. Carmina lee el fax de Omar.
     FAX de: Omar Álvaro Vallejas.
     CARMINA: Carmina, vi a Tomás esta mañana con su tutor. Según un alumno, Tomás robó un estéreo personal en El Corte Inglés. Tomás insistió que no es verdad. Después, volvió a clase. Omar.

3   NARRADOR: Son las seis y media. Otro mail de Carmina a Omar.
     OMAR: Omar – más noticias. La señora de enfrente vio a Tomás. Volvió a casa a las once, cogió su mochila, y salió casi en seguida. Carmina. ¿Pero adónde fue Tomás?

4   NARRADOR: Son las ocho menos veinticinco. Isabel manda un mensaje de texto a Carmina.
     CARMINA: Tía Carmina, ¡urgente! Mi amigo José vio a Tomás – ¡en el autobús que va al aeropuerto! Isabel.

5   NARRADOR: Son las ocho y diez de la tarde. Carmina recibe un fax.
     CARMINA: FAX de Iberia, Aeropuerto de Sevilla. Confirmación: Venta de billete de avión a Tomás Willoughby a las 14.45. Vuelo IB 562 Sevilla–Londres (Heathrow). Salida a las 16.00 horas. ¡Tomás ha ido a Londres! Debo llamar a Michael ... ¿qué va a decir Teresa?

2   **El viaje de Tomás**

An open-ended writing activity in which students use cues to describe Tomás' trip in their own words, using the preterite tense.

Gramática

Students are referred to the grammar summary, sections 20 (p.151) and 21 (p.152) and could practise the preterite verb drills in Acción: lengua 14, p.133 before attempting Activity 2.

Acción: lengua 14, page 133

Practice of the preterite tense.

1   ◗ Students fill in the correct first person of the preterite tense for the different verbs.

◆ Students put a series of verbs from a paragraph written in the present, into the preterite tense.

Answers: ◗ *1 – Cogí, visité; 2 – compré; 3 – salí, fui; 4 – comí; 5 – vi.*

◆ *Fui; Monté; hice; tomó; nadó; salí; fue; compró.*

2   ◗ Students pick the correct preterite tense verb from the alternatives.

◆ Students pick the correct verbs and put them into the preterite tense.

Answers: ◗ *Jugaste; Tomé; Sacaste; leí; pasó; practicó.*

◆ *1 – fue; 2 – saqué; 3 – leyó; 4 – llegó; 5 – salió.*

3   ◆ Students read the poem and put the verbs into the correct form in the preterite tense.

Answers: *salí; conociste; compró; compraste; cenamos; cogisteis; fuisteis.*

Objectives

Students learn – to say what country they are from
– to say what nationality they are, and to ask others

Key language

¿de qué nacionalidad eres?
yo soy …
nací en …
nació allí
Alemania
Escocia
Canadá
Estados Unidos
Francia
Gales
Gran Bretaña
Irlanda del Norte
Italia
India
Inglaterra
Marruecos
América del Sur
Paquistán
Portugal
alemán / alemana
americano/a
británico/a
canadiense
escocés / escocesa
español/a
francés / francesa
galés / galesa
indio/a
paquistaní
inglés / inglesa
italiano/a
marroquí
portugués / portuguesa

Skills / Strategies

Learning more about adjective agreement

ICT opportunities

Student's Book, Activity 4 (follow-up): word-process ID forms and peripheral information

Ways in

Picture story in Student's Book, page 134

Assessment opportunities

AT1,3   Student's Book, Activity 3a: students listen and pick the correct nationality

AT2,4   Student's Book, Activity 4b: students talk with their partner, in the roles of people from Activity 4a.

AT3,1   Student's Book, Activity 2: students read the grid and Worksheet 15.1, and then fill in the grid on the worksheet.

AT4,2   Student's Book, Activity 2: students fill in the grid.

STUDENT'S BOOK, pages 134–135

1 **La policía**

Students listen to the text, which presents the vocabulary for some of the various nationalities being introduced here, and answer a series of true / false / impossible to tell questions.

Answers: *1 – verdad; 2 – mentira; 3 – mentira; 4 – no se sabe; 5 – no se sabe; 6 – verdad.*

> GUARDIA: ¿Tú eres la hermana de Tomás?
> ISABEL: Sí.
> GUARDIA: ¿De qué nacionalidad eres?
> ISABEL: Yo soy británica. Nací en Inglaterra, como Tomás.
> OMAR: El padre de Tomás e Isabel es inglés …
> ISABEL: … pero mi madre es española.
> PILAR: El pobre Tomás – ¿dónde está?

2 **Las nacionalidades**

Students fill in the gaps on a grid showing the nouns and adjectives connected with nationality. Worksheet 15.1 can be used to support students. They can also refer back to Acción: lengua 4 (p.37) to revise feminine adjectives.

Answers: *galés / galesa; inglés / inglesa; irlandés / irlandesa; francés / francesa; portugués / portuguesa; indio; italiano/a; norteamericano/a; sudamericano/a; alemán / alemana.*

3 **¿De dónde es?**

a Students listen to various people talking and pick each person's nationality.

Answers: *Azahar – MA; Catarina – I; David – GB; Hugo – E; Peter – D; Ismael – IND; Julio – P.*

AZAHAR	
VOZ:	Azahar, ¿de qué nacionalidad eres?
AZAHAR:	Soy marroquí. Nací en Marruecos.
CATARINA	
VOZ:	¿Y tú, Catarina?
CATARINA:	Yo nací en Italia. Soy italiana.
DAVID	
VOZ:	David, ¿de qué nacionalidad eres?
DAVID:	Soy británico. Nací en Gran Bretaña. Mi hermana nació allí también.
HUGO	
VOZ:	Hugo, eres español, ¿no?
HUGO:	Sí. Nací en Burgos, en el norte.
PETER	
VOZ:	Peter, ¿de qué nacionalidad eres?
PETER:	Soy alemán. Nací en Berlín, en Alemania.
ISMAEL	
VOZ:	Ismael, naciste en la India, ¿verdad?
ISMAEL:	Sí, soy indio.
JULIO	
VOZ:	Julio, eres español, ¿no?
JULIO:	No, soy portugués. Nací en el sur de Portugal.

b Now students write three brief sentences about each person, using the information given.

Answers:	
	Azahar – Me llamo Azahar. Soy de Marruecos. Soy marroquí.
	Catarina – Me llamo Catarina. Soy de Italia. Soy italiana.
	David – Me llamo David. Soy de Gran Bretaña. Soy británico.
	Hugo – Me llamo Hugo. Soy de España. Soy español.
	Peter – Me llamo Peter. Soy de Alemania. Soy alemán.
	Ismael – Me llamo Ismael. Soy de India. Soy indio.
	Julio – Me llamo Julio. Soy de Portugal. Soy portugués.

4 Los jóvenes

a Students read the sentences about people's origins, and look at the accompanying photos to try to identify who is who.

Answers:	1 – Guillermo; 2 – Zeneida; 3 – Laura; 4 – Kamal; 5 – Zeneida; 6 – Kamal.

b A pairwork activity in which students use the information from Activity 4a to form the basis of four dialogues.

SUPPORT MATERIALS

Worksheet 15.1 Las nacionalidades

This sheet is for use in conjunction with Activity 2 on p.134 of the Student's Book. Students fill in the gaps on a grid showing the nouns and adjectives connected with nationality

Objectives

Students learn – to make formal and informal introductions
         – to invite someone to eat and drink
         – Grammar: indirect object pronouns; the personal *a*

Key language

¿conoce usted a mi mujer ...?
¿qué quiere tomar?
¿qué quieres tomar?
¿quiere comer algo?
¿quieres comer algo?
¿un café?
¿un pastelito?
¿una galleta?
buenas tardes
encantado/a
igualmente
siéntese / siéntate aquí
te / le presento a mi mujer ...
lo / la conozco
para mí, nada, gracias
con mucho gusto
te presento a ...

Skills / Strategies

Students learn – to use formal and informal terms of address
              appropriately

Ways in

Picture story in Student's Book, page 136

Assessment opportunities

AT1,3   Student's Book, Activity 2 ◑: students work out who the speakers know and who they don't.

AT1,3   Student's Book, Activity 2 ◓: students work out who is a boy and who is a girl.

AT2,3   Student's Book, Activity 4 ◑: students adapt the conversation from the preceding activity.

AT2,3   Student's Book, Activity 4 ◓: students invent new scenarios, using the appropriate forms of address.

AT3,3   Student's Book, Activity 3: students listen and read, and select the appropriate one of two alternatives for each sentence.

STUDENT'S BOOK, pages 136–137

1 **El invitado**

◑ Students read and listen to the picture story, and answer a set of true or false questions exploiting the text.

◓ Students correct the sentences that are incorrect.

Answers: ◑ *1 – mentira; 2 – verdad; 3 – mentira; 4 – mentira; 5 – mentira; 6 – verdad.*

◓ *1 – El Señor Gómez es el tutor de Tomás; 3 – El Señor Gómez no conoce a Carmina; 4 – El señor Gómez quiere beber algo caliente (toma un café); 5 – El Señor Gómez no quiere algo de comer.*

OMAR:	¡Señor Gómez!
SEÑOR GÓMEZ:	Buenas tardes.
OMAR:	Pase, pase ... ¿Conoce usted a mi mujer, Carmina?
SEÑOR GÓMEZ:	No, no la conozco.
OMAR:	Señor Gómez, le presento a mi mujer, Carmina.
CARMINA:	Encantada.
SEÑOR GÓMEZ:	Igualmente.
CARMINA:	Siéntese aquí.
OMAR:	¿Qué quiere tomar? ¿Un café?
SEÑOR GÓMEZ:	Sí, con mucho gusto.
CARMINA:	¿Quiere comer algo?
SEÑOR GÓMEZ:	Para mí, nada, gracias.
SEÑOR GÓMEZ:	Roberto ... El Corte Inglés ... robo ... no es verdad ...
ISABEL:	¡Tomás es inocente!

Gramática

Students are referred to the grammar summary, section 24, p.152 for a brief summary of the personal *a* – used with verbs *ver* and *conocer*, with no equivalent in English. There are also practice activities on *Acción: lengua 15, p.141.*

2 **La expedición**

◑ Two students on an international camp are looking at the list of groups and their members and discussing whether they know them or not. Students note whether the people are known to the speakers or not.

◓ Students listen again and decide whether each person mentioned is male or female.

Answers: ◑ *1 – X; 2 – ✓; 3 – X; 4 – X; 5 – ✓; 6 – ✓; 7 – ✓; 8 – ✓; 9 – ✓; 10 – X.*

◓ *1 – m; 2 – f; 3 – m; 4 – m; 5 – f; 6 – f; 7 – m; 8 – m; 9 – f; 10 – f.*

VOZ 1:	¿Tienes la lista de participantes?
VOZ 2:	Sí, la tengo aquí. A ver quién está en nuestro grupo.
VOZ 1:	Vamos a ver ...
VOZ 2:	Número uno – Adiel. ¿Adiel?
VOZ 1:	No le conozco.
VOZ 2:	Yo tampoco.
VOZ 2:	Número dos es Erandi.
VOZ 1:	Erandi, sí la conozco. Está en mi grupo. Es amable.
VOZ 1:	Número tres es ...
VOZ 2:	Lloys. ¿Le conoces? Yo no.
VOZ 1:	No le conozco, no.
VOZ 1:	Y el número cuatro tampoco.
VOZ 2:	Raymi. Ni idea. No le conozco yo.
VOZ 1:	Número cinco es Fiorel.
VOZ 2:	¿Fiorel? La conozco. Estudia italiano, creo.
VOZ 1:	Número seis, Itxero. ¿La conoces?
VOZ 2:	Sí la conozco. Está en el grupo de mi hermana.
VOZ 2:	Número siete, Jahil.
VOZ 1:	Le conozco yo, porque está en mi grupo de gimnasia. También muy amable.
VOZ 2:	Número ocho, Kepa.
VOZ 1:	¿Kepa? Sí, le conozco. Está en mi grupo de deporte. ¡Es súper inteligente!
VOZ 2:	Nueve, Zafiro. ¡Qué bien – me gusta mucho Zafiro!
VOZ 1:	¿De dónde la conoces?
VOZ 2:	Come en nuestra mesa en la cantina.
VOZ 1:	¿Y Sarli?
VOZ 2:	No, no la conozco.
VOZ 1:	Yo tampoco la conozco. ¡Bueno, conocemos a algunos, por lo menos!

Gramática

A brief reminder that the indirect object pronouns are featured in the grammar summary, section 16, p.151. There are also practice activities in Acción: lengua 15, p.141.

3 **Pilar, Raquel y Juan**

Students listen and read. Raquel is visiting Pilar, who introduces her to her brother Juan. A multiple-choice activity in which students write the number of the phrase or expression heard.

Answers: 3, 4, 6, 9, 10.

PILAR:	¡Raquel! ¡Pasa, pasa!
RAQUEL:	¡Hola!
PILAR:	¿Conoces a mi hermano, Juan?
RAQUEL:	No, no le conozco.
PILAR:	Bueno, Juan, te presento a Raquel.
RAQUEL:	Hola, Juan.
JUAN:	Encantado. Siéntate aquí.
PILAR:	¿Qué quieres tomar? ¿Un café?
RAQUEL:	Un café solo, por favor.
JUAN:	¿Quieres comer algo? ¿Un pastelito? ¿Una galleta?
RAQUEL:	Un pastelito, gracias.

4 **Te toca a ti**

○ Students now use the script from Activity 3 as the stimulus for their own conversations in groups of three – referring to the information box on the right for details.

○ Students invent another scenario, but this time with adults as well as young people, taking care to ensure that they use the correct form *tú* or *usted*.

SUPPORT MATERIALS

Worksheet 15.2 ¡Hola!

a ○ Students listen to the recording and pick a visual for each conversation.

Answers: A–4; C–3; D–5; E–1; F–2;
(B is the distractor).

b ○ Students listen again and pick a sentence for each person.

Answers: Claudia 6; Julia 4; Señora Hernández 5; David 3;
Enrique 1.

1	ANA:	¡Claudia! ¡Qué gusto verte!
	CLAUDIA:	Hola Ana. Pasa, pasa ...
	ANA:	Claudia, ¿conoces a mi amigo Santi?
	CLAUDIA:	No, no le conozco. Hola, Santi. Pero creo que conozco a tu hermano.
	SANTI:	Encantado.
2	SEÑORA:	Julia, ¿quieres tomar algo? ¿Una galleta? ¿Un pastelito?
	JULIA:	No, gracias.
	SEÑORA:	¿No te gustan? ¿Te puedo ofrecer otra cosa?
	JULIA:	No, es que no puedo tomar trigo.
3	SEÑOR:	Bienvenida, Señora Hernández. ¿Quiere tomar algo? ¿Un té? ¿Solo, con limón ...?
	SEÑORA:	La verdad es que me gustaría más un refresco. Algo de limón, ¿o una naranjada si hay?
	SEÑOR:	Claro que hay. Marta, ¿nos traes un poco de hielo?
4	EVA:	¡Pasa, pasa!
	CHICO:	Hola, Eva. ¿Conoces a David? Es de Marruecos.
	EVA:	Encantada, David. ¿Estás aquí de vacaciones?
	DAVID:	No, estoy aquí para estudiar en la universidad.
5	LUZ:	Enrique, ¿quieres tomar un café?
	ENRIQUE:	Sí, gracias. Ah ... no quiero leche, gracias.
	LUZ:	Ah, sí, es verdad. Eres alérgico, ¿no?
	ENRIQUE:	Sí.

Objectives

Students learn – to use exclamations
– to apologise, to thank and congratulate others

Key language

¡ay, perdón!
¡ay, qué bien!
¡ay, qué ilusión!
¡felicitaciones!
¡qué amable!
¡qué asco!
¡qué suerte!
¡y qué ...!
¡qué bien!
¡qué disgusto!
¡qué horario más desagradable!
¡qué horror!
¡qué ilusión!
¡qué pena!
¡qué rollo!
¡qué sorpresa!
¡ay, qué susto!
¡qué suerte!
¿qué tal está ...?
lo siento (mucho)
(muchísimas) gracias por todo
no hay de qué
no importa (ahora)
te pido perdón por ...

ICT opportunities

Students can – use a word-processing package to write a letter
of introduction about themselves, using the letter
on Worksheet 15.4 as a model

Ways in

Use photos of famous people as impromptu stimuli for
introductions (with real or made-up information!); Picture story on
page 138

Assessment opportunities

AT1,3 Student's Book, Activity 2 ○ : students list the
apologies and exclamations.
AT1,3 Student's Book, Activity 2 ✿ : students listen and do a
multiple-choice activity.
AT3,4 Student's Book, Activity 3a: students read the text and
fill in the gaps.
AT4,4 Student's Book, Activity 3b: students write a response to
the letter.

STUDENT'S BOOK, pages 138–139

1 Las exclamaciones

a Students firstly read a list of exclamations and decide if
they are positive or negative.

Answers: *1 – positiva; 2 – positiva; 3 – negativa;*
4 – positiva; 5 – negativa; 6 – negativa;
7 – negativa; 8 – positiva; 9 – negativa;
10 – negativa; 11 – positiva; 12 – negativa.

b Students now listen to various people using the
exclamations in dialogues, and check their answers.

1 RAFA:	No sé si te va a gustar ...	
MARTÍN:	¡Qué amable! Una bufanda del Fútbol Club. Gracias, Rafa ...	
2 MAMÁ:	... y luego el sábado por la tarde, vamos a la costa.	
SOFÍA:	¿A la costa? ¡Qué bien!	
3 PEDRO:	¡Qué horario más desagradable! ¡Tenemos dos horas de matemáticas el lunes por la mañana!	
JUAN:	¡Qué horror!	
4 ANA:	¿Está Mari Carmen?	
MAMÁ:	Sí, un momento. ¡Mari Carmen!	
MARI CARMEN:	Ya voy, Mamá. ¡Ana! ¡Qué sorpresa!	
5 FELIPE:	¡Hola, Reme!	
REME:	¡Felipe! ¡Ay, qué susto! Es que no te oí entrar ...	
6 PACA:	¡... y lo peor es que tenemos tres horas de deberes que hacer para mañana!	
JOSÉ:	¿Tres horas? ¡Qué rollo!	
7 PAPÁ:	¡No puedes ir de excursión con tu clase a Gibraltar!	
MARINA:	¿No puedo ir a Gibraltar? ¡Qué disgusto!	

8 MAMÁ:	Oye, Antonio ...	
ANTONIO:	¿Qué?	
MAMÁ:	¿Te gustaría ir a Londres este verano?	
ANTONIO:	¿A Londres? ¡Qué ilusión!	
9 MILA:	Así que, no puedo venir al cine el sábado.	
TOMÁS:	¿No puedes venir al cine? ¡Qué pena!	
10 CONCHI:	¡Ignacio! ¿Quieres una hamburguesa?	
IGNACIO:	¿Una hamburguesa? ¡Puaj! ¡Qué asco! Pero Conchi, ¿no sabes que soy vegetariano?	
11 EDUARDO:	... en agosto vamos a Los Estados Unidos, y luego bajamos a México y Perú.	
AMALIA:	¡Un viaje a América! ¡Qué suerte!	
12 PAPÁ:	¡Marta, tu dormitorio está hecho una pocilga!	
MARTA:	¡Y qué ...!	

2 Llegadas

Picture story

Carmina comes in through the kitchen door which bangs
into Isabel who is holding a cup of coffee, but Carmina has
some good news for Isabel

○ Students read and listen to the picture story, and make
two lists – one of apologies and another of exclamations.

✿ Students listen and choose the correct alternative in
each sentence.

Answers: ○

Disculpas	*Exclamaciones*
¡Ay perdón!	*¡Felicitaciones!*
te pido perdón	*¡Qué bien!*
Lo siento mucho	*¡Qué ilusión!*
	¡Qué suerte!
	No importa
	No hay de qué

✿ *1 – una hija; 2 – ilusionada; 3 – una hermana;*
4 – contenta; 5 – pide perdón.

CARMINA:	¡Ay, perdón!
ISABEL:	Lo siento mucho, tía Carmina ...
CARMINA:	No importa, Isabel. ¡Felicitaciones!
ISABEL:	¿Por qué?
CARMINA:	¡Por el bebé de tu mamá!
ISABEL:	¡Ay, qué bien!
PILAR:	¡Ay, qué ilusión!
ISABEL:	¿Y Mamá?
CARMINA:	Está bien, Isabel.
ISABEL:	¿Qué es – niño o niña?
CARMINA:	Es una niña.
PILAR:	¡Qué suerte! Yo no tengo ninguna hermana.
ISABEL:	¿Quién es? ... ¡Papá!
PILAR:	¡Y Tomás!
OMAR:	Tomás, te pido perdón por lo del estéreo personal.
TOMÁS:	Vale. No importa ahora.
CARMINA:	Muchísimas gracias por todo, Michael. Tomás está aquí otra vez.
MICHAEL:	No hay de qué. ¿Qué tal está Teresa?
CARMINA:	¡Tienes una hija – y tú, Tomás, una hermana!
ISABEL:	Bueno, ¡al hospital, todos!

3   Muchísimas gracias

a A substitution activity involving reading a letter, looking at picture cues and selecting the correct word to replace the pictures.

Answers: *1 – carta; 2 – regalo; 3 – CD; 4 – paquete; 5 – tarjeta; 6 – foto; 7 – jersey; 8 – camiseta.*

b Students reply to an imaginary letter which encloses a present and an invitation to go to Spain. The letter from Activity 3a may be used as a model if wished, and in addition some support is given in the form of a help box on the page.

SUPPORT MATERIALS

Worksheet 15.3 Muchísimas gracias

This sheet has removable English rubrics at the bottom.

1   Disculpas y gracias

Students fill in the crossword by filling in the blanks in the set phrases 1–7.

Answers:

		7					
1	i	m	p	o	r	t	a
	2	p	e	r	d	ó	n
		3	g	r	a	c	i	a	s
4	e	n	v	i	a	d	o
5	i	g	u	a	l		
	6	p	o	r			

2   Lo pasé bien

a Students match up fragments from letters with the appropriate pictures.

Answers: *1 – c; 2 – a; 3 – f; 4 – e; 5 – d; 6 – b.*

b Students sequence the paragraphs in Activity 2a according to subject matter.

Answers: *Gracias: d; Otros regalos: c; Actividad (de día): f; Por la noche: e; Opinión: b; Planes para el fin de semana: a.*

Worksheet 15.4 ¡Qué bien!

1   Mari Paz

a Students listen to Mari Paz being interviewed on a radio programme and decide whether each visual relates to last week (SP), the future (F), or if an activity is normally done (N).

b Students listen again and answer a series of true / false / impossible to say questions.

Answers: ♣ *a – N; b – F; c – N; d – SP; e – F; f – SP; g – N.*

         ♣ *1 – ✗; 2 – ✓; 3 – ✓; 4 – ?; 5 – ✗; 6 – ✓.*

ENTREVISTADOR:	Mari Paz, háblanos de tu cumpleaños. Acabas de cumplir dieciséis años, ¿no?
MARI PAZ:	Sí, la semana pasada.
ENTREVISTADOR:	¿Y qué tal lo pasaste?
MARI PAZ:	Normalmente, no hago mucho. Suelo ir al cine con mis amigos, o cojo el tren y voy de compras a Madrid.
ENTREVISTADOR:	Pero este año no fue así.
MARI PAZ:	¡No! Mis padres me dieron un vale-regalo.
ENTREVISTADOR:	Pero un vale-regalo para algo especial.
MARI PAZ:	Sí. Un vale-regalo para un vuelo en globo.
ENTREVISTADOR:	¡En globo!
MARI PAZ:	Sí. Fue muy emocionante. Subí en el globo a las cinco de la tarde, y el viaje duró unas dos horas. ¡Me encantó!
ENTREVISTADOR:	¿Tienes ganas de hacerlo otra vez?
MARI PAZ:	No, fue una experiencia inolvidable, pero me gustaría probar otra cosa. El año que viene, quiero hacer un vuelo en un avión pequeño, o en un planeador.
ENTREVISTADOR:	¡Muy atrevido!
MARI PAZ:	Sí, ahora tengo mucho más confianza en mí misma. El mes que viene, voy a hacer espeleología.
ENTREVISTADOR:	¿Espeleología? ¿Es decir, explorar una gruta o una caverna?
MARI PAZ:	Sí. ¡No tengo miedo de nada! Ir debajo de la tierra no me importa ahora. Las alturas tampoco. El fin de semana pasado, hice alpinismo por primera vez, y me divertí mucho.
ENTREVISTADOR:	Así que este vale-regalo de tus padres te ha cambiado la vida.
MARI PAZ:	¡Sí! Fue un regalo estupendo. Ir a la discoteca, o dar una vuelta con mis amigos – que es lo que hago normalmente el fin de semana – me parece ahora muy aburrido.

2   Muchas gracias

A reading activity based on a thank-you letter. Students fill in the blanks by eliciting information from the letter.

Answers: *1 – 15 de abril; 2 – camiseta; 3 – viernes; 4 – discoteca; 5 – la música; 6 – el dolor de cabeza; 7 – ir a la playa; 8 – venir a Gran Bretaña.*

Objectives

Students learn – to use further exclamations

Key language

iqué bonita!
iqué guapa es!
iqué ilusión!
iqué sorpresa!
la boda
el bautizo

Ways in

Picture story on page 140

Assessment opportunities

AT1, 4   Student's Book, Activity 1 ◐: students listen and do a true or false activity.

AT4,4   Student's Book, Activity 1 ♣: students correct the false sentences.

STUDENT'S BOOK, page 140

1 **La invitación**

A rounding-off activity for the language presented in the unit, which introduces some more exclamatory phrases. Carmina receives an invitation to her niece's wedding in Mexico.

◐ Students listen to the recording and read the picture story. They then answer the six true / false / impossible to tell questions based on the text.

♣ Students correct the sentences that are false.

Answers: ◐ *1 – verdad; 2 – mentira; 3 – mentira; 4 – no se sabe; 5 – Amaya: verdad, Martín: no se sabe; 6 – no se sabe.*

♣ *2 La tarjeta es de la hermana de Teresa; 3 Hay también una invitación a una boda.*

TERESA:	¡Michael!
MICHAEL:	Hola, Teresa ...
TERESA:	¿Qué te parece tu hija?
MICHAEL:	¡Qué guapa es!
PILAR:	Tía Teresa – una carta para ti.
TOMÁS:	De México.
TERESA:	Oye, Tomás – ¿me dejas la carta, por favor? Mira, una tarjeta de mi hermana.
ISABEL:	¡Qué bonita!
TERESA:	¡Qué sorpresa! ¡Una invitación a la boda de Amaya y Martín!
ISABEL:	¡México, qué ilusión!
PILAR:	¡Qué suerte!
TOMÁS:	¿Amaya y Martín?
TERESA:	Amaya es la hija de mi hermana. Tiene veinte años ...
MICHAEL:	¿Te gustaría ir a México, Tomás?
TOMÁS:	¿Vienes tú, Papá?
MICHAEL:	Bueno, no lo sé.
TERESA:	Es que depende ...

Acción: lengua 15, page 141

Practice of direct object pronouns and the personal *a*.

1 ◐ Students insert the correct object pronoun.

♣ Students rewrite each of the six sentences relating the same information but in a different way – i.e. placing *le, la, les* or *las* either before or after the verb.

Answers: ◐ *1 – la; 2 – le; 3 – les; 4 – las; 5 – la.*

♣ *1 – Paca le va a pedir salir;*
2 – Estoy enfadada con Paca. No quiero verla;
3 – Juan está en casa. Debo llamarle;
4 – Le voy a decir que yo sé lo que pasa;
5 – No quiero darle la impresión de que me importa;
6 – Pero en realidad, ¡quiero matarles!

2 Use of the preposition *a* before a direct object if the object is a person. Students insert *a* where necessary.

Answers: *1 – a; 2 – not needed; 3 – not needed; 4 – a; 5 – a; 6 – a, a; 7 – a; 8 not needed.*

¡Repaso! 11-15

A review and revision section concentrating on Units 11–15. As with the previous *¡Repaso!* sections, it may be used for on-going assessment and analysis of students' progress.

STUDENT'S BOOK, pages 142–143

1 **¿Dónde estamos?**

Students listen and pick the appropriate location for each conversation.

Answers: *1–h; 2–f; 3–d; 4–a; 5–c; 6–e; 7–g.*

1	VOZ 1:	¿Quién es? ¡Sebastián! ¡Qué bien verte! Pasa, pasa. ¡Marta!
	MARTA:	¿Sí? ¡Hola!
	VOZ 1:	Sebastián, ¿conoces a mi mujer, Marta?
	SEBASTIÁN:	No, no la conozco.
	MARTA:	Encantada, y bienvenido a nuestra casa.
2	VOZ 1:	Buenos días, ¿qué desea?
	VOZ 2:	¿Cuánto cuestan las naranjas?
	VOZ 1:	Un euro cincuenta y cinco el kilo.
	VOZ 2:	Dos kilos, entonces.
	VOZ 1:	¿Algo más?
	VOZ 2:	Un kilo de patatas, por favor.
	VOZ 1:	Muy bien.
3	VOZ 1:	¿Qué quieres comprar?
	VOZ 2:	No sé. El plato es bonito ...
	VOZ 1:	Sí, ¡pero mira el precio!
	VOZ 2:	¿Por qué no compras un póster de la ciudad?
	VOZ 1:	Mm ... no sé ... Me gusta este cinturón, también.
4	VOZ 1:	¿Quieres venir a nadar?
	VOZ 2:	No, gracias. No tengo ganas de nadar.
	VOZ 1:	El agua está muy buena.
	VOZ 2:	Sí, ya lo sé. Véte, tú. Yo me quedo aquí. Prefiero tomar el sol.
	VOZ 1:	Bueno, como quieras. ¡Pero qué lástima venir a la costa y no nadar!
5	VOZ 1:	¿Qué te pasa?
	VOZ 2:	Me duele el estómago.
	VOZ 1:	¿Tienes fiebre?
	VOZ 2:	No, no lo creo.
	VOZ 1:	Bueno, quédate aquí un rato. ¿Qué clase tienes ahora?
	VOZ 2:	Matemáticas.
	VOZ 1:	Bueno, toma un poco de agua.
6	VOZ 1:	Buenos días, ¿qué desea?
	VOZ 2:	¿Tiene algo para un dolor de cabeza?
	VOZ 1:	Tengo aspirinas. Son muy buenas.
	VOZ 2:	Vale, una caja pequeña, entonces. ¿Cuánto es?
	VOZ 1:	Son un euro diez céntimos.
7	CAMARERO:	Buenos días, señores. ¿Qué desean?
	VOZ 1:	De primero, la sopa de fideos.
	VOZ 2:	Para mí, una ensalada mixta.
	CAMARERO:	¿De segundo?
	VOZ 2:	Quisiera un filete, con patatas fritas y guisantes.
	VOZ 1:	Y para mí, tortilla de champiñones.
	CAMARERO:	Muy bien.

---

2 **¿Qué tal las vacaciones?**

a An activity based on a postcard noticeboard. Students work out which person is referred to by each picture.

Answers: *1–Raúl; 2–Ángel; 3–Ángel; 4–Marina; 5–Ana; 6–Marina; 7–Raúl.*

---

b Students work out who answers each of the questions 1–5.

Answers:

Ana	1–✓;	2–✗;	3–✗;	4–✓;	5–✗.
Raúl	1–✗;	2–✓;	3–✗;	4–✓;	5–✓.
Marina	1–✓;	2–✓;	3–✗;	4–✓;	5–✓.
Ángel	1–✓;	2–✗;	3–✓;	4–✓;	5–✗.

c Students prepare answers to questions 1–5 in Activity 2b and then ask and answer them together with a partner.

3 **La carta de Maite**

a Students read Maite's letter, using a dictionary if necessary to look up the meaning of unfamiliar words, in preparation for the activities that follow.

b Students identify which paragraph corresponds to the topics listed.

 Students join up the sentence halves, based on the same letter.

Answers: *1–párrafo b; 2–párrafo c; 3–párrafo e; 4–párrafo d; 5–párrafo f; 6–párrafo b.*
   1–d; 2–f; 3–a; 4–b; 5–e; 6–c.

c Students write a letter using Maite's as a model, including the specified information.

SUPPORT MATERIALS

Worksheet 15.5 ¿Qué tal las vacaciones?

 A worksheet to support Activity 2 on Student's Book p.142. Students study the postcards on p.142 again and write down who each sentence refers to.

Answers: *Raúl–3, 2, 7, 10; Marina–6, 8; Ángel–1, 5, 9; Ana–4.*

Worksheet 15.6 ¿Cómo fue?

 A summative sheet in which students give their opinions on learning Spanish for the first year. They copy out the grid and fill in the three columns with the appropriate sentences.

 Students write a paragraph about their experiences learning Spanish for a year, using a set of given prompts.

STUDENT'S BOOK, pages 144–145

Lectura

There are five texts for reading for pleasure. Encourage students to choose at least one and use their dictionaries to look up any unfamiliar words.

a Chistes – three jokes.

b La tortilla española – recipe and instructions.

c Las vacaciones en España – information about school holidays in Spain.

d ¿Eres atrevido/a? – a personality questionnaire asking students a series of questions relating to how daring they are. After choosing their answers, students add up the points they have scored and read what it says about their personality. Students could also jot down the answers they think their partners may give, and compare them to see whether they agree.

e Poema de amor – a short poem.

STUDENT'S BOOK, page 146

Táctica: lengua

Two learning strategies designed to help students to develop their language skills.

Buscando pistas / Looking for clues

Advice about how to read quickly for gist before reading more intensively for detail. By first of all searching for clue words in a text, students will be able to gain a rough idea of what it is about, and this will enable them to understand the text as a whole. Two short passages are offered in which students can practise looking for clue words. Different students will produce different lists of familiar words and cognates. They should compare notes with a friend to see which words stood out most for each person. You might like to limit their choice of clue words to a certain number, or ask them to suggest the minimum number of words they need to know in order to get a good grasp of the meaning of the passage.

Verbos / Verbs

One of the most difficult problems students face is looking up verbs in the dictionary. This activity helps students to find the infinitive forms, working backwards from the present and preterite tense endings.

Answers: *1 – pasar, ver;*
2 – merendar, buscar;
3 – decidir, encontrar, hacer;
4 – alquilar, subir.

STUDENT'S BOOK, page 147

Práctica: lengua

Some summative grammar practice activities based on the grammar items encountered in the past five units.

1 ○ Students insert the correct indirect object pronoun into each sentence.

♣ Students write the correct direct object pronoun in each gap.

Answers: ○ *1 – le; 2 – te; 3 – Me; 4 – te; 5 – Le; 6 – me.*

♣ *1 – La; 2 – los; 3 – las; 4 – Lo; 5 – les; 6 – Las; 7 – la.*

2 Students insert the correct formal command forms into a rap.

Answers: *1 – Tome; 2 – coga; 3 – Suba; 4 – baje; 5 – Cruce; 6 – siga; 7 – Pase.*

3 ○ Students put a passage about Cinderella into the preterite (first person singular form).

♣ Students put the verbs into the correct preterite tense form.

Answers: ○ *1 – Recogí, hice; 2 – Salí, compré; 3 – Lavé, saqué; 4 – Limpié, planché; 5 –Comí, bebí; 6 – Ayudé; 7 – fui.*

♣ *llegó; Fue; criticó; gustó; preparé; examinó; miró; perdí; protesté; dejó.*

Answers to Assessments

ASSESSMENT A UNITS 1–2
(Total 100 marks – (4 × 25 marks))

Listening AT1/1

1 Las instrucciones

a 3   c 4   e 5   f 2
(2 marks each. Total 8 marks. 6 marks or more = level 1)

Listening AT1/2

2 Ahora

a 2 c   3 b   4 b   5 c
b a 4   d 5   e 3   f 6   g 2
(1 mark per question. Total 9 marks. 7 marks or more = level 2)

Listening AT1/3

3 La excursión

a Excursión a: Segovia
   Día: viernes
   Fecha: 25 de julio
   Autobús número: 19
   Importante traer: (1) carpeta
                       (2) dinero

b Marcos 🙂

   La profesora 🙁

(1 mark per question. Total 8 marks. 6 marks or more = level 3)

Speaking AT2/1

1 ¿Qué?

a 1 una pluma   2 un lápiz   3 un cuaderno
   4 una regla   5 un sacapuntas
b 1 un magnetofón   2 un estante   3 una puerta
   4 un borrador   5 una mesa
*(1 mark per item mentioned. Total 8 marks.
6 marks or more = level 1)*

Speaking AT2/2

2 Instrucciones a tu pareja

a Pon la silla bien.   b Enciende la luz.   c Abre la puerta.
d Cierra la puerta.   e Limpia la pizarra.
*(2 marks per item mentioned. Total 8 marks.
6 marks or more = level 2)*

Speaking AT2/3

3 Los alumnos nuevos

*(2 marks per response, plus 1 mark for fluency / pronunciation.
Total 9 marks. 6 marks or more = level 3)*

Reading AT3/1

1 ¿En la mochila o en el aula?

En una mochila: 2, 4, 5, 8
En el aula: 3, 6, 7
(1 mark per question. Total 7 marks. 5 marks or more = level 1)

Reading AT3/2

2 En clase

2 e   3 g   4 a   5 d   6 b
(2 marks per question. Total 10 marks. 8 marks or more = level 2)

Reading AT3/3

3 Por correo electrónico

2 J   3 B   4 D   5 H   6 I   7 C   8 A   9 F
(1 mark each. Total 8 marks. 6 marks or more = level 3)

Writing AT4/1

1 Copia correctamente

b catorce   c quince   d un cuaderno   e una hoja de papel
f marzo   g abril   h mayo
(1 mark each. Total 7 marks. 5 marks or more = level 1)

Writing AT4/2

2 ¿Qué hay que hacer?

No tengo sacapuntas.
¡Silencio la clase. Callaos!
Enciende el ordenador, por favor.
Mira la pizarra.
Cierra la puerta, por favor.
*(2 marks each. Total 10 marks. 8 marks or more = level 2).

> *2 marks = whole message communicated,
> 1 mark = message partially communicated,
> 0 marks = fails to communicate message

Writing AT4/3

3 ¡Tú eres autor!

a Muy bien / Regular gracias / ¡Fatal! ¿Y tú? (if ¿Y tú? omitted,
   award 1 mark only)
b Sí, toma / Lo siento, no tengo / No, no tengo regla.
c Se me ha olvidado.
d Es el doce de mayo
*(2 marks each. Total 8 marks. 6 marks or more = level 3).

ASSESSMENT B UNITS 3–5
(Total 100 marks – (4 × 25 marks))

Listening AT1/1

1 Me presento

b ✗   c ✗   d ✓   e ✗   f ✓   g ✗   h ✓   i ✗
(1 mark each. Total 8 marks. 6 marks or more = level 1)

Listening AT1/2

2 ¿De qué hablan?

a 2   b 6   c 3   d 9   e 4   f 8   h 7   j 5
*(1 mark each, including distractor. Total 9 marks.
6 marks or more = level 2)*

Listening AT1/3

3 Julio e Irene

2 A   3 E   4 G   5 F   6 L   7 N   8 I   9 J
(1 mark each. Total 8 marks. 6 marks or more = level 3)

Speaking AT2/1

1 Los animales

una serpiente, un perro, un pez, una rata, una tortuga,
un hámster, un conejo
*(1 mark per response. Total 8 marks. Do not penalise faulty
gender. 6 marks or more = level 1)*

Speaking AT2/2

2 En el instituto

*(2 marks per response (both subject and opinion). Total 8 marks.
6 marks or more = level 2)*

Speaking AT2/3

3 Tú y tu familia

*(2 marks per response (4 questions only)). Total 8 marks.
6 marks or more = level 3.

Answers to Assessments

Reading AT3/1

1 Detalles

b 9　c 6　d 8　e 11　f 7　g 10　h 2　i 5　j 1
(1 mark each. Total 9 marks. 7 marks or more = level 1)

Reading AT3/2

2 En los vestuarios

b P　c N　d P, N　e P　f P　g N, P　h N　i N
(1 mark per question. Total 8 marks. 6 marks or more = level 2)

Reading AT3/3

3 Problemas

1 A　2 C　3 A　4 B　5 C　6 A　7 A　8 B
(1 mark per question. Total 8 marks. 6 marks or more = level 3)

Writing AT4/1

1 Me gusta, y no me gusta ...

*(1 mark each. Total 7 marks. 5 marks or more = level 1.
Remove support from sheet with a very able group)*

Writing AT4/2

2 Nuria

*(2 marks for each sentence. Total 10 marks.
8 marks or more = level 2)*

Writing AT4/3

3 El horario

**(2 marks for each response. Total 8 marks.
6 marks or more = level 3.*

ASSESSMENT C UNITS 6–8
(Total 100 marks – (4 × 25 marks))

Listening AT1/1

1 ¿Dónde?

2 I　3 D　4 H　5 G　6 E　7 F　8 C　9 J
(1 mark each. Total 8 marks. 7 marks or more = level 1)

Listening AT1/2

2 El tiempo

Potes 5　Marbella: 1, 7　La Coruña 3, 2　Alicante 1, 4, 6
(1 mark each. Total 8 marks. 6 marks or more = level 2)

Listening AT1/3

3 Mi barrio

Andrés　☺　en un piso en el centro
Lourdes　☹　está a media hora andando
Jaime　☺　su dormitorio
Estela　☹　es ruidoso
　　　　Hay un bar abajo / en la planta baja
(1 mark per response. Total 9 marks. 7 marks or more = level 3)

Speaking AT2/1

1 La casa

*(1 mark for each piece of information successfully
communicated. Do not penalise faulty gender.
Total 8 marks. 5 marks or more = level 1)*

Speaking AT2/2

2 ¿Qué se puede hacer en la región?

*(2 marks for each phrase; choose 1 set.
Total 8 marks. 6 marks or more = level 2.
2 marks = communicating verb and noun, 1 mark = just noun)*

Speaking AT2/3

3 En mi opinión

**(2 marks per response; choose 1 dialogue. Total 8 marks, plus
1 mark for fluency / pronunciation. 6 marks or more = level 3.*

Reading AT3/1

1 En mi calle hay ...

b 8　c 2　e 7　f 1　g 6　h 9　i 5　j 3
(1 mark each. Total 8 marks. 6 marks or more = level 1)

Reading AT3/2

2 Busco ...

2 C　3 B　4 A　5 C　6 A
(1 mark per question. Total 10 marks. 8 marks or more = level 2)

Reading AT3/3

3 Arancha

2 nuevo　3 terraza　4 encima　5 no le gusta　6 lejos
7 bonito　8 comprar
(1 mark per question. Total 7 marks. 5 marks or more = level 3)

Writing AT4/1

1 Tu dormitorio

*(1 mark for each item listed. Total 9 marks.
7 marks or more = level 1)*

Writing AT4/2

2 Un pueblo bonito

*(2 marks for each sentence. Total 8 marks. 6 marks or more =
level 2. 1 mark for phrase from Assessment copied correctly, $\frac{1}{2}$
mark for each word that replaces the picture)*

Writing AT4/3

3 ¿Y tú?

*(2 marks each. Total 8 marks. 6 marks or more = level 3)

ASSESSMENT D UNITS 9–10
(Total 100 marks – (4 × 25 marks))

Listening AT1/2

1 Por la mañana

Desayuno ... a
Voy al instituto ... c
Tengo que ... a
Vuelvo a casa a ... c
(2 marks each. Total 8 marks. 6 marks or more = level 2)

Listening AT1/3

2 Los temas de conversación

Sentimientos / emociones b, f
Quehaceres c, g
Tiempo libre d, h
Instituto / Estudios e, i
(1 mark each. Total 8 marks. 6 marks or more = level 3)

Listening AT1/4–5

3 Luis y Raquel

a　2 L　3 L　4 R　5 R　6 L　7 L　8 R
b　9 ir al cine　10 estudiar
*(1 mark each. Total 9 marks. 5 marks or more = level 4.
Questions 9 and 10 = level 5, (if full marks achieved in part a)*

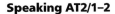

Speaking AT2/1–2

1 Por la tarde

(1 mark per question. Total 8 marks. 6 marks or more = level 2)

Speaking AT2/3

2 Problemas

(2 marks per response, plus 1 extra for time phrases. Total 7 marks. 5 marks or more = level 3.
2 marks = verb + noun, 1 mark = noun only)

Speaking AT2/4–5

3 La invitación

(2 marks each utterance. Choose 1 dialogue. Total 10 marks. 6 marks or more = level 4. Last question = level 5)

Reading AT3/2

1 El sábado

c	9:00	Desayuno
g	10:00	Quehaceres
a	11:00	Jardín con papá
f	12:00	Centro comercial
	13:30	Comida
e	15:00	Deberes
b	17:00	Piscina
h	20:30	Ver la tele
d	21:30	Discoteca con Quino y Alicia.

(1 mark each. Total 7 marks. 5 marks or more = level 2)

Reading AT3/3

2 Salir o no salir

	Anita	Martín	Gari	Elsa	Nuria	Luz
¿Sale o no? ✓ ✗	✗	✗	✓	✗	✗	✓
¿Qué tal? ☺ ☹	☹	☺	☺	☹	☹	☺

(2 marks each. Total 10 marks. 8 marks or more = level 3)

Reading AT3/4–5

3 Querida Corazón

a 1 madre 2 ser 3 vuelve 4 preparar 5 ayudar 6 volver
b 1 enfadado 2 cansada 3 deprimido
(1 mark each. Total 8 marks. 6 marks or more = level 4)

Writing AT4/1–2

1 ¿Qué opinas?

hacer la cama
lavar la ropa
recoger mi dormitorio
sacar la basura
pasar la aspiradora
poner y quitar la mesa
lavar los platos
(1 mark each. Total 7 marks. 5 marks or more = level 2.
Level 1 = correct copying of individual words from the phrases)

Writing AT4/3

2 Por correo electrónico

*(2 marks per phrase. Total 8 marks. 6 marks or more = level 3)

Writing AT4/4–5

3 El fin de semana ideal

(Total 10 marks. 8 marks or more = level 4. Up to 5 marks for content and 5 for range of vocabulary and accuracy)

ASSESSMENT E UNITS 11–13
(Total 100 marks – (4 × 25 marks))

Listening AT1/2

1 La consulta

1 a   2 e, k   3 c, i   4 f, h   5 b, g
(1 mark per ailment. Total 9 marks. 7 marks or more = level 2)

Listening AT1/3

2 En la tienda de recuerdos

PROBLEMA	aburrido	demasiado grande	odia la música pop	no le gusta	muy caro
SOLUCIÓN	un vale-regalo	una camiseta	un libro	un plato cerámico	(ir al) hipermercado

(1 mark per detail. Total 8 marks. 6 marks or more = level 3)

Listening AT1/4–5

3 Comer fuera

b pan   c productos lácteos   d náuseas   e dolor de cabeza
f ir al médico   g está alérgica   h ir a los grandes almacenes
i descansar (en el patio)
(1 mark per detail. Total 8 marks. 6 marks or more = level 4)

Speaking AT2/2

1 Perdone …

*(Total 8 marks. 2 marks for A, 3 marks each for B and C. 5 marks or more = level 2)

Speaking AT2/3

2 En la cafetería

*(2 marks per response. Total 8 marks. 6 marks or more = level 3)

Speaking AT2/4–5

3 Hablando con el / la médico/a

(Total 9 marks. 1 mark for first question, 2 marks for each of the rest. 5 marks or more = level 4. For level 5, the immediate future is needed in the last question)

Reading AT3/2

1 ¿Qué voy a tomar?

2 g   3 d   4 a   5 h   6 e   7 c   8 b
(1 mark each. Total 7 marks. 5 marks or more = level 2)

Reading AT3/3

2 ¿Te gusta ir de tiendas?

2 mercado	3 no es caro	4 regalos / camisetas
5 camisetas	6 el supermercado	7 aburrido
8 buenas	9 (en la) esquina	10 los bombones

(1 mark per question. Total 9 marks. 7 marks or more = level 3)

Reading AT3/4–5

3 Eva

2 mentira   3 verdad   4 mentira   5 mentira   6 no dice
7 verdad   8 no dice   9 verdad   10 mentira
(1 mark per question. Total 9 marks. 6 marks or more = level 4)

Answers to Assessments

Writing AT4/1–2

1 ¡Vamos a comprar!

(1 mark per gap filled. Total 7 marks. 6 marks or more = level 2)

Writing AT4/3

2 El intercambio

(2 marks per phrase. Total 8 marks. 6 marks or more = level 3)

Writing AT4/4–5

3 Los consejos

(Total 10 marks. 8 marks or more = level 4. Up to 5 marks for content, and 5 marks for range of vocabulary and content)

ASSESSMENT F UNITS 14–15
(Total 100 marks – (4 × 25 marks))

Listening AT1/1

1 ¿Quieres tomar …?

2 b   3 a   4 c   5 d
(1 mark per question. Total 4 marks. 3 marks or more = level 1)

Listening AT1/2

2 ¿Cuál es la pregunta correcta?

a 3   c 6   e 5   f 2   g 4
(1 mark per question. Total 5 marks. 4 marks or more = level 2)

Listening AT1/3

3 ¿Qué tal lo pasaste?

	🐴	🏖	🍽	💰	✈👥
😊	6		1		4
☹	2	5	3		

(1 mark each. Total 5 marks. 4 marks or more = level 3)

Listening AT1/4

4 En Gran Bretaña

		ORDEN	OPINIÓN: P, N, P+N
a	La comida	5	P+N
b	Conocer a los jóvenes británicos	1	P
c	Las instalaciones deportivas	4	P
d	Las tiendas		
e	Quedarse con una familia británica	2	P+N
f	El transporte público	3	N

($\frac{1}{2}$ mark per answer. Total 4 marks. 3 marks or more = level 4)

Listening AT1/5–6

5 En mi tiempo libre

jogging N   swimming N   feeling unwell P
reading P   homework P   relaxing F   TV F
(1 mark each. Total 7 marks. Identifying 2 past activities or 2 future activities = level 5, identifying 2 past and 2 future activities = level 6)

Speaking AT2/2

1 ¿Cómo viajas?

(1 mark for each place, 1 mark for each method of transport, plus one extra mark for fluency and accuracy. Total 8 marks. 7 marks or more = level 2)

Speaking AT2/3

2 La llegada del intercambio

(2 marks per question. Total 8 marks. 6 marks or more = level 3)

Speaking AT2/4–6

3 De vacaciones

(Total 9 marks. 5 marks or more = level 4. For levels 5 and 6 good use of tenses is needed)

Reading AT3/1

1 ¡Y qué!

algo bueno: b, d, h, i
algo malo: c, e, f, g, j, k
($\frac{1}{2}$ mark each. Total 5 marks. 4 marks or more = level 1)

Reading AT3/2

2 La bolsa

b 5   c 2   e 4   f 1   g 6
(1 mark each. Total 5 marks. 4 marks or more = level 2)

Reading AT3/3

3 La visita

amigos ✗   tiempo ✗   trabajo ✓   excursión ✓   opinión ✗
(1 mark each. Total 5 marks. 4 marks or more = level 3)

Reading AT3/4

4 Las recomendaciones

a   2 sí   3 no   4 no
b   1 b   2 c
(1 mark each. Total 5 marks. 4 marks or more = level 4)

Reading AT3/5

5 Las vacaciones

2 este año   3 el año pasado   4 este año   5 el año pasado
6 este año
(1 mark each. Total 5 marks. 4 marks or more = level 5)

Writing AT4/1–2

1 Preguntas

(1 mark per sentence. Total 7 marks. 5 marks or more = level 2. With more able students, suggestions at the bottom of the page can be removed)

Writing AT4/3

2 El campamento

(2 marks per sentence. Choose I set. Total 8 marks. 6 marks or more = level 3)

Writing AT4/4–5

3 Mi cumpleaños

(Total 10 marks. Up to 5 marks for content, and 5 marks for vocabulary and accuracy. Minimum of 3 marks in each area needed for level 4)

ASSESSMENT G UNITS 1–15
(Total 100 marks – (4 × 25 marks))

Listening AT1/1

1 ¡Hola!

b 4   c 2   d 1   e 3
(1 mark per question. Total 4 marks. 3 marks or more = level 1)

Listening AT1/2

2 ¿Dónde estamos?

a 3   d 6   f 5   g 2   h 4
(1 mark per question. Total 5 marks. 4 marks or more = level 2)

Listening AT1/3

3 ¿Qué opinas?

	😊	😐	🙁
viernes	f	c	
sábado	a		d
domingo		e	b

(1 mark each. Total 5 marks. 4 marks or more = level 3)

Listening AT1/4

4 Por teléfono

Mensaje para:	Sr Domínguez
Día y hora:	Miércoles, 11.45
Lugar de reunión:	en la entrada
De parte de:	Sra Gallaiztegui
Teléfono:	918 879 502
Traer a la reunión:	carpeta roja

(Total 5 marks. 1 mark per piece of information, $\frac{1}{2}$ mark each where 2 pieces of information needed. 4 marks or more = level 4)

Listening AT1/5

5 ¿Qué quieres hacer?

Joaquín N   Marisa N   Adrián F   Pablo F   Teresa F
Rebeca N
($\frac{1}{2}$ mark each. Total 3 marks. 2 marks or more = level 5)

Listening AT1/6

6 Italia

Años anteriores e
Normalmente f, g
Este año c, b, a
($\frac{1}{2}$ mark each. Total 3 marks. 2 marks or more = level 6)

Speaking AT2/1

1 El dormitorio

($\frac{1}{2}$ mark per item mentioned; Total 4 marks.
3 marks or more = level 1)

Speaking AT2/2

2 En la cafetería

(Total 5 marks. Choose 1 dialogue. $\frac{1}{2}$ mark for each response plus an extra mark for fluency and accuracy gives total of 8.
3 marks or more = level 2)

Speaking AT2/3

3 El instituto

(Total 5 marks. Choose 1 dialogue. $\frac{1}{2}$ mark for each response plus an extra mark for fluency and accuracy.
3 marks or more = level 3)

Speaking AT2/4

4 La rutina

(Total 5 marks. 2 marks for each response to any 5 questions to give total of 10, then divide by 2.
4 marks or more = level 4)

Speaking AT2/5–6

5 El tiempo libre

(2 marks per response. Choose 2 questions.
3 marks = communicates past, present and future (level 6);
2 marks for 2 tenses despite errors (level 5); 1 mark for 1 tense)

Reading AT3/1

1 Buen tiempo, mal tiempo

Buen tiempo: Cádiz, Alicante
Mal tiempo: Burgos, Santiago
(1 mark each. Total 4 marks. 3 marks or more = level 1)

Reading AT3/2

2 En casa

1 c   2 g   4 i   5 e   6 f   7 d   8 h   10 b
($\frac{1}{2}$ mark each. Total 4 marks. 3 marks or more = level 2)

Reading AT3/3

3 Mi región

a Gari   b Milagros   e Ali   f Julia   g Javier
(1 mark each. Total 5 marks. 4 marks or more = level 3)

Reading AT3/4

4 ¿La vida sana?

b mentira   c verdad   d no dice   e verdad   f mentira
(1 mark each. Total 5 marks. 4 marks or more = level 4)

Reading AT3/5–6

5 El nuevo polideportivo

D, H, A, C, E, J, G
(1 mark each. Total 7 marks. Correct answers for present tense and either future or preterite = level 5, correct answers for all tenses = level 6)

Writing AT4/1

1 La fiesta

($\frac{1}{2}$ mark per word. Total 4 marks. 3 or more marks = level 1)

Writing AT4/2

2 Muchas gracias

($\frac{1}{2}$ mark for each word and $\frac{1}{2}$ mark if the sentence is copied correctly. Total 5 marks. 4 marks or more = level 2)

Writing AT4/3

3 La postal

*(Total 5 marks. 2 marks per phrase, then divide total in half.
3 marks or more = level 2)

Writing AT4/4

4 Yo y mi familia

(Total 5 marks. Mark out of 10, then divide by 2)

Writing AT4/5–6

5 ¿Qué pasó?

(Total 6 marks)
TENSES   3 marks = communicates past, present and future (level 6)
2 marks = present tense and one other (level 5)
1 mark = some correct verbs
RANGE   3 marks = wide vocab, complex sentences (level 6)
2 marks = competent use of vocab, some errors (level 5)
1 mark = simple vocab, repetitive, lots of errors

Assessment tapescripts

Assessment A

(Units 1–2)

1 Las instrucciones

1	PROFE.:	Apaga la luz, por favor.
2	PROFE.:	Limpia la pizarra, Juana.
3	PROFE.:	¡Marta!
	MARTA:	¿Sí?
	PROFE.:	Pon la silla bien, por favor.
4	PROFE.:	Paco, cierra la puerta. Gracias.
5	PROFE.:	Apaga el ordenador. ¡Ahora!

2 Ahora

a

1	CHICO:	¿Qué se hace ahora, señor?
	PROFE.:	Sacad los cuadernos, por favor. Sí, los cuadernos.
2	ANA:	¡Pssst! ¡Pilar!
	PROFE.:	Ana, ¿qué pasa? ¿No tienes regla?
	ANA:	Sí, tengo. Es que no tengo sacapuntas.
3	PROFE.:	Ignacio, ciérrala, por favor.
	IGNACIO:	¿La puerta?
	PROFE.:	No, no. Cierra la ventana. Gracias.
4	CHICA:	Oye, ¿qué página es?
	CHICO:	Es la página quince.
	CHICA:	Vale, gracias.
5	CHICA:	Podemos escribir con lápiz, ¿no?
	PROFE.:	No. Escribid con bolígrafo, por favor.

b

1	CHICO:	¡Hola, Susana!
	CHICA:	Gabi, ¡hola!
	CHICO:	¿Qué tal?
	CHICA:	¿Yo?
2	PROFE.:	¡Shhh! ¡La clase! ¡Silencio, por favor …!
3	CHICA:	¿Qué día de la semana es?
	CHICO:	¿Qué día es? ¿No sabes? ¡Qué despistada eres! Hoy es …
4	CHICO:	Mohammed, esta actividad, ¿se hace por delante?
	CHICO:	No, no se hace por delante …
5	CHICO:	Juana, ¿cómo se dice 'deberes' en inglés?
	CHICA:	¿Deberes? Se dice …
6	PROFE.:	Vais a necesitar boli, o lápiz, o pluma.
	CHICO:	¿Rotulador?
	PROFE.:	Si no tienes boli, vale. Bueno, ahora …

3 La excursión

a

PROFE.:	¡Shhh! ¡Escuchad! Escribid los detalles. Excursión a Segovia el veinticinco de julio. El veinticinco de julio.
ALUMNO:	¿Qué día es?
PROFE.:	Viernes. Es viernes. El número del autobús es el diecinueve. Diecinueve.
ALUMNA:	¿Hay que traer algo?
PROFE.:	Es importante traer dos cosas. Uno, una carpeta. Carpeta, por favor. Dos, dinero. Traed un poco de dinero.

b

CHICA:	Una excursión a Segovia, Marcos, ¿qué opinas?
MARCOS:	¡Estupendo!
CHICA:	¿Y usted, señora? – ¿qué opina de la excursión a Segovia?
PROFESORA:	¿Yo y treinta alumnos en un autobús? ¡Fatal! ¡Qué horror!

Assessment B

(Units 3–5)

1 Me presento

a	CHICO:	¡Hola! Me llamo Antonio.
b	CHICO:	Tengo quince años.
c	CHICO:	¿Mi cumpleaños? Es el veinte de marzo.
d	CHICO:	Tengo un ratón, que se llama Kiri.
e	CHICO:	Tengo un hermano y una hermana.
f	CHICO:	¿Mis padres? No tengo madre. Sólo tengo a mi padre.
g	CHICO:	Mi día favorito es el martes.
h	CHICO:	¿El azul? Me encanta el azul.
i	CHICO:	¿Qué hora es? ¿Son las nueve menos cuarto ya? ¡Rápido! ¡A clase!

2 ¿De qué hablan?

1	CHICO:	Juana, ¿cuándo es tu cumpleaños?
	JUANA:	Es el catorce de julio. ¿Por qué?
2	CHICO:	¿Y cómo eres? ¿Alto?
	CHICO:	No. No muy alto. Pero no soy muy bajo tampoco.
3	CHICO:	¿Vives con tus padres?
	CHICO:	No, mis padres están divorciados. Vivo con mi madre.
4	CHICO:	¿No te gusta?
	CHICA:	No. Odio el francés y el inglés, pero me gusta el dibujo y el deporte.
5	CHICA:	¿Vas a pintar tu dormitorio en rojo?
	CHICO:	Sí. Me encantan el rojo y el negro.
	CHICA:	¡Qué horror!
6	CHICO:	Me gustaría mucho tener una lagartija o una serpiente.
	CHICO:	¿Sí? A mí no. Prefiero los conejos.
7	CHICA:	Es muy simpática.
	CHICA:	Sí, es muy graciosa y habladora también.
8	CHICO:	¿Cuántas clases de tecnología tenemos a la semana?
	CHICO:	Dos. El lunes a las nueve, o el jueves a las doce.
9	CHICA:	No me gusta mucho. Es muy antiguo. Hay un patio, pero no hay campo de deporte, ni gimnasio.

3 Julio e Irene

JULIO

ENTREVISTADOR:	¿Qué tal tu horario este año, Julio?
JULIO:	Bastante bien, sí. No está mal. Tengo tres horas de inglés a la semana, pero sólo dos de francés.

ENTREVISTADOR:	¿No te gusta el francés?
JULIO:	No mucho. Ni la historia. ¡Detesto la historia!
ENTREVISTADOR:	¿Qué asignaturas te gustan?
JULIO:	La química, la física, la biología. Me gustan muchísimo.
ENTREVISTADOR:	¿Qué tal las matemáticas este año?
JULIO:	No son fáciles. Son muy difíciles.

IRENE

AMIGA:	¿Es verdad que tienes novio, Irene?
IRENE:	Sí.
AMIGA:	¿Cómo es? ¡Cuéntame todo!
IRENE:	De estatura, es alto. Bastante alto.
AMIGA:	Ana dice que también es gordito.
IRENE:	¡No es verdad! No es gordito. Lo contrario.
AMIGA:	Y de carácter, ¿cómo es?
IRENE:	Es muy simpático.
AMIGA:	¡Quiero conocerle!
IRENE:	Es un poco tímido.
AMIGA:	No como tú. Tú eres muy graciosa y extrovertida.

Assessment C

(Units 6–8)

1 ¿Dónde?

1	CHICO:	Vivo en el norte.
2	CHICA:	¿Yo? Vivo en el sur.
3	CHICO:	Mi pueblo está en la sierra.
4	CHICA:	Vivo en el suroeste.
5	SEÑORA:	La ciudad está en el este.
6	CHICO:	Vivo en la costa.
7	SEÑOR:	Está en el centro, en el campo.
8	CHICA:	Vivo en el noreste.
9	CHICO:	¿Mi pueblo? Está en el sureste, junto al río.

2 El tiempo

A POTES

VOZ:	¿Qué tiempo hace en Potes hoy?
VOZ:	Hace frío. Mucho frío. Y hay niebla también.

B MARBELLA

VOZ:	Vamos ahora a Marbella, en el sur. ¿Qué tiempo hace allí, en Marbella?
VOZ:	Hace calor hoy. Pero hace mucho viento.

C LA CORUÑA

VOZ:	La Coruña, ¿qué tal allí?
VOZ:	Pues, bastante bien. Hace mucho sol. Lo malo es que hace frío.

D ALICANTE

VOZ:	Y Alicante. ¿Qué tiempo hace en Alicante?
VOZ:	Hace calor.
VOZ:	¿Calor? ¡Qué bien!
VOZ:	Sí, pero llueve mucho. Hay tormentas por toda la región.

3 Mi barrio

TINA

CHICO:	Tina, ¿qué tal tu nueva casa?
TINA:	Me encanta. Es muy bonita.
CHICO:	¿Qué tipo de casa es, Tina?
TINA:	Es un chalé.
CHICO:	¡Qué suerte tienes, hija! A mí me gustaría mucho vivir ...

ANDRÉS

CHICA:	Andrés, tú vives en las afueras de Medellín, ¿no?
ANDRÉS:	Sí.
CHICA:	Mis padres quieren comprar una casa allí. ¿Cómo es?
ANDRÉS:	No está mal. El barrio es moderno, hay un parque ... Pero, ... no sé.
CHICA:	¿Dónde preferirías vivir?
ANDRÉS:	Me gustaría más un piso en el centro.
CHICA:	¿Por qué?
ANDRÉS:	No tengo amigos allí ...

LOURDES

CHICO:	Oye, Lourdes, ¿qué tal tu piso nuevo?
LOURDES:	El piso está bien. Pero el barrio ... no hay mucha diversión. No hay nada que hacer.
CHICO:	Pero hay una piscina nueva en ese barrio, ¿no?
LOURDES:	Sí. Es estupenda. Lo malo es que está a media hora andando.
CHICO:	¿No hay autobuses?

JAIME

CHICA:	Tu casa está muy bien, Jaime.
JAIME:	Sí. Y el barrio es bonito también.
CHICA:	Y tienes jardín. ¡Qué bien! Nosotros no tenemos.
JAIME:	No me interesa mucho el jardín. Lo que más me gusta, ¡es mi dormitorio!
CHICA:	Es enorme. Y tienes tu propio cuarto de baño ...

ESTELA

ESTELA:	El barrio es feo, la calle es sucia ...
CHICO:	Pero es una calle muy tranquila.
ESTELA:	¡Qué va! ¡Esto es el problema! Es muy ruidosa.
CHICO:	¿Por qué? No hay mucho tráfico.
ESTELA:	El piso está en la primera planta. Y hay un bar abajo, en la planta baja.
CHICO:	Ah. Entiendo. Supongo que está abierto hasta muy tarde ...

Assessment D

(Units 9–10)

1 Por la mañana

1	CHICO:	¿A qué hora tienes que levantarte tú, Iñigo?
	ÍÑIGO:	A las siete y media normalmente.
2	CHICA:	¿Desayunas, Marta, o no?
	MARTA:	Sí, desayuno. Cereales y un zumo de naranja.
3	CHICO:	¿Cómo vienes al instituto?
	CHICO:	Tengo que venir andando. No hay autobús.

4 TÍO: ¿Qué tal tu instituto nuevo, Luis?

LUIS: Lo malo es que tengo exámenes pronto, y tengo que leer muchos libros.

5 MADRE: ¡Toñi!

TOÑI: ¿Qué? ¿Qué?

MADRE: ¿A qué hora vuelves a casa?

TOÑI: A las dos menos cuarto, Mamá.

2 Los temas de conversación

a CHICO: ¿Sales mucho por la tarde?

CHICA: Depende del tiempo. A veces, salgo con mis amigos o voy al polideportivo. ¿Por qué me lo preguntas?

b MADRE: ¿Qué te pasa, Edu?

EDU: ¡Estoy harto!

MADRE: ¿Por qué?

EDU: Porque tengo que levantarme todos los días a las seis y media para coger el autobús. ¿No me puedes llevar en coche, Mamá?

c CHICO: ¿Tú tienes que ayudar en casa, Felipe?

FELIPE: Sí. Tengo que recoger mi dormitorio todos los días y lavar los platos.

d CHICA: ¿Qué haces por la tarde?

CHICO: Juego al fútbol en el parque, y los viernes voy al club de jóvenes.

CHICA: ¿Puedo ir contigo al club ...?

e PADRE: ¿Trabajas mucho en clase, Bernardo?

BERNARDO: ¡Sí! Hay que escribir mucho, sobre todo en la clase de historia.

f MADRE: Elena, pareces muy preocupada.

ELENA: Sí, Mamá, es verdad.

MADRE: ¿Te puedo ayudar?

ELENA: ¿Conoces a Marisa? No está muy bien. No sonríe, no come, no quiere hablar ...

g CHICO: ¿Tu padre ayuda en casa?

CHICO: Sí. Mucho. Lava la ropa, plancha, pasa la aspiradora ...

h CHICA: ¿Qué te gusta hacer por la noche cuando no estudias?

CHICO: Veo la tele, o escucho música.

CHICA: ¿Te gustaría salir al cine conmigo?

i CHICO: Tengo que trabajar mucho para los exámenes: seis horas durante el día, y luego tres horas de deberes por la tarde.

3 Luis y Raquel

a

RAQUEL: ¡Hola, Luis! ¡Qué tarde! ¡Son las ocho y media ya!

LUIS: Ya lo sé.

RAQUEL: ¿Qué tal estás?

LUIS: ¡Cansado!

RAQUEL: ¿Por qué?

LUIS: Porque mi casa está a tres kilómetros y tengo que venir andando. ¡Tú vienes en autobús!

RAQUEL: ¡Está bien, hacer un poco de ejercicio físico, Luis! Yo hago footing y natación cada mañana.

LUIS: Tienes suerte. A las seis de la mañana, yo estoy haciendo los quehaceres de la casa.

RAQUEL: ¿Sí?

LUIS: Mi madre no está bien. Yo tengo que preparar el desayuno para mis hermanos y recoger la casa. No tengo tiempo para desayunar yo mismo. ¿Tú no tienes que ayudar en casa?

RAQUEL: ¿Yo? No hago nada. Mis padres lo hacen todo. Bueno, rápido, ¡a clase!

b

LUIS: Raquel, ¿vas a ir a la discoteca el viernes?

RAQUEL: No. Vienen mis abuelos. Pero voy a ir al cine el sábado por la tarde. ¿Quieres venir?

LUIS: Mm ...

RAQUEL: Ah, me acuerdo. Normalmente vas al club de jóvenes, ¿no?

LUIS: Sí. Pero este fin de semana no puedo. Tengo que estudiar. Tenemos exámenes en mayo.

RAQUEL: Ya lo sé, pero nos quedan un mes todavía ...

Assessment E

(Units 11–13)

1 La consulta

1 MÉDICO: ¿Qué te pasa?

PACIENTE: Me duelen los oídos.

MÉDICO: ¿Me dejas ver?

PACIENTE: Y tengo fiebre también.

2 PACIENTE: No me siento bien. Tengo la fiebre del heno.

MÉDICA: Mm ... difícil en verano.

PACIENTE: Y me duele el pecho también.

3 PACIENTE: Tengo un catarro.

MÉDICO: ¿Sí? Vamos a ver ...

PACIENTE: Y me duele la nariz también.

4 MÉDICA: ¿Qué le pasa?

PACIENTE: Tengo una picadura. Duele mucho.

MÉDICA: Mmm ... ¿Tiene otros síntomas?

PACIENTE: Tengo dolor de cabeza.

5 PACIENTE: No me siento bien.

MÉDICO: ¿No? ¿Qué te pasa?

PACIENTE: Tengo tos.

MÉDICO: ¿Desde hace cuánto tiempo?

PACIENTE: Una semana. Y tengo una ampolla enorme en el pie.

MÉDICO: Bueno, vamos a ver ...

Assessment tapescripts

2 En la tienda de recuerdos

1 CHICA: ¿Algo para tu padre? ¿Por qué no le compras un CD?

CHICA: Estos son todos de música pop. No le gusta.

CHICA: ¿Un libro, entonces?

2 CHICO: ¿No te gusta este cinturón?

CHICO: No, no mucho. Es un regalo aburrido, un cinturón.

CHICO: Tal vez la mejor solución es un vale-regalo.

3 CHICA: Mira, ¡qué bonito! ¿No te gusta este jersey?

CHICA: Sí, me gusta, ¿pero has visto el precio? Cincuenta euros. ¡Es muy caro!

CHICA: Todo es caro aquí.

CHICA: Bueno, vamos al hipermercado, entonces.

4 CHICO: Vamos a ver ... Un regalo para tu novia. ¿Le gustaría este reloj?

CHICO: Mm ... no creo. Es demasiado grande para una chica.

CHICO: Hace una hora que estamos aquí – ¿no ves nada?

CHICO: Bueno, tal vez una camiseta. ¿Dónde están las camisetas?

5 CHICO: Algo para tu abuela ... ¿Bombones de chocolate?

CHICA: No le gusta el chocolate.

CHICO: ¿No? ¡Qué raro!

CHICA: Tal vez un pieza de cerámica. Un plato de cerámica sería ideal.

3 Comer fuera

LUIS: Está bien, este restaurante.

INÉS: Sí. Es nuevo. A mí me gusta.

LUIS: ¿Quieres un poco de pan?

INÉS: No, gracias. No tomo de momento.

LUIS: ¿No?

INÉS: Y no tomo productos lácteos tampoco.

LUIS: ¿Por qué, Inés?

INÉS: No me siento muy bien cuando los tomo.

LUIS: ¿Qué te pasa?

INÉS: Si tomo mucho pan, tengo náuseas.

LUIS: ¿Y los productos lácteos?

INÉS: Después de tomarlos, tengo un dolor de cabeza horrible. Tal vez debería ir a la farmacia. ¿Qué opinas tú?

LUIS: Creo que debes ir al médico.

INÉS: ¿Te parece algo grave?

LUIS: No necesariamente. Tal vez seas alérgica a la leche. O alérgica al trigo.

INÉS: ¡O a los dos! Sí, debo ir a ver a alguien.

LUIS: Bueno, ¡basta de comida! ¿Qué planes tienes para la tarde? ¿Vas al mercado aquí cerca?

INÉS: Es un poco tarde. Cierra a las dos. Voy a ir a los grandes almacenes en la Plaza Mayor. ¿Y tú? Sé que normalmente vas al gimnasio los jueves.

LUIS: Sí, pero después de una comida fuerte como ésta, no puedo. ¡Voy a descansar en el patio!

Assessment F

(Units 14–15)

1 ¿Quieres tomar ...?

1 CHICO: ¿Mi nacionalidad? Soy español.

2 CHICO: Mi padre es marroquí. Nació en Marruecos.

3 CHICO: Quisiera un agua mineral, por favor.

4 CHICO: ¿De comer? Nada para mí, gracias.

5 CHICO: ¿Conoces a mi hermana menor?

2 ¿Cuál es la pregunta correcta?

1 SEÑORA: Estuve casi quince días. Me quedé una semana en un hotel y el resto del tiempo en casa de una amiga.

2 SEÑORA: Tomé el sol en la playa, nadé en la piscina, visité a amigos – hizo muy buen tiempo.

3 SEÑORA: Fui a Francia, al sur del país. Es una región que no conozco, y es muy bonita.

4 SEÑORA: Un hotel cuesta mucho. Puede ser muy caro. Si te quedas con amigos, es más barato.

5 SEÑORA: Sí. Mi marido tiene que trabajar mucho, y mi hija tiene exámenes. Por eso no fui con la familia.

6 SEÑORA: No. Viajé en tren hasta la frontera y luego en autocar. Pasamos cerca de los Pirineos – ¡fue muy bonito!

3 ¿Qué tal lo pasaste?

1 CHICA: ¿Qué hiciste allí?

CHICA: No mucho. Nadé. Nadé por la mañana y otra vez por la tarde.

CHICA: ¿No fue un poco aburrido?

CHICA: No, lo pasé muy bien.

2 CHICO: Y luego el jueves, monté a caballo.

CHICO: ¿A caballo?

CHICO: Sí. Pero al día siguiente, me dolía la espalda. Todavía tengo un dolor de espalda terrible.

CHICO: ¡Qué pena!

3 CHICA: Fuimos por la noche. Mi familia, y la familia de al lado.

CHICO: ¿Cómo fue?

CHICA: La mesa en la terraza, bien. Y el jardín fue muy bonito. Pero la comida ...

CHICO: ¿No te gustó?

CHICA: De primero, sopa. Estaba fría, con mucha grasa.

CHICO: ¡Qué asco!

4 CHICO: Y luego salimos al centro para ver una película.

CHICA: ¿Una película inglesa?

CHICO: Sí.

CHICA: ¡A qué no entendiste nada!

CHICO: ¡Todo lo contrario! Entendí mucho. Lo pasé bomba.

Assessment tapescripts

5 CHICA: ¿Hiciste un poco de relax, entonces?
CHICA: Sí. Tomé el sol en la playa todo el día.
CHICA: ¡Qué bien!
CHICA: Bueno, no, porque pasé demasiado tiempo en el sol. Cogí una insolación. Tuve que quedarme tres días en la cama.
CHICA: ¡Qué disgusto!

6 CHICO: ¿No fuiste al centro comercial con Íñigo y Gabi?
CHICO: No. No me interesa mucho, ir a comprar. Fui a la escuela de equitación allí enfrente del camping.
CHICO: ¿Te gustó?
CHICO: Fuimos de paseo por el campo. Lo pasé muy bien. Voy a volver mañana.

4 En Gran Bretaña

ENTREVISTADOR: ¿Qué opinas de tu estancia en Gran Bretaña, Mateo?
MATEO: Conocí a muchos jóvenes, todos simpáticos. Salí con ellos, y lo pasé muy bien.
ENTREVISTADOR: ¿Qué tal la vida familiar?
MATEO: En general fue una buena experiencia quedarse en casa de una familia británica, pero a veces me aburría.
ENTREVISTADOR: ¿Visitaste otras regiones de Gran Bretaña?
MATEO: Sí. Viajé en tren a la costa y a la capital, pero fue muy difícil. Los trenes siempre llegaban tarde, y nunca salían a tiempo.
ENTREVISTADOR: Cuando salías, ¿qué hacías?
MATEO: Íbamos al polideportivo o a la piscina. Había un campo de deporte y un parque bonito cerca de casa. ¡Qué suerte tienen los jóvenes allí!
ENTREVISTADOR: ¿Qué tal la comida?
MATEO: La familia comía muchas patatas fritas, y hamburguesas – la comida tenía demasiada grasa para mí. Pero la hija era vegetariana, y preparaba unos platos de verduras estupendas.

5 En mi tiempo libre

AMIGO: Débora, tú conoces la pista de hielo, ¿no? ¿Cómo es?
DÉBORA: Está bien – moderna, amplia. Voy allí cada semana. ¿Por qué?
AMIGO: Me gustaría ir. ¿Puedo ir contigo?
DÉBORA: Sí, pero no voy este fin de semana. ¡Voy a descansar!
AMIGO: ¿Por qué? ¿No estás bien?
DÉBORA: Ahora sí. Pero el fin de semana pasado, no. Pasé todo el día con náuseas. Y tuve que estudiar – escribí dos redacciones para la clase de lengua, pero me sentí fatal.

AMIGO: ¡Qué pena! ¿Qué pasó con tu programa de footing? ¿Tuviste que dejarlo?
DÉBORA: No, hago footing y natación todos los días como siempre. Pero no voy al gimnasio de momento.
AMIGO: Débora, ¿tienes el libro de poesía para la clase de literatura?
DÉBORA: ¿De Machado? Sí, lo leí el sábado pasado.
AMIGO: ¿Leíste todo el libro? ¡Uf! ¿Me lo puedes prestar? No sé dónde está el mío.
DÉBORA: Claro. ¿Quieres venir aquí el sábado por la tarde? Voy a quedarme en casa a ver la tele.
AMIGO: Vale. ¿Sobre las siete?
DÉBORA: Perfecto. ¡Hasta luego!
AMIGO: Hasta luego. Adiós.

Assessment G

(Units 1–15)

1 ¡Hola!

a CHICA: ¿Qué tal estás?
CHICO: Fatal.
b CHICA: ¿Por qué?
CHICO: No me gusta la casa nueva. Es un chalé.
c CHICA: ¿Dónde está?
CHICO: Al sureste.
d CHICO: Está en el campo.
e CHICO: Es muy tranquilo.

2 ¿Dónde estamos?

1 VOZ: Buenos días, ¿qué desea?
VOZ: Quisiera diez pastelitos, por favor.
VOZ: Muy bien. ¿Quiere usted éstos de chocolate ...

2 VOZ: Buenas tardes. ¿En qué le puedo ayudar?
VOZ: ¿Tiene una crema para las picaduras?
VOZ: ¿Una crema antiséptica? Sí, tenemos ésta ...

3 VOZ: ¡Martín, siéntate, por favor! ¿Qué te pasa?
VOZ: No tengo bolígrafo. No puedo escribir.
VOZ: Ana, ¿tienes un boli o un lápiz ...?

4 VOZ: ¿Cuánto cuesta jugar al squash?
VOZ: ¿Al squash? Cuesta tres euros por hora.
VOZ: No sé si tengo bastante dinero ...

5 VOZ: Buenos días, señora. ¿Qué desea?
VOZ: Filetes de ternera, si hay.
VOZ: ¿Cuánto quiere?
VOZ: Quinientos gramos, por favor.
VOZ: Muy bien. ¿Algo más?

6 VOZ: Quiero café descafeinado, por favor. Un paquete pequeño.
VOZ: Muy bien. ¿Algo más?
VOZ: Sí. Una botella de limonada también.
VOZ: Muy bien. ¿Es todo?

3 ¿Qué opinas?

CHICA: ¿Tienes que ayudar en casa, Felipe?

FELIPE: Sí, ¡el fin de semana! El viernes después de las clases, tengo que pasar la aspiradora por toda la casa.

CHICA: ¿Te gusta hacerlo?

FELIPE: No está mal.

CHICA: ¿Es todo?

FELIPE: No. También tengo que quitar la mesa después de la cena. Pero me gusta hacer esto porque es rápido.

CHICA: ¿Y el sábado?

FELIPE: Por la mañana, saco al perro. Me encanta ir de paseo, así que lo paso bien. Pero después de comer me toca a mí lavar los platos. ¡Qué aburrido!
El domingo …

CHICA: ¿Tienes que ayudar el domingo?

FELIPE: Sí. Tengo que quitar el polvo primero. No está mal. Y luego ayudar a Mamá lavar la ropa – ¡qué rollo es eso!

4 Por teléfono

SEÑORA: ¡Oiga! Mensaje para el señor Domínguez. Hay una reunión de nuestro grupo el miércoles, a las doce menos cuatro. Miércoles, las doce menos cuarto. ¿Nos vemos en la entrada cinco minutos antes?
Yo soy la señora Gallaiztegui. Se escribe G-A-dos les – A-I-Z-T-E-G-U-I. Repito, escribe G-A-dos les – A-I-Z-T-E-G-U-I. Mi número de teléfono es el nueve, uno, ocho … ocho, siete, nueve … cinco, zero, dos.
No tengo mi carpeta roja. Creo que la dejé en la oficina. ¿Puede usted traer mi carpeta roja a la reunión? Bueno, vale, gracias. ¡Hasta luego!

5 ¿Qué quieres hacer?

JOAQUÍN: Idaira, ¿qué quieres hacer el sábado por la noche?

IDAIRA: Voy a ir a la pista de hielo. ¿Quieres venir, Joaquín?

JOAQUÍN: No, no tengo ganas, gracias.

MARISA: Nunca quieres venir con nosotros, Joaquín.

JOAQUÍN: Ya lo sé. Es que todos los sábados me quedo en casa y estudio. ¿Qué haces tú los sábados, Marisa?

MARISA: ¿Yo? De día, trabajo en una tienda de alimentación.

ADRIÁN: ¿La tienda en la Plaza del Mercado?

MARISA: Sí, Adrián. ¿La conoces?

ADRIÁN: Sí. ¿Qué bien! Voy a ir a verte este sábado entonces.

MARISA: ¡Por favor, no, Adrián!

ADRIÁN: Voy a comprar un montón de cosas y ¡luego decirte que no tengo dinero!

MARISA: ¡Qué tonto eres! ¡Pablo! ¡Hola! ¿Qué vas a hacer tú el sábado?

PABLO: Teresa y yo vamos a visitar a su padre en Gijón. ¿Por qué?

MARISA: ¿No hay nadie que quiera venir al cine? ¿Rebeca?

REBECA: No, lo siento. Los sábados recojo mi habitación, y ayudo a mi madre.

MARISA: ¿No sales el sábado por la noche?

REBECA: No, por lo general, no. Veo la tele con Mamá, o leo.

MARISA: ¡Qué aburridos sois todos!

6 Italia

SEÑOR: ¿Vas a visitar Italia? ¡Qué suerte! ¿Cómo vas a ir?

SEÑORA: En avión, creo. Normalmente viajo en autocar pero de aquí a Siena son muchos kilómetros.

SEÑOR: ¿Dónde vas a quedarte?

SEÑORA: En casa de una amiga. Ella vive en la sierra, en un pueblo muy bonito.

SEÑOR: ¿No quieres ir a la playa?

SEÑORA: No. Siempre voy a la playa. ¡Estoy harta de playa! Este año quiero hacer algo diferente.

SEÑOR: Conoces Italia ya, ¿no? ¿No fuiste hace dos años?

SEÑORA: Bueno, fui al sur, pero este año voy a ir al norte. Lo pasé muy bien allí.